Fifth Workshop on the Use of Computational Methods in the Study of Endangered Languages (ComputEL-5)

Dublin, Ireland
26-27 May 2022

ISBN: 978-1-7138-6730-2

Printed from e-media with permission by:

Curran Associates, Inc.
57 Morehouse Lane
Red Hook, NY 12571

Some format issues inherent in the e-media version may also appear in this print version.

Printed with permission by Curran Associates, Inc. (2023)

For permission requests, please contact the Association for Computational Linguistics at the address below.

Association for Computational Linguistics
209 N. Eighth Street
Stroudsburg, Pennsylvania 18360

Phone: 1-570-476-8006
Fax: 1-570-476-0860

acl@aclweb.org

Additional copies of this publication are available from:

Curran Associates, Inc.
57 Morehouse Lane
Red Hook, NY 12571 USA
Phone: 845-758-0400
Fax: 845-758-2633
Email: curran@proceedings.com
Web: www.proceedings.com

COMPUTEL-5 2022

Fifth Workshop on the Use of Computational Methods in the Study of Endangered Languages

Proceedings of the Workshop

May 26-27, 2022

Introduction

These proceedings contain the papers presented at the 5th Workshop on the Use of Computational Methods in the Study of Endangered Languages, held as a hybrid event May 25-26, 2022 in Dublin, Ireland, and co-located with the 60th Association of Computational Linguistics (ACL) conference. As the name implies, this is the fifth workshop held on the topic—the first meeting was co-located with the ACL main conference in Baltimore, Maryland in 2014 and the second, third, and fourth ones in 2017, 2019, and 2021 were co-located with the 5th, 6th, and 7th editions of the International Conference on Language Documentation and Conservation (ICLDC) at the University of Hawai'i at Mānoa. This is the second time this workshop has been co-located with the ACL main conference and it enhances ACL 2022's Theme Track: "Language Diversity: from Low-Resource to Endangered Languages".

The workshop covers a wide range of topics relevant to the study and documentation of endangered languages, ranging from technical papers on working systems and applications, to reports on community activities with supporting computational components.

The purpose of the workshop is to bring together computational researchers, documentary linguists, and people involved with community efforts of language documentation and revitalization to take part in both formal and informal exchanges on how to integrate rapidly evolving language processing methods and tools into efforts of language description, documentation, and revitalization. The organizers are pleased with the range of papers, many of which highlight the importance of interdisciplinary work and interaction between the various communities that the workshop is aimed towards.

We received 36 submissions as papers or extended abstracts. After a thorough review process, 23 submissions were selected to be published in the ACL Anthology. Twelve submissions were accepted as posters and twelve for oral presentations.

The Organizing Committee would like to thank the Program Committee for their thoughtful review of the submissions. We are also grateful to the Social Sciences and Humanities Research Council (SSHRC) of Canada for supporting the workshop through their Partnership Grant #895-2019-1012. We would moreover want to acknowledge the support of the organizers of ACL 2022.

Organizing Committee

Organizers

Sarah Moeller, University of Florida, USA
Antonios Anastasopoulos, George Mason University, USA
Antti Arppe, University of Alberta, Canada
Aditi Chaudhary, Carnegie Mellon University, USA
Atticus Harrigan, University of Alberta, Canada
Josh Holden, University of Alberta, Canada
Jordan Lachler, University of Alberta, Canada
Alexis Palmer, University of Colorado Boulder, USA
Shruti Rijhwani, Carnegie Mellon University, USA
Lane Schwartz, University of Illinois, USA

Program Committee

Program Committee

Alexandre Arkhipov, Universität Hamburg
Alexis Michaud, CNRS
Alexis Palmer, University of Colorado, Boulder
Anna Kazantseva, National Research Council Canada
Antti Arppe, University of Alberta
Borini Lahiri, Indian Institute of Technology Kharagpur
Borui Zhang, University of Florida
Christopher D Cox, Carleton University
Claire Bowern, Yale University
Daan van Esch, Leiden University
Daisy Rosenblum, University of British Columbia
Dorothee Beermann, Norwegian University of Science and Technology
Elizabeth Salesky, Johns Hopkins University
Emily M. Bender, University of Washington
Emily Prud'hommeaux, Boston College
Emmanuel Schang, Université d'Orléans
Francis M. Tyers, Indiana University, Bloomington
František Kratochvíl, Palacky University
Gary F Simons, SIL International
Jean Maillard, Facebook AI
Jeffrey Good, State University of New York at Buffalo
Jordan Lachler, University of Alberta
Jörg Tiedemann, University of Helsinki
Josh Holden, University of Alberta
Judith Lynn Klavans, University of Maryland, College Park
Lane Schwartz, University of Alaska Fairbanks
Lori Levin, School of Computer Science, Carnegie Mellon University
Luke Gessler, Georgetown University
Martin Benjamin, Kamusi Project International
Meladel Mistica, The University of Melbourne
Menzo Windhouwer, University of Amsterdam
Olga Lovick, University of Saskatchewan
Olivia Sammons, First Nations University of Canada
Paul Trilsbeek, Max Planck Institute for Psycholinguistics
Rebecca Knowles, National Research Council Canada
Richard Sproat, Massachusetts Institute of Technology
Ritesh Kumar, Dr. Bhimrao Ambedkar University
Robert Forkel, Max-Planck Institute for Evolutionary Anthropology
Roland Kuhn, National Research Council of Canada
Sakriani Sakti, Japan Advanced Institute of Science and Technology
Sonal Sinha, Google
Steven Bird, Charles Darwin University
Worthy Martin, University of Virginia, Charlottesville
Yves Scherrer, University of Helsinki
Zahra Azin, Carleton University

Zoey Liu, Boston College

Table of Contents

Development of the Siberian Ingrian Finnish Speech Corpus

Ivan Ubaleht
Omsk State Technical University
ubaleht@gmail.com

Taisto-Kalevi Raudalainen
Estonian Academic Society of Ingria
taika.rauta@gmail.com

Abstract

In this paper we present the speech corpus for the Siberian Ingrian Finnish language. The speech corpus includes: audio data, annotations, software tools for data processing, two databases and a web application. We have published part of the audio data and annotations. The software tool for parsing annotation files and feeding a relational database is developed and published under a free license. A web application is developed and available. At this moment, about 300 words and 200 phrases can be displayed using this web application.

1 Introduction

Many of endangered languages have the following specific features: (i) there are no writing system and stable orthography; (ii) there are very few available speech data and texts. These features should be considered when working on speech corpora. Since we plan to document and revitalize several endangered languages from our region, we are developing software – the Lexeme.Net system, at www.lexeme.net that is adapted to our requirements and goals.

Our requirements: (i) all source code and data should be accessible on GitHub and licensed under one of a free license; (ii) speech corpora should be available to users via the Internet without installing additional software; (iii) speech corpora should be convenient not only for linguists, but also for speakers of endangered languages, language activists and software developers; (iv) speech corpora should have a powerful system of requests to data (for example, search by grammatical categories, regular expression search). At present, there are solutions that meet these requirements: the “Tsakorpus” corpus platform[1] (for example, the project INEL uses the “Tsakorpus” corpus platform (Arkhangelskiy et al., 2019)), Kwaras and Namuti (Caballero et al., 2019), LingSync & the Online Linguistic Database (Dunham et al., 2014), Kratylos (Kaufman and Finkel, 2018), the IATH ELAN Text-Sync Tool (Dobrin and Ross, 2017).

Since we wanted a very flexible solution, we decided to develop own project. We chose the .NET Framework[2] and Microsoft SQL Server[3] for the implementation of the project. Siberian Ingrian Finnish was chosen as the first endangered language for the Lexeme.Net system.

We briefly review the Siberian Ingrian Finnish in section 2. We describe the design of the Siberian Ingrian Finnish speech corpus in section 3. In section 3 we describe the general structure of the speech corpus, annotation tiers, the data model of the fieldwork database and the web application.

2 An overview of the Siberian Ingrian Finnish language

The Siberian Ingrian Finnish Language is an Ingrian Finnish – Ingrian (Izhorian) mixed language. The ancestors of the speakers of Siberian Ingrian Finnish spoke Lower Luga Ingrian Finnish (so-called the dialect of the Kurkola peninsula) and Lower Luga Ingrian varieties (Kuznetsova et al., 2015). They migrated from the Lower Luga area to Siberia in 1803-1804.

Siberian Ingrian Finnish (Russian: Сибирский ингерманландский идиом) is the term introduced by D.V. Sidorkevich. D.V. Sidorkevich who researched and documented Siberian Ingrian

[1] https://github.com/timarkh/tsakorpus

[2] https://dotnet.microsoft.com/

[3] https://www.microsoft.com/sql-server

Proceedings of the Fifth Workshop on the Use of Computational Methods in the Study of Endangered Languages, pages 1 - 4
May 26-27, 2022 ©2022 Association for Computational Linguistics

Finnish (Sidorkevich, 2011; Sidorkevich, 2014) in 2008-2014. The language was also studied by N.V. Kuznetsova (Kuznetsova, 2016) and M.Z. Muslimov.

In 2022, there is still a group of people of elder generation who use Siberian Ingrian Finnish in the domestic sphere of communication in Ryzhkovo settlement (Krutinsky District of Omsk Oblast). The villagers of Ryzhkovo also use Siberian Ingrian Finnish for communication with their relatives from Estonia by phone. There is also a small group of people in Omsk who use this language occasionally. According to our estimates, about 15 native speakers of this language now live in Russia and Estonia. The number of semi-speakers is about 30-60.

Siberian Ingrian Finnish has a number of distinctive features such as word-final vowel reduction and the emergence of a large number of consonant phonemes. The language has no writing system, stable orthography and texts.

3 The design and development of the speech corpus

3.1 The general structure of the speech corpus

In this subsection, we briefly describe all components of the Siberian Ingrian Finnish speech corpus. We use ELAN media annotation tool (Wittenburg et al., 2006) to annotate speech data. The structure of the annotation files is shown in subsection 3.3.

Annotation files are XML files, therefore we have developed a software tool to read annotations (see subsection 3.3). After parsing annotations, the object tree with data from annotations is stored in a relational database. Two relational databases are part of the speech corpus (see subsection 3.4). The fieldwork database stores annotations of speech data, timestamps and the attributes of speakers, interviewers, audio files, equipment. The lexical database will store information about grammatical categories, parts of speech, synonyms of words. The lexical database will be used for the Siberian Ingrian Finnish dictionary and for the work of the morphological analyzer. Both of these databases can exchange information.

The next part of the speech corpus is the web application which allows users to play audio fragments according to timestamps from annotation files, display information according to annotations, and also will allow users to make complex queries to database. The web application also will display information about word-forms, morphology and grammatical categories.

3.2 The data collection

The speech data of Siberian Ingrian Finnish are available in our repository on GitHub and licensed under a Creative Commons Attribution 4.0 license (CC BY 4.0). Currently, the part of the audio data from our expeditions has been published. We recorded 15 hours of audio and 2 hours of video from 9 speakers during our expeditions to Ryzhkovo and Mikhailovka settlements (Omsk oblast, Russia) and interviews via phone in 2019-2022. About 5 hours of the audio data were published on GitHub[4].

3.3 The annotations

We use ELAN media annotation tool for annotating speech data. Annotation files are stored in our project repository on GitHub[5]. The structure of the annotation files is shown in Figure 1. On the "Speaker-Speech" tier are the phrases spoken by the speakers of Siberian Ingrian Finnish. Tier "Speaker-Words" displays the words spoken by the speakers. Layers "Speaker-WordsEnTranslation", "Speaker-WordsRu Translation", "Speaker-SpeechEnTranslation" "Speaker-SpeechRuTranslation" display translations of phrases and words into English and Russian. Parts of speech and morphological aspects are described on the tiers: "Speaker-PartOfSpeach", "Speaker-Morph". Questions and phrases of an interviewer are annotated on tiers: "Interviewer-Speech", "Interviewer-SpeechEnTranslation".

ELAN file format is an XML format. We have developed a software tool (the desktop application for Windows) for parsing these XML files (*.eaf files) and transforming annotations into an object tree. Then in accordance with this object tree, our program library generates SQL-insert commands for adding these objects to the relational database. We tested this software tool by parsing an ELAN file with 10,000 lines and tested running about a

[4]https://github.com/ubaleht/SiberianIngrianFinnish

[5]https://github.com/ubaleht/SiberianIngrianFinnish/tree/master/annotations

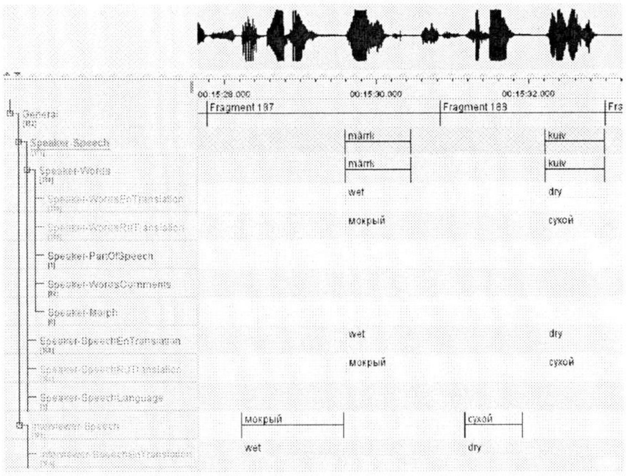

Figure 1: An example of annotated fragment of speech data of Siberian Ingrian Finnish and the list of tiers.

thousand SQL-insert commands [6] to add information from annotations to a relational database in Microsoft SQL Server. This software tool is stable and can be used for other endangered languages. This software is available on GitHub[7] and licensed under the Apache 2.0 License.

3.4 The databases for the speech corpus

The speech corpus uses two relational databases. The fieldwork database stores the characteristics of the recorded fragments of speech and timestamps from annotations as well as characteristics of the speakers. The data model[8] of this database is shown in Figure 2.

The lexical database stores the data for the Siberian Ingrian Finnish dictionary, more precisely, word-forms according to inflectional paradigms. Since the language is under-resourced, we build a part of word-forms hypothetically according to our knowledge of the grammar. We verify the data from the lexical database, using the data from the fieldwork database based on annotations. A key field for linking the two databases is the field "Lemma". The lexical database is necessary for the work of the rule-based morphological analyzer for Siberian Ingrian Finnish.

[6] https://github.com/ubaleht/SiberianIngrianFinnish/tree/master/SpeechDatabase/Data

[7] https://github.com/ubaleht/LexemeELAN

[8] https://github.com/ubaleht/SiberianIngrianFinnish/tree/master/SpeechDatabase/Scheme

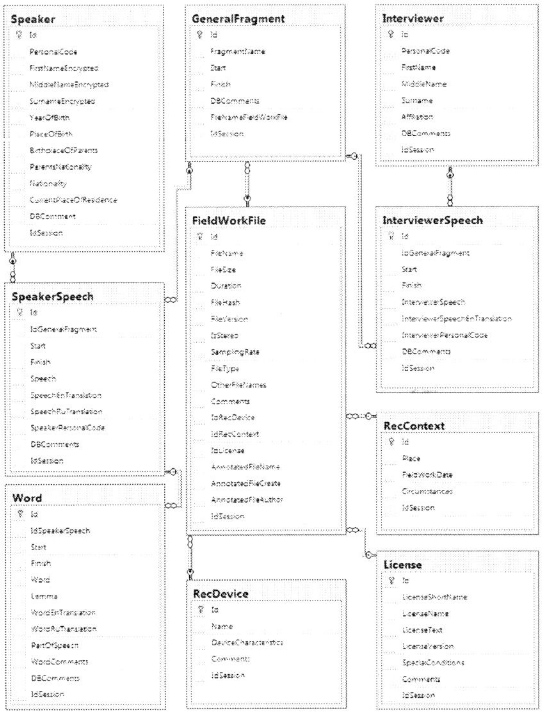

Figure 2: The data model of the fieldwork database.

3.5 The web application

We have developed a web application that, in accordance with user requests, can display information taken from annotation files, which is stored in the database. This web application can play audio fragments according to timestamps obtained from the database. Depending on the user's request, these timestamps can correspond to such fragments as: words, phrases, interviewer questions (in order to better understand the context of words). The source code of the web application is open and available on GitHub[9]. At the moment, web application is available via Internet[10], see Figure 3.

4 The current status of the creation of the speech corpus and conclusion

At this moment, about 300 words (the number of individual pronunciations) and 200 phrases in audio files have been annotated. All these words and phrases were collected from 4 speakers of Siberian Ingrian Finnish. These words are mostly from the 200-word Swadesh list as well as the other basic lexicon. These 300 words and 200

[9] https://github.com/ubaleht/Lexeme

[10] http://lexeme.net/sif

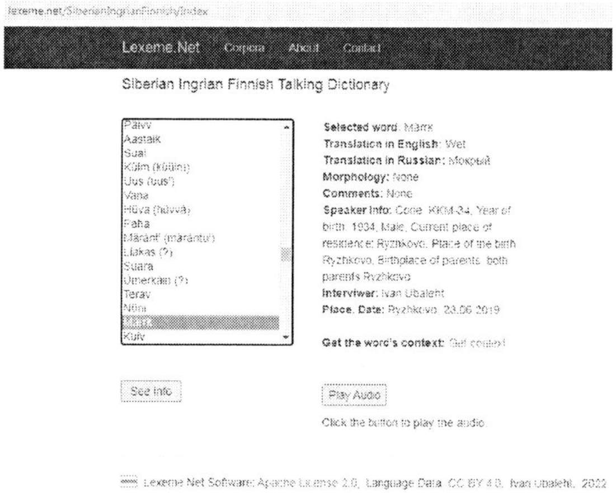

Figure 3: The first version of the web application for the Siberian Ingrian Finnish speech corpus.

phrases can be played in our web-application, and the web-application also displays information from the annotations associated with these audio fragments.

The following results have been achieved:

- Audio data of the Siberian Ingrian Finnish language has been published and licensed under a Creative Commons Attribution 4.0 license (CC BY 4.0).
- The annotations of audio data have been published.
- A software tool for parsing annotation files and feeding a database was created.
- The structure of the fieldwork database has been developed and this database has been filled. Now this database contains information about 300 words and 200 phrases.
- The web application had been created. The source code of the web application is open and available in GitHub. At the moment, the web application is available via Internet.
- The rule-based morphological analyzer and the lexical database of Siberian Ingrian Finnish is under development.

After creating the speech corpus for Siberian Ingrian Finnish, we plan to start creating a speech corpus for the Siberian Tatar language using the software described above.

References

Timofey Arkhangelskiy, Anne Ferger, and Hanna Hedeland. 2019. Uralic multimedia corpora: ISO/TEI corpus data in the project INEL. In *Proceedings of the Fifth International Workshop on Computational Linguistics for Uralic Languages*. Association for Computational Linguistics, pages 115-124. https://doi.org/10.18653/v1/W19-0310.

Lise M. Dobrin and Douglass Ross. 2017. The IATH ELAN Text-Sync Tool: A Simple System for Mobilizing ELAN Transcripts On- or Off-Line. *Language Documentation & Conservation*, 11:94–102.

Joel Dunham, Gina Cook, and Joshua Horner. 2014. LingSync & the Online Linguistic Database: New models for the collection and management of data for language communities, linguists and language learners. In *Proceedings of the 2014 Workshop on the Use of Computational Methods in the Study of Endangered Languages*, pages 24-33. https://doi.org/10.3115/v1/W14-2204.

Gabriela Caballero, Lucien Carroll, and Kevin Mach. 2019. Accessing, managing, and mobilizing an ELAN-based language documentation corpus: The Kwaras and Namuti tools. *Language Documentation & Conservation*, 13:63-82.

Daniel Kaufman and Raphael Finkel. 2018. Kratylos: A tool for sharing interlinearized and lexical data in diverse formats. *Language Documentation & Conservation*, 12:124–146.

Natalia Kuznetsova, Elena Markus, and Mehmet Muslimov. 2015. Finnic minorities of Ingria. *Cultural and linguistic minorities in the Russian Federation and the European Union*, 13: 127-167. https://doi.org/10.1007/978-3-319-10455-3_6.

Natalia Kuznetsova. 2016. Evolution of the non-initial vocalic length contrast across the Finnic varieties of Ingria and adjacent areas. *Linguistica Uralica*, 52(1):1-25. https://doi.org/10.3176/lu.2016.1.01.

Daria V. Sidorkevich. 2014. *Yazyk ingermanlandskih pereselentsev v Sibiri*. Diss. ILIRAN.

Daria V. Sidorkevich. 2011. On domains of adessive-allative in Siberian Ingrian Finnish. In *Proceedings of Institute for Linguistic Studies* 7(3): 575-607.

Peter Wittenburg, Hennie Brugman, Albert Russel, Alexander Klassmann, and Han Sloetjes. 2006. ELAN: A Professional Framework for Multimodality Research. In *Proceedings of Language Resource and Evaluation 2006*, pages 1556–1559.

New syntactic insights for automated Wolof Universal Dependency parsing

Bill Dyer
University of Florida / Dept. of Linguistics 4131
Turlington Hall P.O. Box 115454
Gainesville, FL 32611
wgdyer@ufl.edu

Abstract

Focus on language-specific properties with insights from formal minimalist syntax can improve universal dependency (UD) parsing. Such improvements are especially sensitive for low-resource African languages, like Wolof, which have fewer UD treebanks in number and amount of annotations, and fewer contributing annotators. For two different UD parser pipelines, one parser model was trained on the original Wolof treebank, and one was trained on an edited treebank. For each parser pipeline, the accuracy of the edited treebank was higher than the original for both the dependency relations and dependency labels. Accuracy for universal dependency relations improved as much as 2.90%, while accuracy for universal dependency labels increased as much as 3.38%. An annotation scheme that better fits a language's distinct syntax results in better parsing accuracy.

1 Introduction

Wolof is a language of Senegal, where it is the lingua franca in a nation of more than twelve million people (McLaughlin, 2008). About six million speak Wolof as their first language (Eberhard et al., 2020). However, it is severely underrepresented in print, as well as in digital format. Because French is the official language of the Senegalese state, writing is more commonly practiced in French, while Wolof and other indigenous languages are used more in spoken communication.

Out of the almost 120 languages for which there are universal dependency treebanks available, only eight are indigenous African languages[1]. African languages in particular are not well represented, given Africa's large share of the world's languages and the relatively large populations of even minority language groups. The presence of these annotated treebanks is promising for automated computational tasks, though.

[1] https://universaldependencies.org

The aim of this study is to improve universal dependency (UD) parsing for Wolof. A UD treebank by Cheikh Bamba (Dione, 2019) is available for the Wolof language. The innovation proposed here is not only to train a parser, as (Dione, 2020) has already designed a Wolof language-specific parser. The purpose was to determine whether out-of-the-box parsers would show improvement on the Wolof treebanks after edits to the part of speech and universal dependency syntax annotations. Improved Wolof parser models may be used to inform other African language parsers, whose features can be analyzed on their own terms rather than through the lens of other major languages or existing annotation schemes.

2 Hypothesis

The assignment of syntactic dependencies in the Wolof UD treebank is based on syntactic and morphological analysis from lexical functional grammar (Dione, 2019). In some cases, natural language processing has ignored language-specific features, a sacrifice that is to some degree necessary to create a universal system like UD syntax. This is especially true of languages with less presence in scholarly literature, where tagging or parsing assignments attempt to fit languages into the mold of world languages like English (Tovey, 2019). The dependency structures of determiners, pronouns, and copulas in the Wolof UD Treebank comply with the traditional functions of those categories, but can be realigned to capture broader linguistic generalizations of their behavior while improving accuracy.

2.1 Relative clauses

Wolof determiners and relative clause pronouns are represented by identical morphemes. Determiners follow nouns, as in example 1 (Njie, 1982; Ka, 1994). They consist of a consonant that corresponds with the noun class and a vowel

Proceedings of the Fifth Workshop on the Use of Computational Methods in the Study of Endangered Languages, pages 5 - 12
May 26-27, 2022 ©2022 Association for Computational Linguistics

that corresponds to deictic configuration (Njie, 1982; Robert, 2006). Wolof has a large number of classes (or genders) for nouns (McLaughlin, 1997), and 18 classes are represented in the Wolof UD Treebank. This class of words includes definite determiners and demonstratives that designate the distance of the object from the speaker.

(1) a. *cin* ***l-i***
large.pot LClass-the

'the large pot'

b. *jamono* ***j-ooju***
era JClass-that.far

'that time long ago'

In the Wolof UD Treebank, such determiners are tagged DET in both the universal UD tagset and the Wolof-specific tagset. Their UD dependency label is *det*, and they are dependents of the noun.

Wolof relative clauses appear with an overt noun head, or as 'headless' relative clauses. Examples of headed relative clauses from the training and development data of the Wolof UD Treebank are those in 2.

(2) a. *làkk* ***y-ii*** *ñu*
language YClass-these we
nàmp
learn.as.mother.tongue

'these languages here that we learn as a mother tongue'

In the Wolof UD Treebank, the relative pronouns in headed relative clauses are tagged as PRON in both the universal and Wolof-specific tag assignments. They are given the dependency relation label that corresponds to their role in the embedded clause, such as *nsubj* or *obj*, and are a dependent of the verb embedded in the relative clause.

The examples in 3 are headless relative clauses. The relative clause pronouns are made of the same class consonant and vowel combinations that signify distance from the speaker.

(3) a. ***k-i*** *leen*
ClassK-the them
taxawal-oon
stand.up.against-PAST

'the one who stood against them'

The relative pronoun in these headless relative clauses are also given the PRON tag in the Wolof UD Treebank, for both their universal part-of-speech (POS) tag, as well the Wolof tagging system established by Dione. Unlike the dependency relation for headed relative pronouns, the embedded relative clause verb is a dependent of the relative pronoun. Alternatively, adopting an SUD annotation scheme would also result in parallel structures where the closed class determiner is the head. SUD provides further evidence that the strict application of UD syntactic policy does not always result in the most accurate parsing (Gerdes et al., 2018).

There are other clauses that are have the same structure as relative clauses, such as temporal and conditional clauses beginning with *bu* or *su* (Torrence, 2013). If relative clauses are uniformly assigned a similar dependency structure, regardless of whether they have a head or not, the parser should be able to better recognize them. The idea that the relative pronoun should consistently be represented as a functional head with the same position in the syntax is clear from minimalist syntax as outlined by (Chomsky, 1996).

Furthermore, all definite determiners, demonstratives, relative pronouns and quantifiers follow nouns, provide more information about the noun and agree in noun class. As such, I hypothesize that if they are all labeled with the same tag, the part-of-speech tagger in the parser pipeline will be more accurate.

An annotation scheme where the definite-determiner-like morpheme is a complementizer should result in a better trained parser than one where it is a determiner, following the syntactic analysis of (Torrence, 2013).

2.2 The existence of copulas

A similar trend occurs with those words that have been tagged COP in the Wolof language specific tags, all of which are AUX in the universal tag set. Syntactic analyses have identified several copulas in Wolof (Torrence, 2013), although each are associated with other function words. *La* indicates complement (as opposed to subject or verb) focus in a clause. *Di* (and its allomorph *y*) indicates progressive aspect. The examples in 4 show them in copular sentences. The *-a-* morpheme in 4b indicates subject focus. Capital letters represent focus of any kind in the glosses.

(4) a. *Kolle sama mag la*
Kolle my older.sibling FOCUS

'Kolle is my OLDER SISTER"

b. *Abdu mo-o-y sama mag.*
Abdu he-FOCUS-is my older.sibling

'ABDU is my older brother'

The examples in 5, however, show the use of *la* and *di* as verbal auxiliaries that indicate focus and progressive aspect, respectively (Ka, 1994). In such cases, *la* is tagged as INFL in the Wolof tagset, and *di* is tagged as AUX. Both are tagged as AUX in the universal tagset.

(5) a. *Kolle kànj la jënd.*
Kolle okra FOC.he sell

'Kolle has sold OKRA.'

b. *Kolle kànj la-y jënd.*
Kolle okra FOC-he-is sell

'Kolle is selling OKRA.'

c. *Kolle mo-o jënd kànj.*
Kolle he-FOC sell okra

'KOLLE has sold okra.'

d. *Kolle mo-o-y jënd kànj.*
Kolle she-FOC-is sell okra

'KOLLE is selling okra.'

Wolof does allow null copulas, which must be the case in sentences like 5c. It is more likely that the function morphemes assigned as copulas are in fact function morphemes in all cases, and that there are no overt copular verbs, a phenomenon attested in many languages. While the interpretation of lexical functional grammar presented by (Dione, 2019) would attempt to match the function of a verb with the words present, the minimalist analysis elaborated by (Chomsky, 1996) does not require an overt lexical item to occupy a syntactic position. The verb position may be empty in certain cases, allowing the focus complementizer morphemes like *la*, following (Martinović, 2017), and imperfect morphemes like *di* to consistently maintain their roles rather than be circumstantially designated as verbs. Attempts to make a language fit the mold of other languages more commonly tested in natural language processing are what (Tovey, 2019) predicts will increase confusion in tasks like part-of-speech tagging.

The function words that determine focus and verbal aspect are consistent in their syntactic distribution, whether used in copular contexts or not.

3 Methods

The original data in the Wolof UD Treebank (Dione, 2019) consists of 42,832 tokens across 2,107 sentences. These sentences are from four different Wolof sources online: the Organisation Sénégalaise dAppui au Développement (Senegalese Aid and Development Organization) web site, Wolof Online, Wolof Wikipedia, and the news site Xibaaryi. They were divided by Dione into training, test, and development sets.

Table 1: Sources of Corpora for the Wolof UD Treebank (Dione, 2019)

Source	# Doc.	# Tok.	# Sent.
OSAD	6	6,269	265
Wolof Online	18	12,988	673
Wolof Wikip.	12	9,232	500
Xibaaryi	17	15,095	669

Using Python, the test, development, and test files of the Wolof UD Treebank were edited to assign certain lemmas new tags in certain environments and assign new UD labels and hierarchies.

3.1 DEF model with relative pronoun dependency labeled 'mark'

First, the universal dependency relations of headless relative clauses were edited. Examples of headed and headless relative pronouns can be seen in 6 and 7 respectively, illustrating the structural difference in the baseline.

(6) Headed Relative Clause

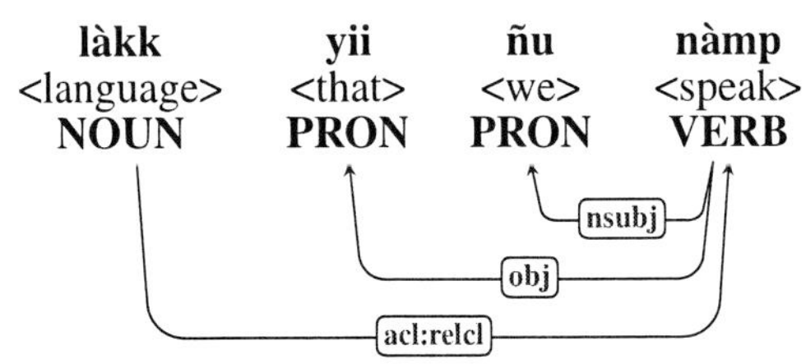

(7) Headless Relative Clause

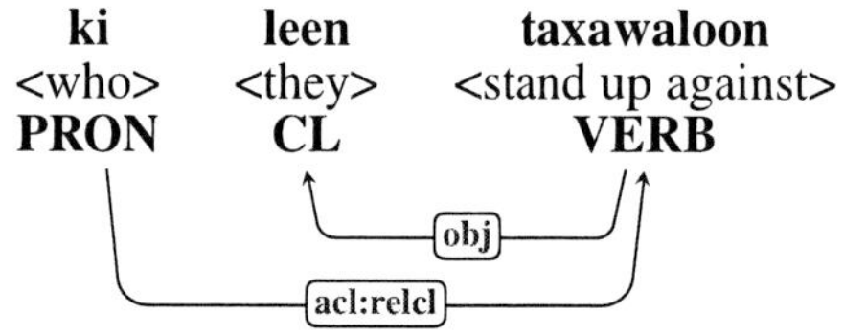

Following the hypothesis that similar syntactic structures will have similar dependency structures, headless relative clauses like 7 were edited to take on the dependency hierarchy in 8. In this way, all relative clauses are given the same dependency structure, whether they have an overt noun head or not.

(8) Adjusted dependency relations for headless relative clauses to match headed relative clauses

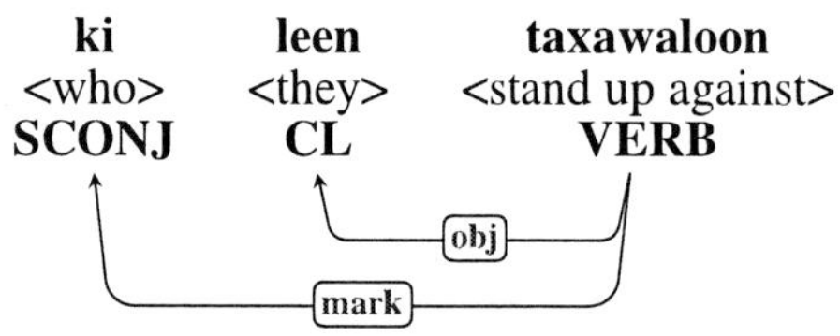

The tags of each definite determiner, relative pronoun, post-nominal quantifier, or clausal complementizer that agrees in noun class are changed from DET, PRON, and COMP to a new class; DEF. The universal equivalent of the Wolof-specific COMP tag is SCONJ. This includes the complementizers *bu* and *su*, which (Torrence, 2013) analyzes as being the relative pronouns of headless conditional relative clauses. The edited treebanks will be the input for the first parser model.

In this model, all relative pronouns in headed and headless relative clauses are labeled as the universal dependency relation *mark*, which signifies complementizers in the UD annotation. Even the headed relative clauses had their part-of-speech tags and universal dependency relation labels changed.

(9) Adjusted dependency relations for headed relative clauses

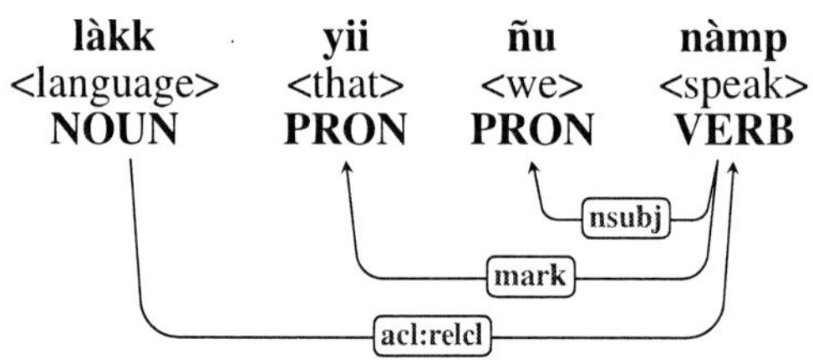

3.2 DEF model with relative pronoun dependency labeled 'det'

The analysis of the relative pronoun as complementizer is the one that Torrence favors, but another hypothesis that he tests is that they are determiners. This competing analysis is tested computationally by a second parsing model. The edited treebanks for this model use the label *det* for relative clause pronouns rather than *mark*.

3.3 Relabeled copula model

All copular tags are edited in treebanks designated to be the input to a third model. In this model, all COP tags for selected lemmas are changed to INFL and AUX. These are lemmas that are assigned INFl and AUX tags in non-copular contexts. The assignment of AUX or INFL is somewhat changed, however, based on the category of the lemma. The following lemmas that sometimes acted as copulars are given with their alternate POS in Table 2.

Table 2: Alternative tag assignment for select lemmas when not assigned COP

INFL		AUX	
Lem.	Funct.	Lem.	Funct.
la	Compl. Foc	ngi	Prog. Asp.
da	Verb. Foc	du	Neg.
daan	Pst. Hab Asp., foc. cl.	daan	Pst. Hab Asp., non-focus cl.
		di	Imp. Asp.

One issue with this classification is that it divides AUX and INFL into irregular categories. Some of the lemmas in each category designate focus, while others designate aspect. Instead, AUX and INFL are reassigned to these lemmas based on the classification given in Table 3. INFL will be assigned for focus particles and negative *du*, which appears in the same syntactic position as focus elements do. AUX will be assigned to auxiliaries denoting aspect, but is also used for particles that are not used as copulas and are not on this list. The universal tags for these lemmas goes unchanged, as the Wolof-specific tags for AUX and INFL are both labeled AUX in the univeral tag system.

Table 3: Category reassigned to selected lemmas previously assigned COP, AUX, or INFL tag

INFL		AUX	
Lem.	Funct.	Lem.	Funct.
la	Comp. foc.	ngi	Prog. Asp.
da	Verb. foc.	daan	Pst. Hab. Asp.
du	Neg	di	Imp, Asp.

Words that were originally assigned as COMP are retagged, as well as those lemmas in the table that were assigned INFL or AUX. This leads into somewhat reduced granularity in part of speech tags, but there is a diverse distribution of each dependency structure outside of copulas.

The dependencies in subject focus constructions are also conflated into a similar structure. Nominals are treated as roots in copular clauses with subject focus and a nominal complement, as in 10. However, in copular clauses with subject focus and a clausal complement, as in 11, the imperfect auxiliary *di* is treated as the root.

(10) *Di* copula with nominal complement

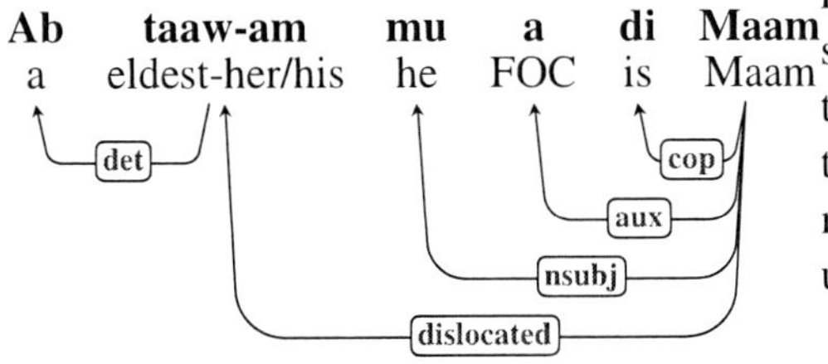

(11) *Di* copula with clausal complement

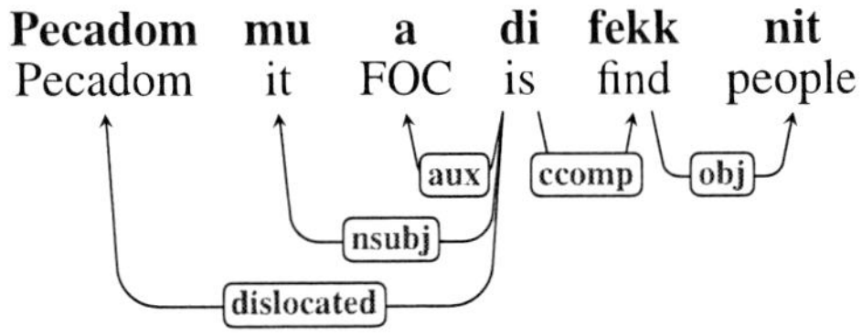

The dependencies for sentences like 11 will be changed into the structure in 12 in the treebanks for the third model.

(12) Reassigned dependency for clausal *di* copula to match nominal complement

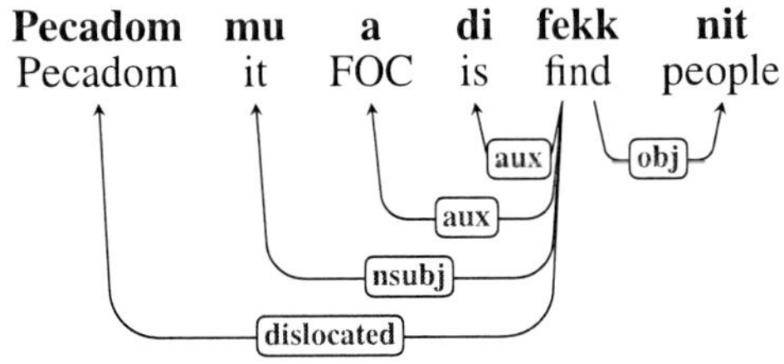

The relative clause verb *fekk*, 'find,' is now the root. In the UD system, the verb of the clause acts as the root, meaning that copular verbs can be roots. In Diones lexical functional grammar analysis (Dione, 2019), the subject focus morphemes (*mooy* = *mu*+*a*+*di*) in 11 act as a copula. The copula implies a cleft, such as the English translation "Its Pecadom who finds people that are sick in their house." I reject the cleft analysis, and follow Martinovics analysis for the similar *la* complement focus construction (Martinović, 2017). Like *la*, the *-a* in 11 and 12 are complementizers. *Di* is a morpheme that marks imperfect aspect. It is not a copula and does not result in a cleft. The main verb in 12 is *fekk*, 'find', rather than a copula, making it the root.

3.4 Parser pipelines

After the treebanks are edited, they are prepared for either the spaCy parser pipeline, or the TreeTagger+MaltParser parser pipeline.

3.5 The SpaCy pipeline

For spaCy, the treebank UD treebanks for all three models are converted to .json format. There are separate treebanks for the train, development, and test data. The parser is trained using each of the three sets of edited treebanks. A baseline parser model was also trained using the data from the unedited Wolof UD Treebank.

Four separate models have been created; one baseline model, one model from the DEF tag treebanks with relative pronouns as *mark*, a third from the DEF tag treebanks with relative pronouns as *det*, and a fourth from the treebanks that are edited to replace the COP tag. The trained models are evaluated using Python. The accuracy of the universal dependency label assigned was measured against the baseline, as well as the accuracy of the universal dependency hierarchies.

3.6 The MaltParser pipeline

The second parser consisted of two separate tools: TreeTagger (Schmid, 1994) and MaltParser (Nilsson and Nivre, 2008). The baseline and all three edited treebanks were used to train TreeTagger models. TreeTagger requires the tag SENT for punctuation marking the end of the sentence. The Wolof tags PERIOD, EXL-POINT, SEMICOLON, ELLIPSIS and INT-MARK were changed to SENT for use on TreeTag, as their corresponding lemmas '.', '!', ';', '...', and '?'

were used to separate sentences in the Wolof UD Treebank. After models were trained, a treebank file was produced that tagged the words from the test Wolof UD Treebank. The treebank file took combined tags from a universal tagger and Wolof-specfic tagger that were trained for each parser pipeline model. A baseline tagger was also trained based on the original Wolof UD Treebank.

The treebank files only contained the word number, word form, lemma, universal POS tag, and Wolof POS tag for each word. This is all that could be produced by the tagger. After a treebank file was prepared for each model, it was used as input into MaltParser. A MaltParser model was trained on the baseline Wolof UD Treebank training data, as well as the edited treebank data for each model. The trained edited models were all tested against the baseline; for accuracy of the UD labels as well as the UD structural hierarchy.

3.7 Combination of DEF+'det' model and Relabeled Copulas model

After testing was completed, the COP model and the DEF tag model that showed the highest improvement in accuracy are combined. A combined model was made for both spaCy and the TreeTagger-MaltParser pipeline.

4 Results

Accuracy was improved for the models made for each parser pipeline; the spaCy and the TreeTagger+Malt Parser pipelines. Table 5 shows the results for both the labels assigned to the universal dependency relations, as well as the hierarchical structure of the universal dependencies.

Table 4: Accuracy for UD labels and relations with spaCy pipeline

#	Annot.	UD Label	Univ. Dep.
0	Baseline	76.4%	71.1%
1	DEF tag, RC pron as *det*	77.9%	71.7%
2	DEF tag, RC pron as *mark*	77.8%	71.4%
3	Copulas Relabeled	77.4%	71.2%
4	Combination of #1 and #3	78.0%	71.4%

Table 5: Accuracy for UD labels and relations with TreeTagger+MaltParser pipline

#	Annot. Label	UD Dep.	Univ.
0	Baseline	72.7%	70.4%
1	DEF tag, RC pron as *det*	74.9%	72.9%
2	DEF tag, RC pron as *mark*	74.0%	73.2%
3	Copulas Relabeled	73.9%	70.7%
4	Combination of #1 and #3	76.1%	73.3%

Models 1 and 2 with the DEF tag showed drastic improvement in SpaCy UD Label, the Malt UD Label, and the Malt universal dependency accuracies when compared to the test data. The SpaCy UD label increased 1.5% for the model with the *det* label, the Malt UD labels increased 2.2%, and the Malt universal dependencies increased 2.5%. The model with the *mark* label improved SpaCy UD labels by 1.4%, Malt UD labels by 1.3%, and Malt universal dependencies by 2.8%. Targeting a separate set of syntactic dependencies, relabeling copulas also showed across the board increases in accuracy. Accuracy for the SpaCy UD labels improved 1%, .8% for the Malt UD labels, and .3% for the Malt universal dependencies. Improvement was less in the SpaCy universal dependencies, which showed a maximum of .6% improvement. When the changes made to the best DEF model treebanks were made to the Relabeled Copula treebanks, the SpaCy UD label accuracy increased 1.6%, SpaCy universal dependency accuracy increased by .3%, Malt UD label accuracy increased by 3.4%, and Malt universal dependencies increased by 3.3%.

Relative clauses pronouns were relabeled as determiners (det), which show an increase in recall and f1-score. As relative clause pronouns were made determiner dependents of the relative clause verb, and no longer confused with subjects (nsubj), objects (obj), obliques (obl), and indirect objects (idobj), their precision, recall and f1-scores increase in the improved parser. There are no copula dependency labels in the improved parser, and the relabeling of 182 copulas in the auxiliary (aux) category resulted in an increase in precision, recall, and f1-score for auxiliaries (aux).

5 Analysis

Overall, adopting a unified and streamlined syntactic approach to assigning UD relations improves accuracy in Wolof. Two different parsers both showed improvement in parsing when a DEF tag was added to definite noun modifiers, headless relative clauses had the same structure as headed ones, and copulas were relabeled to capture their universal function. This suggests that improved accuracy was not simply due to the parsers.

The results supported the hypothesis that a unified UD syntax for headed and headless relative clauses improves the accuracy in parsing universal dependencies and their labels. The hypothesis that treating definites as one part of speech category would improve parsing was supported by the results. The hypothesis the relative pronoun is a complementizer due to theoretical syntactic analysis was not supported by the data. In fact, the model that treats the relative pronoun as *det*, an extracted determiner, results in more accurate parsing.

The copular analysis carried over from English does not seem to 'fit' Wolof. The data from Wolof does not contradict an analysis where *di* and its allomorphs universally indicates imperfect aspect, rather than acting in some instances as a copula. The subject and object focus morphemes are the same whether the sentence is copular or not, suggesting that they are not copulas in copular sentences. The copula should be instead attributed to some null morpheme. Improved parsing accuracy resulting from the reassigning of copula tags and dependency relations in the Wolof UD Treebank supports this hypothesis.

As (Dione, 2019) mentions, the morphosyntactic assignments of the Wolof UD treebanks, and the universal dependency program in general, are based on lexical functional grammar. In this view, whatever lexical item is the semantic head of the relative clause must have the rest of the relative clause as its dependents. The same is true for morphemes that were labeled as copulas; the subject, object and other arguments of the sentence would be dependents of this morpheme. In other cases, however, the same lexical item would be swapped and the dependency relationship completely inversed. These cases involve the same lexical items, but apply the semantic role of another missing element to them.

By adopting syntactic assumptions from the minimalist syntax formalism (Chomsky, 1996), a unified structure can be preserved with the UD framework. The minimalist framework allows for the assumption that the missing element is simply not overtly pronounced. Although common in many languages, the need for a copular verb or overt relative clause head need not outweigh the evidence that verbs or relative clause heads may simply be null items. A legitimate UD structure can still be attained while maintaining a consistent roll for these words. Such consistency better reflects the findings of (Tovey, 2019) that language-specific particularities should not be diluted in annotation to accommodate more commonly analyzed languages.

As editing the treebanks improves parsing from the baseline, the morphological and syntactic annotations made here should improve future parsers. (Dione, 2020) trained a Wolof-specific lexical functional grammar parser with 67% recall, 93% precision and an f-score of 78%. The most accurate parser model in this study had 78% recall, 78% precision, and an f-score of 78%. The significance of this study is not the accuracy of the parser itself, but the improvement from the baseline. The baseline-trained spaCy parser had 76% recall, 76% precision, and an f-score of 76%, meaning that each measure improved by 2%. This improvement should carry over if implemented with future Wolof UD parsers.

6 Conclusion

This study proposed considerations for improving the parsing of Wolof, one of the few African languages represented in a UD treebank. In the cases of relative clauses, assigning tags and dependency relations of definites based on their distribution and features provides a better parse than trying to distinguish them as pronoun in certain cases and determiners and demonstratives in others, following patterns from Indo-European languages. Positing a unified dependency structure for relative clauses also improves parsing. The idea of a copula imported from copular sentences in other languages does not fit the syntax of Wolof. Rather, classifying part-of-speech tags and labels based on their function in the clause results in a more accurate parse.

Although the UD framework is lexically oriented, and is more readily translated from lexical functional grammar, insights from the minimalist framework can inform morphological and syntactic annotation. These edited treebank annotations lead to improved parsing in the case of Wolof, and are likely to be useful for related African languages.

While the Wolof UD parser by (Dione, 2019) has similar accuracy, the fact that two out-of-the-box parsers showed improvements with the edited annotations is promising. The final accuracy achieved by this parser is similar to Dione's, and suggest that future parsers can attain even greater accuracy if these treebank annotation edits were combined with Dione's parser. Wolof is a low-resource language with only one treebank, also created by (Dione, 2019). 2% is a small but valuable improvement given accuracies of 75%-80% and a smaller treebank relative to langauges like English, French, and Russian. The improvements made to parsing compared to the baseline provide guidance for future annotation of African language treebanks, which are not proportionally represented in the UD project.

References

Noam Chomsky. 1996. *The Minimalist Program*. Current Studies in Linguistics. MIT Press.

Cheikh Bamba Dione. 2019. Developing universal dependencies for wolof. In *Third Workshop on Universal Dependencies (UDW, SyntaxFest 2019)*, Paris, France.

Cheikh Bamba Dione. 2020. Implementation and evaluation of an lfg-based parser for wolof. In *Proceedings of the 12th Conference on Language Resources and Evaluation (LREC 2020)*, pages 5128–5136, Marseille, France. European Language Resources Association (ELRA).

David M. Eberhard, Gary F. Simons, and Charles D. Fenning, editors. 2020. *Ethnologue: Languages of the World*, 23 edition. SIL International, Dallas, Texas USA.

Kim Gerdes, Bruno Guillaume, Sylvain Kahane, and Guy Perrier. 2018. SUD or surface-syntactic Universal Dependencies: An annotation scheme near-isomorphic to UD. In *Proceedings of the Second Workshop on Universal Dependencies (UDW 2018)*, pages 66–74, Brussels, Belgium. Association for Computational Linguistics.

Omar Ka. 1994. *Wolof phonology and morphology*. University Press of America.

Martina Martinović. 2017. Wolof wh-movement at the syntax-morphology interface. *Natural Language and Linguistic Theory*, 35:205–256.

Fiona McLaughlin. 1997. Noun classification in wolof: When affixes are not renewed. *Studies in African Linguistics*, 26(1):1–28.

Fiona McLaughlin. 2008. Senegal: the emergence of a national lingua franca. In Andrew Simpson, editor, *Language and National Identity in Africa*, pages 79–97. Oxford.

Jens Nilsson and Joakim Nivre. 2008. Malteval: An evaluation and visualization tool for dependency parsing. In *Sixth international conference on Language Resources and Evaluation*, Marrakech, Morocco.

Codu Mbassy Njie. 1982. *Description Syntaxique du Wolof de Gambie*. Les Nouvelles Éditions Africaines.

Stéphane Robert. 2006. Deictic space in wolof: discourse, syntax and the importance of absence. In Maya Hickmann and Stéphane Robert, editors, *Space in languages: linguistic systems and congnitive categories*, volume 66 of *Typological Studies in Language*, pages 155–174. John Benjamins.

Helmut Schmid. 1994. Probabilistic part-of-speech tagging using decision trees. In *Proceedings of International Conference on New Methods in Language Processing*, Manchester, UK.

Harold Torrence. 2013. *The Clause Structure of Wolof*. John Benjamins, Philadelphia.

Bethan Siân Tovey. 2019. You're not the pos of me: part-of-speech tagging as a markup problem. In *Proceedings of Balisage: The Markup Conference 2019*, volume 23 of *Balisage Series on Markup Technologies*, Washington, DC USA. Basilage: The Markup Conference 2019.

A Data availability statement

The data that support the findings of this study are openly available in the directory wolofUDParsing at `https://github.com/BillDyer/wolofUDParsing`.

Corpus Development of Kiswahili Speech Recognition Test and Evaluation sets: Preemptively Mitigating Demographic Bias Through Collaboration with Linguists

Kathleen Siminyu[⋆] **Kibibi Mohamed Amran**[†] **Abdulrahman Ndegwa Karatu**[‡]
Mnata Resani[#] **Mwimbi Makobo Junior**[α] **Rebecca Ryakitimbo**[⋆] **Britone Mwasaru**[⋆]
[⋆]Mozilla Foundation [†]County Government of Mombasa
[‡]Hekaya Arts Initiative [#]Dodoma University
[α]Independent
kathleensiminyu@gmail.com

Abstract

Language technologies, particularly speech technologies, are becoming more pervasive for access to digital platforms and resources. This brings to the forefront concerns of their inclusivity, first in terms of language diversity. Additionally, research shows speech recognition to be more accurate for men than for women(Tatman, 2017) and more accurate for individuals younger than 30 years of age than those older(Sawalha and Abu Shariah, 2013). In the Global South where languages are low resource, these same issues should be taken into consideration in data collection efforts to not replicate these mistakes. It is also important to note that in varying contexts within the Global South, this work presents additional nuance and potential for bias based on accents, related dialects and variants of a language. This paper documents: i) the designing and execution of a Linguists Engagement for purposes of building an inclusive Kiswahili Speech Recognition dataset, representative of the diversity among speakers of the language, ii) the unexpected yet key learning in terms of socio-linguistcs which demonstrate the importance of multidisciplinarity in teams developing datasets and NLP technologies, iii) the creation of a test dataset intended to be used for evaluating the performance of Speech Recognition models on demographic groups that are likely to be underrepresented.

1 Introduction

Language technologies, particularly speech technologies, are becoming more pervasive for access to digital platforms and resources. This brings to the forefront concerns of their inclusivity, first in terms of language diversity. Additionally, research shows speech recognition to be more accurate for men than for women and more accurate for individuals younger than 30 years of age than those older. In the Global South where languages are low resource, these same issues should be taken into consideration in data collection efforts to not replicate these mistakes. It is also important to note that in varying contexts within the Global South, this work presents additional nuance and potential for bias based on accents, related dialects and variants of a language.

Kiswahili is a language widely spoken in East Africa and is one of the official languages of the East African Community in addition to being a national language in Tanzania, Kenya, the Democratic Republic of Congo and Uganda. Kiswahili has over 200 million speakers[1]. It is the most widely spoken African language. In 2021, Mozilla Foundation kicked off efforts to build a Kiswahili dataset on Common Voice. Common Voice(CV) (Ardila et al., 2019) is a massively multilingual speech corpus developed for Automatic Speech Recognition purposes but can be useful in other domains such as language identification. Common Voice 8[2], the latest release of CV as of February 2022, is the most diverse multilingual open speech corpus in the world. It is now 18,000 hours, and 13 million voice clips - generated entirely by 200,000+ volunteer contributors around the world.

The inclusion of Kiswahili on CV is intended to democratise and diversify voice technology. Beyond the effort to include a language community previously left out of voice technology development, we are sensitive to the fact that even among marginalised communities, there is the possibility of having subsets of the entire population excluded based on characteristics such as age, gender, accent and dialect and we are working to mitigate these possible effects from the outset. This is the main reason we sought to include linguists in the planning and development stages of our work.

This paper documents:

1. the designing and execution of a Linguists

[1]Swahili gaining popularity globally

[2]Mozilla Common Voice dataset grows by 30% and reaches 87 languages

May 26-27, 2022 ©2022 Association for Computational Linguistics

Engagement for purposes of building an inclusive Kiswahili Speech Recognition dataset, representative of the diversity among speakers of the language

2. the unexpected yet key learning in terms of socio-linguistcs which demonstrate the importance of multi-disciplinarity in teams developing datasets and NLP technologies

3. the creation of a test dataset intended to be used for evaluating the performance of Speech Recognition models on demographic groups that are likely to be underrepresented

2 Linguists Engagement

2.1 Preliminary Preparation

In order to understand how best to invite linguists' participation, we took stock of some of the things we knew, in addition to drawing up what outputs we wanted to get from the process.

There are nuanced differences that occur in speech which to a native of East Africa, hint to a speaker's ethnic background or where they have spent a considerable amount of time so as to significantly impact how they speak. While these nuances are perceptible to locals, we were interested in determining whether linguists have codified these linguistic differences and, if yes, whether these would potentially be useful labels in a speech recognition dataset.

We considered already known to us that:

- 'Standard' Kiswahili is one of several Swahili dialects which have varying levels of mutual intelligibility, therefore dialectal differences should be considered

- Speakers for whom Kiswahili is a second-language may have their pronunciations affected by their mother-tongue

- Due to the multilingual nature of different geographical contexts within East Africa, code-switching and the influence of other languages spoken has given rise to variations of the language

As output that would be useful in the context of model training and development, we wanted:

- to identify dominant Kiswahili dialects and variants, based on number of existing speakers

- to select several from among these that we would then collaboratively build word lists and sentences for, as resources demonstrative of the dialectal differences

- to identify dominant Kiswahili accents and the features demonstrative of their distinctions

We invited expressions of interest from linguists and language experts within the EA region, looking to create a team that would balance a spread of various factors:

- Demonstration of a familiarity of the content of interest to us with regards to the language

- Geographical spread of Kenya, Tanzania, the Democratic Republic of Congo and possibly the Comoros would be good to ensure we have people connected to the dialects/communities

- Gender diversity

- Their personal contributions to the Kiswahili language community

We identified and worked with a team of 4 from Kenya, Tanzania and the DRC.

2.2 Methodology

2.2.1 Discussions

We had a series of discussions which were an interactive platform where we invited thoughts and opinions from the language experts based on their expertise and experience on a variety of topics. We recorded the discussions to enable us transcribe and extract the information we needed from them. Once data collection had taken place, these discussions were also a platform via which linguists could review and validate each others' work. Each discussion had a topic shared in advance to enable participants do preliminary research and prepare their thoughts. These topics included:

- Introduction to the Common Voice project - so as to introduce linguists and language experts to our work, why their contributions are important and how we will use the outputs

- Dominant Kiswahili Dialects - What are they? Why do they differ? Geographical regions where they are spoken, estimated number of speakers and what is the level of mutual intelligibility between them

Dialect	Region(Originated)	Classification
Kimiini (Mwiini, Barawa)	Sounthern Somalia	Northern dialect
Kitikuu (Bajuni, Gunya)	Border of Kenya and Somalia	Northern dialect
Kisiu	Pate Island	Northern dialect
Kipate	South West region of Pate island	Northern dialect
Kiamu	Northern region of Lamu Island	Northern dialect
Kishela	Lamu Island	Northern dialect
Kimatondoni	Southern region of Lamu Island	
Kimvita	Mombasa and Kilifi	Central dialect
Kijomvu	Mombasa	Central dialect
Kingare	Mombasa	Central dialect
Chifundi (Kisharazi)	Mombasa and Funzi Island	Central dialect
Kivumba (Kivanga)	Border of Kenya and Tanzania	Central dialect
Kichwaka	Shimoni	
Kimtang'ata (Kimrima)	Tanga	Southern dialect
Kipemba	Pemba Island	Southern dialect
Kiunguja (Kimji)	Mjini, Zanzibar	Southern dialect
Kitumbatu	Tumbatu Island	Southern dialect
Kijambiani	Zanzibar	
Kimakunduchi (Kikae)	Southern Zanzibar	Southern dialect
Kimgao	Southern coast of Tanzania	Southern dialect
Kimwani	Northern Msumbiji	
Kingwana	Shaba province of the DRC	

Table 1: Kiswahili dialects and their regions of origin. The 13 highlighted have been most used in writing.

- Dominant Kiswahili Accents, as well as the impact of other languages spoken in Eastern Africa and their impact on the use of the Kiswahili language eg. code-switching and the borrowing of words.
- Use case resource creation
- Validation of data resources created

2.2.2 Linguists' Field Work

The team of linguists and language experts was encouraged to develop the data resources in collaboration with native speakers. They were able to reach out to individuals and hold focus group discussions with groups of people from the relevant dialects, and through these, created the word and sentence lists expected as outputs. Using common words in English as a starting point, the task at hand was for us to identify their equivalents, synonyms or perhaps translations in the various dialects and variants that we selected to work on. These words were then used as a basis for the creation of sentences, with native speakers asked to compose sentences using the words. Discussions on various topics, were also facilitated and later transcribed to create text content. The linguists used various methods of engaging with the local populations;

- Relying on their own subjective experiences having moved from various diverse linguistic spaces. This was employed particularly where the language variants were concerned, as these more commonly vary with geographic location and age
- Watching video content(eg. on YouTube) and listening to audio content that has been created in the respective dialects and variants
- Engaging everyday people belonging to the dialects in conversation, asking them questions and transcribing relevant aspects of the conversation
- Focus groups where groups of people were invited and discussion prompts used to facilitate conversations on certain topics
- The use of communication platforms to reach native speakers in instances where they were not within physical reach eg. WhatsApp

Dialect/Variant	Words and Phrases	Sentences
Kiunguja	904	206
Kitumbatu	295	143
Kiswahili Sanifu	1413	-
Kiswahili cha Bara ya Tanzania	932	205
Kiswahili cha Bara ya Kenya	1311	-
Kipemba	475	183
Kingwana	776	-
Kimvita	2589	665
Kimakunduchi	464	204
Kibajuni	1510	566
Total	10669	2172

Table 2: Resources created for the 10 dialects/variants we focused on.

3 Qualitative Results

3.1 Origin Theories of the Kiswahili Language

Kiswahili is a widely spoken language, in East Africa and beyond. The matter of its origin is still an open question with several existing theories and continues to be a topic of research. There are two main origin stories of the Kiswahili language. The first is that Kiswahili is a pidgin, or creole, of Arabic and Bantu languages and that it came about when the Arabs came to Eastern Africa(EA) for trade purposes and began interacting with locals, who were Bantu speakers in the 19th century. *Linguistic studies show that situations of contact, where two linguistic communities interact, leads to the emergence of pidgins (simplified registers) that allow the two or more distinct linguistic groups to communicate.* (Nesbitt, 2018) Further to this are theories that it is a pidgin or a mixture that includes several other languages, Portuguese, Indian and Persian, as these are some of the other nationalities that were present along the EA coast for trading purposes. The second theory states that the term 'Kiswahili' is what is of Arabic origin, while the language itself is Bantu. That when the Arabs came to EA and found those living there, along the coast, they referred to them as 'Saheel', which is Arabic for 'the coast', and that over time this term evolved to become Kiswahili for the language and Swahili(or Waswahili in plural), referencing the people. (LaViolette, 2008) Further to the claim that Kiswahili is a Bantu language, the researchers support this theory, through demonstrating that linguistic features present in Kiswahili are similar to and also present in many other Bantu languages. Evidence of Kiswahili as a Bantu language dates back to as early as the 2nd century AD in a document called 'Periplus of Erythrean Sea' written by an anonymous Greek author detailing the early expansion of Swahili civilisations towards Somalia, Kenya and Zanzibar. (Maganda and Moshi, 2014)

3.1.1 The Politics of Language

The Standard Kiswahili, or Kiswahili Sanifu, we know today was created through the standardisation of a dialect known as *Kiunguja*, which originated from the Zanzibar and Pemba Islands. In the book *'Machozi Yameniishia'*, the poet Mohammed Ghassani, is critical of the choice of Kiunguja as the basis for Kiswahili Sanifu, and many Kiswahili writers and academics share this sentiment. The process was entirely owned by colonial authorities without the involvement of native speakers. The topic of standardising Kiswahili was driven by missionary groups. On one hand were German missionaries who were keen on using the dialects from Mombasa, Pate and Tanga, which are areas where they were stationed. On the other hand were English missionaries keen on using Kiunguja only because it was the language where they were stationed, on Zanzibar and neighbouring islands. In 1930 the Inter-territorial Language Committee chose the Zanzibari Kiswahili dialect, Kiunguja, as the source of Standard Kiswahili (Thomas, 2013), a decision influenced by British colonial rule over East African territories. In his book *Decolonising the Mind: The Language of African Literature*, Ngugi wa Thiong'o talks about the fact that language is an important tool, both for the coloniser and for the colonised. The making of Kiswahili Sanifu was primarily as a tool for the coloniser, so that they could understand the thoughts of the colonised and be understood amongst them. The Inter-territorial Language Committee, to ensure the propagation of Kiswahili Sanifu, would approve textbooks used to teach the language in schools, and this committee was entirely European. Textbooks were written and reviewed by Europeans and through this vocabulary changed, with some words being shortened and completely changing their meaning(Mbaabu, 2007). Therefore the more this language was standardised, the further it drifted away from what native Kiswahili speakers knew as Kiunguja. (Mbaabu, 2007) argues that Europeans completely changed and destroyed the language. Some see the standardisation as a tool to massacre other dialects. Its use and calculated propagation is schools led to reduced use of other related dialects.

Post-independence, Kiswahili Sanifu has been used as a national language in Tanzania, Kenya, the DRC and Uganda, and even as the medium of instruction in schools in Tanzania. The language has enjoyed great government support in the region, particularly in Tanzania. One of the greatest contributions of Julius Nyerere, the first president of Tanzania, was to push for the growth of Kiswahili in East and Central Africa as he believed that it could promote African unity, as it had done in Tanzania. Kiswahili scholars in EA continue to actively grow the language with literature departments at universities and research bodies continuing to publish new editions of Kiswahili dictionaries. Language bodies such as Baraza la Kiswahili la Taifa(BAKITA) in Tanzania and Chama cha Kiswahili cha Taifa(CHAKITA) in Kenya are responsible for the promotion of the Kiswahili language and publishing houses, notably in Tanzania, contribute to a growing body of literary works in circulation in the language.

It is important for us to acknowledge this history and process of standardisation since in our work, we view Kiunguja and Kiswahili Sanifu as two different languages, despite the former being the basis of the latter. Both languages are included in the selected group of languages that we further build upon. Knowledge of this history also justifies the decision to work on dialects related to Kiswahili and to ensure they are able to benefit from the wider work done for Kiswahili Sanifu.

3.2 Kiswahili Dialects

The term dialect refers to a variety of a language that is characteristic of a particular group of the language's speakers. These differences in language use may be caused by differences in age, gender, the clan or lineage of the speakers and geographical separation or distance between the relevant groups.

There are 23 major dialects of Kiswahili. These are listed in Table 1. Of these, 13 dialects have been used widely in writing and therefore more widespread in use. These 13 are highlighted in grey on the table.

Kiswahili dialects are classified into 3 major linguistic categories, clusters which cover the EA coast from north to south. There are Northern dialects, Central dialects and Southern dialects.(Whiteley, 1993) In addition to geographic proximity, there is greater mutual intelligibility within these clusters. This classification of dialects is also indicated in Table 1.

3.3 Kiswahili Variants

Our discussions surfaced the fact that languages are in a constant state of evolution and that for this work to be relevant to current use of Kiswahili in different geographical areas, beyond seeking to be inclusive of dominant and widely spoken (historical) dialects, it was necessary to also identify variants of the language used in different locales. In this work, we use the term linguistic variants to refer to regional, social or contextual differences in the ways that a particular language is used. We identified 5 main variant clusters that are largely based on geographical regions. These are:

- Coastal Kiswahili or Kiswahili cha Pwani, referring to the EA coast where the Swahili people are from.
- Inland Kiswahili in Kenya or Kiswahili cha Bara ya Kenya
- Inland Kiswahili in Tanzania or Kiswahili cha Bara ya Tanzania
- Northern DRC Kiswahili or Kiswahili cha DRC Kaskazini
- Southern DRC Kiswahili or Kiswahili cha DRC Kusini

There are many others, and infact each of these broad categorisations could potentially be further subdivided. However due to limited time and resources, we have chosen to work with these clusters and selected Kiswahili cha Bara ya Kenya and Kiswahili cha Bara ya Tanzania to include in resource development efforts in our work at this stage.

4 Quantitative Results

Our time with the linguists and language experts involved working to develop textual data that is representative of 10 dialects and variants of Kiswahili. In comparison to the work being done for the wider Kiswahili dataset, these subsets will be significantly smaller and our intention is to have the texts and the audios collected from the respective communities, be subsets of the whole.

The dialects and variants we focused on are as listed in Table 2, in addition to the number of resources created for each. We selected these 10 in a bid to balance out several characteristics.

- it is important that the dialects and variants selected have a significant number of speakers as our work is intended to build tools of use in present day settings
- we worked to ensure national representation of dialects and variants, considering Kenya, Tanzania and the Democratic Republic of Congo
- we worked to ensure linguistic diversity by including dialects from each of the 3 major linguistic categories of the language; Northern dialects, Central dialects and Southern dialects

These subsets will have 2 main purposes.

1. to help us quantitatively evaluate how our models and downstream applications perform on related dialects and variants. We would like to work towards models with equal performance across various variant and dialect speakers, not forgetting the gender and age aspects as well, and a first step will be figuring out if there is indeed degraded performance for the different groups
2. In the event that the performance is degraded for different demographics, we would like to make resources available to developers, so that depending on the particular local contexts they are building applications for, they will be able to fine-tune so as to improve performance if necessary.

The texts have been uploaded to GitHub[3] and text as well as audio resources will be made available in future releases of the Common Voice dataset.

5 Future Work

Future work will include further expansion of these text resources, particularly at a sentence level with a target of getting 5,000 unique sentences for each of the dialects and variants of focus. We will then proceed with data collection efforts for the voice component. Beyond the dialects and variants of focus in this work, we would encourage others to replicate these efforts for those that we have not been able to focus on. Additionally, the scope of our work does not include variants that make use of code-switching, such as *sheng*, a slang common among the youth of Nairobi, Kenya that mixes Kiswahili and English, and the variant clusters in the DRC, *Kiswahili cha DRC Kaskazini* and *Kiswahili cha DRC Kusini* which mix Kiswahili and French. The inclusion of these will be key for linguistic equity moving forward.

References

Rosana Ardila, Megan Branson, Kelly Davis, Michael Henretty, Michael Kohler, Josh Meyer, Reuben Morais, Lindsay Saunders, Francis M Tyers, and Gregor Weber. 2019. Common voice: A massively-multilingual speech corpus. *arXiv preprint arXiv:1912.06670*.

Adria LaViolette. 2008. Swahili cosmopolitanism in africa and the indian ocean world, ad 600–1500. *Archaeologies*, 4(1):24–49.

DM Maganda and LM Moshi. 2014. The swahili people and their language: A handbook for teaching. *London: Addonis & Abbey*.

Ireri Mbaabu. 2007. *Historia ya usanifishaji wa Kiswahili*. Taasisi ya Uchunguzi wa Kiswahili, Chuo Kikuu cha Dar es Salaam.

Francis Nesbitt. 2018. Swahili creolization and post-colonial identity in east africa. In *Creolization and Pidginization in Contexts of Postcolonial Diversity*, pages 116–131. Brill.

M Sawalha and M Abu Shariah. 2013. The effects of speakers' gender, age, and region on overall performance of arabic automatic speech recognition systems using the phonetically rich and balanced modern standard arabic speech corpus. In *Proceedings of the 2nd Workshop of Arabic Corpus Linguistics WACL-2*. Leeds.

[3] Kiswahili Dialects Data

Rachael Tatman. 2017. Gender and dialect bias in youtube's automatic captions. In *Proceedings of the first ACL workshop on ethics in natural language processing*, pages 53–59.

Jamie Arielle Thomas. 2013. *Becoming Swahili in Mexico City and Dar es Salaam: Identity in the learning of a globalized language through an African studies program*. Michigan State University.

Wilfred Howell Whiteley. 1993. *Swahili: the rise of a national language*. Gregg Revivals.

CLD^2: Language Documentation Meets Natural Language Processing for Revitalising Endangered Languages

Roberto Zariquiey* **Arturo Oncevay†** **Javier Vera‡**
*Dep. of Humanities, Linguistics Unit, Pontificia Universidad Católica del Perú, Perú
†School of Informatics, University of Edinburgh, Scotland
‡Escuela de Ing. Informática, Pontificia Universidad Católica de Valparaíso, Chile
rzariquiey@pucp.edu.pe, a.oncevay@ed.ac.uk, javier.vera@pucv.cl

Abstract

Language revitalisation should not be understood as a direct outcome of language documentation, which is mainly focused on the creation of language repositories. Natural language processing (NLP) offers the potential to complement and exploit these repositories through the development of language technologies that may contribute to improving the vitality status of endangered languages. In this paper, we discuss the current state of the interaction between language documentation and computational linguistics, present a diagnosis of how the outputs of recent documentation projects for endangered languages are underutilised for the NLP community, and discuss how the situation could change from both the documentary linguistics and NLP perspectives. All this is introduced as a bridging paradigm dubbed as Computational Language Documentation and Development (CLD^2). CLD^2 calls for (1) the inclusion of NLP-friendly annotated data as a deliverable of future language documentation projects; and (2) the exploitation of language documentation databases by the NLP community to promote the computerization of endangered languages, as one way to contribute to their revitalization.

1 Introduction

There are around 6,500 mutually unintelligible languages in the world (Hammarström et al., 2018). However, several thousand minority languages are in danger of being lost forever without leaving systematic records. In response to this, in the last decades *Documentary Linguistics* has become a major and vibrant field in Linguistics, which attempts to produce permanent records of the linguistic and cultural practices of the most threatened speech communities (Himmelmann (2012); Austin (2010); Woodbury (2011), among many others).

The outcomes of documenting a language in the frame of contemporary Documentary Linguistics often comprise large amounts of audio and video recordings, featuring collections of texts (often transcribed, translated and interlinearized), as well as lexical repertoires, framed as vocabularies or dictionaries, with different degrees of detail. These data are often deposited in international language archives, from which they can be accessed by scholars and members of speech communities. Transcription of texts is often conducted in the ELAN software (Max Planck Institute for Psycholinguistics, 2021), and interlinearization if often conducted using software tools, such as FLex (Summer Institute of Linguistics, 2021a) and Toolbox (Summer Institute of Linguistics, 2021b). The ideal outcome of this process are time-aligned parsed transcriptions with information about the morphological structure and the part-of-speech class of each lexical unit. Texts are often presented in .txt or .htlm formats.

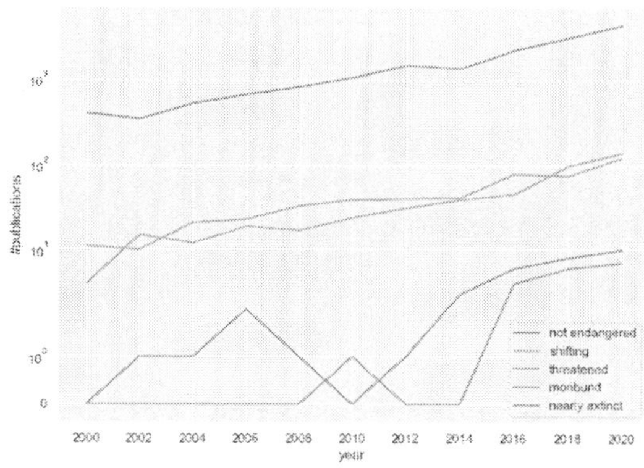

Figure 1: Number of publications in the ACL Anthology where languages are explicitly named in the title or abstract, and they are classified by their vitality from the Agglomerated Endangerment Status (Seifart et al., 2018). Vertical axis is in log-scale.

International language archives comprises documentation databases for several hundred languages. For instance, the Endangered Language Archive (ELAR) includes collections for 695 languages[1],

[1] https://www.elararchive.org/

Proceedings of the Fifth Workshop on the Use of Computational Methods in the Study of Endangered Languages, pages 20 - 30
May 26-27, 2022

each of which may comprise several hours of transcribed and parsed speech, which represent several thousands of fully annotated sentences. These data has been produced in the frame of collaborative documentation projects with high ethical standards in terms of their methods, their outcomes and their dissemination. Thus, in principle, the data available through international language archives have been published with the permission of the linguistic communities involved, and therefore it is expected that they will be incorporated into new research, education and revitalisation projects, ideally with the participation of members of the communities culturally and linguistically linked to the data (Bird, 2020).

Language databases, however, are often underexploited for further developments. Although field linguists very often incorporate revitalisation components in their documentation projects, language *documentation* and language *revitalisation* are not equivalent in terms of their frames, methods and outcomes. Language revitalisation will surely take advantage of the data produced in language documentation projects, by actively using such records in community-based revitalisation programs, which may take various shapes according to the needs of the community and/or the scope of the project. Although it is true that creating a language repository alone cannot revert language endangerment or decay, there are several ways in which documentation data can be integrated into revitalisation projects. Here, we focus on one, associated with the perspective of language technologies. Language technologies offer a promising perspective for language revitalisation, not only because technological gadgets such smart phones are becoming more popular even in rural areas, but also because they are inexpensive. The concern about language endangerment is a fundamental issue in contemporary approaches to Computational Linguistics, and in the last years, the "computerisation" of minority languages has become a growing field in NLP research (Berment, 2002). NLP developments' potential contribution to revitalising endangered languages is high, but there is still moderate interaction between Documentary Linguistics and NLP research for language revitalisation.

In this paper, we reflect on the necessity of increasing the interactions between Documentary Linguistics and NLP. This is not a novel point in the literature (see particularly (Levow et al., 2017)), but to our knowledge this is the first attempt to put some ideas on this topic together in a position paper. We hope that the proposals we dubbed here as Computational language Documentation and Development (CLD²) will stimulate debate and more vibrant interactions between documentary linguists and NLP developers.

2 Language documentation and language revitalisation

Language documentation (or documentary linguistics) emerged at the end of the last century as a research program whose primary motivation lies in the concern about the accelerating loss of language diversity in the world. As a response, language documentation aims to create permanent records of the linguistic and cultural practices of the most threatened speech communities (Himmelmann, 1998; Austin, 2010; Woodbury, 2011). These records are framed as databases, ideally including several hours of audio and video recordings of monologue and dialogue texts belonging to various genres and topics (e.g. traditional tales and myths, verbal art, jokes, historical facts, life stories, cultural knowledge, among others). A good portion of these recordings is transcribed, translated and parsed. Each transcribed sentence is expected to be time-aligned and to include an orthographic or IPA representation, a morphemic parse, glossing, information about parts of speech and a free translation.

Producing such linguistic databases is a long-term and time-consuming task that may take several years and requires considerable funding. The expectation is that these linguistic databases, conceptualised as multipurpose repositories deposited and curated in international archives, will be preserved for posterity and thus will support community-based revitalisation projects in the future. Although it is true that language documentation projects very often incorporate revitalisation components, they are inevitably marginal since the documentation itself is the main focus of documentary linguistics. Therefore, the contribution of language documentation to language revitalisation is potentially significant but mainly indirect: the linguistic repositories produced in the frame of language documentation projects can indeed contribute to future revitalisation projects, but crafting and archiving a repository is not expected to have an inherent positive impact on the vitality status of an endangered language.

`collections/`, consulted on February, 28th, 2022

3 Language documentation and computational linguistics

Most interactions between computational linguistics and documentary linguistics relate to the release of software tools for language documentation, processing and archiving (van Esch et al., 2019; Anastasopoulos et al., 2020). Computational linguists and computer scientists have developed advanced software tools to assist field linguists in the various processes of contemporary language documentation, making them less time-consuming, more efficient and more systematic. These tools have been crucial for the exponential growth of language documentation on a global scale.

Contemporary language documentation implies a large amount of technical sophistication for managing, annotating, processing and archiving lasting and large repositories (Himmelmann, 2006; Austin, 2006; Woodbury, 2003, among many others). This could not be achieved without the contribution of computer scientists (particularly software developers). In the last decades, we have witnessed the release of specialised software tools nowadays customary for language documentation, speech analysis and linguistic fieldwork. Field linguist's Toolbox (before "Shoebox") (Summer Institute of Linguistics, 2021a) and more recently Fieldworks (FLex) (Summer Institute of Linguistics, 2021b) are data management and analysis tools for field linguists developed by the Summer Institute of Linguistics, which are used in language documentation and taught in linguistics schools worldwide. Toolbox and Flex allow to create dictionaries, which can be used for morphosyntactic parsing and annotation of transcribed texts. Transcription is often conducted in a different and nowadays very popular software called ELAN (Max Planck Institute for Psycholinguistics, 2021), developed by the Max Planck Institute for Psycholinguistics. ELAN allows to visualise and play audio and video files in order to create time-aligned transcriptions and translations. ELAN can also be used for morphological parsing, but most linguists prefer to conduct such tasks in Toolbox or FLex since ELAN transcriptions can be easily exported into these programs. In Toolbox or Flex, each sentence in an ELAN file (containing a transcription and a free translation) can receive morphemic parsing, morpheme-by-morpheme glossing and parts of speech tags, among any other relevant information in the frame of a specific project. The resulting Toolbox/Flex files are text files that can be opened back in ELAN, in PRAAT (a phonetics analyser) (Boersma and Weenink, 2001), or to be processed in Python or any other programming language as plain texts. This is shown in Figure 2.

In sum, there have been several attempts from the computational side trying to create or incorporate intelligent components in language documentation tools and procedures (Good et al., 2014; Arppe et al., 2017, 2019; van Esch et al., 2019; Anastasopoulos et al., 2020). We find a one-direction application (computation into language documentation), but there are still few developments in the other direction (language documentation into computation). One of our takes in this paper is that language documentation can significantly contribute to computational linguistics by providing data and insights to develop NLP tools for endangered languages.

4 NLP has not really met endangered language documentation

As mentioned before, NLP has mainly focused on aiding the language documentation pipeline. However, has NLP taken advantage of the outputs of the documentation projects, especially for endangered languages?

4.1 Data

To address that question, we looked into the central repository of NLP publications: the ACL Anthology[2], the language inventory of massive multilingual datasets in NLP research (UniMorph (McCarthy et al., 2020), Universal Dependencies (Nivre et al., 2020), Tatoeba (Tiedemann, 2020))[3], and the central database of language documentation projects for endangered languages: The Endangered Languages Archive, or ELAR, which is supported by the Endangered Languages Documentation Programme or ELDP[4].

Besides, we work with the list of languages from Glottolog 4.4 (Hammarström et al., 2021), which is an extended inventory of living and extinct languages, including metadata such as geographical location and other properties. Moreover, we use the Agglomerated Endangerment Status (AES) classification proposed by Seifart et al. (2018) to distinguish the vitality status of the language inventory.

[2] https://aclanthology.org/

[3] We chose these datasets as they are the most diverse collections according to their language inventory.

[4] https://www.eldp.net/

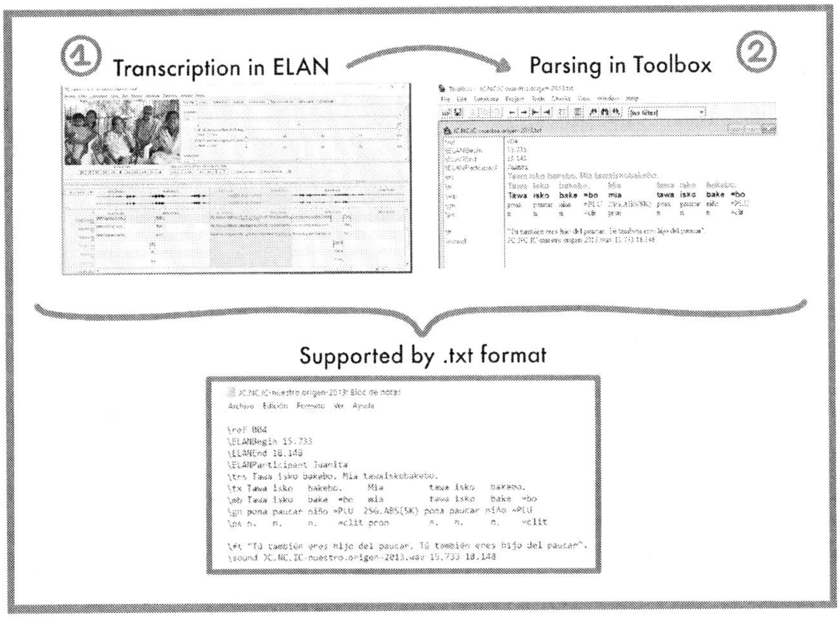

Figure 2: Graphic representation of the standard computational frame of language documentation: transcription is conducted in ELAN; ELAN files are imported into Toolbox or FLex where they are fully parsed and glossed. Crucially, we are dealing with .txt files throughout the process, which enormously facilitates their manipulation in any programming language

The classes are, from more to less vital: not endangered, shifting, threatened, moribund, nearly extinct and extinct[5].

4.2 Processing

With the language inventory and their vitality status, we first identified all the publications in the ACL Anthology (both conference and workshop proceedings) whose title or abstract explicitly includes the name of a language[6]. We manually clean false positives, such as concise language names (less than five characters) that can be confused with English words or acronyms.

A similar procedure is done with the ELAR database: all the projects are extracted, the language names are matched with the Glottolog inventory, and we manually curated potential false positives. From all the 570 projects published in the ELAR database, we identified 307 language names matching with the Glottolog database. With this, we obtained geographical information for 286 languages.

The procedure is similar for the massively multilingual (MM) datasets (Unimorph, Universal Dependencies and Tatoeba), and the language identifiers (ISO códe or name) are matched with the Glottolog inventory. Details of the considered languages are shown in Table 1[7].

4.3 Results

First, we look into how the NLP literature has considered endangered languages across time. Figure 1 shows that, in the current century, there is a considerable growth of publications for languages across different revitalisation status. For instance, articles about languages with shifting or threatened status have increased from ten to a hundred papers annually, but there is a very shy increase of the moribund or nearly extinct languages (from zero to ten annually), which are the most endangered ones. This is highly contrasted by the continuous increment of NLP publications for not endangered languages (from hundreds to thousands annually).

Then, we observe the overlap of the language coverage between the ELAR database, the ACL Anthology and the language inventory of massive multilingual datasets above-mentioned. Figure 3 shows the cross-over in a map. The very low over lapping was expected: from the ELAR inventory

[5] We do not consider the extinct languages in our analysis

[6] We are aware that this was not an extended practice previously, but the Bender's Rule (Bender, 2011) has remarked it recently. Moreover, if a work does not specify which language is working on, we can expect the target to be English or very well-known established multilingual datasets.

[7] Data is published in https://github.com/aoncevay/cld2

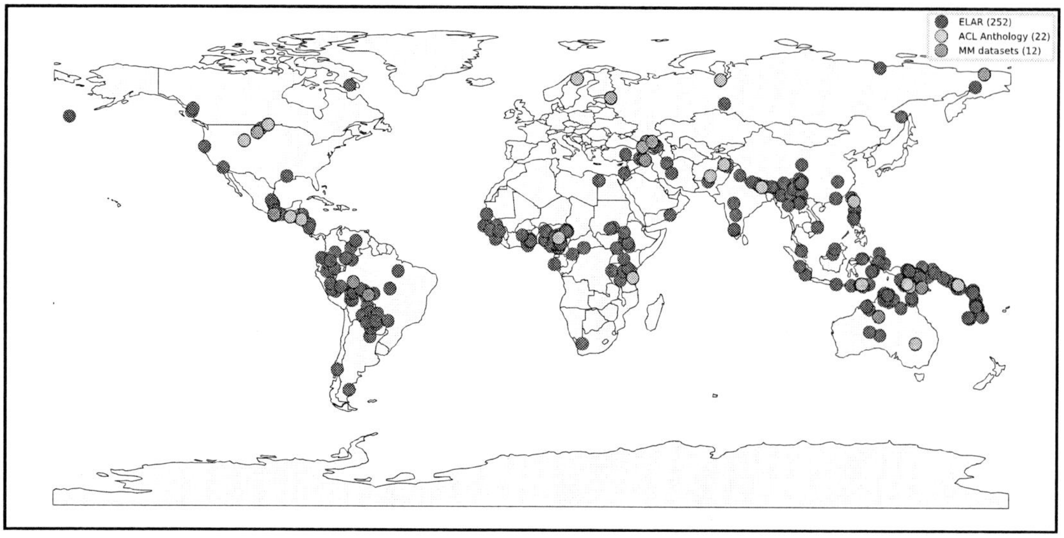

Figure 3: World map with languages in ELAR database and ACL Anthology. For the the present study, we only consider the languages of the ELAR database (570), whose names appear in *Glottolog* (version 4.4). This selection consists in 286 languages with geographical information. With this, 252 languages only belong to ELAR database (in blue); 22 languages belong to both ELAR database and ACL Anthology (in orange); and 12 languages belong to both ELAR database and massively multilingual (MM) datasets (Unimorph, Universal Dependencies and Tatoeba) (in red).

(286)[8], there are only 22 languages with at least one entry in the ACL Anthology (7.7%), and also 12 languages from this inventory included in at least one massive multilingual NLP dataset (4.2%). This two lists of languages overlaps only in 5 languages (Lakota, Laz, Chechen, Chukchi and Ingrian). Moreover, the geo-localisation allows us to observe the potential of these under-utilised resources in terms of representation for NLP research. Geographical areas such as the Americas, Africa, South-East Asia or Australia are better covered by language documentation projects than NLP resources and studies. Regional initiatives, such as Masakhane for Africa (Nekoto et al., 2020), or AmericasNLP (Mager et al., 2021), must look towards these still unexplored resources for extending their language coverage.

4.4 Discussion

The NLP community is recently more aware of the importance of language diversity in their research (Bender, 2009, 2011). Typologically-diverse language data allows to discuss results more broadly and to identify potential flaws of the proposed methods in languages with typologically uncommon grammatical properties and categories (O'Horan et al., 2016; Ponti et al., 2019). Furthermore, it has been pointed out that minority languages are indeed expected to exhibit unusual typological trends and non-prototypical degrees of complexity (Trudgill, 2011, 2010). Therefore, accessing and processing databases of a wide sample of endangered languages data would be beneficial for the NLP agenda.

However, as we observed, this has not been a priority. Why? We argue that this is mainly because of the visibility, accessibility, and readability of the data (from the NLP perspective):

Visibility Language documentation archives are mostly known in the linguistic community. The NLP community should look for data beyond the usual repositories. Besides ELAR, other famous repositories are the Archive of the Indigenous Languages of Latin America (AILLA)[9] from the University of Texas, The Language Archive (TLA)[10] from the Max Planck Institute for Psycholinguistics, and the Pacific and Regional Archive for Digi-

[8]We do not consider all languages in ELAR inventory (570) because languages in ELAR database are identified in most cases only by their names (and not by ISO codes), which match with the Glottolog database for 307 languages.

[9]`https://ailla.utexas.org/`

[10]`https://archive.mpi.nl/tla/`

tal Sources in Endangered Cultures (PARADISEC). [11]

Accessibility Most of the language documentation databases are open-source, but one often needs to become a registered user in order to access the materials deposited in the language archives. Furthermore, some linguists block fully public access to their records as a way to protect speech community's rights.

Readability Although most language documentation outputs video, audio and text files (plain texts or interlineal glossed texts, known as IGT), they are not labelled or processed for immediate use for NLP developments. If we observe the example in Figure 2, we can quickly identify potential resources for morphological segmentation and analysis, part-of-speech tagging, and machine translation. However, IGT is partially standardised, as not all the annotations follow the same label schema.

In sum, NLP is not taking advantage of all the resources potentially available for different applications. Moreover, from the three previously explained factors, readability is the hardest to overcome. One of our takes in this paper is to push the NLP community to focus more on the parsing and processing of the already published data, which is unlikely to be modified, unfortunately[12]. For instance, there should be paid more attention to IGT parsing research (Lewis and Xia, 2010; Round et al., 2020) or to the establishment of a more universally-readable IGT schema (Palmer and Erk, 2007). All this is complementary to the last point of Section 3, as we expect that, ideally, future deliverables of documentation projects could consider the annotation schema and resources that are more easily readable for NLP research.

5 CLD²: Computational Language Documentation and Development

Computational linguistics and language documentation share not only the assumption that technology plays an important role in the design and development of language-related projects, but also a crucial concern about language endangerment and loss. This concern is obvious from the perspective of language documentation, in the sense that it assumes itself as a response to language endangerment Himmelmann (2006, 5). A similar shift towards minority languages can be found in contemporary approaches to computational linguistics. Berment (2002) regrets that less than 1% of the world's languages have been correctly "computerised". That is, for Berment (2002), the fact that 99% of the world's languages lack computational tools (NLP tools as spell-checking or machine translation) requires immediate attention. Since the seminal article by Krauss (1992), language endangerment and language dormancy is a major concern for both current language documentation and computational linguistics.

This paper takes the shared interest in linguistic diversity found in language documentation and computational linguistics further by proposing a paradigm that assumes an intense and multifaceted interaction between the two: Computational Language Documentation and Development (CLD²). CLD² assumes, following (Berment, 2002), that "computerisation" should be understood as one main task in language documentation and, at the same time, proposes a basic protocol to carry out this task. This basic protocol is based on a straightforward idea according to which any documentation project, in addition to its customary outcomes (audio and video recordings, transcriptions, morphological parsing and glossing, and free translations), should include NLP-friendly annotated data as its deliverables:

1. Monolingual and parallel corpora[13] in a digital format, ideally taken from a specific domain or discourse that is relevant for the language speaker community;
2. A public representative set of sentences annotated in universal frameworks for morphology and syntax, such as Universal Morphology (McCarthy et al., 2020) and Universal Dependencies (Nivre et al., 2020)[14], which are well-known in the NLP field; and
3. A communication describing the main characteristics of the released Universal Depen-

[11] https://www.paradisec.org.au

[12] Most of the language documentation projects that are published might do not have extra funding allocated for any update, or new funding will be required for the job.

[13] Translations paired with English or another relevant language spoken in the specific region, such as Spanish in Latin America.

[14] The identification of syntax dependencies and their annotation is not common in language documentation projects. However Croft et al. (2017) have argued that the UD scheme shares crucial principles with typological research. Indeed, research on linguistic typology may benefit from the development of an annotation scheme like UD and vice-versa.

dencies (Nivre et al., 2020) treebank and Universal Morphology (McCarthy et al., 2020) dataset, so that NLPers can understand the particularities and challenges of the data.

We attempt then to draw documentary and computational linguists' attention towards the potentialities of a more integral and systematic collaboration between them. On the one hand, field linguists may get involved in creating relevant products from the NLP perspective (e.g. preparing representative treebanks taking as a starting point their own data). On the other hand, NLPers can get involved in the development of processes and protocols that may contribute to the transformation of linguistic data of the traditional sort into formats that may support NLP developments.

According to Forcada (2006, 1), one feature for a language to be considered as a minor one is the few to zero availability of machine-readable resources. There are features such as the number of speakers or literacy speakers that may support the definition of a minor language in a general overview, but we want to emphasise the computational perspective in Forcada's statement. Dictionaries, translated text or annotated corpora, that are currently part of a standard language documentation process, are instances of machine-readable data. We consider that linguistic corpora are insufficient to disentangle the relationship between a language and its characterisation as a minor language. We claim the need to develop more multiple resources to support a consistent revitalisation of the language. However, we do not mean that all language documentation processes should include a massive technology development by itself. The magnitude of such a project would be cost-prohibitive. Nevertheless, we have identified some elements that might be included in a documentation process that could drive a "computerisation" effect in the studied language.

We want to emphasise the development of multipurpose linguistic databases, specifically aiming at language technologies, whose implementation will not radically increment the amount of expected work for the linguist. Language technologies are purpose-specific programmes that try to address language-related tasks from spell- or grammar-checking to automatic machine translation. Based on such databases, NLPers and field linguists may work together to develop NLP toolkits for minority languages. An NLP Toolkit is a set of different tools made to computerise a language fully. We then take inspiration from the Basic Language Resource Kit (Krauwer, 2003) and also consider established annotation frameworks, such as UD or UniMorph, and current state-of-the-art methods in NLP, such as transfer learning. With transfer learning protocols, especially multilingual pretraining (Lauscher et al., 2020; Ebrahimi and Kann, 2021), CLD² projects might automatise learning tasks by taking advantage of larger amounts of multilingual data and tools. A learning task in this context may refer to a specific NLP or functionality, such as a dependency parser, which has been trained to learn how to parse the syntax in a textual sentence. Finally, we list the main tools that such basic toolkits could have:

1. Morphological tools: such as morphological analysis, to determine the base form or lemma of an inflected word and its morphological features; morphological segmentation, to identify the canonical or surface morphemes (Mager et al., 2020); and morphological reinflection (Pimentel et al., 2021), which exploits UniMorph data. Morphological knowledge is usually crafted in language documentation projects (see Figure 2), so these deliverables could be the most manageable.
2. Spell-checker: to detect and automatic correct of spelling errors. Dictionary-based spell-checkers can be easily retrieved from a documentation project with a lexicon as an output, whereas rule-based ones can be adapted from a finite-state morphological analyser. Data-driven spell-checking is also possible to develop from monolingual data only.
3. Syntactic parser: to analyse the relationships between the words and phrases that compose a text. A dependency syntax parser can be developed using UD annotated data, and is also benefited for transfer learning and pre-training approaches (Lauscher et al., 2020). Current language documentation projects do not usually focus on this kind of annotation, but we emphasise that it might be relevant for research not only on NLP but also in linguistic typology (Croft et al., 2017).
4. Part-of-Speech tagger and Named Entity Recognition: both tasks are sequence taggers, and are two of the tasks that have been benefited the most from multilingual pretraining, and few- or zero-shot learning (Lauscher et al.,

2020; Ebrahimi and Kann, 2021). POS tagging could be easily adapted from the current glossing annotation, whereas NER annotation can be quickly extended or marked in the glosses.

Besides these tools, further developments that can be achieved for endangered languages, such as machine translation, are very appealing. However, we also need to point out that, despite the progress of the pretraining approaches and the use of few labelled examples, a translation system (or other kinds of NLP tools) should not be deployed with low-quality outputs, as it can mislead the user. Limitations of their usage should be assessed according to the annotated data used and the purpose of the systems.

6 Conclusion

CLD² calls for an enrichment of language documentation projects by means of incorporating components, outcomes and methods from NLP research, as a strategy to promote the computarisation and revitalisation of minority languages. This paper shows that most of the interactions between computational linguistics and language documentation are framed as software developments that facilitate the various processes involved in documenting a language. The potential contributions of language documentation and language repositories to NLP research are under-exploited and deserve urgent attention from the NLP community. At the same time field linguists may also incorporate into the outcomes of their projects, data crafted into paradigms that can be automatically used for NLP developments (Universal Dependencies and/or Universal Morphology, for instance).

This will benefit not only language documentation and computational linguistics scholars but also typologists and speech communities, as research in NLP has recently paid some attention to linguistic typology as a substantial source of linguistics knowledge to improve performance in different algorithms and technologies (O'Horan et al., 2016; Ponti et al., 2019). Indigenous communities, in turn, are highly enthusiastic about the computerisation of their languages as a political strategy that vindicates their languages and demonstrates that they are as valuable as major European languages. CLD² can significantly contribute to this aim by promoting productive exchanges among field linguists, NLP researchers and members of indigenous communities as part of multi-component projects that put language revitalisation at their core.

7 Acknowledgements

The first author acknowledges the support of CONCYTEC-ProCiencia, Peru, under the contract 183-2018-FONDECYT-BM-IADT-MU from the funding call E041-2018-01-BM.

References

Antonios Anastasopoulos, Christopher Cox, Graham Neubig, and Hilaria Cruz. 2020. Endangered languages meet Modern NLP. In *Proceedings of the 28th International Conference on Computational Linguistics: Tutorial Abstracts*, pages 39–45, Barcelona, Spain (Online). International Committee for Computational Linguistics.

Antti Arppe, Jeff Good, Mans Hulden, Jordan Lachler, Alexis Palmer, and Lane Schwartz, editors. 2017. *Proceedings of the 2nd Workshop on the Use of Computational Methods in the Study of Endangered Languages*. Association for Computational Linguistics, Honolulu.

Antti Arppe, Jeff Good, Mans Hulden, Jordan Lachler, Alexis Palmer, Lane Schwartz, and Miikka Silfverberg, editors. 2019. *Proceedings of the 3rd Workshop on the Use of Computational Methods in the Study of Endangered Languages Volume 1 (Papers)*. Association for Computational Linguistics, Honolulu.

Peter K Austin. 2006. Data and language documentation. *Essentials of language documentation*, 178:87.

Peter K. Austin. 2010. Communities, ethics and rights in language documentation. In Peter K. Austin, editor, *Language documentation and description*, volume 7, pages 34–54. London: School of Oriental and African Studies.

Emily M. Bender. 2009. Linguistically naïve != language independent: Why NLP needs linguistic typology. In *Proceedings of the EACL 2009 Workshop on the Interaction between Linguistics and Computational Linguistics: Virtuous, Vicious or Vacuous?*, pages 26–32, Athens, Greece. Association for Computational Linguistics.

Emily M Bender. 2011. On achieving and evaluating language-independence in nlp. *Linguistic Issues in Language Technology*, 6(3):1–26.

Vincent Berment. 2002. Several directions for minority languages computerization. In *COLING 2002: The 17th International Conference on Computational Linguistics: Project Notes*.

Steven Bird. 2020. Decolonising speech and language technology. In *Proceedings of the 28th International Conference on Computational Linguistics*, pages 3504–3519, Barcelona, Spain (Online). International Committee on Computational Linguistics.

Paul Boersma and David Weenink. 2001. Praat, a system for doing phonetics by computer. *Glot International*, 5(9/10):341–345.

William Croft, Dawn Nordquist, Katherine Looney, and Michael Regan. 2017. Linguistic typology meets universal dependencies. In *TLT*, pages 63–75.

Abteen Ebrahimi and Katharina Kann. 2021. How to adapt your pretrained multilingual model to 1600 languages. In *Proceedings of the 59th Annual Meeting of the Association for Computational Linguistics and the 11th International Joint Conference on Natural Language Processing (Volume 1: Long Papers)*, pages 4555–4567, Online. Association for Computational Linguistics.

Mikel Forcada. 2006. Open source machine translation: an opportunity for minor languages. In *Proceedings of the Workshop "Strategies for developing machine translation for minority languages", LREC*, volume 6, pages 1–6.

Jeff Good, Julia Hirschberg, and Owen Rambow, editors. 2014. *Proceedings of the 2014 Workshop on the Use of Computational Methods in the Study of Endangered Languages*. Association for Computational Linguistics, Baltimore, Maryland, USA.

Harald Hammarström, Thom Castermans, Robert Forkel, Kevin Verbeek, Michel A. Westenberg, and Bettina Speckmann. 2018. Simultaneous visualization of language endangerment and language description. *Language Documentation & Conservation*, 12:359–392.

Harald Hammarström, Robert Forkel, Martin Haspelmath, and Sebastian Bank. 2021. Glottolog 4.4. Leipzig: Max Planck Institute for Evolutionary Anthropology. Available at `http://glottolog.org`. Accessed on 2021-05-20.

Nikolaus Himmelmann. 1998. Documentary and descriptive linguistics. *Linguistics*, 36:161–195.

Nikolaus Himmelmann. 2012. Linguistic data types and the interface between language documentation and description. *Language Documentation & Conservation*, 6:187–207.

Nikolaus P Himmelmann. 2006. Language documentation: What is it and what is it good for. *Essentials of language documentation*, 178(1).

Michael Krauss. 1992. The world's languages in crisis. *Language*, 68(1):1–10.

Steven Krauwer. 2003. The basic language resource kit (blark) as the first milestone for the language resources roadmap. In *Proceedings of SPECOM*, volume 2003, pages 8–15.

Anne Lauscher, Vinit Ravishankar, Ivan Vulić, and Goran Glavaš. 2020. From zero to hero: On the limitations of zero-shot language transfer with multilingual Transformers. In *Proceedings of the 2020 Conference on Empirical Methods in Natural Language Processing (EMNLP)*, pages 4483–4499, Online. Association for Computational Linguistics.

Gina-Anne Levow, Emily M. Bender, Patrick Littell, Kristen Howell, Shobhana Chelliah, Joshua Crowgey, Dan Garrette, Jeff Good, Sharon Hargus, David Inman, Michael Maxwell, Michael Tjalve, and Fei Xia. 2017. STREAMLInED challenges: Aligning research interests with shared tasks. In *Proceedings of the 2nd Workshop on the Use of Computational Methods in the Study of Endangered Languages*, pages 39–47, Honolulu. Association for Computational Linguistics.

William D Lewis and Fei Xia. 2010. Developing odin: A multilingual repository of annotated language data for hundreds of the world's languages. *Literary and Linguistic Computing*, 25(3):303–319.

Manuel Mager, Özlem Çetinoğlu, and Katharina Kann. 2020. Tackling the low-resource challenge for canonical segmentation. In *Proceedings of the 2020 Conference on Empirical Methods in Natural Language Processing (EMNLP)*, pages 5237–5250, Online. Association for Computational Linguistics.

Manuel Mager, Arturo Oncevay, Abteen Ebrahimi, John Ortega, Annette Rios, Angela Fan, Ximena Gutierrez-Vasques, Luis Chiruzzo, Gustavo Giménez-Lugo, Ricardo Ramos, Ivan Vladimir Meza Ruiz, Rolando Coto-Solano, Alexis Palmer, Elisabeth Mager-Hois, Vishrav Chaudhary, Graham Neubig, Ngoc Thang Vu, and Katharina Kann. 2021. Findings of the AmericasNLP 2021 shared task on open machine translation for indigenous languages of the Americas. In *Proceedings of the First Workshop on Natural Language Processing for Indigenous Languages of the Americas*, pages 202–217, Online. Association for Computational Linguistics.

Max Planck Institute for Psycholinguistics. 2021. *ELAN (Version 6.2)*. The Language Archive, Nijmegen. Https://archive.mpi.nl/tla/elan.

Arya D. McCarthy, Christo Kirov, Matteo Grella, Amrit Nidhi, Patrick Xia, Kyle Gorman, Ekaterina Vylomova, Sabrina J. Mielke, Garrett Nicolai, Miikka Silfverberg, Timofey Arkhangelskiy, Nataly Krizhanovsky, Andrew Krizhanovsky, Elena Klyachko, Alexey Sorokin, John Mansfield, Valts Ernštreits, Yuval Pinter, Cassandra L. Jacobs, Ryan Cotterell, Mans Hulden, and David Yarowsky. 2020. UniMorph 3.0: Universal Morphology. In *Proceedings of the 12th Language Resources and Evaluation Conference*, pages 3922–3931, Marseille, France. European Language Resources Association.

Wilhelmina Nekoto, Vukosi Marivate, Tshinondiwa Matsila, Timi Fasubaa, Taiwo Fagbohungbe,

Solomon Oluwole Akinola, Shamsuddeen Muhammad, Salomon Kabongo Kabenamualu, Salomey Osei, Freshia Sackey, Rubungo Andre Niyongabo, Ricky Macharm, Perez Ogayo, Orevaoghene Ahia, Musie Meressa Berhe, Mofetoluwa Adeyemi, Masabata Mokgesi-Selinga, Lawrence Okegbemi, Laura Martinus, Kolawole Tajudeen, Kevin Degila, Kelechi Ogueji, Kathleen Siminyu, Julia Kreutzer, Jason Webster, Jamiil Toure Ali, Jade Abbott, Iroro Orife, Ignatius Ezeani, Idris Abdulkadir Dangana, Herman Kamper, Hady Elsahar, Goodness Duru, Ghollah Kioko, Murhabazi Espoir, Elan van Biljon, Daniel Whitenack, Christopher Onyefuluchi, Chris Chinenye Emezue, Bonaventure F. P. Dossou, Blessing Sibanda, Blessing Bassey, Ayodele Olabiyi, Arshath Ramkilowan, Alp Öktem, Adewale Akinfaderin, and Abdallah Bashir. 2020. Participatory research for low-resourced machine translation: A case study in African languages. In *Findings of the Association for Computational Linguistics: EMNLP 2020*, pages 2144–2160, Online. Association for Computational Linguistics.

Joakim Nivre, Marie-Catherine de Marneffe, Filip Ginter, Jan Hajič, Christopher D. Manning, Sampo Pyysalo, Sebastian Schuster, Francis Tyers, and Daniel Zeman. 2020. Universal Dependencies v2: An evergrowing multilingual treebank collection. In *Proceedings of the 12th Language Resources and Evaluation Conference*, pages 4034–4043, Marseille, France. European Language Resources Association.

Helen O'Horan, Yevgeni Berzak, Ivan Vulić, Roi Reichart, and Anna Korhonen. 2016. Survey on the use of typological information in natural language processing. In *Proceedings of COLING 2016, the 26th International Conference on Computational Linguistics: Technical Papers*, pages 1297–1308, Osaka, Japan. The COLING 2016 Organizing Committee.

Alexis Palmer and Katrin Erk. 2007. IGT-XML: An XML format for interlinearized glossed text. In *Proceedings of the Linguistic Annotation Workshop*, pages 176–183, Prague, Czech Republic. Association for Computational Linguistics.

Tiago Pimentel, Maria Ryskina, Sabrina J. Mielke, Shijie Wu, Eleanor Chodroff, Brian Leonard, Garrett Nicolai, Yustinus Ghanggo Ate, Salam Khalifa, Nizar Habash, Charbel El-Khaissi, Omer Goldman, Michael Gasser, William Lane, Matt Coler, Arturo Oncevay, Jaime Rafael Montoya Samame, Gema Celeste Silva Villegas, Adam Ek, Jean-Philippe Bernardy, Andrey Shcherbakov, Aziyana Bayyr-ool, Karina Sheifer, Sofya Ganieva, Matvey Plugaryov, Elena Klyachko, Ali Salehi, Andrew Krizhanovsky, Natalia Krizhanovsky, Clara Vania, Sardana Ivanova, Aelita Salchak, Christopher Straughn, Zoey Liu, Jonathan North Washington, Duygu Ataman, Witold Kieraś, Marcin Woliński, Totok Suhardijanto, Niklas Stoehr, Zahroh Nuriah, Shyam Ratan, Francis M. Tyers, Edoardo M. Ponti, Grant Aiton, Richard J. Hatcher, Emily Prud'hommeaux, Ritesh Kumar, Mans Hulden, Botond Barta, Dorina Lakatos, Gábor Szolnok, Judit Ács, Mohit Raj, David Yarowsky, Ryan Cotterell, Ben Ambridge, and Ekaterina Vylomova. 2021. Sigmorphon 2021 shared task on morphological reinflection: Generalization across languages. In *Proceedings of the 18th SIGMORPHON Workshop on Computational Research in Phonetics, Phonology, and Morphology*, pages 229–259, Online. Association for Computational Linguistics.

Edoardo Maria Ponti, Helen O'Horan, Yevgeni Berzak, Ivan Vulić, Roi Reichart, Thierry Poibeau, Ekaterina Shutova, and Anna Korhonen. 2019. Modeling language variation and universals: A survey on typological linguistics for natural language processing. *Computational Linguistics*, 45(3):559–601.

Erich Round, Mark Ellison, Jayden Macklin-Cordes, and Sacha Beniamine. 2020. Automated parsing of interlinear glossed text from page images of grammatical descriptions. In *Proceedings of the 12th Language Resources and Evaluation Conference*, pages 2878–2883, Marseille, France. European Language Resources Association.

Frank Seifart, Nicholas Evans, Harald Hammarström, and Stephen C. Levinson. 2018. Language documentation twenty-five years on. *Language*, 94(4e):324–345.

Summer Institute of Linguistics. 2021a. *Field linguist's Toolbox (Version 1.6.4)*. Http://www.fieldlinguiststoolbox.org/?i=1.

Summer Institute of Linguistics. 2021b. *Fieldworks (Version 9.0)*. Https://software.sil.org/fieldworks/.

Jörg Tiedemann. 2020. The tatoeba translation challenge – realistic data sets for low resource and multilingual MT. In *Proceedings of the Fifth Conference on Machine Translation*, pages 1174–1182, Online. Association for Computational Linguistics.

Peter Trudgill. 2010. Contact and sociolinguistic typology. In Raymond Hickey, editor, *The Handbook of Language Contact*, pages 299–319. Oxford: Wiley-Blackwell.

Peter Trudgill. 2011. *Sociolinguistic Typology: social determinants of linguistic complexity*. Oxford: Oxford University Press.

Daan van Esch, Ben Foley, and Nay San. 2019. Future directions in technological support for language documentation. In *Proceedings of the 3rd Workshop on the Use of Computational Methods in the Study of Endangered Languages Volume 1 (Papers)*, pages 14–22, Honolulu. Association for Computational Linguistics.

Anthony Woodbury. 2011. Language documentation. In Peter Austin and Julia Sallabank, editors, *Handbook of Endangered Languages*, The Cambridge Handbook of Endangered Languages, pages 159–186. Cambridge: Cambridge University Press.

Anthony C Woodbury. 2003. Defining documentary linguistics. *Language documentation and description*, 1(1):35–51.

A AES status for massively multilingual datasets

AES status	Tatoeba	Unimorph	UD
not endangered	164	60	52
threatened	71	25	16
shifting	44	17	16
moribund	11	4	2
nearly extinct	7	4	1
extinct	24	17	11

Table 1: Agglomerated Endangerment Status (AES) (Seifart et al., 2018) statistics for MM databases (Tatoeba, Unimorph and Universal Dependencies).

One Wug, Two Wug+s: Transformer Inflection Models Hallucinate Affixes

Farhan Samir
University of British Columbia
fsamir@mail.ubc.ca

Miikka Silfverberg
University of British Columbia
msilfver@mail.ubc.ca

Abstract

Data augmentation strategies are increasingly important in NLP pipelines for low-resourced and endangered languages, and in neural morphological inflection, augmentation by so called data hallucination is a popular technique. This paper presents a detailed analysis of inflection models trained with and without data hallucination for the low-resourced Canadian Indigenous language Gitksan. Our analysis reveals evidence for a concatenative inductive bias in augmented models—in contrast to models trained without hallucination, they strongly prefer affixing inflection patterns over suppletive ones. We find that preference for affixation in general improves inflection performance in "wug test" like settings, where the model is asked to inflect lexemes missing from the training set. However, data hallucination dramatically reduces prediction accuracy for reduplicative forms due to a misanalysis of reduplication as affixation. While the overall impact of data hallucination for unseen lexemes remains positive, our findings call for greater qualitative analysis and more varied evaluation conditions in testing automatic inflection systems. Our results indicate that further innovations in data augmentation for computational morphology are desirable.

1 Introduction

Data augmentation strategies, for instance, back-translation (Sennrich et al., 2016) and mixed sample data augmentation (Zhang et al., 2018; Guo et al., 2020), are increasingly important components of NLP pipelines (Feng et al., 2021). These strategies often form the cornerstone of modern NLP models for lower-resourced and endangered languages and dialects in particular (e.g., Kumar et al., 2021; Hauer et al., 2020; Zhao et al., 2020; Ryan and Hulden, 2020), where models can otherwise badly overfit due to the paucity of training data.

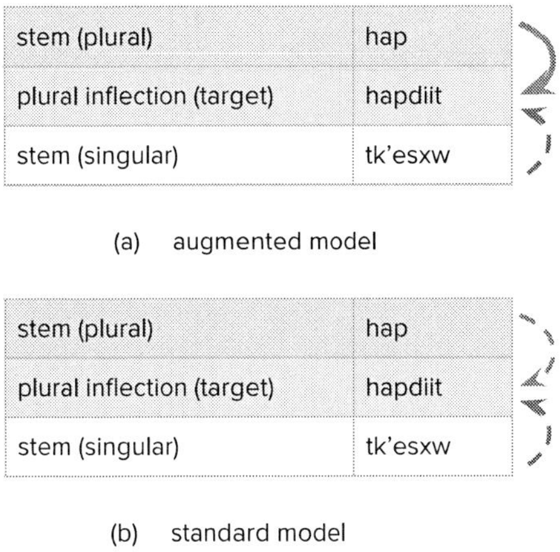

Figure 1: Predicting a plural inflection for a lexeme using two possible source forms (singular stem and plural stem). **(a)** A Transformer model trained with data hallucination prefers the plural form as the source (depicted by a thicker arrow, representing model confidence). **(b)** The same model trained without hallucination exhibits no preference.

Consider the task of low-resource morphological inflection: high-capacity neural models trained without data augmentation are prone to collapsing at test time, achieving as little as 0% accuracy (Silfverberg et al., 2017). Conversely, those very same models trained on artificially augmented data can generalize respectably. Unfortunately, there is little research on understanding why these augmentation strategies work. We know little about the changes they cause in the model – are they simply a form of weight regularization? Do they alleviate class imbalance? Or do they provide a task-specific inductive bias?

In this paper, we investigate the data hallucination strategy, a relatively commonplace strategy (Anastasopoulos and Neubig, 2019; Silfverberg et al., 2017) for increasing the size of small morphological datasets. We conduct our study in the context of developing a Paradigm Cell-Filling (PCFP; Ackerman et al., 2009; Silfverberg and Hulden, 2018) system for the Gitksan language – a critically

Proceedings of the Fifth Workshop on the Use of Computational Methods in the Study of Endangered Languages, pages 31 - 40
May 26-27, 2022

endangered language with an estimated 300-850 speakers (Dunlop et al., 2018) – that can be used for applications such as developing pedagogical noun and verb conjugation exercises and further computer-assisted language learning applications.

Given a partial inflectional paradigm with n filled slots and a number of empty slots, the task is to complete the paradigm by predicting all the missing slots from the given ones. Following previous work on PCFP (Silfverberg and Hulden, 2018; Liu and Hulden, 2020), we leverage morphological reinflection models to complete PCFP. Specifically, we employ the one-source model of Liu and Hulden (2020): We use each of the n given forms in turn to predict the form in an empty target slot, giving n output forms (see Fig. 1, where $n = 2$). We then select one of the output forms as our prediction for the empty slot: We pick the predictions that the model makes with the highest confidence, a decision strategy we denote MAX.[1]

Given the relatively small size of our paradigm dataset, further described in Section 2, we investigate whether data hallucination is an effective strategy for mitigating overfitting. In accordance with recent results (Liu and Hulden, 2021), we find that data hallucination improves performance in "wug test" (Berko, 1958) like conditions: where no inflectional variant of a lexeme was witnessed during training. Surprisingly, however, we also find that data hallucination significantly worsens performance for lexemes which were partially observed during training; that is at least one of the inflectional variants of the lexeme was present in the training data.

These findings motivated a controlled error analysis of our PCFP system to discover why data hallucination generalizes to the unobserved test setting but seemingly slashes performance in the observed test setting. This analysis yields two major insights. First, we find that the model trained without hallucination is "often right for the wrong reason" (McCoy et al., 2019): our error analysis reveals that a unaugmented Transformer model exhibits undesirable memorization to a significant degree, even when incorporating recently prescribed parameter settings for inflection (Wu et al., 2021; Liu and Hulden, 2020). This allows the model to memorize lexeme-specific inflection patterns, rather than learning the morphophonological structure of the language. That is, we find that the model trained without hallucination relies on a brittle memorization strategy.

[1]Note that other decision strategies such as randomly selecting an output form or taking the majority vote are also possible. These alternative strategies consistently underperform MAX, so we exclude them from the main text.

MSD	Form
ROOT	we / wa
ROOT-1PL.II	wa'm
ROOT-3.II	wet / wat

Table 1: A partial paradigm for the word meaning "name" in Gitksan. The paradigm has two entries (ROOT and ROOT-3.II) that each have two dialectal variants attested in the data. Four different one-to-one (MSD to Form) realizations of the paradigm are possible.

Second, we find evidence that data hallucination introduces an inductive bias towards concatenative morphology: where inflection is accomplished by appending affixes to a word stem. We find that the MAX strategy combined with data hallucination selects a simpler transformation: In Fig. 1, the augmented model prefers the simple transformation of appending *diit* to *hap* to predict the target *hapdiit* over the unpredictable transformation from *tk'esxw* to *hapdiit*. Conversely, the model trained without hallucination exhibits no strong preference over either transformation. Since concatenative morphology is the dominant inflection process in Gitksan, this inductive bias serves the hallucination model well in inflecting unfamiliar lexemes during testing.

Data hallucination, however, can be damaging depending on the morphophonological phenomena at hand. We find, for instance, that it dramatically reduces performance in inflections involving reduplication, a transformation that requires copying of phonological material rather than a simple concatenation (Haspelmath and Sims, 2013). While the overall effect of data augmentation in inflection has been reported as overwhelmingly positive (e.g., Lane and Bird, 2020; Anastasopoulos and Neubig, 2019; Liu and Hulden, 2021), our detailed analysis reveals that it carries both benefits and drawbacks and should therefore be applied with caution. Furthermore, our findings call for greater qualitative analysis and more varied evaluation conditions in testing automatic inflection systems.

2 Data

Our dataset comprises paradigms that were programatically extracted from an interlinear-glossed dataset of $18,000$ tokens (Forbes et al., 2017). Details of the gloss to paradigm conversion procedure can be found in Appendix B. The interlinear glosses were collected during still-active language documentation efforts with Gitksan speakers.

The Gitksan-speaking community recognizes two dialects: Eastern (Upriver) and Western (Downriver), and our dataset comprises forms from both dialects. Although the two dialects are largely mutually intelligible, some lexical and phonological differences manifest, with the most prominent being a vowel shift. Consider the Gitksan translation for the word "name" in Table 1. The dialectal variation manifests as several entries for a given morphosyntactic description (henceforth MSD) in the paradigm: *we* (Western) vs. *wa* (Eastern).

Instead of attempting to model one-to-many (MSD to form) paradigms, we adhere to the simplifying constraint that each paradigm have a single realization per morphosyntactic description. In order to convert a one-to-many paradigm to a one-to-one paradigm, we aim to select a single form for each MSD so that, taken together, the inflected forms are maximally similar to each other. In the partial paradigm for for Table 1, the inflection from `wa` to `wa'm` is a simpler transformation than `we` to `wa'm`, making it simpler for a neural inflection model to acquire generalizable inflection rules. Thus, in Table 1 we would select a one-to-one paradigm with the forms *wa*, *wa'm*, and *wat*.

To obtain maximally similar inflected forms, we apply the following algorithm to a one-to-many paradigm. First, we generate all possible one-to-one realizations of the paradigm. For instance, for Table 1 one paradigm could comprise the MSD-to-form mappings: *ROOT:wa*, *ROOT:-1PL.II:wa'm*, *ROOT-3.II:wet*; there would be four possible one-to-one paradigms in total. Next, given a candidate one-to-one paradigm, we construct a fully-connected graph where each inflectional form is a vertex and every (undirected) edge is weighted by the Levenshtein distance. We then compute the weight of the minimum spanning-tree of the graph. Finally, we return the one-to-one paradigm that has the minimum-spanning tree with the lowest weight.[2]

We divide the resulting paradigms into four disjoint subsets. (1) A dataset for training a morphological reinflection model Π_{train} that will be used for the PCFP task; (2) A test set containing partial paradigms Π_{obs} so that **some** of the lexemes' inflectional variants were seen during training while the other inflectional variants are used only for testing; A validation set Π_{dev} constructed in the same manner as Π_{obs}; (4) A test set simulating the conditions of a "wug test" (Liu and Hulden, 2021; Berko, 1958) containing complete paradigms (Π_{wug}) so that **none** of the lexemes' inflectional variants were observed during training.

In order to train or evaluate a reinflection system for PCFP, we first need all the paradigms to have at least two entries. This is necessary since a reinflection datapoint is of the form *src_form:src_msd;tgt_form:tgt_msd*. Thus, our first step is to drop all paradigms that only have a single entry, providing us with 459 paradigms. Next, we randomly sample paradigms (without replacement) and add them to Π_{wug} until Π_{wug} contains 10% of the 1303 forms in our dataset.[3] This procedure guarantees that no forms in paradigms belonging to Π_{wug} are ever observed during training.

For the remaining paradigms π, we split them into two disjoint sets: π_{train} and $\pi_{hold-out}$. The forms in π_{train} are added to the training set Π_{train}. The forms in $\pi_{hold-out}$ are added either to the development set Π_{dev} or partially observed test set Π_{obs}. This way, the model is allowed to observe some of the forms belonging to the (partial) paradigms in Π_{dev} and Π_{obs} during training. However, it is guaranteed not to have observed the particular forms in Π_{dev} and Π_{obs} during training.[4]

More concretely, for a paradigm of size n, between 2 and $n-1$ forms (inclusive) are placed into train and the remaining forms are all placed into test (or all placed into dev). We obtain the following number of inflectional variants in each disjoint subset: $|\Pi_{train}| = 927$, $|\Pi_{dev}| = 124$, $|\Pi_{obs}| = 125$, $|\Pi_{wug}| = 131$. In the next section, we describe our procedure for employing these four sets of (partial) paradigms for training and evaluating a PCFP system.

[2]Note that the resulting paradigms are not necessarily free of dialectal variation. For instance, a paradigm where only the Western dialect form was observed for the *ROOT* and the Eastern dialect was observed for *ROOT-3.II* would still contain forms from both dialects.

[3]Strictly speaking, it will containly slightly more than 10%, since the last sampled paradigm may have more forms than the desired amount.

[4]More specifically, it has never seen the *MSD:form* pairs occurring in the training set.

3 Experiments and Results

Having split our paradigm dataset into the desired disjoint subsets Π_{train}, Π_{obs}, Π_{dev}, Π_{wug}, we can train Transformers in morphological reinflection that can, in turn, be used for the PCFP task.[5]

Training. We form reinflection training pairs by using the given forms in each paradigm in Π_{train}. Concretely, for every $\pi \in \Pi_{train}$, we take the cross product of the entries in π and learn to reinflect each given form in the paradigm to another form in the same paradigm as demonstrated in Fig. 2.[6] Counting reinflection datapoints over all paradigms, we obtain 1365 datapoints in the training set for the reinflection system.

We train two Transformer models. First, we train a "standard" Transformer model on the aforementioned 1365 datapoints using the parameter settings described in Wu et al. (2021) and Liu and Hulden (2020); see Appendix A. Next, we train a second "augmented" Transformer model, using the same hyperparameter settings, on the original 1365 datapoints in addition to $10,000$ datapoints hallucinated from the original training dataset. We obtain the hallucination method, number of hallucinated examples ($10,000$), and implementation from Anastasopoulos and Neubig (2019).

Evaluation. We evaluate the models both on paradigms describing lexemes whose inflections were partially observed (Π_{obs}) and lexemes that are entirely unfamiliar (Π_{wug}). Since most of our paradigms are very sparse, containing only contain a few forms, we do a leave-one-out style evaluation procedure where, for every target form in either Π_{wug} or Π_{obs} that belongs to paradigm π, we predict it using every other form that belongs to the same paradigm π.[7] This gives us $|\pi| - 1$ predictions for a target form, where $|\pi|$ is the total number filled slots in the paradigm.

Finally, we use the MAX strategy to select the form that was predicted with the highest likelihood averaged across output characters. We consider a paradigm π as correctly predicted if all forms for the paradigm that are present in Π_{obs} or Π_{wug} were correctly predicted.

Results and Discussion. We make a number of observations regarding the results in Fig. 3. First, we observe that there is a significant reduction in performance for the unfamiliar lexemes (Π_{wug}) relative to the familiar lexemes (Π_{obs}) – replicating observations made in the context of the SIGMORPHON shared tasks (Goldman et al., 2021; Cotterell et al., 2017; Liu and Hulden, 2021). We find that the augmented model reduces the deficit to 10%. That hallucination improves performance on unfamiliar lexemes has been previously observed (Liu and Hulden, 2021).

We also find, however, that hallucination worsens performance on familiar lexemes. In both cases, the aggregate accuracy scores glean little insights into these surprising results. Why does accuracy drop by nearly 50% for the non-hallucination model across the two testing conditions? How does hallucination improve performance on unfamiliar lexemes? And why does hallucination reduce performance on familiar lexeme paradigms? To understand these differences in performance between the two models and testing conditions, we turn to an analysis of the errors.

4 Error analysis

To reveal insights into the behaviour of the two Transformer models, we look into the case of Gitksan pluralization, which is instantiated as suppletion or reduplication depending on the lexeme, enabling us to investigate whether either Transformer can learn two disparate inflectional strategies. This error analysis enables us to systematically characterize the effects hallucination has on the Transformer model in inflection, demonstrating that the effects can be both beneficial and adverse.

Unaugmented Transformers memorize inflection patterns. We begin by analyzing the models' behaviour on suppletive forms; Gitksan uses suppletion as a productive strategy for pluralization. For instance, the stem for singular forms for "laugh" is *tk'esxw*, but the plural stem is *hap*. The transformation from a singular form to a suppletive plural form is unpredictable (*ts'ehlx* $\rightarrow$ *hapdiit*); the model must instead rely on other plural source forms (e.g., *hap* $\rightarrow$ *hapdiit*). Even if the model is unable to produce the correct suppletive plural inflection, it should be able to perform the simpler task of placing higher confidence in the prediction from the plural source form (*hap*) over the singular source form (*ts'ehlx*). Failing to exhibit this preference would indicate that the model is simply

[5]All code and results for this paper are available at: <anonymized for review>.

[6]Note that this means that we filter out identity pairs.

[7]We also predict from forms that belong to the training set if forms from paradigm π were included in the training set, but we only evaluate performance on the forms in Π_{wug} and Π_{obs}.

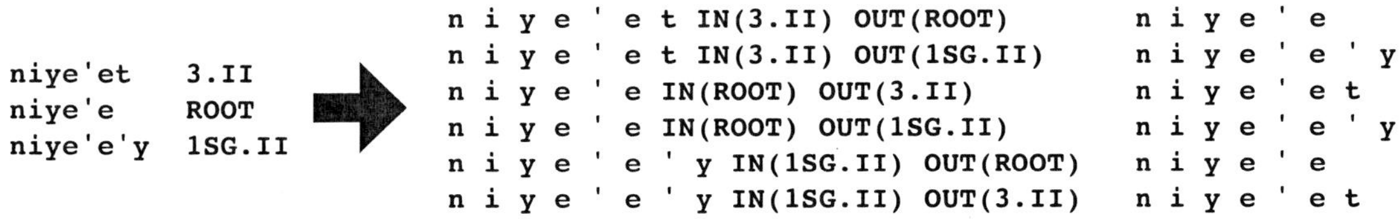

Figure 2: From a paradigm in the training data spanning three forms, we can generate six reinflection training examples. Forms are tokenized into individual characters. Further, we distinguish tags for the input form from tags for the output form.

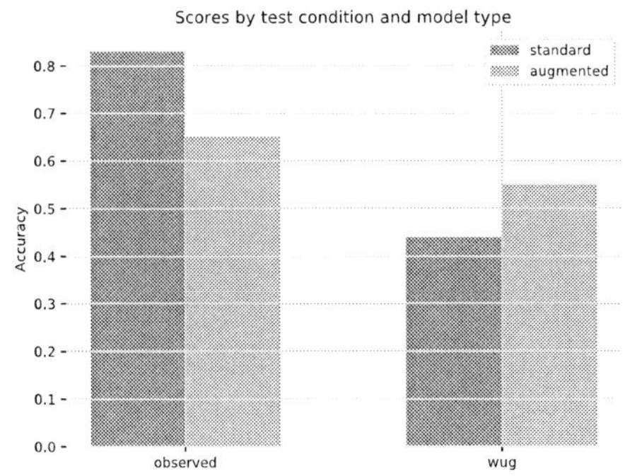

Figure 3: Performances of the augmented and standard models using the MAX decision strategy on Π_{obs} and Π_{wug} test sets.

memorizing target inflectional forms, rather than trying to acquire the morphophonological structure of the language.

Concretely, we acquire all of the 95 suppletive plurals in either Π_{wug} or Π_{obs}. We then follow our leave-one-out procedure, where every other form in the same paradigm π as the target suppletive plural form is used as a source to try to predict the target form. Instead of evaluating whether the target form was correctly predicted, we test whether the model assigns higher likelihoods to the reinflection examples where the source form is also a suppletive plural (*hap*) over examples where the source form is singular (*tk'esxw*).

This analysis can be interpreted as a binary classification task when we hold the target suppletive form (*hapdiit*) fixed. The task is then to classify the source suppletive plural forms as positive instances and the source singular forms as negative instances. We can then use standard binary classification metrics to quantify performance. We use weighted Average Precision (Murphy, 2012), where the weight is the total number of suppletive forms in the paradigm π. We use the Average Precision implementation from `scikit-learn` (Pedregosa et al., 2011).[8]

We find that the augmented model performs significantly better in this task, achieving a weighted Average Precision of .89 while the unaugmented model achieves .52. This analysis provides evidence that the unaugmented model is memorizing the target suppletive plural form (*hapdiit*), rather than attending to and copying the suppletive plural stem (*hap*) and concatenating the appropriate affix ("diit"). This result can explain, in part, the substantial drop in performance of the unaugmented model from Π_{obs} to Π_{wug}: memorization is unlikely to generalize well for inflecting unfamiliar lexemes. Further, it can explain the stronger performance of the hallucination model in predicting forms in Π_{wug}: this inductive bias towards concatenative morphology can generalize well to unfamiliar lexemes given the prevalence of concatenative morphology in the Gitksan dataset.

Augmented Transformers struggle with non-concatenative morphology. Our Gitksan paradigm dataset comprises more than just concatenative morphology, however. Another pluralization strategy in Gitksan, albeit rarer, is reduplication, where number is indicated by copying a part of the word stem. For example, *wat* ("name") and *hu-wat* ("name+PL"). The copied stem segment frequently undergoes further phonological alternations in the case of partial reduplication (as opposed to full reduplication; Haspelmath and Sims, 2013). While reduplication bears superficial resemblance to affixation, it cannot be analyzed as a concatenation of a stem and affix.

This resemblance, however, is sufficient to confuse prominent data hallucination techniques (Anastasopoulos and Neubig, 2019; Silfverberg et al., 2017). Consider the Gitksan word *dew* ("freeze") which is pluralized using full reduplication: *dewdew*. The hallucinated form of this data-

[8] `https://scikit-learn.org/stable/modules/generated/sklearn.metrics.average_precision_score.html`

point would have random characters substituted for the stem: e.g., *txu* -> *dewtxu*. Clearly, this hallucinated datapoint does not preserve the reduplicative structure. Unfortunately, the hallucination strategy could impair the model's ability to perform reduplication, given that the number of examples of reduplication would become smaller relative to the size of the complete dataset.

Indeed, we find strong evidence that the hallucination model is unable to perform reduplication. We find that the standard model is able to predict the 12 instances of reduplication in Π_{wug} and Π_{obs} with .92 accuracy, while the hallucination model slashes this proficiency to a mere .25. Our analysis emphasizes the need for data-augmentation techniques that preserve reduplicative structure, given the phenomenon's typologically robust prevalence (Haspelmath and Sims, 2013).

Reduplication is pronounced in the Gitksan dataset and causes problems for current data hallucination methods. However, it is by no means the only phenomenon where data hallucination can generate incorrect inflection patterns. Consider the example of lenition in our paradigm dataset where the final consonant undergoes voicing between vowels: *ayook + 3.II* -> *ayook+'m* -> *ayooga'm*. Hallucination identifies *ayoo* as the stem here due to the k/g alternation. If a hallucinated stem ending in a consonant like *dap* is used, we get an example *dapk* -> *dapga'm*, where *k* is no longer surrounded by vowels but is still voiced when the *a'm* affix attaches, contrary to the morphophonology of Gitksan. Thus, it is possible that hallucination's inability to preserve morphological phenomena like reduplication and lenition explain the drop in performance on the observed paradigms.[9] Approaches that try to perform data hallucination incorporating the target language's structure have been explored (Lane and Bird, 2020), but it's unclear how to generalize this method without expert knowledge of the target language.

5 General Discussion

In this paper, we explore the effect of data hallucination on the Gitksan language that is currently underserved in NLP. Given the low amount of training data for the model, inflection models are likely to encounter many unfamiliar lexemes during test time. Thus, it is important to assess the model's ability to make adequate morphological generalizations for such lexemes. To this end, we tested the model's ability to generalize for lexemes on a cline of familiarity from familiar (Π_{obs}) to unfamiliar (Π_{wug} Section 2).

Under these disparate conditions, we find that a data-augmented model and a standard model exhibit drastically different behaviours. We found that the standard model, a Transformer model trained under recommended parameter settings (Wu et al., 2021), memorizes inflection patterns to a significant degree (Section 3 and Section 4). At the same time, we find that data hallucination alleviates the need for memorization significantly, generalizing well to unfamiliar lexemes (Section 3) with an inductive bias towards concatenative morphology (Section 4). Data hallucination, however, is not universally beneficial: we find it reduces the model's capacity to recognize common morphophonological phenomena (Section 4), limiting the performance improvements it can bring.

Although our study was conducted on a single language, we note that our characterization of data hallucination could be informative for languages other than Gitksan. As Section 4 demonstrates, data hallucination can encourage the model to apply voicing in incorrect contexts. Such effects are not limited to Gitksan. In English, data hallucination could give rise to erroneously conditioned allomorphy: for instance, hallucination can generate a synthetic past tense inflection example *mar* -> *mard* from a gold standard training example such as *like* -> *liked*. The desired hallucinated past tense form is of course *mared*. Overall, our work suggests common data augmentation strategies for NLP like data hallucination merit closer inspection and that further innovations in data augmentation for computational morphology are desirable.

[9]It could also explain why we don't see a greater increase in performance on the Π_{wug} test set with the augmented model.

References

Farrell Ackerman, James P Blevins, and Robert Malouf. 2009. Parts and wholes: Implicative patterns in inflectional paradigms. *Analogy in grammar: Form and acquisition*, pages 54–82.

Antonios Anastasopoulos and Graham Neubig. 2019. Pushing the limits of low-resource morphological inflection. *arXiv preprint arXiv:1908.05838*.

Jean Berko. 1958. The child's learning of english morphology. *WORD*, 14:150–177.

Ryan Cotterell, Christo Kirov, John Sylak-Glassman, Géraldine Walther, Ekaterina Vylomova, Patrick Xia, Manaal Faruqui, Sandra Kübler, David Yarowsky, Jason Eisner, and Mans Hulden. 2017. Conll-sigmorphon 2017 shared task: Universal morphological reinflection in 52 languages. In *CoNLL Shared Task*.

Britt Dunlop, Suzanne Gessner, Tracey Herbert, and Aliana Parker. 2018. Report on the status of BC First Nations languages. Report of the First People's Cultural Council. Retrieved March 24, 2019.

Steven Y. Feng, Varun Gangal, Jason Wei, Sarath Chandar, Soroush Vosoughi, Teruko Mitamura, and Eduard Hovy. 2021. A survey of data augmentation approaches for NLP. In *Findings of the Association for Computational Linguistics: ACL-IJCNLP 2021*, pages 968–988, Online. Association for Computational Linguistics.

Clarissa Forbes, Henry Davis, Michael Schwan, and the UBC Gitksan Research Laboratory. 2017. Three Gitksan texts. In *Papers for the 52nd International Conference on Salish and Neighbouring Languages*, pages 47–89. UBC Working Papers in Linguistics.

Omer Goldman, David Guriel, and Reut Tsarfaty. 2021. (un) solving morphological inflection: Lemma overlap artificially inflates models' performance. *arXiv preprint arXiv:2108.05682*.

Demi Guo, Yoon Kim, and Alexander Rush. 2020. Sequence-level mixed sample data augmentation. In *Proceedings of the 2020 Conference on Empirical Methods in Natural Language Processing (EMNLP)*, pages 5547–5552, Online. Association for Computational Linguistics.

Martin Haspelmath and Andrea Sims. 2013. *Understanding morphology*. Routledge.

Bradley Hauer, Amir Ahmad Habibi, Yixing Luan, Arnob Mallik, and Grzegorz Kondrak. 2020. Low-resource G2P and P2G conversion with synthetic training data. In *Proceedings of the 17th SIGMORPHON Workshop on Computational Research in Phonetics, Phonology, and Morphology*, pages 117–122, Online. Association for Computational Linguistics.

Sachin Kumar, Antonios Anastasopoulos, Shuly Wintner, and Yulia Tsvetkov. 2021. Machine translation into low-resource language varieties. In *ACL/IJCNLP*.

William Lane and Steven Bird. 2020. Bootstrapping techniques for polysynthetic morphological analysis. *arXiv preprint arXiv:2005.00956*.

L. Liu and Mans Hulden. 2020. Analogy models for neural word inflection. In *COLING*.

Ling Liu and Mans Hulden. 2021. Can a transformer pass the wug test? tuning copying bias in neural morphological inflection models. *arXiv preprint arXiv:2104.06483*.

Tom McCoy, Ellie Pavlick, and Tal Linzen. 2019. Right for the wrong reasons: Diagnosing syntactic heuristics in natural language inference. In *Proceedings of the 57th Annual Meeting of the Association for Computational Linguistics*, pages 3428–3448, Florence, Italy. Association for Computational Linguistics.

Kevin P Murphy. 2012. *Machine learning: a probabilistic perspective*. MIT press.

Myle Ott, Sergey Edunov, Alexei Baevski, Angela Fan, Sam Gross, Nathan Ng, David Grangier, and Michael Auli. 2019. fairseq: A fast, extensible toolkit for sequence modeling. In *NAACL*.

F. Pedregosa, G. Varoquaux, A. Gramfort, V. Michel, B. Thirion, O. Grisel, M. Blondel, P. Prettenhofer, R. Weiss, V. Dubourg, J. Vanderplas, A. Passos, D. Cournapeau, M. Brucher, M. Perrot, and E. Duchesnay. 2011. Scikit-learn: Machine learning in Python. *Journal of Machine Learning Research*, 12:2825–2830.

Zach Ryan and Mans Hulden. 2020. Data augmentation for transformer-based G2P. In *Proceedings of the 17th SIGMORPHON Workshop on Computational Research in Phonetics, Phonology, and Morphology*, pages 184–188, Online. Association for Computational Linguistics.

Rico Sennrich, Barry Haddow, and Alexandra Birch. 2016. Improving neural machine translation models with monolingual data. In *Proceedings of the 54th Annual Meeting of the Association for Computational Linguistics (Volume 1: Long Papers)*, pages 86–96, Berlin, Germany. Association for Computational Linguistics.

Miikka Silfverberg and Mans Hulden. 2018. An encoder-decoder approach to the paradigm cell filling problem. In *EMNLP*.

Miikka Silfverberg, Adam Wiemerslage, L. Liu, and Lingshuang Jack Mao. 2017. Data augmentation for morphological reinflection. In *CoNLL*.

Shijie Wu, Ryan Cotterell, and Mans Hulden. 2021. Applying the transformer to character-level transduction. In *EACL*.

Hongyi Zhang, Moustapha Cisse, Yann N. Dauphin, and David Lopez-Paz. 2018. mixup: Beyond empirical risk minimization. In *International Conference on Learning Representations*.

Xingyuan Zhao, Satoru Ozaki, Antonios Anastasopoulos, Graham Neubig, and Lori Levin. 2020. Automatic interlinear glossing for under-resourced languages leveraging translations. In *Proceedings of the 28th International Conference on Computational Linguistics*, pages 5397–5408, Barcelona, Spain (Online). International Committee on Computational Linguistics.

A Transformer training details

We train all models using the implementation of Transformer in the `fairseq` package (Ott et al., 2019). Both the encoder and decoder have 4 layers with 4 attention heads, an embedding size of 256 and hidden layer size of 1024. We train with the Adam optimizer starting of the learning rate at 0.001. We chose the batch size (400) and maximum updates (5000) based on the highest accuracy on the development data. Our model setting resembles the work of Wu et al. (2021) who found that a relatively large batch size is beneficial for morphological inflection. Prediction is performed with the best checkpoint model, according to validation accuracy score, and a beam of width 5.

B Database of Gitksan Inflection Tables

We perform all experiments on a database of Gitksan inflection tables. In total, there are 1055 inflection tables containing 2125 inflected forms. An interlinear-glossed corpus of Gitksan narratives Forbes et al. (2017) forms the basis of our database. The Gitksan corpus is glossed at the root level meaning that word forms are broken down into roots, derivational morphemes and inflectional morphemes. This level of description is too fine-grained for our purposes and we, therefore, combine roots and potential derivational material into word stems. The inflected forms for each noun and verb stem are gathered into inflection tables. In total, there are 33 possible inflected forms and each inflection table will contain a subset of these forms. And example table is shown in Appendix C.

C Sample inflection table

A Gitksan inflection table for *jok* ('to dwell') generated from IGT and displayed in TSV format. Each row in the table contains five cells: (1) a morphosyntactic description, (2) an English translation, (3) a gloss with an English lemma, (3) a canonical segmented output form, (4) the surfce word form, and (5) a gloss with a Gitksan lemma. Many cells in the table are empty since they were unattested in the IGT data.

```
ROOT dwell jok jok jok
ROOT-SX dwell-SX jok-it jogat jok-SX
ROOT-SX dwell-SX jok-it jogot jok-SX
ROOT-PL _ _ _ _
ROOT-3PL _ _ _ _
ROOT-ATTR _ _ _ _
ROOT-3.II dwell-3.II jok-t jokt jok-3.II
ROOT-PL-SX PL~dwell-SX CVC~jok-it jaxjogat PL~jok-SX
ROOT-PL-SX PL~dwell-SX CVC~jok-it jaxjogot PL~jok-SX
ROOT-1SG.II dwell-1SG.II jok-'y jogo'y jok-1SG.II
ROOT-2SG.II _ _ _ _
ROOT-2PL.II _ _ _ _
ROOT-3PL.II dwell-3PL.II jok-diit jokdiit jok-3PL.II
ROOT-1PL.II dwell-1PL.II jok-'m jogo'm jok-1PL.II
ROOT-PL-3PL _ _ _ _
ROOT-TR-3.II _ _ _ _
ROOT-PL-3.II PL~dwell-3.II CVC~jok-t jaxjokt PL~jok-3.II
ROOT-PL-ATTR _ _ _ _
ROOT-PL-2SG.II _ _ _ _
ROOT-TR-1SG.II _ _ _ _
ROOT-PL-3PL.II PL~dwell-3PL.II CVC~jok-diit jaxjokdiit PL~jok-3PL.II
ROOT-PL-1SG.II _ _ _ _
ROOT-TR-1PL.II _ _ _ _
ROOT-PL-1PL.II PL~dwell-1PL.II CVC~jok-'m jaxjogo'm PL~jok-1PL.II
ROOT-TR-2PL.II _ _ _ _
ROOT-TR-3PL.II _ _ _ _
ROOT-TR-2SG.II _ _ _ _
ROOT-PL-TR-3.II _ _ _ _
ROOT-PL-TR-2SG.II _ _ _ _
ROOT-PL-TR-3PL.II _ _ _ _
ROOT-PL-TR-1SG.II _ _ _ _
ROOT-PL-TR-1PL.II _ _ _ _
ROOT-PL-TR-2PL.II _ _ _ _
```

Automated speech tools for helping communities process restricted-access corpora for language revival efforts

Nay San[1,2], Martijn Bartelds[3], Tolúlọpẹ́ Ògúnrẹ̀mí[4], Alison Mount[2], Ruben Thompson[2], Michael Higgins[2], Roy Barker[2], Jane Simpson[2], and Dan Jurafsky[1,4]

[1]Department of Linguistics, Stanford University
[2]ARC Centre of Excellence for the Dynamics of Language, Australian National University
[3]Department of Computational Linguistics, University of Groningen
[4]Department of Computer Science, Stanford University
nay.san@stanford.edu

Abstract

Many archival recordings of speech from endangered languages remain unannotated and inaccessible to community members and language learning programs. One bottleneck is the time-intensive nature of annotation. An even narrower bottleneck occurs for recordings with access constraints, such as language that must be vetted or filtered by authorised community members before annotation can begin. We propose a privacy-preserving workflow to widen both bottlenecks for recordings where speech in the endangered language is intermixed with a more widely-used language such as English for meta-linguistic commentary and questions (e.g. *What is the word for 'tree'?*). We integrate voice activity detection (VAD), spoken language identification (SLI), and automatic speech recognition (ASR) to transcribe the metalinguistic content, which an authorised person can quickly scan to triage recordings that can be annotated by people with lower levels of access. We report work-in-progress processing 136 hours archival audio containing a mix of English and Muruwari. Our collaborative work with the Muruwari custodian of the archival materials show that this workflow reduces metalanguage transcription time by 20% even with minimal amounts of annotated training data: 10 utterances per language for SLI and for ASR at most 39 minutes, and possibly as little as 39 seconds.

1 Introduction

In speech recorded for language documentation work, it is common to find not only the target language that is being documented but also a language of wider communication, such as English. This is especially so in early-stage fieldwork when the elicitation may centre around basic words and phrases from a standard word list (e.g. the Swadesh List: Swadesh, 1955). In these mixed-language recordings, utterances in the language of wider communication are largely metalinguistic questions and commentary (e.g. *What is the word for 'tree'?, This word means 'soft'*), which appear inter-mixed with the utterances of interest in the target language. In this paper, we propose a workflow to help process hundreds of hours of unannotated speech of this genre.

We describe a use case where the language of wider communication is English (ISO 639-3: eng), and the documented language is Muruwari (ISO 639-3: zmu), an Aboriginal language traditionally spoken in north western New South Wales, Australia. As illustrated in Figure 1, we leverage voice activity detection (VAD) to detect speech regions, then spoken language identification (SLI) to distinguish between Muruwari and English regions, and then automatic speech recognition (ASR) to transcribe the English. The uncorrected transcriptions offer a rough but workable estimate of the contents in a given recording.

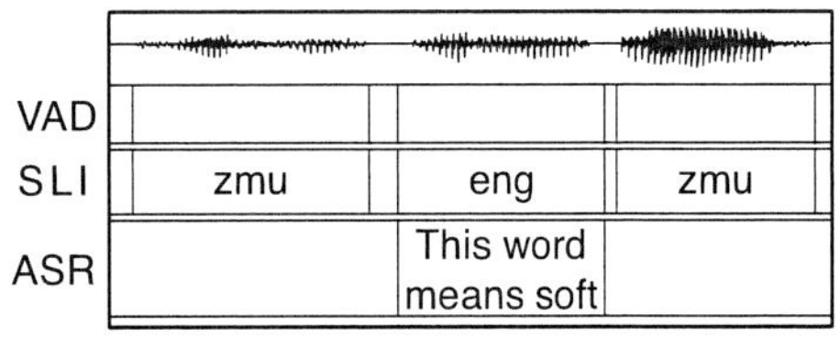

Figure 1: Deriving transcriptions of English in mixed-language speech using voice activity detection (VAD) and spoken language identification (SLI) to identify speech regions and the language spoken (zmu: Muruwari or eng: English) and automatic speech recognition (ASR) to transcribe English speech.

We use this workflow to help process 136 hours of predominantly single-speaker recordings made in the 1970s by the last first language (L1) speaker of Muruwari, James 'Jimmie' Barker (1900-1972). The generated transcriptions can

Proceedings of the Fifth Workshop on the Use of Computational Methods in the Study of Endangered Languages, pages 41 - 51
May 26-27, 2022 ©2022 Association for Computational Linguistics

be used by the data custodian and Muruwari elder, Roy Barker (author RB; grandson of Jimmie Barker), to triage the recordings and make initial decisions on which recordings can be listened to by people with lower levels of access who can then correct the transcriptions. The corrected transcriptions provide approximate locations where certain Muruwari words and phrases are being discussed, providing an index of the corpus from which language learning materials can be produced. In this way, we are able to support ongoing language revival initiatives through a strategic deployment of machine and human efforts in a manner that adheres to the level of privacy required.

For the benefit of other projects, we also conducted SLI and ASR experiments to determine the minimum amounts of annotated data required to implement this workflow. Through our SLI experiments we show that 1) only 10 example utterances per language are needed to achieve reliable single-speaker SLI performance, and 2) speech representations for SLI such as those from SpeechBrain (Ravanelli et al., 2021) can be used as-is as input to a simple logistic regression classifier without needing compute-intensive adaptation methods requiring a graphics processing unit (GPU).

Through our ASR experiments we show that transcriptions for 39 seconds of Jimmie's Australian English was sufficient to increase the accuracy of an ASR system trained for American English (Robust wav2vec 2.0: Hsu et al., 2021). To our surprise, timed transcription tasks revealed that the fine-tuned models offered no meaningful reduction in transcription correction time over an off-the-shelf model. Nevertheless, the machine-assisted workflow integrating the VAD, SLI, and ASR systems offers a 20% reduction in annotation time, requiring 2.36 hours of correction time per 30-minute recording compared to 2.95 hours of work to produce the same annotations manually, with ASR-assisted transcription responsible for the majority of the time savings.

With the exception of the archival audio and transcriptions, which we do not have permission to openly release, all experiment artefacts, model training/deployment scripts, and data preparation instructions developed for this project are publicly available on GitHub.[1]

The remainder of this paper is organised as follows. We first provide the project background in §2. Subsequently, in §3, we formulate the research questions we sought to address with our experiments and then describe the data we used for them in §4. The following three sections detail the methods and results of our SLI (§5) and ASR (§6) experiments, and the timed annotation tasks (§7). In §8, we discuss how this workflow assists in the ongoing documentation of the Muruwari language. Finally, in §9, we summarise and conclude this work, making clear its limitations and outlining directions for future research.

2 Project background

Muruwari is an Aboriginal language traditionally spoken in north western New South Wales, Australia and belongs to the Pama-Nyungan family of Australian languages (Oates, 1988). Oates (1988), which comprises the largest extant single work on Muruwari, describes it as a relative isolate compared to the neighbouring Pama-Nyungan languages, Yuwaaliyaay, Yuwaalaraay, Barranbinya, Ngiyampaa (Ngemba), Guwamu and Badjiri.

James 'Jimmie' Barker (1900–1972), the last first language (L1) speaker of Muruwari, produced in the early 1970s a total of 136 hours of reel-to-reel tape recordings consisting of a mix of Muruwari and meta-linguistic commentary on the Muruwari language in English. The now digitised recordings are held at the Australian Institute of Aboriginal and Torres Strait Islander Studies and access to these materials depend on permission from the custodian and Muruwari elder, Roy Barker (author RB; grandson of Jimmie Barker).

To date, RB has manually auditioned approximately 40 of the 136 hours over the course of 4 years to determine regions of speech appropriate for general access and those requiring restricted access (e.g. for only the Muruwari community, or only the Barker family). At this rate of roughly 10 hours per year, the remaining 96 hours may require nearly a decade of manual review by RB.

Parallel to the review of the remaining recordings, a subset of the recordings that have already been cleared by RB is being used to search for excerpts that may be useful for learning materials and those that can inform the development of a standardised orthography for Muruwari. To assist these ongoing initiatives, we investigated how SLI and ASR can be leveraged to allow for the review process and excerpt searches to be done more strategically and efficiently.

[1] `https://github.com/CoEDL/vad-sli-asr`

3 Research questions

There has been growing interest in leveraging speech processing tools to assist in language documentation workflows, including the formulation of shared tasks (e.g. Levow et al., 2021; Salesky et al., 2021).[2] Aimed at making unannotated fieldwork recordings more accessible, Levow et al. (2017) proposed a family of shared tasks, dubbed the "Grandma's Hatbox", which include SLI and ASR. In our work, we additionally leverage VAD to make the system fully automatable and, to derive a rough index of the corpus, we transcribe all speech regions detected as English (in the shared task formulation, ASR was intended to transcribe only the metadata preamble in the recordings).

The performance of speech processing systems can be poor when there are mismatches between the speech on which they were trained and that on which they are deployed. Commenting on such poor deployment-time performance of SLI systems, Salesky et al. (2021) concluded that what is necessary for real-world usage are methods for system adaptation with a few examples from the target speakers/domains. Accordingly, we sought to answer the following questions: 1) How many utterances of English and Muruwari are needed to adapt an off-the-shelf SLI system? 2) Is it possible to make use of such a system without compute-intensive adaptation methods requiring a graphics processing unit (GPU)?

Regarding this latter question, we were inspired by a recent probing study on various speech representations showing that logistic regression classifiers performed on-par with shallow neural networks for two-way classification of speech, e.g. distinguishing between vowels and non-vowels (Ma et al., 2021). Hence, we examined through our SLI experiments whether using a logistic regression classifier suffices for the two-way classification of the speech data, i.e. distinguishing between English and Muruwari.

Turning now to ASR, the typical use case in language documentation work has been to develop ASR systems to help transcribe the target language (e.g. Adams et al., 2018; Shi et al., 2021; Prud'hommeaux et al., 2021). By contrast, our use of ASR more closely aligns with recent work exploring techniques such as spoken term detection to help locate utterances of interest in untranscribed speech corpora in the target languages (Le Ferrand et al., 2020, 2021; San et al., 2021). In this work, however, we take advantage of the mixed-language speech in the corpus, and leverage SLI and ASR to transcribe the English speech as a way to derive a rough index.

We opted to use the Robust wav2vec 2.0 model (Hsu et al., 2021) to reduce the mismatch in audio quality between the training and the deployment data (i.e. noisy archival recordings). This model is pre-trained not only on LibriSpeech (960 hours: Panayotov et al., 2015) and CommonVoice English (700 hours: Ardila et al., 2019), but also on noisy telephone-quality speech corpora (Fisher, 2k hours: Cieri et al., 2004 and Switchboard, 300 hours: Godfrey et al., 1992), and also fine-tuned on 300 hours of transcribed speech from Switchboard. With our ASR experiments, we sought to answer the following questions: 1) What amount of transcribed speech is sufficient to reliably achieve better than off-the-shelf performance? 2) Using the same amount of transcribed speech, to what extent can ASR system performance be further increased when supplemented with a language model trained on external texts?

4 Data: the Jimmie Barker recordings

To gather training and evaluation data for the two speech processing tasks, we obtained 6 archival recordings of Jimmie Barker's speech cleared by RB. For each recording, we used the off-the-shelf Robust wav2vec 2.0 (Hsu et al., 2021),[3] to simply transcribe all speech regions detected by the Silero VAD system,[4] and generated an .eaf file for ELAN.[5] Using ELAN, three annotators (2 recordings per annotator) then erased the spurious text for the Muruwari utterances (i.e. for SLI, we simply used blank annotations to denote Muruwari regions, given the orthography is still in development) and manually corrected the English transcriptions for ASR (i.e. for SLI, any non-blank region with text was considered English). While the machine-generated annotations for the training and evaluation data were human-corrected, we have yet to establish inter-annotator agreement or conduct error analyses.

[2] Aimed to help drive system development, shared tasks are competitions in which teams of researchers submit competing systems to solve a pre-defined challenge.

[3] https://huggingface.co/facebook/wav2vec2-large-robust-ft-swbd-300h

[4] https://github.com/snakers4/silero-vad

[5] https://archive.mpi.nl/tla/elan

When correcting the English transcriptions, speech was transcribed verbatim with no punctuation except for apostrophes, i.e. including false starts (e.g. *we we don't say*) and hesitations (e.g. *and uh it means steal*). To facilitate searches, transcriptions were made in lower-case with the exception of proper nouns (e.g. *uh the Ngiyaamba has it uh*) and words that were spelled out by Jimmie (e.g. *you've got B U at the end of a word*). For ASR training, the transcriptions were automatically converted to all upper-case to normalise the text to a 27-character vocabulary (26 upper-case letters + apostrophe) that matches vocabulary with which the wav2vec 2.0 Robust model was originally trained. As we report in Appendix A, not re-using the original vocabulary required significantly more fine-tuning data to achieve the same performance.

Based on the corrected annotations, we extracted the speech regions into individual 16-bit 16 kHz .wav files and all the transcriptions for the English utterances into a single tab-delimited file. A summary of the data used in this paper is given below in Table 1. Overall, the yielded speech content contained more English than Muruwari (78% English by duration or 66% by number of utterances), reflecting the relatively more numerous and longer nature of the meta-linguistic commentary in English compared to the Muruwari words and phrases being commented upon.

Recording ID	**Speech (mins)**	
(Running time, mins)	eng	zmu
33-2162B (65)	23.2	2.06
31-1919A (65)	16.3	6.28
25-1581B (65)	15.5	4.75
25-1581A (65)	12.1	4.34
28-1706B (64)	7.00	2.06
25-1582A (35)	6.92	2.68
Total: 5.98 hours	81.0 mins	22.2 mins
4864 utts.	3243 utts.	1621 utts.

Table 1: Duration and number of utterances (utts.) of English and Muruwari speech yielded from labelling 6 archival recordings

Notably, only a third of the total running time of the recordings was found to be speech content on average, with frequent inter- and intra-phrase pauses arising from the semi-improvised linguistic self-elicitation being undertaken by Jimmie. A consequence of these pauses is that the VAD system segments Jimmie's speech into sequences of sentence fragments, e.g. *This word..., This word means soft..., And also softly*. We will return to these data characteristics in our discussion of the timed annotation tasks §7.

Finally, we note that having had few prior experimentally-informed estimates of the minimum amounts of data required, we chose to label for our initial implementation of this workflow this specific set of 6 recordings in accordance with other project priorities. While our deployed models are those trained on all the data, we opted to run detailed analyses on how much of the labelled data was actually necessary for adapting the SLI and ASR models to help establish estimates regarding the minimum amounts of labelled data needed to apply this workflow in other settings, and timed the annotation tasks using models trained on these minimum amounts of data.

5 Spoken Language Identification

We are interested in finding the minimum amount of training utterances required to obtain a performant system for same-speaker SLI. As training a system with very few utterances can lead to a large variance in its performance on unseen utterances, we were particularly interested in determining the training set size at which the variance was functionally equivalent to training on all available data.

5.1 Method

For our SLI experiments, we first extracted speech representations from each of the 4864 English and Muruwari utterances using the SpeechBrain toolkit (Ravanelli et al., 2021), which includes a state-of-the-art SLI model trained on 107 languages of the VoxLingua107 dataset (Valk and Alumäe, 2021).[6] We then performed 5000 iterations of training and evaluating logistic regression classifiers. At each iteration, the dataset was shuffled and 20% of the data (972 utterances) was held out as the test set. The remaining 80% of data (3892 utterances) was designated as the 'All' training set and from which we sampled 5 additional subsets (1, 5, 10, 25, and 50 utterances per language). We trained separate logistic regression classifiers using each of the 6 datasets (5 subsets + All), and then measured SLI performance of

[6]While the model was trained to identify English (dialects unspecified), we found that the included, off-the-shelf classifier could not consistently identify Jimmie's Australian English utterances, which were most frequently classified as Welsh (497/3243: 15.3%) or English (321/3243: 9.8%).

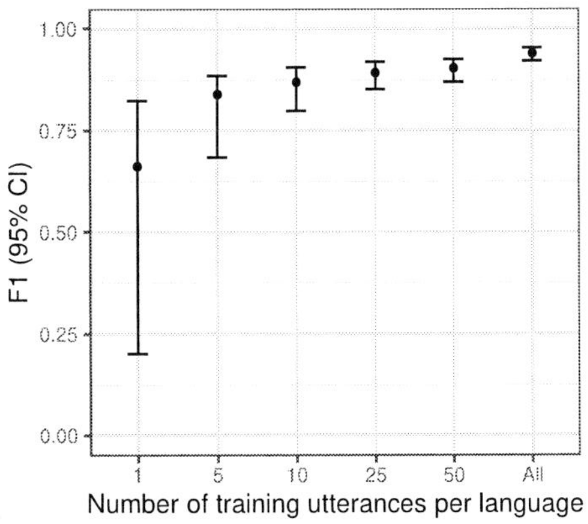

Figure 2: Two-way spoken language identification performance (English vs. Muruwari) using logistic regression classifiers trained on SpeechBrain SLI embeddings (Ravanelli et al., 2021) using varying dataset sizes (1, 5, 10, 25, 50 utterances per language, and All available data: 3892 utterances). Points represent mean F1 and error bars the 95% bootstrap confidences intervals over 5000 iterations.

each classifier on the same test set using the F1 score.[7] Finally, we also calculated the differences between the F1 scores for the classifier trained on all the training data and each of those trained on the smaller datasets (All vs. 1, All vs. 5, All vs. 10, All vs. 25, All vs. 50).

5.2 Results

Figure 2 displays the mean F1 scores for each of the training dataset sizes. The error bars represent the 95% bootstrap confidence interval (CI) for the mean obtained over 5000 iterations. Using all the training data resulted in the highest SLI performance of 0.93 [95% CI: 0.91, 0.95]. Of the smaller dataset sizes, the 50-, 25-, and 10-utterance training subsets performed similarly with mean F1 scores of 0.90 [95% CI: 0.87, 0.93], 0.89 [95% CI: 0.85, 0.92], and 0.87 [95% CI: 0.79, 0.91], respectively. The smallest two dataset sizes showed yet lower SLI performance with mean F1 scores for 5 utterances at 0.84 [95% CI: 0.69, 0.89] and 1 utterance at 0.66 [95% CI: 0.20, 0.82].

Table 2 displays the mean differences and the corresponding confidence intervals for the mean differences in F1 scores for the classifier trained on all the training data (All) and each of those trained on the smaller datasets (1, 5, 10, 25, 50 utterances per language). On average, using only 1 utterance of English and Muruwari results in a system that is 28 percentage points worse than using all the data (Table 2 a). While using 5 or 10 utterances resulted in similar average differences compared to using all the data (10 vs 7 percentage points, respectively), the difference is nearly twice as variable when only 5 utterances per language are used (CI width: 20 percentage points).

Comparison	Difference in F1 Mean, [95% CI]: CI width
a. All vs. 1	0.28, [0.11, 0.74]: 0.63
b. All vs. 5	0.10, [0.05, 0.25]: 0.20
c. All vs. 10	0.07, [0.03, 0.14]: 0.11
d. All vs. 25	0.05, [0.02, 0.09]: 0.07
e. All vs. 50	0.04, [0.01, 0.07]: 0.06

Table 2: Mean difference in F1 and 95% bootstrap confidence intervals (lower and upper bounds, and width) for the difference in means for the performance on a spoken language identification task using logistic regression classifiers trained of varying dataset sizes (1, 5, 10, 25, 50 utterances per language, and All available training data: 3892 utterances)

Answering our SLI-related questions, then: 1) using 10 utterances per language yields systems whose average performance is within 10 percentage points of using all the data (3892 utterances). 2) a logistic regression classifier suffices for two-way same-speaker SLI using off-the-shelf speech embeddings for SLI (Ravanelli et al., 2021).

6 Automatic Speech Recognition

Recall that for ASR, we seek to answer the following questions: 1) What amount of transcribed speech is sufficient to reliably achieve better than off-the-shelf performance for transcribing Jimmie's Australian English? 2) Using the same amount of transcribed speech, to what extent can ASR system performance be further increased when supplemented with a language model trained on external texts? In this section, we report on experiments conducted in order to answer these questions.

6.1 Method

In all our fine-tuning experiments, we fine-tuned the Robust wav2vec 2.0 model over 50 epochs, evaluating every 5 epochs (with an early-stopping patience of 3 evaluations). All training runs started from the same off-the-shelf checkpoint and we

[7] Ranging between 0 (worst) and 1 (best), the F1 score is a measure of a classification system's accuracy, taking both false positives and false negatives into account.

kept constant the training hyperparameters, all of which can be inspected in the model training script on GitHub. We varied as the independent variable the amount and samples of data used to fine-tune the model and measured as the dependent variable the word error rate (WER).[8]

In all our experiments, we split the total 81 minutes of transcribed English speech into an 80% training set (65 minutes) and a 20% testing set (16 minutes). The training split of 65 minutes was designated as the 100% training set from which we sampled smaller subsets consisting of 52 minutes (80% of training split), 39 minutes (60% of training split), 26 minutes (40% of training split), 13 minutes (20% of training split), 6.5 minutes (10% of training split), 3.25 minutes (5% of training split), and 0.65 minutes (1% of training split).

We fine-tuned 8 separate models with varying amounts of data and evaluated their performance on the same test set to obtain a first estimate of an amount of data sufficient to achieve better than off-the-shelf performance. We then created 10 new 80/20 training/testing splits for cross-validation in order to establish the variability in WER when only using that minimal amount of data.

We were also interested in whether supplementing the ASR system with a language model further reduced the WER. Our initial labelling work revealed that many errors made by the off-the-shelf system were particularly related to domain- and region-specific English words (e.g. *spear*, *kangaroo*). With permission from the maintainers of the Warlpiri-to-English dictionary, we extracted 8359 English translations from example sentences to obtain in-domain/-region sentences in English, e.g. *The two brothers speared the kangaroo*.

We used this data to train a word-level bigram model using KenLM (Heafield, 2011). While we opted to extract sentences from the Warlpiri-to-English dictionary given it is the largest of its kind for an Australian language, this corpus of sentences still only amounts to 75,425 words (4,377 unique forms), and as such we opted for a bigram model over a more conventional 3- or 4-gram model. With the only change being the inclusion of the language model, we then fine-tuned 10 additional models using the same training and testing splits.

[8]Ranging from 0% (best) to 100% (worst), word error rate (WER) is a measure of the accuracy of an ASR system, taking into account substitutions (wrongly predicted words), additions (erroneous extra words) and deletions (missing words).

Training set size	WER	CER
a. 65 minutes (100%)	10.1%	4.2%
b. 52 minutes (80%)	10.1%	4.4%
c. 39 minutes (60%)	11.8%	5.2%
d. 26 minutes (40%)	12.3%	5.5%
e. 13 minutes (20%)	13.2%	6.1%
f. 6.5 minutes (10%)	13.4%	6.1%
g. 3.25 minutes (5%)	15.1%	6.7%
h. 0.65 minutes (1%)	19.1%	8.8%
i. Off-the-shelf (0%)	36.3%	21.5%

Table 3: Word error rates (WERs) achieved from fine-tuning the same wav2vec 2.0 model (large-robust-ft-swbd-300h) over 50 epochs using various subsets of data from 65 minutes of Australian English archival audio data.

6.2 Results

Table 3 displays the word error rates (WERs) achieved by a Robust wav2vec 2.0 model fine-tuned with various amounts of transcribed speech. The baseline WER achieved by the off-the-shelf model with no additional fine-tuning is 36.3%. Training with all 65 minutes of data yielded a topline WER of 10.1%. Remarkably, training with less than 1 minute of speech was sufficient to decrease the WER to 19.1%. As a first estimate, the amount of training data that sufficiently improves on the off-the-shelf model appears to be 0.65 minutes of transcribed speech.

To verify that fine-tuning with only 1% of our training data does consistently yield a better than off-the-shelf WER, we conducted cross-validation experiments using 10 additional 80/20 training/testing splits, each time using only 1% of the data from the training split (0.65 minutes or 39 seconds on average).

Figure 3 displays the results of our cross-validation experiments. First, evaluating the off-the-shelf model on the 10 test sets, we found the baseline mean WER to be 35.6% (standard deviation, SD: 1.48%; range: 33.8–37.9%). The mean WER of the models fine-tuned with only 1% of data and without a language model was found to be 18.2% (SD: 0.99%; range: 16.7–19.5%). These results demonstrate that fine-tuning with less than 1 minute of speech consistently yields better than off-the-shelf performance.

When a bigram language model was used for decoding, we found that the mean WER increased to 20.0% (SD: 1.48%; range: 17.8–21.9%) for

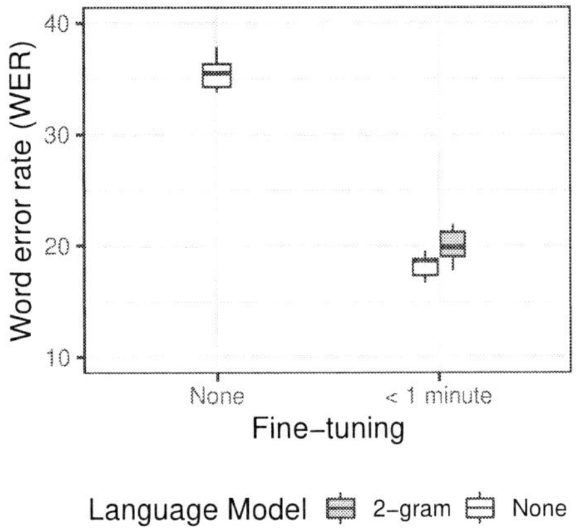

Figure 3: Variability in word error rates of training and testing Robust wav2vec 2.0 models over 10 iterations using different samples in the training and testing datasets, holding constant the size of the training set (1% of training set = 0.65 minutes or 39 seconds, on average) and testing set (16 minutes). The off-the-shelf model without fine-tuning was also evaluated on the same 10 testing sets.

the fine-tuned models. These results are inconsistent with our earlier experiments (reported in Appendix A), where we fine-tuned the same off-the-shelf model with 39 minutes of data. In these experiments, decoding with the same bigram model did lead to WER improvements, suggesting that more careful calibration and weighting of the language model may be required in near-zero shot adaptation scenarios.

To answer our ASR-related questions, then: 1) 39 seconds on average of speech on average is sufficient to achieve a better than off-the-shelf performance for transcribing Jimmie's Australian English speech. 2) the effect on ASR performance of a language model is inconclusive (cf. Appendix A).

7 Timed annotation tasks

In addition to helping provide estimates of the contents of recordings for review by an authorised person, another purpose of this workflow is to help reduce the time required to annotate speech in such a way that excerpts from cleared recordings can be easily extracted for use in relevant initiatives, e.g. creating language learning materials.

The initial process of annotating speech for this purpose involves two tasks: segmentation and transcription, which we illustrate in Figure 4 using two clips of Jimmie's speech. In segmentation, the annotator identifies regions of speech and non-speech and also which of the speech regions is English or Muruwari. For a sequence of English sentence fragments such as those in Clip a), the utterances can simply be merged into one. For mixed-language regions such as those in Clip b), separate utterances should be created to allow the Muruwari speech to be easily extracted for use in language learning materials. To create transcriptions for indexing, the annotator transcribes the English segments, given regions segmented and identified as English. We conducted a set of timed annotation tasks to evaluate to what extent the machine-assisted workflow reduces the time taken to perform these two tasks.

As detailed in Table 4, we gathered for our timed annotation tasks three different recordings

Time taken in minutes (Annotator)

Recording ID (Running time, mins)	**Segmentation only**		**Transcription only**			
	Manual	Assisted VAD+SLI	Manual	Assisted: ASR systems, A–C: A	B	C
33-2171A/S1 (31)	88 (A1)	81 (A2)	-	-	54 (A4)	53 (A3)
33-2163A/S1 (33)	83 (A2)	84 (A1)	-	-	57 (A3)	66 (A4)
33-2167B/S2 (32)	-	-	96/87 (A1/A2)	55/71 (A3/A4)	-	-
Mean time taken, in minutes	**85.5**	**82.5**	**91.5**	**63.0**	**55.5**	**59.5**

Table 4: Time taken to annotate recordings by four annotators (A1–A4) with and without machine assistance. In the segmentation task, annotators corrected the segmentations by the voice activity detection (VAD) and spoken language identification systems (SLI: trained on 10 utterances per language), or they manually annotated speech regions. In the transcription task, annotators were given intervals of English speech without any accompanying text (manual transcription), or text generated by one of three ASR (A, B C) systems differing in accuracy. System A was an off-the-shelf Robust wav2vec 2.0 model (Hsu et al., 2021) with no fine-tuning (word error rate/character error rate: 36/22). Systems B (19/7) and C (14/6) were Robust wav2vec 2.0 models fine-tuned on 39 minutes of transcribed English speech, and System C supplemented with a bigram language model trained on external texts.

approximately 30 minutes in length that were not part of the training and evaluation recordings in the previous experiments. For each timed task, annotators were asked to perform only segmentation or only transcription. For segmentation, they either manually created all time boundaries or corrected machine-derived ones from the VAD and SLI systems. For transcription, they either manually typed in the transcriptions for English speech or corrected machine-derived ones from an ASR system. We tested ASR systems developed earlier in our research (reported in Appendix A), that was fine-tuned on 39 minutes of Jimmy's Australian English speech, and reached a WER/CER of 19/7, as well as a version of the same system augmented with a bigram language model which reached a WER/CER of 14/6. The three recordings and the four annotators and the six annotation tasks were counter-balanced such that each annotator listened to each recording for a given task exactly once.

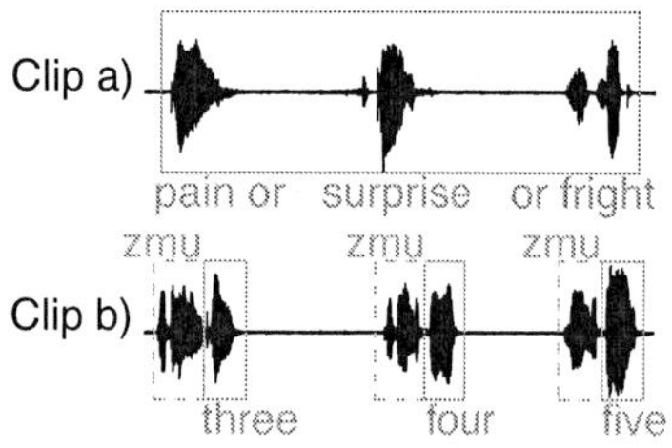

Figure 4: Desired annotations for two excerpts of speech from the Jimmie Barker recordings. Clip a) shows a sequence of sentence fragments in English, to be annotated as a single utterance. Clip b) shows alternating Muruwari (zmu) and English speech, to be annotated as 6 utterances.

The segmentation task took 85.5 minutes of work for a 30-minute recording without machine assistance and 82.5 minutes when assisted. That is, correcting time boundaries, inserting missing intervals or removing erroneous ones, and merging/splitting machine-derived segmentations takes nearly the same amount of time as placing these boundaries manually. The waveforms in Figure 4 illustrate how the acoustics of alternating Muruwari and English separated by brief pauses look indistinguishable from English sentence fragments separated by similar amounts of pauses — leading to sub-optimal segmentations using a standard, sequential VAD-then-SLI pipeline. The mixed-language nature of this speech may require jointly optimising the VAD and SLI steps.

The transcription task took 91.5 minutes of work for a 30-minute recording without machine assistance and on average 59.3 minutes when assisted (a 35% reduction). We found no meaningful difference between the correction times for transcriptions generated by ASR systems with different levels of accuracy. For transcriptions produced by an off-the-shelf system (WER/CER: 36/22), the correction time was 63 minutes. For systems fine-tuned with 39 minutes of transcribed speech, WER/CER: 19/7 and 14/6, the correction times were 55.5 and 59.5 minutes, respectively.

The closeness in transcription correction times may relate to how an English ASR system whose WER is 30% or less produces good enough transcriptions for editing, according to a crowd-sourced study (Gaur et al., 2016). Here, our transcribers' tolerance for the relatively less accurate off-the-shelf system (WER 36%) may be attributable to their familiarity with the speech domain and speaker (Sperber et al., 2017), having collectively spent nearly 40 hours correcting transcriptions of Jimmie's English by the time we conducted the timed tasks. These results suggest that, where correction is permissible by L1-speaking transcribers of the metalanguage, the time savings over manual transcription could still be gained using an off-the-shelf system that achieves a WER of 30–36% or less for the metalanguage in the recordings.

Nevertheless, we find that the machine-assisted workflow does offer time savings over a fully manual workflow (in line with previous work, e.g.: Sperber et al., 2016, 2017). Specifically, we find that the machine-assisted workflow offers a 20% reduction in overall time to identify regions in the target language and metalanguage and also transcribe the latter, requiring 2.36 hours (82.5 + 59.3 mins) of correction time for a 30-minute recording compared to a fully-manual one which requires 2.95 hours (85.5 + 91.5 mins). Unlike the manual workflow, the fully-automatable workflow can derive first-pass transcriptions to help an authorised person triage recordings.

8 Towards a Muruwari orthography

As mentioned above, the Muruwari orthography is still currently in development. In this section, we provide a brief overview of how transcriptions of the English metalanguage are being used to aid in the development of the Muruwari orthography.

A key source of information on Muruwari phonemes and words of interest to the current Muruwari community are two 1969 recordings in which Jimmie Barker discusses an early Muruwari wordlist (Mathews, 1902). This wordlist was created by linguist R.H. Mathews and consists of Muruwari words in his romanisation along with English translations. Using this wordlist, the documentation team is able to shortlist Muruwari words whose romanisation is suggestive of containing sounds of interest (e.g. dental consonants), and then quickly locate in these recordings Jimmie's pronunciation of the words and associated commentary using the time-aligned English transcripts generated for the two recordings. Here, the English transcripts provide significantly more streamlined access to untranscribed Muruwari utterances than browsing the recordings in real time. Once verified of containing the sounds of interest, the documentation team is able to extract snippets of these words to be included in the community consultation process.

9 Conclusion

Many hours of unannotated speech from endangered languages remain in language archives and inaccessible to community members and language learning programs. The time-intensive nature of annotating speech creates one bottleneck, with an additional one occurring for speech in restricted access corpora that authorised community members must vet before annotation can begin. For a particular genre of recordings where speech in the endangered language is intermixed with a metalanguage in a more widely-used language such as English, we proposed a privacy-preserving workflow using automated speech processing systems to help alleviate these bottlenecks.

The workflow leverages voice activity detection (VAD) to identify regions of speech in a recording, and then spoken language identification (SLI) to isolate speech regions in the metalanguage and transcribes them using automatic speech recognition (ASR). The uncorrected transcriptions provide an estimate of the contents of a recording for an authorised person to make initial decisions on whether it can be listened to by those with lower levels of access to correct the transcriptions, which, collectively, help index the corpus. This workflow can be implemented using a limited amount of labelled data: 10 utterances per language for SLI and 39 seconds of transcribed speech in the metalanguage for ASR. The workflow reduces metalanguage transcription time by 20% over manual transcription and similar time savings may be achievable with an off-the-shelf ASR system with a word error rate of 36% or less for the metalanguage in the target recordings.

Given our use case, the present demonstration of the workflow was limited to the scenario of processing single-speaker monologues with a mix of Muruwari and English, the latter of which made possible the use of a state-of-the-art model trained for English ASR (Robust wav2vec 2.0: Hsu et al., 2021) and also for transcriptions to be corrected by first language speakers of English. Our work also revealed that VAD and SLI systems require further optimisation for mixed-language speech.

We hope our demonstration encourages further experimentation with model adaptation with limited data for related use cases. For dialogues between a linguist and language consultant, for example, speaker diarisation could be added via few-shot classification using speech representations for speaker recognition (e.g. SpeechBrain SR embeddings: Ravanelli et al., 2021). With user-friendly interfaces like Elpis (Foley et al., 2018), for which wav2vec 2.0 integration is underway (Foley, pers. comm.), we hope to see more streamlined access to pre-trained models for language documentation workflows and, consequently, more streamlined access to the recorded speech for community members and language learning programs.

References

Oliver Adams, Trevor Cohn, Graham Neubig, Hilaria Cruz, Steven Bird, and Alexis Michaud. 2018. Evaluating phonemic transcription of low-resource tonal languages for language documentation. In *LREC 2018 (Language Resources and Evaluation Conference)*, pages 3356–3365.

Rosana Ardila, Megan Branson, Kelly Davis, Michael Henretty, Michael Kohler, Josh Meyer, Reuben Morais, Lindsay Saunders, Francis M Tyers, and Gregor Weber. 2019. CommonVoice: A massively-multilingual speech corpus. *arXiv preprint arXiv:1912.06670*.

Christopher Cieri, David Miller, and Kevin Walker. 2004. The Fisher corpus: A resource for the next generations of speech-to-text. In *LREC*, volume 4, pages 69–71.

Ben Foley, J Arnold, R. Coto-Solano, G. Durantin, T. M. Ellison, D. van Esch, S. Heath, F. Kratochvíl, Z. Maxwell-Smith, David Nash, O. Olsson, M. Richards, Nay San, H. Stoakes, N. Thieberger, and J Wiles. 2018. Building Speech Recognition Systems for Language Documentation: The CoEDL Endangered Language Pipeline and Inference System (Elpis). In *The 6th Intl. Workshop on Spoken Language Technologies for Under-Resourced Languages (SLTU)*, pages 200–204.

Yashesh Gaur, Walter S Lasecki, Florian Metze, and Jeffrey P Bigham. 2016. The effects of automatic speech recognition quality on human transcription latency. In *Proceedings of the 13th International Web for All Conference*, pages 1–8.

John J Godfrey, Edward C Holliman, and Jane McDaniel. 1992. SWITCHBOARD: Telephone speech corpus for research and development. In *Acoustics, Speech, and Signal Processing, IEEE International Conference on*, volume 1, pages 517–520. IEEE Computer Society.

Kenneth Heafield. 2011. KenLM: Faster and smaller language model queries. In *Proceedings of the sixth workshop on statistical machine translation*, pages 187–197.

Wei-Ning Hsu, Anuroop Sriram, Alexei Baevski, Tatiana Likhomanenko, Qiantong Xu, Vineel Pratap, Jacob Kahn, Ann Lee, Ronan Collobert, Gabriel Synnaeve, et al. 2021. Robust wav2vec 2.0: Analyzing domain shift in self-supervised pre-training. *arXiv preprint arXiv:2104.01027*.

Eric Le Ferrand, Steven Bird, and Laurent Besacier. 2020. Enabling interactive transcription in an indigenous community. In *Proceedings of the 28th International Conference on Computational Linguistics*, pages 3422–3428, Barcelona, Spain (Online). International Committee on Computational Linguistics.

Eric Le Ferrand, Steven Bird, and Laurent Besacier. 2021. Phone based keyword spotting for transcribing very low resource languages. In *Proceedings of the The 19th Annual Workshop of the Australasian Language Technology Association*, pages 79–86.

Gina-Anne Levow, Emily P Ahn, and Emily M Bender. 2021. Developing a shared task for speech processing on endangered languages. In *Proceedings of the Workshop on Computational Methods for Endangered Languages*, volume 1, pages 96–106.

Gina-Anne Levow, Emily M Bender, Patrick Littell, Kristen Howell, Shobhana Chelliah, Joshua Crowgey, Dan Garrette, Jeff Good, Sharon Hargus, David Inman, et al. 2017. Streamlined challenges: Aligning research interests with shared tasks. In *Proceedings of the 2nd Workshop on the Use of Computational Methods in the Study of Endangered Languages*, pages 39–47.

Danni Ma, Neville Ryant, and Mark Liberman. 2021. Probing acoustic representations for phonetic properties. In *ICASSP 2021-2021 IEEE International Conference on Acoustics, Speech and Signal Processing (ICASSP)*, pages 311–315. IEEE.

R. H. Mathews. 1902. Amendments in Murawarri: The Murawarri and Other Australian Languages. *Royal Geographical Society of Australasia*, 18:52–68.

Lynette Oates. 1988. *The Muruwari Language*. Dept. of Linguistics, Research School of Pacific Studies, The Australian National University.

Vassil Panayotov, Guoguo Chen, Daniel Povey, and Sanjeev Khudanpur. 2015. LibriSpeech: an ASR corpus based on public domain audio books. In *2015 IEEE international conference on acoustics, speech and signal processing (ICASSP)*, pages 5206–5210. IEEE.

Emily Prud'hommeaux, Robbie Jimerson, Richard Hatcher, and Karin Michelson. 2021. Automatic speech recognition for supporting endangered language documentation. *Language Documentation & Conservation*, 15:491–513.

Mirco Ravanelli, Titouan Parcollet, Peter Plantinga, Aku Rouhe, Samuele Cornell, Loren Lugosch, Cem Subakan, Nauman Dawalatabad, Abdelwahab Heba, Jianyuan Zhong, et al. 2021. SpeechBrain: A general-purpose speech toolkit. *arXiv preprint arXiv:2106.04624*.

Elizabeth Salesky, Badr M Abdullah, Sabrina J Mielke, Elena Klyachko, Oleg Serikov, Edoardo Ponti, Ritesh Kumar, Ryan Cotterell, and Ekaterina Vylomova. 2021. SIGTYP 2021 shared task: robust spoken language identification. *arXiv preprint arXiv:2106.03895*.

Nay San, Martijn Bartelds, Mitchell Browne, Lily Clifford, Fiona Gibson, John Mansfield, David Nash, Jane Simpson, Myfany Turpin, Maria Vollmer, et al. 2021. Leveraging pre-trained representations to improve access to untranscribed speech from endangered languages. *arXiv preprint arXiv:2103.14583*.

Jiatong Shi, Jonathan D Amith, Rey Castillo García, Esteban Guadalupe Sierra, Kevin Duh, and Shinji Watanabe. 2021. Leveraging end-to-end ASR for endangered language documentation: An empirical study on Yoloxóchitl Mixtec. *arXiv preprint arXiv:2101.10877*.

Matthias Sperber, Graham Neubig, Satoshi Nakamura, and Alex Waibel. 2016. Optimizing computer-assisted transcription quality with iterative user interfaces. In *Proceedings of the Tenth International Conference on Language Resources and Evaluation (LREC'16)*, pages 1986–1992, Portorož, Slovenia. European Language Resources Association (ELRA).

Matthias Sperber, Graham Neubig, Jan Niehues, Satoshi Nakamura, and Alex Waibel. 2017. Transcribing Against Time. *Speech Communication*, 93C:20–30.

Morris Swadesh. 1955. Towards greater accuracy in lexicostatistic dating. *International journal of American linguistics*, 21(2):121–137.

Jörgen Valk and Tanel Alumäe. 2021. VoxLingua107: a dataset for spoken language recognition. In *2021 IEEE Spoken Language Technology Workshop (SLT)*, pages 652–658. IEEE.

A Fine-tuning with a re-initialised vocabulary

In this section, we describe an earlier set of ASR fine-tuning experiments which were analogous to those reported in §6, except for the manner in which vocabulary (i.e. character set) was configured. Following recommended fine-tuning practice,[9] we initialised a linear layer whose output size corresponds to set of characters to be predicted (e.g. 'A', 'B', ...) and is derived from the target training dataset. However, this guidance presupposes that the pre-trained model being fine-tuned is one with no prior fine-tuning for ASR on the same language.

Given the size of our available training data (total 65 minutes), we chose to continue to train the Robust wav2vec 2.0 model,[10] already fine-tuned for English ASR on 300 hours of Switchboard (Godfrey et al., 1992). The results of fine-tuning this model using various-sized subsets of our training data is reported below in Table 5. Notably, fine-tuning with only 13 minutes of data resulted in a significantly worse than off-the-shelf performance (98% vs. 37%, off the shelf). By deriving labels for the linear layer from our training dataset, the label mappings were scrambled (e.g. from Output 4 = 'E' to Output 4 = 'C'), yielding gibberish predictions during initial fine-tuning. Through this fine-tuning process, 39 minutes of training data were required for the model to (re-)learn the appropriate parameters for English ASR.

By contrast, in our experiments reported above in §6, we adapted our datasets to match the vocabulary of the tokeniser included with the off-the-shelf model. By doing so, we were able to achieve better than off-the-shelf ASR performance using only 39 seconds of training data.

Yet, unlike those experiments reported above, the addition of a language model to models fine-tuned with a re-initialised vocabulary yielded better performance. As shown in Figure 5, the mean WER of the models fine-tuned with 39 minutes of data and without a language model was found to be 19.5% (SD: 2.98%; range: 15–23%). When a bigram language model was included, we found that the mean WER decreased to 14% (SD: 2.30%; range: 11–18%). These findings suggest that while the addition of a language model can be beneficial more experimentation is needed to inform best practices for calibrating and/or weighting the language model in near-zero shot learning scenarios.

Training set size	WER	CER
a. 65 minutes (100%)	11%	5%
b. 52 minutes (80%)	13%	5%
c. 39 minutes (60%)	16%	6%
d. 26 minutes (40%)	37%	14%
e. 13 minutes (20%)	98%	78%
f. Off-the-shelf (0%)	37%	22%

Table 5: Word error rates (WERs) achieved from fine-tuning the same wav2vec 2.0 model (large-robust-ft-swbd-300h) over 50 epochs using various subsets of data from 65 minutes of Australian English archival audio data.

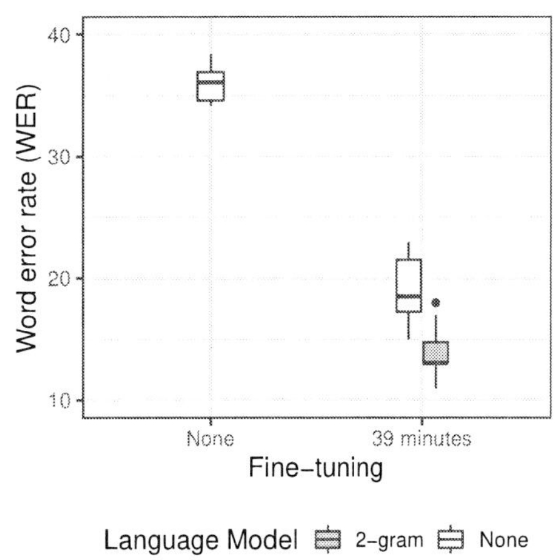

Figure 5: Variability in word error rates of training and testing Robust wav2vec 2.0 models over 10 iterations using different samples in the training and testing datasets, holding constant the size of the training set (39 minutes) and testing set (16 minutes). The off-the-shelf model without fine-tuning was also evaluated on the same 10 testing sets.

[9] https://huggingface.co/blog/fine-tune-wav2vec2-english

[10] https://huggingface.co/facebook/wav2vec2-large-robust-ft-swbd-300h

G_i2P_i: Rule-based, index-preserving grapheme-to-phoneme transformations

Aidan Pine[1] aidan.pine

Patrick Littell[1] patrick.littell

Eric Joanis[1] eric.joanis

David Huggins-Daines[2] dhdaines@gmail.com

Christopher Cox[3] christopher.cox

Fineen Davis[4] fineen.davis@gmail.com

Eddie Antonio Santos[5] eddie.santos@ucdconnect.ie

Shankhalika Srikanth[6] ssrikanth@uvic.ca

Delasie Torkornoo[3] delasie.torkornoo

Sabrina Yu[7] sab.yu@mail.utoronto.ca

Abstract

This paper describes the motivation and implementation details for a rule-based, index-preserving grapheme-to-phoneme engine 'G_i2P_i' implemented in pure Python and released under the open source MIT license[8]. The engine and interface have been designed to prioritize the developer experience of potential contributors without requiring a high level of programming knowledge. G_i2P_i already provides mappings for 30 (mostly Indigenous) languages, and the package is accompanied by a web-based interactive development environment, a RESTful API, and extensive documentation to encourage the addition of more mappings in the future. We also present three downstream applications of G_i2P_i and show results of a preliminary evaluation.

1 Introduction and motivation

G_i2P_i is a library[9] for grapheme-to-phoneme and orthographic transformation, with a particular focus on the needs of digital humanities projects. While libraries for general-purpose G2P exist, we found that our downstream projects had special needs that existing libraries did not entirely meet. In particular,

1. Subject-matter experts for these languages are often teachers or linguists without a background in computer science, who are unfamiliar with the conventions of programming and need more intuitive interfaces to convert their knowledge into executable code (§2.1).

2. Most existing libraries operate on unstructured text, under the assumption that the original document will be discarded after its linguistic information is extracted. Our downstream use-cases, however, often involve the augmentation of the original document with downstream results (e.g., with pronunciations, alternative orthographies, or time-aligned highlighting). We need to be able to trace results backward to their original counterparts (e.g. by using indices as shown in Figure 1), maintaining this information through every step of transduction, so that markup, IDs, punctuation, and other features of the original document can be preserved (§2.2).

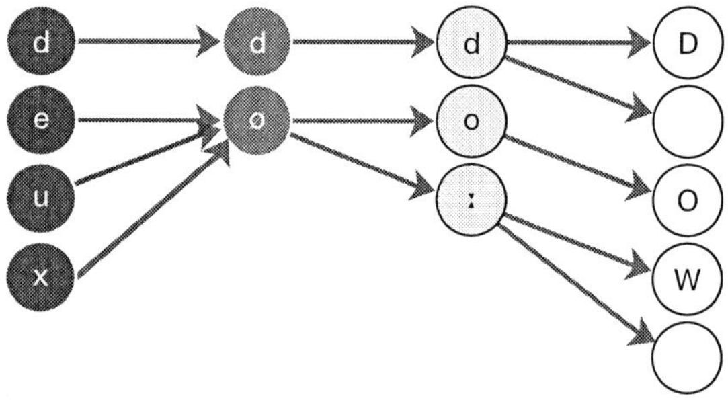

Figure 1: Screenshot from G2P Studio of interactive visualization of the indices preserved when composing transductions of the French word "deux", between the orthographic form, a phonetic representation in the International Phonetic Alphabet (IPA), the closest English phonemes according to PanPhon (Mortensen et al., 2016), and finally to English ARPABET (see §2.3).

3. Software packages for linguistic transformation, and their dependencies, can be difficult to compile and install, or cannot be installed on all operating systems.

The need for such specialized knowledge presents a bottleneck in the development of G2P

[1]National Research Council Canada; @nrc-cnrc.gc.ca
[2]Independent Researcher
[3]Carleton University; @carleton.ca
[4]Wiichihitotaak ILR Inc.
[5]University College Dublin
[6]University of Victoria
[7]University of Toronto
[8]https://github.com/roedoejet/g2p
[9]The package is registered on the Python Package Index as 'g2p' - however to disambiguate our package from the generic NLP task 'G2P', we make specific reference to the index preservation capabilities of our package and refer to the package as G_i2P_i throughout this paper.

Proceedings of the Fifth Workshop on the Use of Computational Methods in the Study of Endangered Languages, pages 52 - 60

engines, particularly when we venture away from the NLP space and into the digital humanities space; experts of a particular language's sound patterns should not necessarily need experience in programming and compiling software in order to translate their knowledge of the language into a machine-readable format.

Meanwhile, however, the languages that we are concentrating on (in particular, Indigenous languages spoken in Canada) do not typically have extensive, publicly-available corpora of parallel orthographic and phonetic renderings, from which we could learn a weighted FST (Novak et al., 2016; Deri and Knight, 2016) or neural model (Rao et al., 2015; Peters et al., 2017). For most of these languages, rule-based approaches based on expert knowledge will be the norm for the foreseeable future. Fortunately, these are mostly languages with regular, linguistically-informed orthographies, such that rule-based approaches are adequate.

In broad strokes, our library is most similar to Epitran (Mortensen et al., 2018), which shares some of these design decisions; it prioritizes ease of installation and adopts a method for defining rule-based G2P mappings inspired by phonological re-write rule syntax that would be familiar to linguists. Our work differs by allowing rules to be written in a spreadsheet format (§2.1), by having a core engine that preserves the indices between inputs and output transductions (§2.2), and by providing a bundled web interface for writing and running G2P mappings (§2.4) with an accompanying RESTful API (§2.6.1).

2 G_i2P_i

This section briefly describes the process for writing rules (§2.1), the motivation and implementation details for preserving indices between inputs and outputs (§2.2), the automatic generation of cross-linguistic phoneme-to-phoneme mappings (§2.3), the 'G2P Studio' development environment (§2.4), a list of currently supported languages (§2.5), documentation information (§2.6), and a description of various applications (§2.7).

2.1 Writing Rules

Rules are written in either a tabular, spreadsheet format or in JSON (See Figure 2). The core functionality of G_i2P_i is expressible in the spreadsheet format (CSV), while the JSON format allows for more functionality. Each mapping is also accompanied by a configuration file written in YAML. In its most basic form, a rule just has an input and an output, like in Figure 2.

```
a,b
```

(a) Minimal CSV Rule

```
{
    "in": "a",
    "out" : "b"
}
```

(b) Minimal JSON Rule

Figure 2: A minimal rule converting 'a' to 'b' expressed in both the CSV syntax (a) and JSON syntax (b)

Context-sensitive rules can also be written which conditionally apply rules based on whether a pattern is matched before or after the input as shown in Figure 3.

```
{
    "in": "a",
    "out" : "b",
    "context_before": "b",
    "context_after": "c"
}
```

Figure 3: A minimal context-sensitive rule in JSON format for converting 'a' to 'b' only when 'a' is preceded by 'b' and followed by 'c'. The equivalent rule written in the CSV format is '`a,b,b,c`'.

Under the hood, these rules are compiled into regular expressions, where the input is the pattern to match, and the 'context before' and 'context after' values are turned into positive lookbehinds and lookaheads respectively. Lookbehinds are first converted to be fixed width and several other preprocessing steps are applied before constructing the regular expression. Namely, any explicit indices (§2.2) are removed, optional case insensitivity flags are applied, Unicode normalization (NFC or NFD) is done, and special characters can be escaped.

A collection of rules with a configuration constitutes a 'mapping' which can then be run in the sequence the rules are defined or in an automatically generated order that runs the rules in reverse order of input length. This mode is intended to help prevent particular rule 'bleeding' relationships where if the input to a hypothetical rule r_1 is a substring

(1)	*baata*	(2)	*baata*
	r_2 bæta		r_1 bəətə
	r_1 bætə		r_2
	bætə		bəətə

Figure 4: Example of rule ordering relationships in a made-up language. r_1 is the rule a → ə, and r_2 is the rule aa → æ. In this made-up language, 'bætə' is the correct transduced form of 'baata', and therefore we want to order rule r_2 before r_1, as shown in (1), so that r_1 does not bleed the context for r_2 to apply, as shown in (2).

of the input to rule r_2 and is ordered to apply first, it will remove, or 'bleed' the context for r_2 to apply, erroneously preventing the application of r_2 as shown in example (2) in Figure 4.

2.1.1 Preventing Feeding Relationships

Another type of rule interaction that can be avoided is a feeding relationship between rules—i.e. where the output of one rule creates the context for another rule to apply. In some situations this is desired, but it can also create problems in your rules. To handle this, we allow `prevent_feeding` to be declared either for an individual rule in a JSON-formatted mapping or for each rule in a mapping. When `prevent_feeding` is set to `true`, the output of a rule is replaced with a character from the Supplementary Private Use Area A Unicode block, offset by the index of the rule in a given mapping. Thus, they will never match the input or context of other rules. After applying all rules in a mapping, these intermediate representations are transformed back into the appropriate values.

2.1.2 Composite Transducers

In practice, many real-world transduction tasks comprise a sequence of simpler transductions. For example, a G2P transduction used in ReadAlong Studio (§2.7.3) might start with converting a font-encoded orthography into a Unicode compliant form, then replacing confusable characters, converting the orthographic form into IPA, mapping those characters onto their closest English equivalents, and finally mapping the English IPA characters into the ARPABET alphabet used by the acoustic model.

G_i2P_i is built with this in mind; an arbitrary number of transducers can be combined, and chains of transducers can be inferred automatically. If the user requests a mapping from one language code[10] to another, e.g., from `alq` (Algonquin) to `eng-arpabet`, and that particular mapping does not exist, the software can search for the shortest possible chain of transducers with those endpoints, and it will act as if it were an ordinary transducer (including maintaining indices between the ultimate inputs and outputs, and all intermediate forms, as seen in Fig. 1).

Fig. 5 on the following page illustrates the current network of transducers possible in G_i2P_i.

This modularity is intended, in part, to help subject-matter experts contribute their domain knowledge (e.g., the pronunciation of their language's orthography) without having to understand the other specialized components of the transduction pipeline (e.g., confusable Unicode characters or ARPABET), or even the structure of the pipeline as a whole. They only have to contribute their particular piece; G_i2P_i can compose the pipeline as a whole, and even auto-generate certain kinds of missing pieces (§2.3).

2.1.3 Debugging

Debugging transductions can be a difficult task when there are multiple mappings involved, each with possibly dozens of rules. In order to help ease the burden on developers, multiple debugging tools have been developed to assist contributors. In the G2P Studio (§2.4), there is an automatic visualization mode which allows users to visualize transductions in an interactive way; Figure 1 is a screenshot of this visualization.

There are also two alternative options for debugging; the `--debugger` flag used in either the CLI or REST API shows each transduction applied in sequence along with any intermediate steps (§2.1.1). Additionally, there is a `g2p doctor` command in the CLI that checks a specific mapping for a list of common errors, such as the declaration of IPA characters not recognized by PanPhon.

2.2 Preserving Indices

The concerns in (§1) are not as pressing when considering a G2P transformation to create artifacts such as training data for a speech recognition

[10]In G_i2P_i, a mapping is a collection of rules with a defined input language code and output language code. By "code" we mean an arbitrary label for the language. By convention we start with the ISO 639-3 code and add a descriptive suffix (e.g. `-ipa` when required.

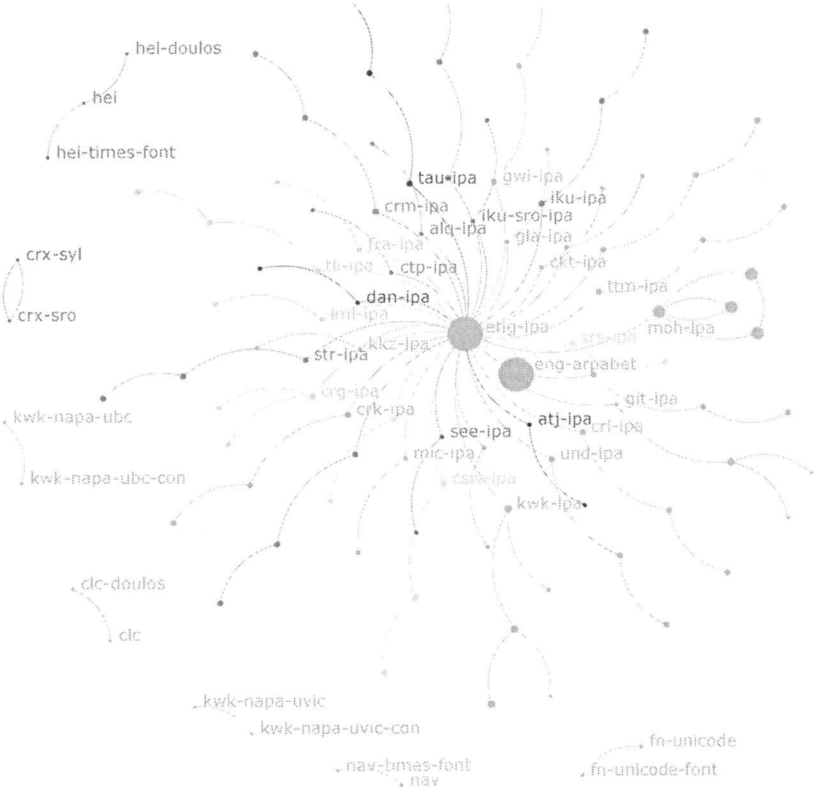

Figure 5: Visualization of the network created by G2P. Nodes represent orthographies or phonetic representations. They are labelled and colour coded according to the associated language's ISO 639-3 code. Arcs represent mappings. Nodes are sized relative to the number of upstream nodes. English (eng) has the largest nodes due to the large number of generated mappings into English for the purpose of the ReadAlong Studio project (see §2.3, §2.7.3).

model. There, once the necessary information has been extracted from the document, features in the original document like punctuation can be ignored, as only the transformed version is used.

However, consider how the project needs differ when force-aligning a storybook with an accompanying recording, such that a beginner reader can see words highlighted when they are read, click to hear words in isolation, etc. If our transformation pipeline has thrown out all non-speech features of the document on the way to the ARPABET needed by the decoder, we are left with timestamps that correspond only to a text document with an unclear relationship with the original structured data. This would be fine if the storybook were only to be used as training data, but if we want to re-associate those timestamps with the original document, we would have an additional problem of re-alignment.

We could potentially try to learn an alignment model between the output and the original document, but data is extremely scarce in most of our target languages, and in any case these alignments are something that the model itself could have maintained. Therefore, we designed the G_i2P_i library to maintain index alignments throughout the process, even when transformations are composed.

This is also true below the level of the word. Many of our target languages are very morphologically complex and long words are the norm. Therefore, educational material in these languages often has subword highlighting. For example, educational material from the Onkwawenna Kentyohkwa immersion school for the Kanyen'kéha (Mohawk) language has a systematic association with particular kinds of morphemes with colors. Another example is when the downstream project involves subword phenomena: a bouncing-ball sing-along video requires syllable-level alignment to get the bounce at the correct place and time.

However, in both of these examples, the unit of transformation is still the word; the word is the domain over which most phonological transformations apply. Splitting the original word into subword units before processing will not necessarily produce correct results, as this would introduce new "word" boundaries. Therefore, we must also keep and compose indices below the level of the word, so that even when transforming whole words we can associate the resulting pronunciations, timestamps, etc. with subword markup in the original

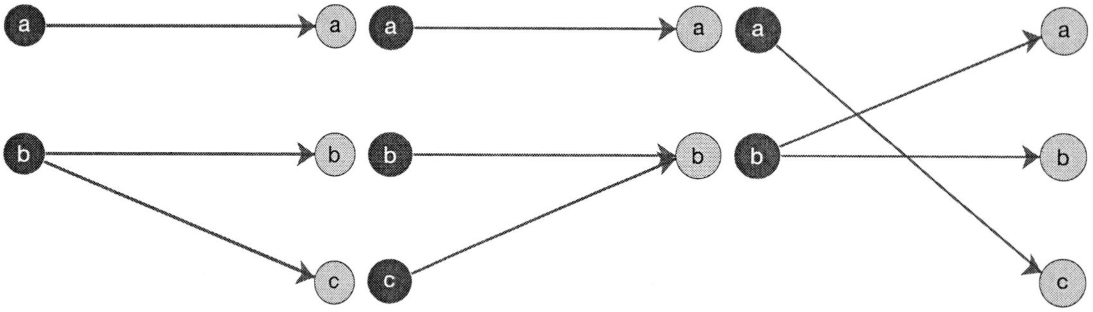

(a) ab → abc (b) abc → ab (c) a{1}b{2} → ab{2}c{1}

Figure 6: Examples of various strategies for assigning indices between inputs and outputs; default assignment of indices is shown in 6a and 6b and explicit assignment of indices is shown in 6c.

document.

Maintaining these indices is also useful for a debugging visualization in the bundled development environment (§2.4), making clear in composed transductions how inputs, intermediate, and output forms correspond to each other (Fig. 1).

2.2.1 Default and Explicit Indexing

The default interpretation of rules is to assign indices evenly between inputs and outputs; if there is a mismatch in length between inputs and outputs, excess characters are assigned the index of the last character of the shorter string, as seen in Figures 6a and 6b.

However, G_i2P_i also allows a more explicit syntax for defining indexing relationships between inputs and outputs: rules can be marked up with curly braces to indicate a specific indexing of characters between inputs and outputs as seen in Figure 6c.

2.3 Automatic Phoneme-to-Phoneme Mappings

Another use of the G_i2P_i library, beyond grapheme-to-phoneme transformation or orthographic transliteration, is to map the sounds of one language onto the sounds of another, for cross-linguistic comparison. This is used, for example, in ReadAlong Studio (§2.7.3) to align text and speech in an arbitrary language using only an English-language acoustic model.

While these mappings can be written by hand, it is somewhat of a specialized art, typically performed by speech technology specialists. Therefore, the G_i2P_i library also includes functionality to automatically generate phone-to-phone mappings, by leveraging the phone-to-phone distance metrics included in PanPhon (Mortensen et al., 2016) to serve as "glue" in a composite transducer (§2.1.2).

For composing a mapping A with a mapping B, where both the output vocabulary of A and in the input vocabulary B represent IPA characters (but not necessarily the same inventory of IPA characters), the G_i2P_i library can generate a mapping in which each character in the output of A is mapped to its nearest neighbor in the input of B, according to the PanPhon's calculated phone-to-phone distance between the characters' phonological feature vector representations. PanPhon allows for a variety of distance metrics between IPA characters; by default we use PanPhon's Hamming distance metric between IPA phonological feature vector representations. This allows non-specialist users to generate cross-linguistic transductions of the sort used in cross-lingual speech synthesis (§2.7.2) or ReadAlong Studio (§2.7.3), without necessarily having to be a linguist familiar with the IPA.

2.4 G2P Studio

In addition to developing rules locally as described in §2.1, writing and running mappings can be performed in a web interface called 'G2P Studio'. The G2P Studio is written using a vanilla JavaScript front-end with Skeleton CSS[11] and a Python backend written in Flask with low-latency, bidirectional communication handled through WebSockets.

The G2P Studio is hosted at `https://bit.ly/g2p-studio` but can also be deployed in a distributed fashion, as the lightweight server/app code is bundled in the Python package.

2.4.1 Visual Programming Rule Creator

In addition to creating rules in spreadsheets or JSON files, G2P Studio includes a visual program-

[11] `http://getskeleton.com/`

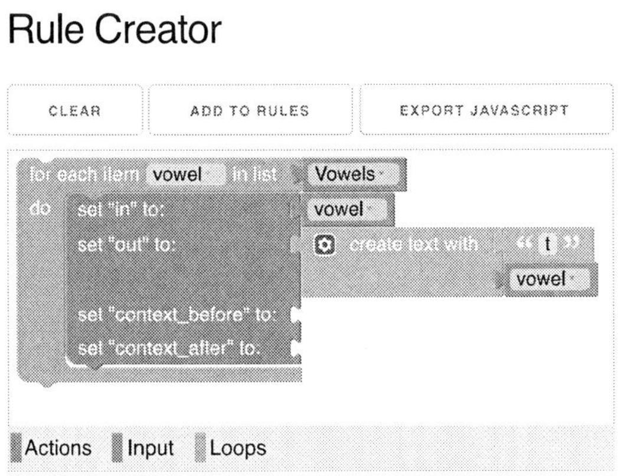

Figure 7: Screenshot of the "Rule Creator" interface in G2P Studio showing a toy set of rules being made that take each vowel in the Vowels variable (declared elsewhere in G2P Studio) as input and return the same vowel prefixed by 't' as output.

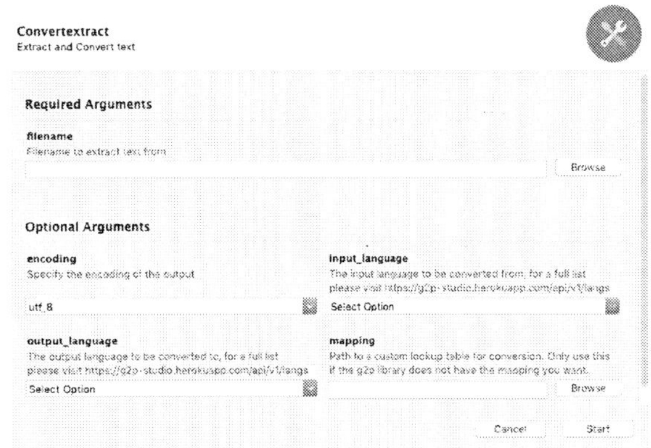

Figure 8: Screenshot of Convertextract GUI for macOS

ming interface for authoring rules (Figure 7). This visual programming interface was created with Blockly[12] (Fraser, 2015; Pasternak et al., 2017).

2.5 Supported Languages

At the time of writing, 30 languages are supported: Anishinàbemiwin (alq), Atikamekw (atj), Michif (crg), Southern & Northern East Cree (crj), Plains Cree (crk), Moose Cree (crm), Swampy Cree (csw), Western Highland Chatino (ctp), Danish (dan), French (fra), Gitksan (git), Scottish Gaelic (gla), Gwich'in (gwi), Hän (haa), Inuinnaqtun (ikt), Inuktitut (iku), Kaska (kkz), Kwak'wala (kwk), Raga (lml), Mi'kmaq (mic), Kanien'kéha (moh), Anishinaabemowin (oji), Seneca (see), Tsuut'ina (srs), SENĆOŦEN (str), Upper Tanana (tau), Southern Tutchone (tce), Northern Tutchone (ttm), Tagish (tgx), Tlingit (tli). G_i2P_i is also bundled with other mappings, such as mappings from font-encoded writing systems in Heiltsuk, Tsilqot'in, and Navajo to Unicode-compliant versions as well a mapping from English IPA to English ARPABET.

2.6 Documentation

Documentation on primary use cases and edge cases is an important part of the G_i2P_i project. Without contributions to the mappings, the project will be less accessible, and more difficult to maintain. Technical documentation is therefore provided through ReadTheDocs[13] as well as a 7-part blog series[14] written for a more general audience.

2.6.1 RESTful API documentation

The core functionality of G_i2P_i is also exposed through a RESTful API. The API and its documentation are generated dynamically using Swagger[15] to provide up-to-date, interactive documentation[16]. The documentation allows users to interactively make requests to the API, see available mappings, and copy the related Curl commands along with other information like the Request URLs, and Response body and headers from their requests.

2.7 Applications

Grapheme-to-phoneme transformations are used in a wide variety of natural language processing tasks, and so G_i2P_i can be used for any such use case. Below, we briefly discuss three projects that are implemented using G_i2P_i.

2.7.1 Convertextract

Convertextract (Pine and Turin, 2018), is a tool that performs find/replace operations on Microsoft Office documents while preserving the original formatting of the file. Convertextract is available for the command line and with a macOS GUI (Figure 8). Integration is fully automated between the libraries—whenever a new version of G_i2P_i is released, it triggers a new build and release of convertextract which is able to perform any conversion between any of the mappings defined in G_i2P_i.

2.7.2 Speech Synthesis Front End

We have built speech synthesis models for SENĆOŦEN, Kanyen'kéha, and Gitksan using

[12] `https://developers.google.com/blockly`
[13] `https://g2p.readthedocs.io/`
[14] `https://blog.mothertongues.org/g2p-background/`
[15] `https://swagger.io/`
[16] `https://bit.ly/g2p-api-docs`

mappings developed with G_i2P_i (Pine et al., 2022). Part of the pipeline for these models involves transforming the orthographic form of utterances to a phonetic representation. This is necessary for the pre-processing step of forced alignment and the phonetic representation of the text is used as input to the feature prediction network in the speech synthesis pipeline. The phonetic form is represented either as one-hot encodings or as multi-hot phonological feature vectors derived from PanPhon. This is another use case for generated mappings (§2.3); a mapping between the IPA symbols of a target language could be mapped on to the IPA symbols of one or more languages in a pre-trained model using G_i2P_i to facilitate fine-tuning on a language that was not present in the pre-trained model. This method allows for a principled rule-based method for mapping between symbol spaces in cross-lingual speech synthesis without the use of a learned phonetic transformation network like the one described by Tu et al. (2019).

2.7.3 ReadAlong Studio

ReadAlong Studio[17] is a library for the creation of time-aligned "read-along" audiobooks, intended to make text/speech alignment easy for non-specialist users. It utilizes a zero-shot speech alignment paradigm in which target-language text is converted to English-language phonemes, and then force-aligned using the default English-language acoustic model from PocketSphinx (Huggins-Daines et al., 2006).

By its nature, this text conversion is a composite transduction (§2.1.2) – first converting the target-language text to target-language phonemes, then converting the target-language phonemes into similar English-language phonemes (§2.3), and finally converting the English-language phonemes into the ARPABET symbols that the aligner expects as shown previously in Figure 1.

While none of these steps is, in itself, difficult to specify by hand, in combination they require a relatively rare expertise: (1) understanding of a specific language's orthography, (2) understanding how sounds map to each other between languages, and (3) familiarity with the ARPABET conventions and the specific phone vocabulary of the English-language acoustic model used.

By automating the second and third steps, and automating their composition, the G_i2P_i library only requires the user to be able to do the first, putting it within reach of a linguistically-informed teacher or other knowledge worker. It *does* require knowledge of the IPA, but this is relatively widespread knowledge, and IPA-equivalence charts for many languages are easy to come by in books and online.

3 Evaluation

As mentioned previously, this paper shares many similarities with Epitran, however we cannot evaluate our system using the same method. Epitran leverages baseline data available in some of the languages it supports to evaluate the system indirectly using the downstream task of developing ASR systems. The word error rates (WER) of ASR systems created using letter-to-sound rules from Epitran are then compared against those created using the available baseline. The primary focus for this library is on extremely low resource languages, and we do not possess baseline data to recreate the evaluation procedure implemented by Epitran.

As a crude replacement, we evaluate two of our mappings by reporting the accuracy of a downstream forced alignment task using ReadAlong Studio (§2.7.3). We manually annotated data from SENĆOŦEN and Kanyen'kéha with word-level alignments in Praat. Given the time-consuming nature of manual alignment, we were limited to a single document from each language; the SENĆOŦEN document is 5:47 long and contains 417 words and the Kanyen'kéha document is 5:07 long and contains 249 words. Both documents are private materials owned by the language communities and shared with us by linguist Timothy Montler and Kanyen'kéha educator Owennatekha Brian Maracle respectively.

We evaluate our hand-written mappings against a baseline zero-shot G2P method. The baseline we use is ReadAlong Studio's fallback method for 'und' (ISO 639-3 for 'undetermined') text. This fallback method uses the text-unidecode[18] package to convert all characters to ASCII equivalents, and then uses a rule-based mapping from ASCII to IPA. For our hand-written SENĆOŦEN and Kanyen'kéha mappings, we use G_i2P_i's built-in automatic mapping functionality to map the IPA inventories to the closest English IPA equivalents (§2.3). All methods are then mapped from IPA to the ARPABET vocabulary used by the decoder.

[17] `https://github.com/ReadAlongs/Studio`

[18] `https://pypi.org/project/text-unidecode/`

Mapping	Lang.	Tolerance (ms) <10	<25	<50	<100
Handmade	moh	0.24	0.43	0.68	0.84
	str	**0.24**	**0.49**	**0.69**	**0.88**
Und	moh	0.24	0.46	0.72	0.86
	str	0.15	0.34	0.49	0.62

Table 1: Results for Kanyen'kéha (moh) and SENĆOŦEN (str) downstream forced alignment task showing alignment accuracy with varying amounts of tolerance for word boundaries for alignments created from handmade G_i2P_i mappings and mappings based on text unidecode ('Und'), measured against hand-labelled alignments.

Similar to McAuliffe et al. (2017), we evaluate the system by reporting the accuracy of the word boundaries predicted by the aligner within thresholds of < 10, < 25, < 50, and < 100 milliseconds; for example, a result of 0.88 with a threshold of <100ms means that 88% of system boundaries were within 100ms of the reference boundaries.

As shown in Table 1, the results for SENĆOŦEN and Kanyen'kéha are not the same. While alignment created from handmade mappings for SENĆOŦEN outperforms the baseline by 26% with a 100ms tolerance threshold, the results from Kanyen'kéha are less clear, and do not show an improvement over the baseline. We suspect this is in part because while the Kanyen'kéha orthography is quite consistent with other Latin-based orthographies, the SENĆOŦEN orthography is considerably different (for example Ć corresponds to the sound /ʧ/), which would affect the text-unidecode library's ability to predict reasonable ASCII equivalents. These results could point to a finding that for simpler[19] orthographies that are strongly aligned with English, the text unidecode technique could be sufficient; however, caution should be applied in interpreting these preliminary results and further evaluation with additional languages, data, and downstream tasks would be needed.

4 Conclusion

In this paper we presented G_i2P_i along with its motivations, and some descriptions of its use cases. The library is written in pure Python to support (relatively) easy installation, with support for 30 different languages, index preservation between inputs and outputs, an accompanying graphical web interface, a RESTful API, and extensive documentation to encourage the development of mappings for more languages in the future.

We recognize that language experts are the best people suited to write mappings between a language's orthography and the IPA, and we hope that through a variety of features that such a contributor would "get for free" by contributing, that G_i2P_i is an attractive option for rule-based G2P. To summarize, by contributing a mapping, a contributor will acquire the following:

- Integration into the broader G_i2P_i transduction network for cross-lingual purposes (§2.1.2)
- Debugging tools (§2.1.3)
- Index preservation for transductions (§2.2)
- A graphical interface (§2.4)
- A RESTful API (§2.6.1)
- Automatic downstream support in Convertextract (§2.7.1) and ReadAlong Studio (§2.7.3)

Each time a mapping is added to G_i2P_i it becomes more useful software, so we have prioritized the developer experience of contributing a mapping through documentation, debugging tools and the features described above. We hope that these measures will make using and contributing to G_i2P_i more accessible and we will measure the success of the project by the number of collaborator contributions of mappings.

Acknowledgements

We would like to acknowledge the Yukon Native Language Centre and the W̱SÁNEĆ School Board for extremely helpful contributions in providing alphabet charts, sample text and other materials that aided in the development of some of the mappings described in §2.5. We would also like to thank Bradley Ellert for his contributions in helping developing mappings.

References

Aliya Deri and Kevin Knight. 2016. Grapheme-to-phoneme models for (almost) any language. In *Proceedings of the 54th Annual Meeting of the Association for Computational Linguistics (Volume 1: Long Papers)*, pages 399–408.

[19] Kanyen'kéha contains fewer than half as many segmental phonemes as SENĆOŦEN

Neil Fraser. 2015. Ten things we've learned from Blockly. In *2015 IEEE Blocks and Beyond Workshop*, pages 49–50.

David Huggins-Daines, Mohit Kumar, Arthur Chan, Alan W Black, Mosur Ravishankar, and Alexander I Rudnicky. 2006. Pocketsphinx: A free, real-time continuous speech recognition system for hand-held devices. In *2006 IEEE International Conference on Acoustics Speech and Signal Processing Proceedings*, volume 1, pages I–I. IEEE.

Michael McAuliffe, Michaela Socolof, Sarah Mihuc, Michael Wagner, and Morgan Sonderegger. 2017. Montreal forced aligner: Trainable text-speech alignment using kaldi. In *Interspeech*, volume 2017, pages 498–502.

David R. Mortensen, Siddharth Dalmia, and Patrick Littell. 2018. Epitran: Precision G2P for many languages. In *Proceedings of the Eleventh International Conference on Language Resources and Evaluation (LREC 2018)*, Paris, France. European Language Resources Association.

David R. Mortensen, Patrick Littell, Akash Bharadwaj, Kartik Goyal, Chris Dyer, and Lori S. Levin. 2016. Panphon: A resource for mapping IPA segments to articulatory feature vectors. In *Proceedings of COLING 2016, the 26th International Conference on Computational Linguistics: Technical Papers*, pages 3475–3484. Association for Computational Linguistics.

Josef Robert Novak, Nobuaki Minematsu, and Keikichi Hirose. 2016. Phonetisaurus: Exploring grapheme-to-phoneme conversion with joint n-gram models in the wfst framework. *Natural Language Engineering*, 22(6):907–938.

Eric Pasternak, Rachel Fenichel, and Andrew N. Marshall. 2017. Tips for creating a block language with Blockly. In *2017 IEEE Blocks and Beyond Workshop*, pages 21–24.

Ben Peters, Jon Dehdari, and Josef van Genabith. 2017. Massively Multilingual Neural Grapheme-to-Phoneme Conversion. In *Proceedings of the First Workshop on Building Linguistically Generalizable NLP Systems*, pages 19–26, Copenhagen, Denmark. Association for Computational Linguistics.

Aidan Pine and Mark Turin. 2018. Seeing the Heiltsuk orthography from font encoding through to Unicode: A case study using convertextract. In Claudia Soria, Laurent Besacier, and Laurette Pretorius, editors, *Proceedings of the LREC 2018 Workshop "CCURL 2018 – Sustaining knowledge diversity in the digital age"*, pages 27–30. European Language Resources Association.

Aidan Pine, Dan Wells, Nathan Thanyehténhas Brinklow, Patrick Littell, and Korin Richmond. 2022. Requirements and Motivations for Low Resource Speech Synthesis. In *Proceedings of ACL 2022*, Dublin, Ireland. Association for Computational Linguistics.

Kanishka Rao, Fuchun Peng, Haşim Sak, and Françoise Beaufays. 2015. Grapheme-to-phoneme conversion using long short-term memory recurrent neural networks. In *2015 IEEE International Conference on Acoustics, Speech and Signal Processing (ICASSP)*, pages 4225–4229.

Tao Tu, Yuan-Jui Chen, Cheng-chieh Yeh, and Hung-yi Lee. 2019. End-to-end Text-to-speech for Low-resource Languages by Cross-Lingual Transfer Learning. In *Interspeech 2019*, pages 2075–2079.

Shallow Parsing for Nepal Bhasa Complement Clauses

Borui Zhang
George A. Smathers Libraries
University of Florida
boruizhang@ufl.edu

Abe Kazemzadeh
Graduate Programs in Software
University of St. Thomas
abe.kazemzadeh@stthomas.edu

Brian Reese
Institute of Linguistics
University of Minnesota
breese@umn.edu

Abstract

Accelerating the process of data collection, annotation, and analysis is an urgent need for linguistic fieldwork and documentation of endangered languages (Bird, 2009). Our experiments describe how we maximize the quality for the Nepal Bhasa syntactic complement structure chunking model. Native speaker language consultants were trained to annotate a minimally selected raw data set (Suárez et al., 2019). Embedded clauses, matrix verbs, and embedded verbs were annotated. We apply both statistical training algorithms and transfer learning in our training, including Naive Bayes, MaxEnt, and fine-tuning the pre-trained mBERT model (Devlin et al., 2018). We show that with limited annotated data, the model is already sufficient for the task[1]. The modeling resources we used are largely available for many other endangered languages. The practice is easy to duplicate for training a shallow parser for other endangered languages.

1 Introduction

Nepal Bhasa (also known as Newari or Newar Language) is an endangered, low-resource language mainly spoken by the indigenous community in Kathmandu Valley, Nepal. The native speaker population has declined from 1,041,090 (Shrestha, 1999) to 860,000 from 1991 to 2011. The current project comprises two interconnected goals. First, we aim to better understand Nepal Bhasa complementation structures in order to explore broader cross-linguistic generalizations. Second, we leverage the available low cost resources and our expertise in language, linguistics, and data science, to build complementation prediction models to facilitate our research on Nepal Bhasa complementation.

2 Linguistic motivation

Every natural language has complementation structures where a clause is embedded within a larger clausal constituent by a clause embedding predicate. Clausal syntactic structure and lexical semantics of clause embedding verbs, therefore, are two major focuses in research on complementation (Moulton, 2009; Bresnan, 1972). We study the Kathmandu Nepal Bhasa dialect (cf. Genetti (2009) for Dolakha Newar) which is generally head-final (OV language). However, embedded complement clauses include both head-final and head-initial complementizers, as shown in (1) and (2) respectively.[2]

(1) Sitā-na [CP Rām-na oṃ nala
sitaana ramna ong nala
Sita-ERG Ram-ERG mango eat.PST
dhakā/dhayā] dhā-u.
dhakaa/dhayaa dhaau
C/C say-PST
'Sita said **that** Ram ate mangos.'

(2) Sitā-na dhā-u [CP **ki** Rām-na
sitaana dhaau ki ramna
Sita-ERG say-PST C Ram-ERG
oṃ nala].
ong nala
mango eat.PST
'Sita said **that** Ram ate mangos.'

[1]The data and code used in this paper are available at github.com/boruizhang/newa

[2]We follow Leipzig glossing conventions: ERG for ergative, PST for past tense, and C for complementizer.

Proceedings of the Fifth Workshop on the Use of Computational Methods in the Study of Endangered Languages, pages 61 - 67
May 26-27, 2022 ©2022 Association for Computational Linguistics

Kathmandu Nepal Bhasa has four surface forms of complementizers: two head-final *dhakā/dhayā*, head-initial *ki*, and null head (Zhang, 2021). In studying clausal complementation (CP) in this language, one would ideally want access to as much language data as possible exemplifying the relevant CP embedding structures. However, in our experience the speed of data collection and the vocabulary range are often limiting factors in traditional linguistic fieldwork. These limitations negatively impact the development of research on endangered languages given the lack of quantitative evidence to test and confirm theoretical claims. Zhang (2021) suggests that different complementizers in Nepal Bhasa contribute different syntactic and semantic properties to a CP even though the surface forms are seemingly interchangeable based on the general meaning of the sentence as in the examples shown in (1) and (2). The data from the first author's Nepal Bhasa fieldwork shows potential morphological restrictions on matrix verbs that may be related to complementizer selections.

Large, structured corpora collected from non-fieldwork study can help validate theoretical linguistic claims. Such corpora provide a wider range of verb forms and more realistic distributions of complementizer uses. Clause-level structural information can be used to retrieve embedded CP constituents (e.g. Universal Dependencies relations or labeled constituent structure parse trees as in the UPenn Treebank (McDonald et al., 2013; Marcus et al., 1993)). However no such resources exist for Nepal Bhasa. Building structured corpora is costly and time-consuming for small research groups. Therefore, the current research investigating Nepal Bhasa CPs is aimed to explore the extent to which NLP techniques can help with accelerating the process of linguistic fieldwork annotation.

3 Data and Annotation

Structured corpora provide naturalistic data with syntactic and semantic annotations and provide an important resource for linguistic research and language documentation (Hovy and Lavid, 2010; de Marneffe and Potts, 2017). Building annotated corpora for endangered languages is particularly beneficial, as linguistic insights are systematically shown in the data, which are directly reusable and can be improved by adjoined efforts over time. However, there is no annotated public corpus resource of Nepal Bhasa currently available. However, the Open Super-large Crawled Aggregated coRpus (OSCAR) (Suárez et al., 2019), a 20TB corpus covering 166 natural languages, does include 5.7MB (16694 sentences) of unannotated Nepal Bhasa data. Two native speaker consultants assisted in the annotation process for the project, providing their language expertise on identifying embedded clauses and verbs in a small, pre-selected set of sentences. We worked closely on reviewing annotation work to improve the annotation quality. A faster annotating work speed was observed in the later annotation sessions. We then used this annotated data to train shallow parsers to predict embedded clauses in Nepal Bhasa.

The study focuses on the CPs that are headed by *dhakā* (head-final) and *ki* (head-initial). Table 1 outlines the pre-processing steps undertaken before annotation, including removing non-Devanagari characters, aligning one sentence per line, and removing sentences that had less than three words in one line, resulting in a total of 16603 clean sentences left for CP extraction.[3] 684 sentences were found containing the keyword *dhakā*, and 2660 sentences were found that contained the keyword *ki*. *Dhakā* is a good morphological cue for the detection of complement sentences in the data, while *ki* is ambiguous between being a complementizer or a phrasal conjunction ('and'). Out of the 3344 sentences (680+2660) that potentially contain CPs, 200 *dhakā*-sentences and 100 *ki*-sentences were randomly selected for the annotation task. See Appendix ?? for the written annotation guidelines.

Among the 300 sentences, 6 true embedded CPs were found in the 100 *ki*-sentences, and more than 190 true embedded CPs were found in the 200 *dhakā* sentences. After the manual annotation, the annotated sentences were converted to the CoNLL-2003 shared NER task format using IBO labels (Abney, 1991), as shown in Table 2.

[3]Data will be made available in Github repo.

Devanagari script data	Sentences
OSCAR-2019 raw sentences	16694
# actual working sentences	16603
# Keyword *'dhakā'*	684
# Keyword *'ki'*	2660
Annotated	
# total manually annotated	300
# total identified non-embedded	101

Table 1: Nepal Bhasa OSCAR corpus status

Tags	Tokens
#I	2332
#O	1933
#B	208

Table 2: Annotation level distribution

Because chunks are by definition non-overlapping sequences of tokens, the models we present below are unable to recognize recursive structures (e.g., a CP embedded in another CP). We found few instances of such structures in the data and chose to label only the embedding CP in such instances.

4 Learning methods

We implemented three CP chunking models for Bhasa Nepal: Naive Bayes, maximum entropy, and mBERT via NERDA. For Naive Bayes and maximum entropy models, we utilized both bigram and trigram features (two and three word token contexts with one and two tag/label contexts, respectively) and we tried predicting labels in forward and reverse directions (using preceding and following n-gram contexts, respectively). For the labels used as features, we used predicted labels as the features when testing to prevent leakage of the true labels into the prediction.

We used the NERDA Python library (Kjeldgaard and Nielsen, 2021) to train a neural chunking model. The package offers an easy to use interface for the NER task with fine-tuning of pretrained large models for any low-resource language.

We fine-tuned the pretrained cased mBERT model 'bert-base-multilingual-cased' for our experiment (Devlin et al., 2018). Nepal Bhasa is reported as being included in the mBERT training process. The data is split into training, validation, and testing sets with a ratio of 7:2:1. The average training time is 3 to 4 minutes with GPU. The hyper-parameter settings 11 epochs, 10 warmups, 7 batches proved to be the best among different trials. A systematic observation is that a larger batch size, 10 for example in this case, significantly lowers the accuracy, which (Keskar et al., 2016) suggest in their study of deep learning structures.

5 Results and discussion

Figure 1 and Table 3 show the token accuracy and chunk precision, recall, and F1 scores. For all the metrics except recall, increasing the n-gram context from bigram to trigram improved the maximum entropy models, whereas the extra trigram context decreased the performance for naive Bayes across all metrics.

We hypothesized that reversing the order of processing would be beneficial for head-final languages like Nepal Bhasa, since the embedded clause appears before the main verb (order: S CP V) in the default position, in contrast to the head-initial word order (order: S V CP) of languages like English. However, the result did not show any benefit to performance, even decreasing the performance (these were omitted from Figure 1 but shown in Table 3). This suggests that using right-to-left processing only may not be an appropriate learning order regardless of the headedness of a natural language. Even the head-final CPs as in (1) show a 'backward' relation between the main verb and the complementizer head of the embedded clause; the remaining sentence elements do not maintain backward relations for every pair.

The mBERT-based NERDA models show comparable performance to the maximum entropy models with trigram features. The NERDA model showed improved accuracy (96% vs. 91% but slightly lower F-score (69% vs. 72%), with NERDA showing higher recall than maximum entropy (77% vs. 69%) but lower precision (63% vs. 75%). We manually reviewed the predictions for every entry in the test set. The NERDA fune-tuning models predict the right edge of the CP with 100% accuracy, and the left-edge with 69% accuracy. The prediction accuracy result matches the language typological feature of

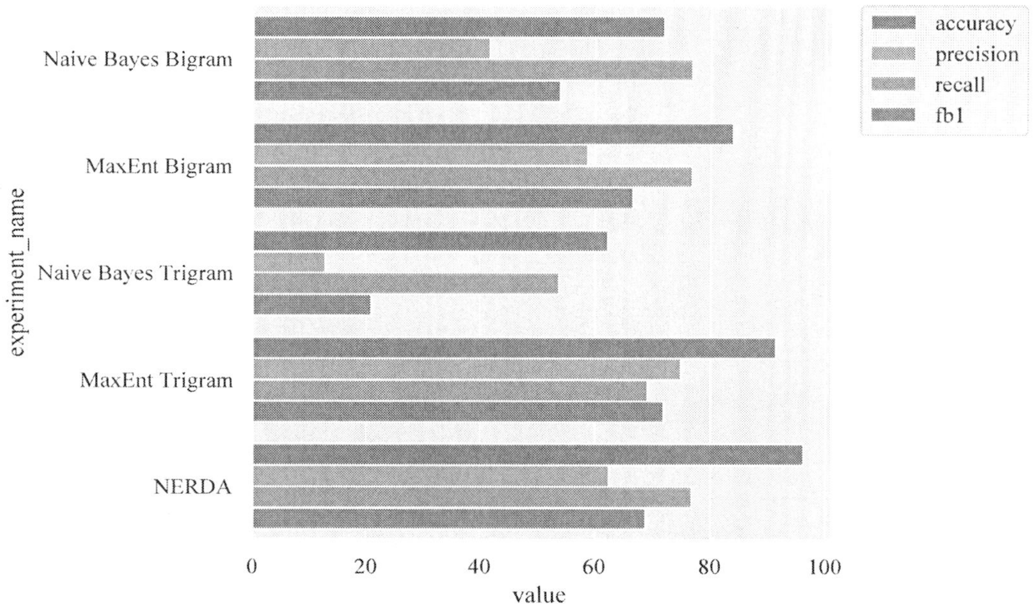

Figure 1: Tag-level accuracy and chunk-level precision, recall and F1 score for top-performing models. Table 3 contains more details of other models.

experiment_name	toks	phrases	corr.	acc.	prec.	rec.	fb1
Naive Bayes Unigram	268	13	1	63.81	2.17	7.69	3.39
MaxEnt Unigram	268	13	0	52.24	0.00	0.00	0.00
Naive Bayes Bigram	268	13	**10**	72.01	41.67	**76.92**	54.05
MaxEnt Bigram	268	13	**10**	83.96	58.82	**76.92**	66.67
Naive Bayes Trigram	268	13	7	62.31	12.96	53.85	20.90
MaxEnt Trigram	268	13	9	91.42	**75.00**	69.23	**72.00**
Naive Bayes Bigram Backward	268	13	1	62.69	7.69	7.69	7.69
MaxEnt Bigram Backward	268	13	6	90.67	40.00	46.15	42.86
Naive Bayes Trigram Backward	268	13	0	56.34	0.00	0.00	0.00
MaxEnt Trigram Backward	268	13	0	60.07	0.00	0.00	0.00
NERDA	242	13	**10**	**96.28**	62.50	**76.92**	68.97

Table 3: Experimental results: number of tokens (toks), number of chunks (phrases), number of correct chunks (corr.), token accuracy (acc.), chunk precision (prec.), chunk recall (rec.), and chunk f-score (fb1).

Nepal Bhasa being head-final. As previously discussed, head-final complementizers syntactically appear on the right periphery of the clause, before the main verb, and therefore the right edge of the clause is more predictable due tothis strong linguistic cue. This could also show the benefit of the mBERT model's bi-directional transformer, which is expected to be good at capturing both head-final CP and other components with different headedness.

In contrast, the difficulty in predicting left CP boundaries may reflect corpus distributional facts. First, the head-initial complementizers are more rarely used in the data set than the head-final ones, even though both kinds are grammatical in this language. Second, other linguistic components, such as noun phrases and adverbials, may occupy the left periphery of an embedded CP structure.

Considering the small size of the training data, the accuracy of the model heavily depends on the training data, as shown by the 10-fold cross validation results in Table 4.

Additionally, we provide counts for matrix (embedding) verbs for the entire annotated data set. (See full list in Appendix B.) Our ongoing linguistic fieldwork data suggests a morphological restriction in Nepal Bhasa matrix verbs in complementation constructions: aspectual suffix morpheme न (a, IPA:[ə]), never appears on embedding verb. The matrix verb distribution shows that the morpheme गु

fold	toks	phrases	corr.	acc.	prec.	rec.	fb1
1	383	16	0	48.56	0	0	0
2	320	16	13	92.50	76.47	81.25	78.79
3	417	16	11	85.37	64.71	68.75	66.67
4	418	16	0	41.15	0	0	0
5	388	16	0	61.86	0	0	0
6	333	17	2	81.08	9.52	11.76	10.53
7	331	19	5	82.78	25	26.32	25.64
8	275	16	11	86.91	64.71	68.75	66.67
9	281	16	15	97.51	93.75	93.75	93.75
10	285	16	11	94.39	55	68.75	61.11
mean	343.1	16.4	6.80	77.21	38.92	41.93	40.32
std	52.3	0.92	5.69	18.72	34.07	35.80	34.84

Table 4: 10-fold cross validation of NERDA model

(u, IPA:[u]), frequently appears in embedding verbs in the corpus which supports the generalization.

6 Conclusion

Our experiments training shallow parsers for Nepal Bhasa complement phrases has shown the potential use of NLP tools in assisting corpus annotation for fieldwork research in endangered languages in general. We successfully achieve some high model performance with the very limited data source (less than 300 manually annotated sentences, 2% of the entire OSCAR Nepal corpus). The procedure may be used as a starting step in developing more structured corpora for fieldworkers.

Furthermore, theoretical linguistic insights also suggest a new perspective to interpret the model performance. For example, we learned that the right boundary of the clause is more predictable than the left boundary of a clause for head-final CPs. This means model performance with the traditional 'IBO' annotation style could show a lower performance than one with an annotation style of 'IEO' ('E': end of the CP clause) for being the exact same model. Therefore, the directions for improving our chunking model performance should not only be seeking higher label accuracy, but also maintaining good linguistic understanding of the language.

Possible future directions can further improve this work. Studies show that annotator expertise has a strong influence on the annotation accuracy and speed (Baldridge and Palmer, 2009). Our language consultants' expertise has grown significantly throughout the experiment. Setting up agreement tests for annotators to review others' annotation work may be helpful to improve future accuracy, although the annotation time might be prolonged and more annotators would be needed. The deep learning NERDA model shows that transfer learning with fine-tuning pre-trained large language model is a promising methodology for low-resource linguistic fieldwork research. However, certain longer sentences were discarded by the training algorithm. Moreover, training models remain independent which makes them easy to share with other fieldworkers, and possibly to combine models to start building more complex structured treebank corpora for low-resource languages.

In additional to transfer learning, active learning featured with actively querying annotators for labels, can provide sufficient information to the annotators without being overwhelmed by a mass of data. More high quality training data can be provided under the productive pipe-line.

Acknowledgements

We thank our Nepal Bhasa native speaker consultants for their time and efforts with providing us the annotation help.

References

Steven P Abney. 1991. Parsing by chunks. In *Principle-based parsing*, pages 257–278. Springer.

Jason Baldridge and Alexis Palmer. 2009. How well does active learning actually work? time-based evaluation of cost-reduction strategies for language documentation. In *Proceedings of the 2009 Conference on Empirical Methods in Natural Language Processing*, pages 296–305.

Steven Bird. 2009. Natural language processing and linguistic fieldwork. *Computational linguistics*, 35(3):469–474.

Joan W Bresnan. 1972. *Theory of complementation in English syntax*. Ph.D. thesis, Massachusetts Institute of Technology.

Marie-Catherine de Marneffe and Christopher Potts. 2017. Developing linguistic theories using annotated corpora. In *Handbook of Linguistic Annotation*, pages 411–438. Springer.

Jacob Devlin, Ming-Wei Chang, Kenton Lee, and Kristina Toutanova. 2018. BERT: pre-training of deep bidirectional transformers for language understanding. *CoRR*, abs/1810.04805.

Carol Genetti. 2009. *A grammar of Dolakha Newar*, volume 40. Walter de Gruyter.

Eduard Hovy and Julia Lavid. 2010. Towards a 'science' of corpus annotation: a new methodological challenge for corpus linguistics. *International journal of translation*, 22(1):13–36.

Nitish Shirish Keskar, Dheevatsa Mudigere, Jorge Nocedal, Mikhail Smelyanskiy, and Ping Tak Peter Tang. 2016. On large-batch training for deep learning: Generalization gap and sharp minima. *arXiv preprint arXiv:1609.04836*.

Lars Kjeldgaard and Lukas Nielsen. 2021. Nerda. GitHub.

Mitchell P. Marcus, Beatrice Santorini, and Mary Ann Marcinkiewicz. 1993. Building a large annotated corpus of English: The Penn Treebank. *Computational Linguistics*, 19(2):313–330.

Ryan McDonald, Joakim Nivre, Yvonne Quirmbach-Brundage, Yoav Goldberg, Dipanjan Das, Kuzman Ganchev, Keith Hall, Slav Petrov, Hao Zhang, Oscar Täckström, et al. 2013. Universal dependency annotation for multilingual parsing. In *Proceedings of the 51st Annual Meeting of the Association for Computational Linguistics (Volume 2: Short Papers)*, pages 92–97.

Keir Moulton. 2009. *Natural selection and the syntax of clausal complementation*. University of Massachusetts Amherst.

Bal Gopal Shrestha. 1999. The newars: The indigenous population of the kathmandu valley in the modern state of nepal. *The Journal of Newar Studies*, 2:1.

Pedro Javier Ortiz Suárez, Benoît Sagot, and Laurent Romary. 2019. Asynchronous pipeline for processing huge corpora on medium to low resource infrastructures. In *7th Workshop on the Challenges in the Management of Large Corpora (CMLC-7)*. Leibniz-Institut für Deutsche Sprache.

Borui Zhang. 2021. *Clausal Complementation in Nepal Bhasa*. Ph.D. thesis, University of Minnesota.

A Nepal Bhasa complement CP annotation guideline

Please follow the three steps to annotate the sentences in this corpus:
(i) If you find a sentence that has an embedded clause, mark the clause by adding a squared bracket '[ ]' around it.
(ii) Select and add the matrix verb of the sentence to a new line.
(iii) Select and add the embedded verb next to the matrix verb.

If the sentence does not have an embedded clause, add '**' in front of the sentence. If you cannot identify which verb to select, please fill it with a 'UNK' label in the of (ii) and (iii).

Embedded clause annotation example:

(3) स्कुलय् ब्वनेगु इलय् धाःगु खः [कि
Skul bwonegu yilaye dhagukha ki
In-school studying time it's-said [that
छुं नं वस्तुया रंग दइमखु]
chunah bastuya ranga daimakhu
any item color does.not.have
'It's said during school time that all items do not have colors.'
Matrix verb: धाःगु ख (dhagukha)
Embedded verb: दइमखु (daimakhu)

B Nepal Bhasa matrix verb list in the annotation set

Table 5 shows the embedding verbs seen in the corpus.

Matrix verb	Meaning	Count
म्हसीकिगु (mhasiku)	introduce	6
वयाच्वंगु दु (bayachogu)	become	5
न्यनेगु (nyanegu)	ask	4
धाइ (dhai)	say	4
उल्लेख यानातःगु दु (ulekh yanatagudu)	describe	3
थुइकेगु (thuikegu)	understand	3
सुचुकेत (suchuketa)	hide	3
तःगु (tagu)	put	3
खनेदु (khanaedu)	see	2
बियातःगु दु (biyatagudu)	give	2
क्यनेगु (kyanegu)	see	2
धयातःगु दु (dhayatagudu)	say	2
ब्वइ (woi)	show	2
सल्लाह बी (sallaha bi)	advice	2
नियन्त्रणय् कयाः (Niyantran kaya)	take charge	2
जुयाच्वंगु (juyachogu)	happen	2
तायेकाच्वंगु (tayekachogu)	keep	2
धयातःगु (dhayatagu)	say	2
तगु खः (tagu kha)	put	2
यानातःगु (yanatagu)	do	2
कनेगु (kanegu)	make to say	1
बिउगु दु (biyougudu)	give	1
दयेकूगु (dayekugu)	give	1
ज्वनेत (jyoneta)	catch	1
धारणा प्वंकेगु (daharana pwakegu)	pour thoughts	1
यानादीगु दु (yanadigudu)	done	1
पिकयादीगु (pikayadingu)	publish	1

Table 5: Embedding verb distribution

Using LARA to create image-based and phonetically annotated multimodal texts for endangered languages*

Branislav Bédi
The Árni Magnússon Institute
for Icelandic Studies, Iceland
branislav.bedi@arnastofnun.is

Hakeem Beedar
The University of Adelaide, Australia
hbeedar@hotmail.com.au

Belinda Chiera
The University of South Australia
Adelaide, Australia
Belinda.Chiera@unisa.edu.au

Nedelina Ivanova
The Communication Centre
for the Deaf and Hard of Hearing, Iceland
nedelina@shh.is

Christèle Maizonniaux
Flinders University
Adelaide, Australia
christele.maizonniaux@flinders.edu.au

Neasa Ní Chiaráin
Trinity College, Dublin, Ireland
Neasa.NiChiarain@tcd.ie

Manny Rayner
FTI/TIM
University of Geneva, Switzerland
Emmanuel.Rayner@unige.ch

John Sloan
FTI/TIM
University of Geneva, Switzerland
sloanjo@tcd.ie

Ghil'ad Zuckermann
The University of Adelaide, Australia
Ghilad.Zuckermann@adelaide.edu

Abstract

We describe recent extensions to the open source Learning And Reading Assistant (LARA) supporting image-based and phonetically annotated texts. We motivate the utility of these extensions both in general and specifically in relation to endangered and archaic languages, and illustrate with examples from the revived Australian language Barngarla, Icelandic Sign Language, Irish Gaelic, Old Norse manuscripts and Egyptian hieroglyphics.

1 Introduction

When people are reading documents written in a language less than completely familiar to them, it can often be useful to present the text in multimedia form. This can give the reader access to annotations — typically audio recordings and translations — with a single click, conferring immediate and obvious advantages compared with reading a printed text and looking words up. Many such frameworks now exist; prominent examples include LingQ[1], Learning With Texts[2], the Perseus Digital Library's Scaife viewer[3] and Clilstore[4]. In our paper from the 2021 edition of this conference, (Zuckerman et al., 2021), we described the Learning and Reading Assistant (LARA; https://www.unige.ch/callector/lara/), another platform of this general nature. What primarily distinguishes LARA from the other frameworks is its strongly open source nature, where new features are added in a bottom-up process driven by the demands of a diverse community involved in many different kinds of language-related projects. We argued that this makes it a good fit to endangered languages, which often pose special requirements, and illustrated with three case studies, for Irish Gaelic, Icelandic Sign Language and the revived Australian Aboriginal language Barngarla (Zuckerman et al., 2021).

The version of LARA from last year's paper represented the document as a text string and al-

* Authors in alphabetical order.

[1] https://www.lingq.com/
[2] https://sourceforge.net/projects/lwt/
[3] https://scaife.perseus.org/
[4] http://multidict.net/clilstore/

Proceedings of the Fifth Workshop on the Use of Computational Methods in the Study of Endangered Languages, pages 68 - 77
May 26-27, 2022

lowed annotations to be attached to units at two levels, words and segments (typically a segment is a sentence). Experience since then has revealed two important ways in which the above needs to be further generalised. First, thinking of a written document abstractly as a text string obscures the important fact that it is also a visual object. For many texts (picture-books, posters, handwritten manuscripts), the visual dimension is as significant as the words. Second, it is often necessary to go below the word level and think about the relationship between sounds and letters or other primitive written signs. If the student is uncertain about the writing system, the sound system, or the relationship between them, annotations at the character level can be helpful. These observations are particularly relevant to endangered languages, and indeed it is largely because of our close interaction with the endangered language community that we have become so aware of them. We will have more to say about this later, when we discuss specific languages.

In the rest of this paper, we will describe recent work where we have extended LARA to allow image-based and phonetic annotations to be added to texts, and we again illustrate with concrete case studies. Section 2 presents the new functionality, after which Sections 3 to 5 present examples of how it has been used for Barngarla, Icelandic Sign Language and Irish Gaelic. Section 6 briefly describes how the same features are also useful for annotating historical texts available in manuscript or related form. The final section concludes and suggests further directions.

2 Supporting image-based and phonetic annotations

In this section, we briefly present the overall architecture of LARA and then describe the new functionality which forms the subject of this paper. Full details are available in the online documentation (Rayner et al., 2020).

2.1 Overview of LARA

For a conventional text-based document, the process of converting it into LARA form goes through three stages. The first step is to add annotations dividing the text into pages and segments, tagging inflected words by lemma, and possibly adding HTML markup including links to images defined by instances of the HTML `<img>` tag. For well-resourced languages, the labour-intensive tasks of segmentation and lemma tagging can be performed automatically by tools already integrated into LARA, followed by some post-editing (Akhlaghi et al., 2020). For smaller languages, where the necessary resources often do not exist, all this work may need to be done manually.

In the second step, the annotated LARA text is passed through a script which internalises it and organises data to support creation of annotations, most obviously translations and audio. Thus for example a script is created which can either be uploaded to an integrated voice recording tool or used to invoke a suitable TTS engine, if available. The annotator fills in this data. In the third step, another script combines the internalised text and the annotations created in the second step and adds metadata to create the final multimodal document. In particular, this metadata includes automatically generated concordances and indexes.

The above steps can either be performed using command-line tools, or carried out through the LARA Portal (`https://lara-portal.unige.ch/`), a free online service which provides a wizard-style interface. Links to LARA documents in many languages can be found on the LARA examples page, `https://www.unige.ch/callector/lara-content`.

2.2 Image-based text

We now describe how the above processing flow has been extended to support image-based text. We first define more exactly what we mean by this term. Intuitively, a piece of LARA image-based text is a portion of a LARA document where the text content and annotations are as they would be in a normal LARA document, but all the visual formatting is determined by an image in JPEG or PNG form. For this to be possible, there needs to be exactly one image for each piece of image-based text, and extra information needs to be supplied to define the image locations with which words in the text are associated. In the compiled LARA document, annotations are accessed by clicking or hovering over the defined locations.

The nature of the visual content at the location associated with a given word is arbitrary. The simplest possibility is that it is a written representation of the word; thus the image could be a page containing a manuscript version of the text, with each text word mapping to the correspond-

(a)

```
<annotated_image>
<img src="restaurant_date.jpg" width="800" height="800"/>
chair man glass ||
table ||
glass woman chair ||
</annotated_image>
```

(b)

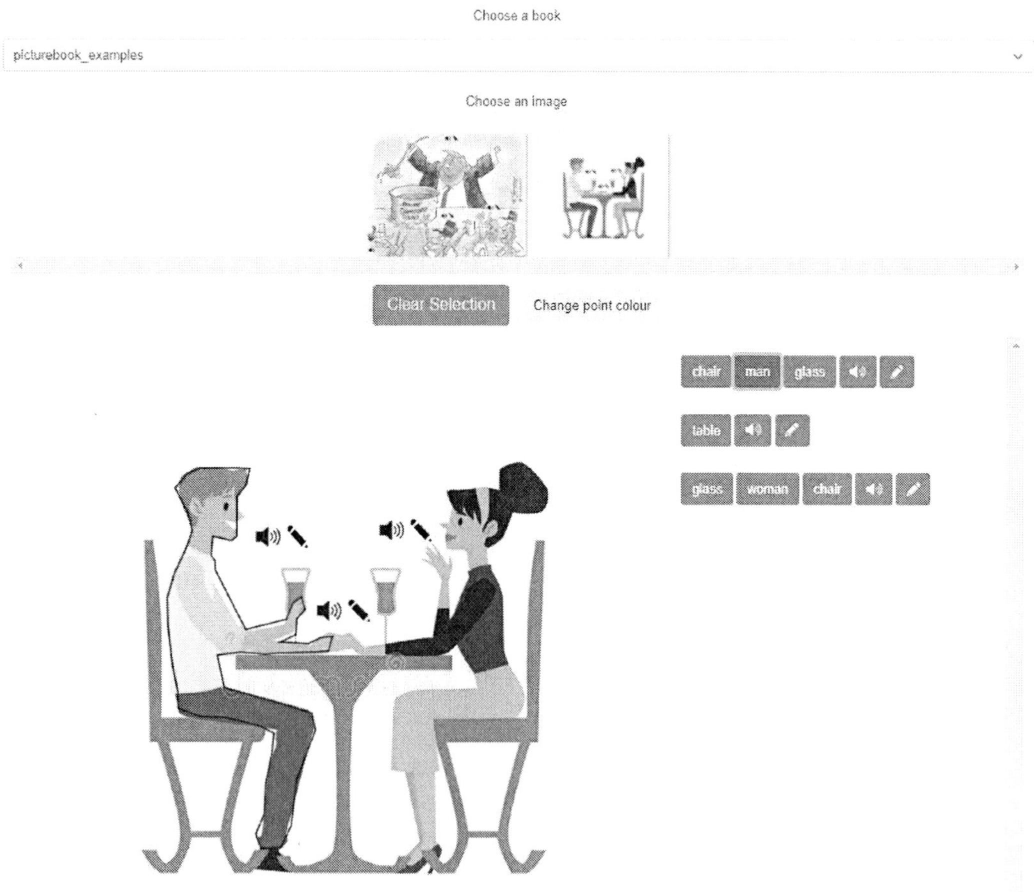

Figure 1: Toy example of a piece of image-based text based on a simple cartoon. The LARA source (a) is given above. The screenshot below (b) shows the tool used to create the word locations file. The top control allows the annotator to choose the text to annotate, after which the slider with the series of thumbnails allows them to choose a page by its image. The bottom left pane presents the selected image, and the bottom right pane the associated words. The annotator can draw a polygon on the left and save it to a word, or select a word on the right to show the current polygon. Here, the annotator has just selected the word "man" on the right, showing the polygon for the picture of the man on the left. The speaker and pencil icons optionally associate audio or text with a whole line. The LARA document is online here.

ing manuscript word. But the visual content can equally well be an image representing the word. Thus for example, in an alphabet book, the text word "apple" could either map to the visual word "apple", or it could map to a part of the image that contains a picture of an apple.

In the concrete LARA implementation, a piece of image-based text is delimited by the tag <annotated_image>. Links between words and locations are defined by a "word locations file", a JSON file with a hierarchical structure whose levels are pages, segments and words. A word is optionally associated with a list of three or more coordinate pairs that specify a polygon. Following the usual LARA processing flow outlined in §2.1, the first processing step creates an uninstantiated or partially instantiated version of the word locations file. This can be efficiently filled in using an online graphical tool. which presents the information and allows the user to draw polygons and associate them with words by pointing and clicking. In the compiled LARA document, hovering over a polygon area outlines it as well as performing the usual LARA functions based on the annotations attached to the area, such as playing audio or displaying translations. Figure 1 presents a toy example with a piece of image-based text and a screenshot showing use of the graphical tool.

2.3 Phonetic annotations

We now move on to describe how we have also extended LARA to support texts annotated at the phonetic level. As outlined in §2.1, a normal LARA text is hierarchically divided into pages, segments and words, where the words are associated with lemmas. In contrast, a *phonetic* LARA text is hierarchically divided into pages, words and letter-groups, where each letter-group is associated with a phonetic value. The same notation is used for both types of text, and nearly all of the processing associated with normal (word-oriented) LARA texts carries over to phonetic texts. In particular, a compiled phonetic text contains a phonetic concordance, giving examples of contexts where each phonetic value occurs.

It would be extremely laborious to construct phonetic LARA texts by hand, and there is a script that converts a normal text into the corresponding phonetic version. This post-processes the internalised text to convert each word into a corresponding phonetic version, while keeping formatting unchanged. For languages which are written completely phonetically (common for endangered languages which only recently have acquired a written form), this only requires the annotator to supply the list of phonetically meaningful letter groups defining the orthography of the language. We present an example for the revived Australian language Barngarla in §3 below.

For languages where online phonetic lexica exist, phonetic versions of most words can be read off the lexicon; free phonetic lexica for many languages are for example available from the IPA-dict project (`https://github.com/open-dict-data/ipa-dict`). The challenge is to align the letters with the phonetic symbols. At the moment, the strategy used is for the conversion script to help the annotator compile an aligned phonetic lexicon, where typical entries are as illustrated in Figure 2. The script creates new entries automatically using a simple dynamic programming method which maximises the number of alignments already seen in the lexicon (this idea is partly inspired by the one from (Jiampojamarn and Kondrak, 2010)), after which a human annotator cleans up the result. Once a few hundred examples of aligned words have been collected, error rates become low and the cleaning-up process is quick. This work will be described in more detail elsewhere.

```
"admirateur"
"a|d|m|i|r|a|t|eu|r"
"a|d|m|i|ʁ|a|t|œ|ʁ"

"ainsi"
"ain|s|i"
"ɛ̃|s|i|"

"alors"
"a|l|o|r|s"
"a|l|ɔ|ʁ|"
```

Figure 2: Examples of entries from French aligned pronunciation lexicon. Several letters can map into one (beginning of `"ainsi"`), and letters can map into the empty string (end of `"alors"`).

2.4 Combining LARA documents

LARA includes functionality that allows multiple LARA documents to be linked together. One possibility is sequential linking: the texts are concatenated in a way that combines their metadata, in particular creating a concordance which includes entries from all the component documents. The practical import is that someone reading a later document will easily be able to see when words also occurred in earlier documents, strengthening memory links across their reading history.

Here, we will be more concerned with a new capability, *parallel* linking. For this to make sense, the linked documents must all be different variants of the same text, organised so that page divisions are consistent. In the compiled versions, links are inserted so that each page in one compiled document is connected to the corresponding pages in the other documents.

2.5 An illustrative example

In order to show how the different functionalities introduced in this section can be usefully combined, we present an example in a familiar language, a multimodal French alphabet book based on *Le petit prince* where each page occurs in three different parallel-linked versions. Figure 3 illustrates. Note that in the second, "phonetic", version, the "picture-book" and "phonetic" functionalities have been combined.

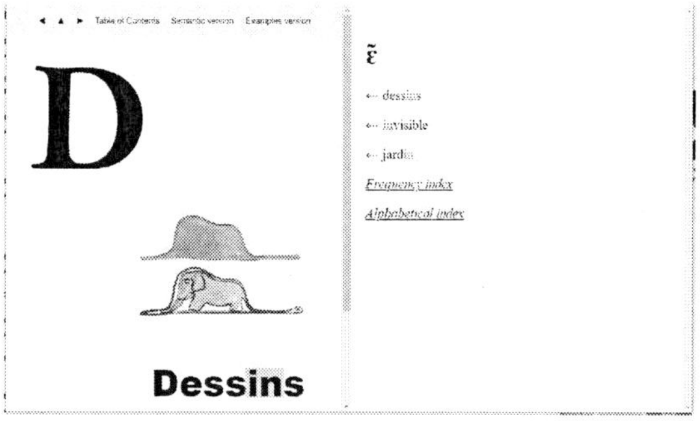

Figure 3: "Phonetic" version of an example page from a "Little Prince" themed LARA alphabet book for French; each page is in three versions, "phonetic", "semantic" and "example". Hovering over the word **Dessins** ("Drawings") outlines phonetically meaningful letter groups; clicking plays audio for the phonetic content selected and shows a phonetic concordance. The student has selected the letter group **in**, showing on the right other words containing the nasalised vowel /ɛ̃/ that this letter group usually represents in French. In the "semantic" version, hovering over the picture on the left outlines it and clicking on it plays audio for the word. The "example" version shows an annotated example sentence. The document can be found here.

3 Barngarla

Barngarla is an Australian Aboriginal language belonging to the Thura-Yura language group, a subgroup of the large Pama-Nyungan language family. Typically for a Pama-Nyungan language, Barngarla has a phonemic inventory featuring three vowels ([a], [i], [u]) and retroflex consonants, an ergative grammar with many cases, and a complex pronominal system.

During the twentieth century, Barngarla was intentionally eradicated under Australian 'stolen generation' policies, the last original native speaker dying in 1960. Language reclamation efforts were launched in 2011 (Zuckermann, 2020). Since then, a series of language reclamation workshops have been held in which about 120 Barngarla people have participated. The primary resource used has been a dictionary, including a brief grammar, written by the German Lutheran missionary Clamor Wilhelm Schürmann (Schürmann, 1844; Clendon, 2015). A number of educational texts have now been constructed using Schürmann material as the base; as described in last year's paper, several of them have been converted into LARA form. This has highlighted two issues, both of which materially contributed to motivating the new functionality we describe here.

First, the original texts are always created as a collaboration between ethnic Barngarla people and non-Barngarla expert linguists: usually, design aspects are the responsibility of the Barngarla members of the team. When converting the texts into LARA form, it is thus important to maintain a format that is as close as possible to the original text layout. Second, even though revised Barngarla is written phonetically, the orthography is not transparent to people whose linguistic heritage is primarily anglophone. A particularly important example is retroflex consonants, which are written using an 'r' before the corresponding non-retroflex version: thus the voiced retroflex plosive [ɖ] (similar to the final sound of Swedish *nord*, "north") is written 'rd' as for example in Barngarla *yarda*, "country". It is however all too easy for the anglophone reader to interpret this as representing a lengthened preceding vowel followed by [d], as for example in the usual Australian pronunciation of "card" or "herd". Another important problem is ambiguous phonetic segmentation. Barngarla orthography contains both the unigraph 'w', representing the velar approximant [w] and the digraph 'aw', representing the diphthong [aʊ]. When Bargarla digraph 'aw' is followed by letters representing a vowel, as for example in the common words *bawoo* ("hello"), *gawoo* ("water"), the anglophone reader most naturally segments the words as `b | a | w | oo`, `g | a | w | oo`; in fact, they should be `b | aw | oo`, `g | aw | oo`.

These issues came to a head during the creation of the latest Barngarla text, *Mangiri Yarda* (Zuckermann and Richards, 2021). The main Barngarla contributor, Emma Richards, invested a substantial amount of effort in the design of the book, and it was clear that the approach used for previous Barngarla LARA texts, trying to reproduce the layout using HTML formatting, would not yield a good result. The issues with pronunciation also became apparent when recording the audio.

The new functionality developed here however made it possible to address both the layout and phonetic issues in a logical way. The draft book is available online here. It is organised as a LARA picture-book exactly reproducing the text layout, in which all the Barngarla words are annotated with audio information, coupled with a parallel track organised as a "phonetic" LARA book, where the reader can spell through each word a letter-group at a time and listen to the associated phonetic value. By the time of the conference, we expect that the book will have been tested with enough Barngarla readers to be able to present initial feedback.

4 Icelandic Sign Language

Icelandic Sign Language (*íslenskt táknmál*; ÍTM) is a natural language and the first language of about 250–300 people in Iceland, almost exclusively Deaf people and their children. A peculiarity of ÍTM, compared to other sign languages, is that hereditary deafness hardly exists in Iceland. This means that Deaf children are much less likely to have Deaf parents than in other countries, rendering more difficult the intergenerational transmission of the language and contributing to its endangered status.

Zuckerman et al., 2021 gave further background and outlined some initial experiments in which LARA was used to create annotated texts for Deaf readers, with audio replaced by signed video. Here, we describe two sample image-based texts of this kind. Both are direct multimodal transpositions of existing paper texts designed for the ÍTM community, whose general purpose is to introduce ÍTM signs, and in particular the handshape inventory, to beginner signers. The signed video content has been taken from YouTube videos linked from Icelandic SignWiki (`https://is.signwiki.org/`).

4.1 Background: handshape inventory

There is a long tradition of using the fingerspelling alphabet in signed conversations. The fingerspelling alphabet is a visual representation of the spoken language's alphabet, and it is used to spell out proper names and other words when a sign is lacking or not known. A sign language's fingerspelling alphabet in no way corresponds to the phonemic inventory of a spoken language. This role is filled by the handshape inventory.

Research on ÍTM's phonemic handshapes has been carried out by Deaf signers and researchers at the Communication Centre for the Deaf and Hard of Hearing. Because there is no corpus for ÍTM, analysis of the frozen lexicon of ÍTM has been slow. In 2019, 33 handshapes were identified as phonemic. Work is still continuing and there may be a slight change in the number of the handshapes. The handshape inventory for ÍTM was developed on the basis of HamNoSys (Schmaling and Hanke, 2001; Smith, 2013). It has two forms, one designed for sign language linguists and one for learners. Further details are available in (Ivanova et al., in press).

4.2 Handshape poster

A poster with the 33 ÍTM handshapes was published in December 2019 in connection with celebrations of the Center's 30 year jubilee. The poster was intended to spread awareness among children, both Deaf and hearing, about the phonemes of ÍTM, and serve as a basic teaching resource. The design was chosen to be colourful and eye-catching, and includes 33 handshapes. For each handshape, there is a drawing representing a sign that exemplifies the handshape in question, together with a disambiguating gloss in Icelandic.

As an initial exercise, we created a LARA version of the poster, linking the 33 shape/picture combinations to Icelandic SignWiki videos so that clicking on a picture plays the video. The result is posted here. Despite the document's very simple construction, we were surprised by the enthusiastic reception it received from the Deaf members of the Center. One memorable comment was "It makes the poster as alive as sign language".

4.3 Pocket dictionary

In 2020 and 2021, the Icelandic Student Innovation Fund, in cooperation with the Center, financed the work of two students for three months each year to develop bilingual ÍTM-Icelandic pocket dictionaries for families of signing children. The model used was the *I am Deaf: Let's talk* series of booklets produced by Deaf Aotearoa[5], in which every sign has an equivalent in written English, a morphological description, a drawing of the sign, and a photo representing the sign's meaning. Six

[5]`https://www.deaf.org.nz/resources/lets-talk-booklets/`

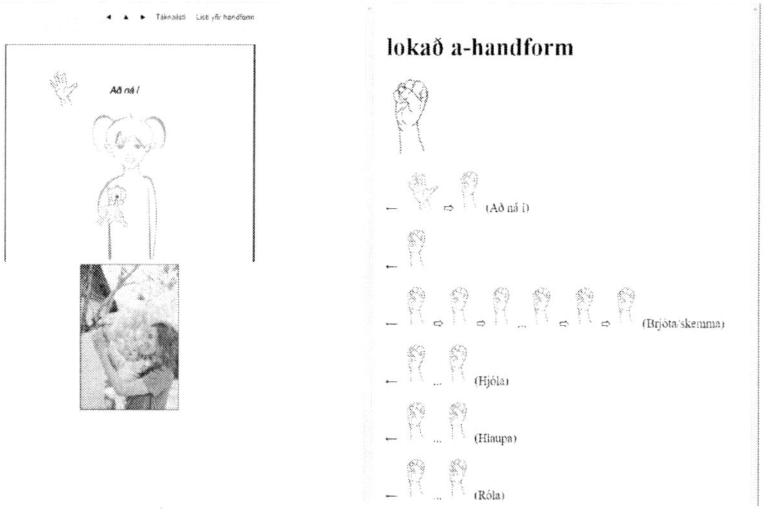

Figure 4: Screenshot of a page from the ÍTM "pocket dictionary"; the user has just clicked on the yellow "closed a-handform" on the upper left, showing examples on the right. The document can be found here.

ÍTM-language booklets were developed, each containing 25 signs grouped by a common theme: "Baby's first signs", "The family's first signs", "Food", "Actions", "Adjectives" and "More signs for the family". The New Zealand model was developed further by adding an image of each sign's handshape and a QR code for SignWiki video. In order to stress that ÍTM is the source language and Icelandic the target language, the signs are not ordered alphabetically but rather by handshape, using the canonical ordering of the handshape inventory and subordered by the movement in the sign.

We converted one of the booklets, "Actions", to LARA form, using a method which tried to respect the core ideas in the project and extend them. Following the principle that sign language is primary, we eliminated all Icelandic text except short phrases naming the actions. Each page (cf. Figure 4) is divided into two halves. The lower half contains the picture illustrating the action; clicking on this picture plays the SignWiki video. The upper half contains the diagram illustrating production of the sign. Here, the reader can click on any hand. This shows the relevant handshape on the right-hand side of the screen, together with a list of other examples where the same handshape is used; the handshapes are shown graphically.

5 Irish

Irish, from the Celtic branch of the Indo-European family, is the first official and national language of the Republic of Ireland and is now a full working language of the EU. English is the second official language in Ireland. Despite the official status of Irish, however, an erosion of first-language speaker communities is clear and according to the UNESCO Atlas of the World's Languages in Danger, the language is considered "definitely endangered" (Moseley, 2012).

Irish is spoken as a community language in pockets in the rural West of Ireland called 'Gaeltacht' areas. Speakers in urban areas tend to be mostly in individual homes and Irish is relatively rarely overheard on the street. Irish is a compulsory subject until school leaving age. There are approximately 700,000 learners of Irish in the education system in the Republic of Ireland (Ní Chiaráin, 2014). There are also large numbers in the education system in Northern Ireland and many learning Irish abroad, although these numbers are more difficult to quantify.

Irish shares distinctive features with other Celtic languages such as a verb-subject-object (VSO) word-order and rich morphology (Stenson, 1981). As in other Celtic languages, initial consonants undergo mutations in specific grammatical contexts, e.g., the lenition of stops to fricatives/approximants; of voiceless stops to voiced stops; of voiced stops to voiced nasals. Verbs are inflected for tense, number and person, while nouns are inflected for number and case. Prepositions can inflect for person and number. Nouns are either masculine or feminine in grammatical gender.

	Labial	Dental	Alveolar	Alveolo-palatal	Palatal	Velar	Glottal
Plosive	pˠ bˠ pʲ bʲ	t̪ˠ d̪ˠ		t̠ʲ d̠ʲ	c ɟ	k ɡ	
Fricative/ Approx.	fˠ w fʲ vʲ		sˠ	ɕ	ç j	x ɣ	h
Nasal	mˠ mʲ	n̪ˠ	n	n̠ʲ	ɲ	ŋ	
Tap			ɾˠ ɾʲ				
Lateral Approx.		l̪ˠ	l	l̠ʲ			

Figure 5: Consonantal system of Irish (Ní Chasaide, 1999), where there is a fundamental contrast between velarised [Cˠ] and palatalised [Cʲ] phonemes

Irish has three main dialects and a number of sub dialects. These dialects differ at many levels, including their structural features, vocabulary and particularly in their pronunciation. A written standard "An Caighdeán Oifigiúil" was first introduced in 1958 and the most recent update to this was published online in 2017. However, as with many minority languages, there is no single spoken standard and all dialect variants hold equally. The fact that the writing system does not match in a simple way to any one of the spoken dialects presents challenges to learners.

A major feature of the Irish sound system is the contrast between palatalised and velarised pairs of consonants as illustrated in Figure 5. The contrast of palatalised and velarised segments not only differentiates words, e.g., /ʟʲoːɴˠ/ leon 'lion' vs. /ʟˠoːɴˠ/ lón 'lunch', but serves for grammatical differentiation of the same lexical item, as in /ʟˠoːɴˠ/ (nominative) vs. /ʟˠoːɴʲ/ (genitive).

Latin script is used for the language's writing system, with an alphabet which is superficially similar to English, excluding j, k, q, v, w, x, y, z, (except in loan words). However, the consonants are not marked for the fundamental contrast of palatalisation and velarisation of Irish; rather, the palatalisation-velarisation difference is shown by the adjacent vowel letter used ('i', 'e', mark palatalisation and 'a', 'o', 'u' mark velarisation). All this makes it very complex for learners to acquire the link between the orthography and the sounds of the language. There is also a contrast between long and short vowels, which differentiates words, e.g. /mʲinʲ/ min '(oat)meal' and /mʲiːnʲ/ mín 'smooth'. Long vowels are orthographically marked with an acute accent, as in: á é í ó ú.

5.1 An Scéalaí

An Scéalaí[6] is a purpose-built iCALL platform for Irish. It builds on the ABAIR initiative, which is concerned with the development of core speech technologies for Irish[7] (particularly TTS to date but ASR development ongoing more recently). *An Scéalaí* deploys core language technologies and presents them to learners in a pedagogically appropriate way. It is currently being used primarily as a writing tool but aims at a holistic approach to language learning, simultaneously training the four skills (for a more detailed description see (Ní Chiaráin et al., 2022)). The intention is to provide a motivational environment for learners to practise writing, and, through having TTS available at the click of a button, brings the spoken language into every aspect of the language learning, helping to compensate for the fact that native speakers are not readily to hand for most learners (one of the most common complaints from learners is the fact that they have limited opportunities to interact through the medium of Irish). As learners practise writing they are encouraged to think of spelling as a phonic-based system (see (Ní Chiaráin and Ní Chasaide, 2019) for more detail). There is an emphasis on self-correction (proofreading and prooflistening) using the available language technology tools and

[6] https://abair.ie/scealai/

[7] https://www.abair.ie

resources for Irish, such as dictionaries[8], TTS, a grammar checker[9], and a grammar database[10], which gives inflected forms of nouns, verbs, adjectives, etc.

5.2 A LARA alphabet book for Irish

We have used the infrastructure described above to create a LARA primer for the sounds of Irish. The format is superficially that of an alphabet book: alphabet books will be regarded by most students as simple and unthreatening, while the introduction of the complex phonetic symbols, as in Figure 5, could be forbidding.

The book's structure presents minimal pairs illustrating key phonemic differences, where words are presented in the context of short sentences combined with pictures and both TTS and human audio. The core goals are to develop phonological awareness of the velarisation-palatalisation contrast in Irish in the hope that learners make the link between the phonological contrasts and the spelling regularities of the language.

Resources of this kind are badly needed, since, remarkably, there is virtually no awareness of consonantal palatalisation/velarisation difference among learners or indeed among many teachers of Irish. It is hardly ever made explicit in teaching, and the difficulty for learners is further compounded by the fact that the L2 learners are English speaking and familiar with the English alphabet and phonics. This undermines the teaching of pronunciation, and fails to highlight the phonic basis of the orthographic system. Pronunciation training is typically not even considered in Irish language instruction.

The LARA Irish alphabet picturebook[11] uses visual and auditory cues to illustrate minimal pairs and help consolidate auditory memory of contrasting forms. It is designed to raise awareness of this fundamental phonological contrast of Irish. This gives a glimpse of a parallel current project *Lón don Leon*, a tablet-based app which is specifically designed to develop phonological awareness and early literacy skills in young learners. This is a multimodal app with a high level of interactivity. To consolidate memorisation and acquisition of the contrasts and of their orthographic realisations, it includes newly composed musical ditties, stories, graphics, quizzes set on a virtual island (see description in (Ní Chasaide et al., 2019)).

We expect the resource to be useful for trainee teachers, at the very least for awareness raising, and for learners at all levels; a recent study carried out by an Irish author of this paper with advanced learners of Irish showed they do not produce the velarisation-palatalisation contrast reliably.

6 Manuscripts and other archaic texts

Although this is not the focus of the current paper, we note in passing that the functionality described here also appears to be relevant to archaic texts in manuscript or inscription form, where the visual appearance of the document is of critical importance. We illustrate with two initial examples. The first is a LARA version of an extract from the Old Norse poem *Völuspá* (Bédi et al., 2020), with each verse presented both in facsimile manuscript and plain text form. The second is an inscription in Ancient Egyptian hieroglyphics taken from (Collier and Manley, 1998), presented in parallel 'word' and 'sign' views. The two examples are posted here and here.

7 Summary and further directions

We have described extensions recently added to the LARA platform to support image-based and phonetically annotated texts, and illustrated with examples from Barngarla, Icelandic Sign Language, Irish, French, Old Norse and Egyptian hieroglyphics. The work was motivated by the demands of these languages, particularly the first three. We are currently liaising with members of other endangered language communities, a leading example being the Austronesian language Iaai.

The implementation of the new functionalities is still at an early stage, and our current priority is to improve their integration into LARA and make them easier to use. In particular, we have started development of an intuitive tool which will enable simple creation of "LARA albums", LARA picture-book/phonetic documents consisting of images paired with short captions. The intention is to lower the bar to entry for people wishing to create LARA texts, so that it can become a routine part of language teaching; this is particularly interesting in the context of the An Scéalaí Irish platform (cf. §5). We hope to be able to report on this work later in 2022.

[8] https://www.teanglann.ie

[9] https://cadhan.com/gramadoir/

[10] https://www.teanglann.ie/en/gram/

[11] https://tinyurl.com/2p8k7zfz

References

Elham Akhlaghi, Branislav Bédi, Fatih Bektaş, Harald Berthelsen, Matthias Butterweck, Cathy Chua, Catia Cucchiarini, Gülşen Eryiğit, Johanna Gerlach, Hanieh Habibi, Neasa Ní Chiaráin, Manny Rayner, Steinþór Steingrímsson, and Helmer Strik. 2020. Constructing multimodal language learner texts using LARA: Experiences with nine languages. In *Proceedings of The 12th Language Resources and Evaluation Conference*, pages 323–331.

Branislav Bédi, Haraldur Bernharðsson, Cathy Chua, Birgitta Björg Guðmarsdóttir, Hanieh Habibi, and Manny Rayner. 2020. Constructing an interactive Old Norse text with LARA. *CALL for widening participation: short papers from EUROCALL*, pages 27–35.

Mark Clendon. 2015. *Clamor Schürmann's Barngarla grammar: A commentary on the first section of A vocabulary of the Parnkalla language*. University of Adelaide Press.

Mark Collier and Bill Manley. 1998. *How to read Egyptian hieroglyphs: a step-by-step guide to teach yourself*. Univ of California Press.

N. Ivanova, R. Sverrisdottir, and G.T. Thorvaldsdóttir. in press. The handshape inventory for Icelandic Sign Language (ÍTM) in early intervention and teaching of ÍTM. *Croatian Review of Rehabilitation Research*, Special issue on Sign Language, Deaf Culture, and Bilingual Education.

Sittichai Jiampojamarn and Grzegorz Kondrak. 2010. Letter-phoneme alignment: An exploration. In *Proceedings of the 48th Annual Meeting of the Association for Computational Linguistics, Uppsala, Sweden*, pages 780–788.

Christopher Moseley. 2012. *The UNESCO atlas of the world's languages in danger: Context and process*. World Oral Literature Project.

Ailbhe Ní Chasaide. 1999. Irish. In *Handbook of the International Phonetic Association*, pages 111–116. Cambridge University Press Cambridge.

Neasa Ní Chiaráin and Ailbhe Ní Chasaide. 2019. An iCALL approach to morphophonemic training for Irish using speech technology. *CALL and complexity*, page 314.

Ailbhe Ní Chasaide, Neasa Ní Chiaráin, Harald Berthelsen, Christoph Wendler, Andrew Murphy, Emily Barnes, and Christer Gobl. 2019. Leveraging phonetic and speech research for Irish language revitalisation and maintenance. In *Proceedings of ICPhS 2019: the 19th International Congress of Phonetic Sciences*, pages 994 – 998, Melbourne, Australia.

Neasa Ní Chiaráin, Oisín Nolan, Madeleine Comtois, Neimhin Robinson Gunning, Harald Berthelsen, and Ailbhe Ní Chasaide. 2022. Using Speech and NLP resources to build an iCALL platform for a minority language: the story of *An Scéalaí*, the Irish experience to date. In *Proceedings of the Fifth Workshop on the Use of Computational Methods in the Study of Endangered Languages*.

Manny Rayner, Hanieh Habibi, Cathy Chua, and Matt Butterweck. 2020. *Constructing LARA content*. `https://www.issco.unige.ch/en/research/projects/callector/LARADoc/build/html/index.html`. Online documentation.

C. Schmaling and T. Hanke. 2001. HamNoSys 4.0. Interface definitions. ViSiCAST Deliverable D5-1. Technical report, University of Hamburg.

Clamor Wilhelm Schürmann. 1844. *A Vocabulary of the Parnkalla Language. Spoken by the natives inhabiting the western shore of Spencer's Gulf. To which is prefixed a collection of grammatical rules, hitherto ascertained*.

Robert Smith. 2013. Hamnosys 4.0 user guide. Technical report, Technical Report. Institute of Technology Blanchardstown Ireland.

Ghil'ad Zuckerman, Sigurður Vigfússon, Manny Rayner, Neasa Ní Chiaráin, Nedelina Ivanova, Hanieh Habibi, and Branislav Bédi. 2021. LARA in the service of revivalistics and documentary linguistics: Community engagement and endangered languages. In *Proceedings of the Workshop on Computational Methods for Endangered Languages*, volume 1, pages 13–23.

Ghil'ad Zuckermann. 2020. *Revivalistics: From the Genesis of Israeli to Language Reclamation in Australia and Beyond*. New York: Oxford University Press.

Ghil'ad Zuckermann and Emma Richards. 2021. *Mangiri Yarda (Healthy Country: Barngarla Wellbeing and Nature)*. Revivalistics Press.

Recovering Text from Endangered Languages Corrupted PDF documents

Nicolas Stefanovitch
Joint Research Centre
European Commission
Ispra, Italy
nicolas.stefanovitch@ec.europa.eu

Abstract

In this paper we present an approach to efficiently recover texts from corrupted documents of endangered languages. Textual resources for such languages are scarce, and sometimes the few available resources are corrupted PDF documents. Endangered languages are not supported by standard tools and present even the additional difficulties of not possessing any corpus availabel over which to train language models to assist with the recovery. The approach presented is able to fully recover born digital PDF documents with minimal effort, thereby helping the preservation effort of endangered languages, by extending the range of documents usable for corpus building.

1 Introduction

Endangered languages usually have extremely scarce linguistic resources available, and even less in a directly usable Unicode-encoded text format. Often the only available resources are PDF documents produced by language preservation efforts or for proselyte purposes by different organisations. Despite the efforts of such organisations to provide text content in endangered languages, it is often the case that the documents they produced are only printable or displayable on screen but totally unusable for automatic text processing purposes. Sometimes the only documents available in these language are contained in such documents, thereby preventing a wider exposure (impossibility to find them with search engines) and study of that language (impossibility to build corpora). The problem this paper tackles is how to recover usable texts from such documents.

There are two main drives behind PDF documents not being exploitable by Natural Language Processing (NLP) systems: 1) the document has a corrupted font to Unicode value translation table - in which case the text can not be extracted as the content of the pasted text is either unavailable or gibberish; 2) the PDF actually contains scanned images - and therefore it is impossible to copy/paste from that document. In this paper we tackle only the first, simpler, problem of born digital PDF document recovery, leaving the second more complex problem for future works.

The alternative of using our approach for such corrupted document is a much more time consuming manual correction of incorrectly OCRed text, or an even more time consuming plain manual transliteration into Unicode of the document content. As such it can be viewed as a lightning fast alternative to manual recovery. Such a work can help speedup corpus creation efforts for endangered languages such as in (Mus and Metzger, 2021).

Despite the general applicability of our approach, we will specifically restrict our attention to the Universal Declaration of Human Right corpus (UDRH), as it is - outside the Bible - the most translated documents whose documents are openly accessible on the internet (Cabatbat et al., 2014). It has to be noted that corrupted PDF documents for endangered languages is a common phenomena: there exists no support for these languages, and very often they posses unique symbols or even use their own writing system. In order to write in these languages the creators of the documents must design their own ad-hoc fonts, which are not publicly available. For all these reasons, the approach we propose in this article particularly relevant for recovering text in endangered languages.

2 Background

2.1 UDHR corpus

The United Nations maintains a website collecting all the different translations of the Universal Declaration of Human Right (UDHR)[1]. The UDHR corpus presents the specificity that most of its texts are present only as PDF documents, without any

[1] https://www.ohchr.org/EN/UDHR/

Proceedings of the Fifth Workshop on the Use of Computational Methods in the Study of Endangered Languages, pages 78 - 82
May 26-27, 2022

Unicode text. At the time of writing of this article, there are 526 translations in the corpus, some of which are the only text openly available in that language. Out of these, 108 (20%) have a content only in form of scanned images and 21 (4%) are corrupted born digital documents containing unrecoverable characters.

A complementary effort has been done by the Unicode Consortium which aims at collecting the Unicode version of the UDHR corpus[2]. As such, many of the documents of the UDHR corpus without extractable content do actually possess a text version in the Unicode consortium repository.

2.2 Document Recovery

Extracting text from documents containing only images can be done with standard Optical Character Recognition (OCR) tools only if the alphabet of the endangered languages is exactly the same as the alphabet of an existing well supported language. However, it is rarely the case, as most endangered languages possess very specific symbols absent from more widely used languages, moreover, such languages sometimes use their own writing system. Finally, as an OCR process is always noisy, a fully automatic text recovery requires to correct the errors by relying on language models (D'hondt et al., 2017). As such even Tesseract-OCR, one of the most popular OCR tool which covers about 100 languages out of the box, is not a workable solution for most endangered languages.

Because of the scarcity of texts in such languages, it is not even possible to correctly train OCR systems, as the only existing realisations of some languages' characters exist only in the Unicode charts [3], and therefore severely lack in diversity as only every Unicode letter has in these charts only one realisation with one font. As such, an OCR system trained solely on Unicode charts would lack the flexibility of dealing with different fonts and realisation of the characters. For these reasons OCR techniques present significant difficulties when dealing with endangered languages, and in this paper we will tackle only with the simpler problem of corrupted fonts in born digital PDF documents.

2.3 PDF documents

In order to understand the solution designed to tackle the problem, it is important to understand

[2]https://www.unicode.org/udhr/

[3]https://www.unicode.org/charts/

Figure 1: Subset of a corrupted font for Nenets, visualised using FontForge

how PDF files are structured. PDF documents do not contain string of Unicode characters that could be directly copied, there is not even an understanding of words as a semantic unit of text (Bandara, 2020). A PDF document actually contains I) a list of fonts, and for each there is a) a mapping between a CID (Characterd IDentifier) and the symbol as a 2D bitmap (glyph), and b) a mapping from CID to Unicode value; II) a list of physical lines, which are themselves made of an ordered list of tuples (page, font, character, bounding box) describing where to to draw each symbols in the 2D coordinates of each pages, as given by the bounding box of that symbol.

2.4 Problem Description

When a PDF document is corrupted, resulting in gibberish being produced when trying to convert the document to text or when trying to copy/paste from it, it is actually only the translation map from CID to Unicode that is corrupted. When using a specialised PDF to text translation tool, such as PDFMiner, characters absent from the map (the map can be only partially corrupted) are extracted as the string `cid:<n>` where `n` is the actual numerical value of the CID. As such all the realisation of a symbol will be linked to the exact same CID, and the task of recovering the document is equivalent to the simpler task of recovering the Unicode translation table.

In Figure 1 we report an example of a corrupted font encoding for Nenets taken from the UDHR corpus: The letters in gray are the Unicode letters associated to the symbol below them. While the dot, the dash and Latin capital letter I are correctly encoded, all the other letters are problematic: Most Cyrillic symbols are not associated with any Unicode character, while some of them are wrongly associated to the characters `1`, `2`, `(` and `)`. Note how both the glyph of the number 2 and of the Cyrillic letter *En with hook* are both translated to the same character.

In Figure 2 we present and instance of a text

Ӄатьгун сик правоғун Декларация
Ниғвӈ иғр̆ раюд

:àòüãóí ñèê ïðàâî4óí Äåêëàðàöèÿ
Ни4в2 и43 раюд

Figure 2: Title of the UDHR in Nivkh, as appearing in the rendered PDF document (top), and as appearing when extracted with a text extraction tool (bottom)

excerpt from a Nivkh document, showing the incorrect result produced by the text extraction tool.

Nevertheless, using extraction tools it is possible to extract correctly the document as a string of CIDs, instead of as a string of Unicode characters. Such a content lends itself to statistical analysis, where the frequency of CID and character ngrams could be used to recover the encoding. However, because of the general unavailability of language models for endangered languages this approach is not possible.

An inspiration to our approach is the work of (Vol et al., 2018), however their system is designed to process documents of undetermined language, while we know the language of the document we want to process; and it relies on OCR of the document for a subset of well supported languages, requiring extensive training material, while there are no such resources in our case as we deal with endangered languages.

Because of all the above constraints, there is no possibility to automatically recover Unicode translation maps for endangered languages. Consequently, human intervention is required, and as such the system we propose is designed to make the recovery process as fast and convenient as possible.

3 Proposed System

The system we designed is an interactive tool that allows the user to recover the text of corrupted document, requiring from a few minutes to a few hours depending on the quantity of symbols to recover, on the knowledge of the user of the target language, and on its ability to input the required characters.

Our system proceeds in two phases: a first fully automatic one that recovers the symbols for space and dot; and a second interactive one that helps the user gradually build the minimal quantity of resources in order to decipher the text.

3.1 Automatic Recovery

Because a font can be only partially corrupted it means that sometimes part of the text can be recovered: several letters as well as spaces and punctuation. However, it may happen that the font is corrupted in a way that the space and dot characters are wrongly attributed to other symbols. As such a font that contains some unattributed CID can not be trusted, and we proceed to the initialisation from scratch of the Unicode translation map, meaning that all documents and all languages are treated the same.

In the automatic phase, the system heuristically recovers which CID corresponds to the space and the dot characters. The space character is determined as the CID which is appears on the most lines, the dot character is determined as the CID that appears the most frequently at the end of a line which ends not at the margin, but specifically between 20% and 80% of the right margin. The left and right margin are determined by the leftmost and rightmost position of a character of that font. Other heuristics to recover the space were tried, such as the most frequent character that do not appear at lines end/beginning, but they did not work consistently and were disregarded.

Because of that reliance on statistics this automatic recovery can not work on very short texts, in which case it can be deactivated and the recovery can proceed only with the interactive phase. However, in case enough text is available to compute the statistics (a few lines), it proves a major time-saver.

3.2 Interactive Recovery

During the interactive phase the user is asked to prompt the system in several ways text as he sees it anywhere in the text. This can be either tokens, in that understanding it is any character sequence separated by spaces, or token sequences. From there, the system automatically tries to match the Unicode sequences that the user inputs to the CID sequences that are extracted from the PDF. Initially the translation map is void but it is filled progressively until there remains no character to be decoded.

If the user inputs a single token, the system will build a regular expression for all the CID sequences of the same length, and substituting the already decoded CID with their Unicode translation. If there is an unique match, the system therefore infers the value of the previously undecoded CID by matching them one by one to the characters entered by

n	1	2	3	4	5	6
niv	10	33	72	93	97	98
yrk	17	29	60	86	98	100

Table 1: Proportion in percent of unique sequences of token lengths for sequence length n in the UDHR for two different languages

language	niv	yrk
unique characters	81	68
text length (words)	1430	1530
input length (words)	57	76

Table 2: Unique character count and total word length for the UDHR declaration in two languages, and the total number of input words necessary for full recovery of these texts

the user. If there is a contradiction with a previously learned translation, the system flags it and the user must review the error and correct its inputs.

Entering a single token is however ineffective when starting the deciphering of a document because of the potentially high number of CID sequence that are of the same size as the token. As such, ii is in practice useful only at latter stages when most of the characters have already been recovered. A much more precise way of matching CID sequences to Unicode sequence is needed.

This problem is solved by letting the user input sequences of consecutive tokens, appearing anywhere on any lines, giving therefore much flexibility to the user. While a token length is an imprecise way of retrieving text, a sequence of token lengths is much more likely to be unique. For non unique sequences it is nevertheless possible to cue to the system its line number. With this minimal information the system can find the correct CID sequence an decipher it in the same fashion as previously.

In Table 1 we report on the uniqueness of such sequences of token length for two languages. For the two illustrated languages, if the user inputs a sequence of 5 words there is at least 97% chance that this sequence is unique, and therefore that all the corresponding letters will be correctly decoded.

In order to help the user, the system determines which CID are the most frequent, and on which lines their are the most unrecovered CID. By using this information the user can reduce to the minimum the number of words he has to input to the system in order to guarantee a full recovery. It also saves considerable time to the user, as this one does not have to search manually through the document for unrecovered characters.

4 Experiments

In the experiments we consider only corrupted documents that do not have an Unicode version even on the Unicode Consortium website. Out of the dozen such documents, we focus our effort on four languages in order to demonstrate the capacity of our approach: Nenets (iso code: yrk, in Cyrillic script), Nivkh (also called Gyliak, iso code: niv - actually the Sakhalin island dialect (Gruzdeva, 2022), in Cyrillic script) is a language isolate spoken by only a few thousands people, Mundari (iso code: unr, in Devanagari script) and a Mongolian dialect (iso code: mvf, in Mongolian script). While there exists significant resources for Mongolian in Cyrillic script, it is not the case for Mongolian script, which is used only to write dialects spoken in China, moreover their difference makes it impossible to exploit transliteration in order to ease the recovery process. The Nivkh language has the particularity that one letter of its alphabet is not even present in Unicode and can be realised only through combining characters. Because of the lack of support for these languages in latex it is impossible to give concrete examples of the rules used when recovering the texts.

In Table 2 we report statistics on the documents: number of unique symbols, number of words; and statistics on the user input: number of words entered in the system. The number of words required by the system is between 4 to 5 % of the total, the number of letters actually input by the user is actually significantly less, as during the text recovery process, it is possible to copy/paste partially recovered sequences of text and only replace the unavailable CID with the correct characters. As such, our approach makes it very efficient to recover the text by requiring to input only a fraction of the original text in order to recover it.

5 Discussion

Our approach allowed us to quickly and efficiently recover the UDHR Unicode text for two languages, requiring less than an hour of work: Nivkh and Nenets. These two documents have been sent to the UDHR page of the Unicode consortium, and are now already publicly available.

One additional advantage of our approach, is that

when dealing with a document collection using the same corrupted font, it is necessary to recover it only once in order to process the other documents, thereby yielding additional time gains for linguists and experts striving to create corpora.

When recovering Mongolian, we have been confronted to the problem that this language is written top down, because PDF documents consider that lines are going exclusively from left to right or right to left, the text extraction tool is totally unable to recover the lines. Consequently, our method can not be applied directly for that language, and instead of relying on an external library, it requires a further ad-hoc vertical segmentation step. This is left for future work.

At the time of the writing, another document is in the process of being recovered: the UDHR in Mundari, which is written in Devanagari script. Devanagari presents one specific difficulty: the long vowel "i" is written in a Unicode text string after the character of the consonant it is attached to, but it is displayed before it when the string is visually rendered. This is because the CID sequence of the symbols of a line is extracted in increasing order of the bounding box coordinates of the characters it contains. In order to deal with that, the user is constrained to input the characters in the same order as the one expected by the CID sequence, and a post-processing step is required to swap the corresponding Unicode characters before rendering the final text.

6 Conclusion

We present an approach that is able to quickly guide a human expert in recovering text from corrupted born digital PDF documents containing text in rare or endangered languages. Such languages impose severe constraints, because often there exists no preexisting corpus to train on, or to compare to the extracted text. Our approach has been designed specifically to operates within these constraints and consists in reconstructing the CID to Unicode translation maps by efficiently leveraging user input in an interactive way. We applied this approach to 4 documents of the UDHR corpus for which there exists no Unicode text, 2 of which where fully recovered, the other ones needing some additional development related to particularities of the writing system they use. The tool is not yet available, but will be released on this repository[4].

[4]https://github.com/nicolasst

Future work will deal in applying the approach to more languages of the UDHR, and to deal with the harder problem of recovering text of endangered language existing solely as pictures. To that intent, we consider exploring image augmentation techniques (Minaee et al., 2021) in order to train ad-hoc OCR system for any scripts solely based on the symbols present in the Unicode charts, with the aim of interactively presenting the user with potential choices.

Our approach is useful to help protect and study endangered languages for which document base exists in born digital PDF format, but for which some of documents, or all of them, are corrupted.

References

RMCV Bandara. 2020. *Content extraction from PDF invoices on business document archives*. Ph.D. thesis.

Josephine Jill T Cabatbat, Jica P Monsanto, and Giovanni A Tapang. 2014. Preserved network metrics across translated texts. *International Journal of Modern Physics C*, 25(02):1350092.

Eva D'hondt, Cyril Grouin, and Brigitte Grau. 2017. Generating a training corpus for ocr post-correction using encoder-decoder model. In *Proceedings of the Eighth International Joint Conference on Natural Language Processing (Volume 1: Long Papers)*, pages 1006–1014.

Ekaterina Gruzdeva. 2022. On the diversification of nivkh varieties. In *The 4th Annual Meeting of Japan*.

Shervin Minaee, Yuri Y Boykov, Fatih Porikli, Antonio J Plaza, Nasser Kehtarnavaz, and Demetri Terzopoulos. 2021. Image segmentation using deep learning: A survey. *IEEE transactions on pattern analysis and machine intelligence*.

Nikolett Mus and Réka Metzger. 2021. Toward a corpus of tundra nenets: stages and challenges in building a corpus. In *Proceedings of the Workshop on Computational Methods for Endangered Languages*, volume 2, pages 4–9.

Mark Vol, Andrey Krutko, Nicolas Stefanovitch, and Denis Postanogov. 2018. Automatic recovery of corrupted font encoding in pdf documents using cnn-based symbol recognition with language model. In *2018 13th IAPR International Workshop on Document Analysis Systems (DAS)*, pages 121–126. IEEE.

Learning Through Transcription

Mat Bettinson and Steven Bird
Northern Institute, Charles Darwin University, Darwin, Australia
matthew.bettinson@cdu.edu.au, steven.bird@cdu.edu.au

Abstract

Transcribing speech for primarily oral, local languages is often a joint effort involving speakers and outsiders. It is commonly motivated by externally-defined scientific goals, alongside local motivations such as language acquisition and access to heritage materials. We explore the task of 'learning through transcription' through the design of a system for collaborative speech annotation. We have developed a prototype to support local and remote learner-speaker interactions in remote Aboriginal communities in northern Australia. We show that situated systems design for inclusive non-expert practice is a promising new direction for working with speakers of local languages.

1 Introduction

Speech transcription is typically motivated by the desire for lasting accessible records of language. However transcription can also be a method for linguistic inquiry and language acquisition (Bowern, 2008; Meakins et al., 2018). In this case it is a form of note-taking as the transcriber strives to make sense of what they hear. This practice is well established in documentary and descriptive linguistics, and it leads to detailed transcriptions that include metalinguistic detail. Computational linguists rely upon these annotated datasets to train language models. Non-specialist outsiders may find their alphabetic decoding skills useful for learning the local languages that are spoken in the places where they live and work, as evidenced by the number of learning resources that depend on having a written representation for these primarily oral languages.

We propose computational support for an activity we call *learning through transcription*. The form we propose is that of a system that supports transcription as a series of learning interactions. The focus of the computation is shifted from automation to computer supported cooperative work. We describe a design and engineering effort to address this need in remote Aboriginal communities in northern Australia.

Here, local people speak one or more local languages, along with various degrees of proficiency in English. Some non-indigenous Australians seek competency in Aboriginal languages to carry out cultural projects with local people. Some locals need to develop literacy in one of the local languages to support knowledge work in art centres, ranger programs, health clinics, schools, tourism operations, and so on. Accordingly, speech transcription is a practice that supports language acquisition and literacy development.

We report on a system for iterative word-level transcription modelled on 'sparse transcription' (Bird, 2020b). Developed through a course of Research-through-Design (cf. RtD in Zimmerman et al., 2007), 'Sparzan' is a vehicle for investigating methods for amplifying human effort in transcribing speech in primarily oral, local languages. We cover data models for learning through transcription, technologies and user interfaces for interactive transcription, and systems engineering.

A topic foregrounded by the COVID-19 pandemic is the tyranny of distance when outsiders seek to conduct fieldwork with people in remote linguistic communities (Williams et al., 2021). We investigate remote collaboration through a novel video messaging appliance which serves as a vector for learner-speaker interactions embedded in transcription work.

This paper is organised as follows. In Section 2 we describe the role of speech transcription for oral languages, including learning through transcription, interactive transcription, and situated systems design. In Section 3 we describe the Sparzan system, including the transcription client, the Lingobox appliance, and an example application. In Section 4 we reflect on the approach and draw lessons for future work.

Proceedings of the Fifth Workshop on the Use of Computational Methods in the Study of Endangered Languages, pages 83 - 92
May 26-27, 2022 ©2022 Association for Computational Linguistics

2 Background

Many local languages, including endangered and Indigenous languages, are purely oral, and there is no naturally-occurring context for deploying text technologies (Bird, 2022). Oral languages are not just languages that lack a writing system; the existence of an oral culture unlimited by writing leads to an entirely different situation (Ong, 1982). Local matters of concern include caring for the country, transmitting ecological knowledge to the next generation, and managing intercultural workplaces. This may mean that there is a need to record and transcribe ancestral knowledge about key places and practices, to compile vocabularies of local flora, fauna, and material culture, and for two-way language learning between the local vernacular and a language of wider communication. Apparently simple tasks like accessing an archive of historical recordings become more complex when one considers that we lack a standardised orthography for a community-agreed reference dialect supported by robust speech recognition. Thus, there is both a need for transcription, and a need to innovate when it comes to making transcriptions, through the design of novel processes and interfaces.

2.1 Learning through transcription

When we speak of language learning, we take a different focus to the usual kind of language learning that depends on previously prepared materials and resources, and that uses methods that are well-described in the field of second language teaching and learning (e.g. Nunan, 1999; Cook, 2016). Australian Aboriginal languages are rarely taught in formal settings, and so non-indigenous people tend to acquire local languages in an independent, self-directed way. One case in point is linguists, whose field methods often incorporate learning.

In one conception of fieldwork on local languages, outsiders enter with their agenda to capture a language, bringing with them a strong focus on creating textual resources for use in linguistic analysis and for training computational models. We immediately run into the so-called 'transcription bottleneck', which is being tackled in various ways, mostly depending on universal phone recognition (Besacier et al., 2014; Hasegawa-Johnson et al., 2016; Adams, 2017; Zanon Boito et al., 2017; Marinelli et al., 2019). Phone recognition for Indigenous languages nevertheless depends on recruiting linguists and local people to create phone level transcriptions. This approach downplays the cultural significance of the content, focussing on idiosyncrasies of form to the point where variations in pronunciation, even speech disfluencies, should ideally be transcribed (Bird, 2020a).

Instead, we begin with the agency of local communities and inquire about what people are already doing. In many Indigenous communities, this includes collaboration with outsiders on culturally meaningful tasks connected to land management, ecological knowledge, and transmitting traditional practices to the next generation. We believe that language work can sit in this space, so long as it is possible to design natural workflows. It may be as simple as shifting the discussion from 'how do we transcribe this utterance using a phonetic alphabet?' to 'what is the cultural significance of this word?' (Bird, 2022).

When we do this, we arrive at a kind of speech transcription which is not based on the idea of exhaustive transcription, but which identifies the significant words and phrases that are useful for organising and accessing audio collections, i.e. sparse transcription (Bird, 2020b). Sparse transcription is particularly suited to situation where newcomers enter a community and begin to learn language in the course of working with local people. Instead of phone recognition, this approach relies on a different off-the-shelf language technology, namely keyword spotting (Garcia and Gish, 2006; Gales et al., 2014; Le Ferrand et al., 2021).

At any stage of this process of learning a language through transcription, we have a personal lexicon of known words and phrases. We can engage speakers in discussions of the meaning of these words, perhaps using the contact language. We can listen to recorded passages with speakers, pick out further key words, elicit their meaning, and add them to the lexicon. This is an approach to language work which is more grounded in local concerns, e.g., interest in transmitting the content, and interest in supporting the learning journey of a newcomer.

2.2 Interactive transcription

The amplification of human effort with machine assistance is a practical approach suited for local languages. Often the most effective form of machine assistance is facilitating collaboration. Systems or *groupware* for computer supported cooperative work (CSCW) are now common in the workplace

(Khoshafian and Buckiewicz, 1995). Language-based CSCW systems have been described and implemented for language documentation and linguistic fieldwork (Hanke, 2017; Cathcart et al., 2012).

Interactive transcription sees the transcriber draw upon machine resources in real-time. Sparzan transcriber (see Sec. 3.2) is a related development to an interactive transcription prototype with an FST language model-backed real-time phone alignment and word completion for a polysynthetic language (Lane et al., 2021). In the present work we deprioritise established language models and metalinguistic analysis, instead focusing on conventional word-level transcription with assistance from keyword spotting and human-to-human language interactions.

2.3 Designing for inclusion

Transcription tools occupy a vital place in the construction of annotated corpora. Transcribers wish for high-quality easy-to-use software, that interoperates with other tools, and that support collaborative workflows (Finlayson, 2016; Thieberger, 2016). In this context we note that production-grade software development is beyond our resources, but some features are relevant as we seek to design for a realistic and useful artefact (rather than a prototype), in accordance with the research-through-design methodology (Zimmerman et al., 2007).

In contrast to the majority of speech transcription tools, our design focus lies not with expert transcribers and the production of annotated corpora, but rather in selective transcription by people working on the ground. Servicing this audience requires supporting non-experts of various types, including Western newcomers to remote Aboriginal communities, along with local people. In recent years there has been growing attention towards updated methodologies and fresh takes on software design to meet these needs. SayMore offered a design aimed at community participants as transcribers, integrating support for audio based workflows over metalinguistic annotation (Hatton, 2013). Similarly, tools developed under the Aikuma umbrella introduce designs for mobile and web-based tools, also aimed at community participation (Bird et al., 2014; Bettinson and Bird, 2017).

It is established practice for field linguists to perform transcriptions with real-time assistance of speakers (Meakins et al., 2018; Sapién, 2018). Yet access to speakers is often limited. Bespoke technology design can help make the most of time spent in the community, chiefly as mediating tools to support face-to-face interactions (Bettinson and Bird, 2021a). There have been proposals for remote collaboration as a form of linguistic crowdsourcing (Hatton, 2013; Bettinson, 2015). The Aikuma-Link prototype explored a mobile-based design to distribute consulting tasks to speaker's phones (Bettinson, 2020, p.87).

The global pandemic has challenged us all to innovate in remote working practice, including interactions with Indigenous language speakers (Williams et al., 2021). The design context of remote Indigenous communities in North Australia is quite different from mainstream culture, urban corporations and the tools that have evolved to serve them. There is rising understanding of the need for technology not to substitute for interaction but rather to support relationships Taylor et al. (2019). A common point of agreement is that video communication supports work practice and relationship maintenance. As a parallel investigation into the general problem of working consultations in remote communities, we developed an appliance-based video messaging service called Lingobox (Bettinson and Bird, 2021b). The design challenge we take up here is to integrate Lingobox as a means to support learner-interactions within a system for collaborative transcription practice.

3 Project Sparzan

In this section we describe a system for collaborative computationally-assisted speech transcription. It is a synthesis of prior work in speech transcription methodology, interactive transcription workflows and remote interaction through tangible technology. The system's working title Sparzan derives from **sparse** tr**an**scription, the fundamental transcription model we adopt here. Two use cases are supported: collaborative lexicon building and individual language acquisition. In both cases, speech is transcribed by non-native speakers as a way to expand their individual and collective understanding, which is why we call this learning through transcription.

The Sparzan architecture is given in Figure 1, comprising a web application including the transcription activity, backed by server 'stack' responsible for the data model logic, data storage and computational agents dispatched as asynchronous

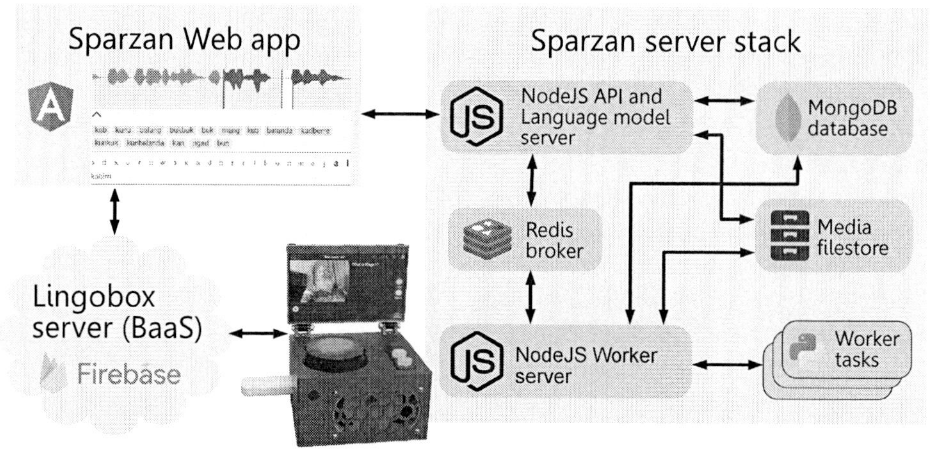

Figure 1: The Sparzan system architecture implementation is similar to common web services. The web-based transcription app is backed by centralised computational resources.

worker processes. Remote language consultation is achieved by integrating the external Lingobox service, hosted on a commercial backend-as-a-service (BaaS). In the following sections we elaborate on key components of the Sparzan system.

3.1 Sparse transcription for learning

Sparse transcription relies on tasks that are well suited to the competencies of the audience in our use case, i.e. as a series of 'interpretive, iterative and interactive processes that are amenable to wider participation' (Bird, 2020b, p713). However, the original proposal does not take asynchronous collaboration into account. For example the tasks of growing and refactoring a glossary (Tasks G and R) presume the existence of a single glossary that is in a perpetual state of motion towards a fully validated and authoritative state.

However, designs to support learning through transcription must recognise the existence of individual understandings of language, or more completely, individual dynamic language systems (De Bot et al., 2007). Systems for computer assisted language learning (CALL, Levy, 1997) often model the knowledge held by individual learners in order to craft personalised learning opportunities (cf. the Input Hypothesis, Krashen, 1992). While the individual strives to acquire the sum of generalised knowledge, the individual *transcriber* is also an actor in incremental processes to extend this knowledge. This observation is not limited to lexical knowledge either, but holds for any type of language knowledge that is being investigated, such as morphosyntax, or sociolinguistic variation. Thus, we need a way to differentiate curated knowledge and individual knowledge.

Accordingly, we extend the sparse transcription model to include two lexical data structures, the glossary (individual) and the lexicon (general). We anticipate one lexicon per language variety but multiple glossaries (one per transcriber). Now we refine the refactoring task to be non-destructive to the glossary, instead using content from the glossary when creating or updating lexical entries during consultation with a language authority.

The lexicon is useful for computationally assisted learning. We use phone-based keyword spotting to identify plausible instances of words in a speech segment and offer a list of suggestions to the learner without prejudice. Should the learner know the word, they may accept the suggestion, thereby establishing a link from the learner's glossary to the lexical entry. Otherwise, if the word be unknown, the suggestion is treated as a learning prompt that supports an exploration of meaning (lexical definition) and usage (concordance views). Crucially, these learning prompts need not be correct; phone-based word spotting errors are typically plausible learner errors in their own right, and thus they are useful as practice to discriminate similar-sounding words (as noted in, Bettinson and Bird, 2021a).

In sum, 'transcription for learning' is a form of computationally-assisted self-study. Learner-speaker interactions are an essential complement to self-study but we must also recognise the reality that time with speakers is limited. Anchoring learner-speaker interaction in context supports the systematic capture of speaker knowledge, reducing

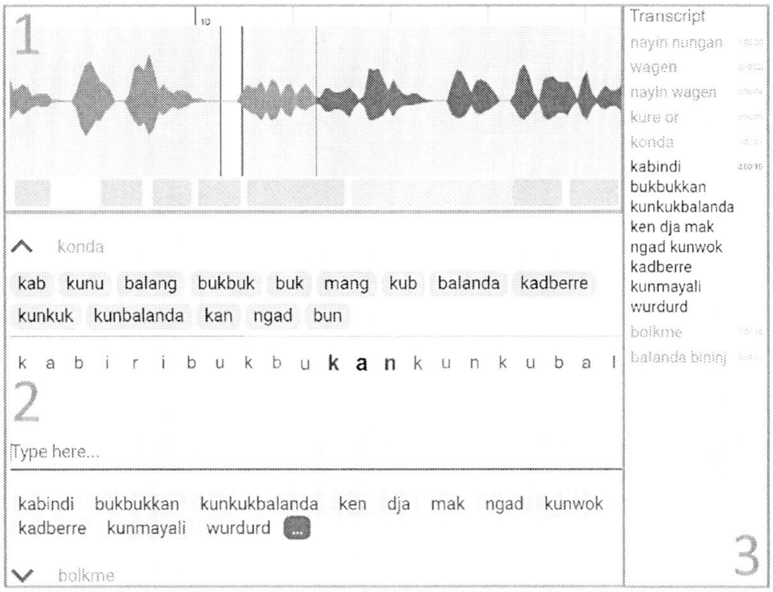

Figure 2: The Sparzan transcriber activity. User interface zones are annotated in red: 1. the signal zone, 2. the segment zone and 3. the transcript zone

repetition and improving learning efficiency and the acquisition of valuable language data. In the next section we illustrate how this is achieved in a transcription activity.

3.2 Sparzan transcriber

In this section we describe the transcription activity of the web app. The design is inspired by prior work in simplified transcription interfaces, particularly those with a focus on oral workflow support such as SayMore and Aikuma-NG. Simplicity is at the heart of the design goals for Sparzan Transcriber for two reasons: as general tactic to increase usability (Nielsen, 1994); and to support transcription as a common resource where consultants and transcribers work together. A natural consequence of co-located tool use is that observers learn to become operators. That is an important design consideration to support the self-sufficiency and digital agency rights of Aboriginal Australians (Carew et al., 2015).

Sparzan Transcriber is split into three zones (Fig. 2): signal, segment and transcript zones. Each zone displays a mapping against time and affords a method of navigation in the media file. The signal zone maps time horizontally, comprising a scrolling waveform (10 second window) and a fixed voice activity (VAD) bar underneath (entire duration). The segment zone maps time vertically, displaying a single speech segment at a time derived from an initial automatic voice activity segmentation. The transcript zone is a vertical map of timestamped transcriptions to offer an uncluttered context of transcription content.

Transcription is achieved by consulting the assistance offered in the segment zone, and typing into a temporary text input box. The current prototype offers phonemically word spotted candidates (yellow chips in Fig. 2) and an automatic phonemic transcription (the text line underneath). When the segment changes, audio playback begins automatically and is reflected in the scrolling signal view and in an animated phone display that highlights phones associated with the current point of playback (visible as the bold 'kan' in Fig. 2).

In contrast to many other transcription tools, transcriptions are not free text. They are a sequence of word tokens rendered as 'chips' so as to support interaction such as querying lexical entries and viewing a concordance of projects associated with the lexicon. A transcription is a sequence of word token chips with an temporary chip mapped to current text input. The transcriber interacts via the temporary text input box and left/right cursors to achieve insert, edit and delete operations.

The operator may request help from a native speaker via the Lingobox service (Sec. 3.4). To do so the operator creates a new Lingobox request by recording a webcam video and customising the Lingobox prompt (Fig. 3). Customisations include

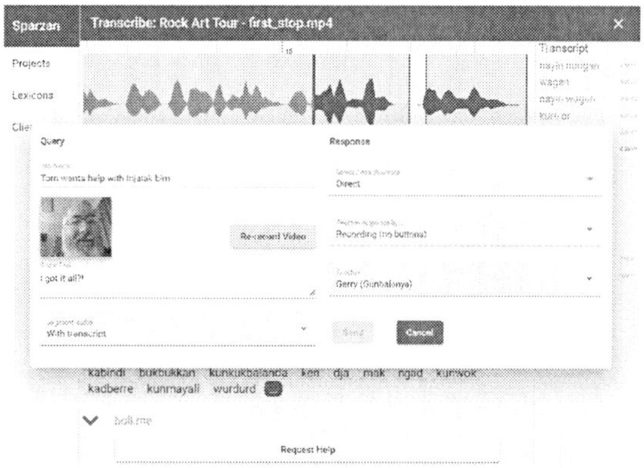

Figure 3: Requesting speaker assistance within a Sparzan transcriber session

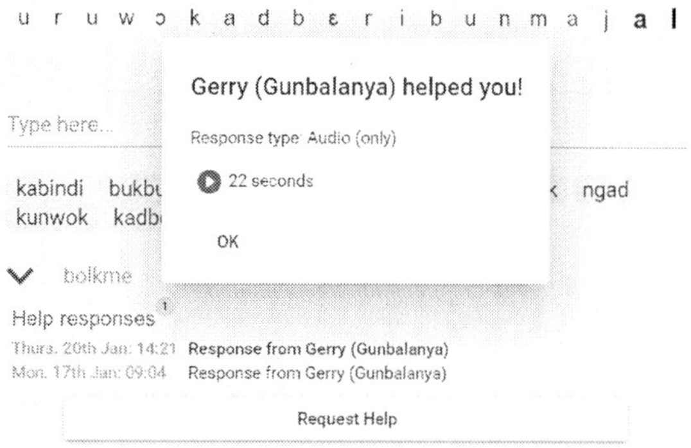

Figure 4: Speaker responses are anchored to transcription spans in Sparzan transcriber

on-screen text, including the segment audio, the recipient of the request (if there are multiple language authorities) and what the type of desired response. Typically one would ask a question about the audio of a current segment, such as confirming a transcription choice. When the speaker has provided a response at a later time, the Sparzan web app indicates the response against a given transcription and clicking on the notification takes the operator directly to the speech transcription segment to access the response (Fig. 4).

3.3 Sparzan server

The server stack comprises two Node.js server apps: a main business logic server, and a 'worker' app. The main server app implements data model transactions and handles client interaction through HTTP and WebSocket APIs. The worker application brokers computational workload via jobs dispatched as asynchronous worker threads, injecting the results back into the database and notifying the main server app on their completion. Structured data is stored in a MongoDB instance while job persistence and inter-app communications are achieved via an in-memory database (Redis).

When the client uploads new media, a media processing job is created which batches up a number of vital tasks: extracting audio peak information, breath group segmentation, automatic phonemic transcription via Allosaurus, customised for Kunwinjku (Li et al., 2020; Le Ferrand et al., 2021) and finally phonemic word spotting of existing lexical entities. These operations must complete before a transcription session may begin, however a phone-based word spotting task is also created, with results to appear in Sparzan transcriber as that operation completes. During normal operations, additional word spotting jobs are executed periodically so that newly added items appear in the candidate suggestions.

User experience of server-backed web applications is highly dependent on network performance. Sparzan's backend supports real-time transcription with a server-based data model with a low-latency WebSocket API transport. This is sufficient to support client transcription in regional centres, but is impractical for supporting transcription sessions in remote communities. On a provisional basis, we support remote community participation through the Lingobox appliance described in the next section. This service utilises a data synchronising strategy designed to function adequately on 'bush internet'.

3.4 Lingobox

Lingobox is an appliance designed to support consulting interactions framed as personal video requests (see Fig. 5) and intended to be deployed in community workplaces, such as language and arts centres, where it behaves much like an answering machine. It was developed to explore an effective replacement for paid consulting interactions that would usually take place in the course of face-to-face fieldwork (Bettinson and Bird, 2021b). We opted to design a custom appliance to solve a number of intractable limitations of mobile devices that have emerged from several years of experience developing stand-alone and server-connected mobile apps. Limitations include poor audio on mobile devices, the need to manage and secure devices, and the low effectiveness of attention strategies such as notifications, and the general lack of prominence and association with a place of work.

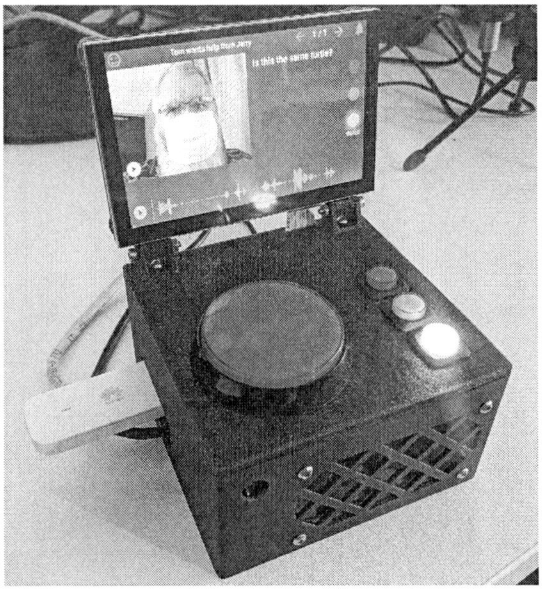

Figure 5: Lingobox, an appliance to support remote interaction in language work

The hardware features illuminated buttons, a tilt-adjustable LCD screen, a integrated cellular modem, and high quality audio recording and playback. Distinct from depersonalised crowdsourcing techniques, the intent here is to support learner-teacher relationships and to place the burden of effort on the person asking for help. New requests are added to a stack of requests with an audible ping, and the large red recording button periodically flashes when there are unanswered requests. Requests are created within the context of ongoing transcription work, and they typically (but optionally) include the segment of audio that is currently being transcribed. Consultants act on requests through a staged process such as: playing the video request, playing the media (e.g. the segment of audio being transcribed), eliciting a spoken response, and conveying it back (Fig. 6). Sparzan provides a rudimentary form of workspace awareness (Gutwin and Greenberg, 1996) to draw attention towards consultant responses. This is achieved through notifications that draw the user directly to the relevant transcription segment.

4 Discussion

Many people have noted the pressing need to bootstrap data collection for primarily oral, local languages. This is largely a human effort, but it can be scaled up with the support of efficient workflows and assistive technologies. For example, having a

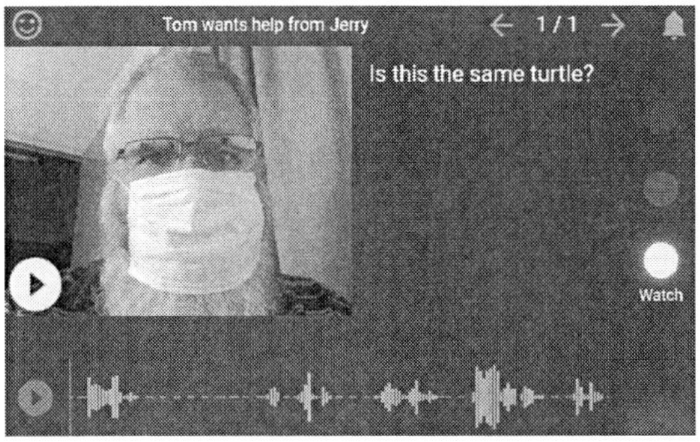

Figure 6: Lingobox on-screen display for a typical transcription-anchored help request

searchable lexicon facilitates updating individual entries. However, piecemeal solutions, where we improve the efficiency of individual tasks, only deliver incremental improvements. Fully integrated solutions allow us to explore broader questions and to exploit fortuitous opportunities.

In the usual pattern of language teaching, learning resources are compiled by 'experts'. Learners with their repetitive mistakes and frequent errors have no role to play in crafting lessons. However for local languages there may be few learning resources of the type expected by western learners, and minimal capacity for creating such resources. Nevertheless, there are still learning resources to be found. In particular, word recognition errors – obstacles for transcription – are plausible learner errors. These are not useless mistakes to be discarded, but potential prompts for learners to consider and correct. *A word that one person has learned and systematically corrected in the course of transcription may become a prompt for another learner.*

The system remains a prototype and we have not yet not been able to test it on the ground because the communities remain closed. This work has some other limitations. Foremost is that the design has been conducted in a university lab, rather than in a co-design process with our partners in the community. A second shortcoming is that the learning potential of collaborative transcription has yet to be explored. Using the resulting data to create learning content for dedicated learning apps is promising direction for future work.

A third shortcoming is the architectural reliance on low-latency networks. Solutions of this type require server infrastructure, but 'bush internet' network conditions rule out the simple convenience of the 'cloud'. One solution is to deploy compact, low-cost server architecture in the field, as we have previously explored with BushPi, a ruggedised battery-powered server to support local use of collaborative language apps (Bettinson and Bird, 2021a). Thus, there is an ongoing need for on-country design and engineering to devise practical, community-based solutions, building on previous attempts in this space (Cathcart et al., 2012; Hanke, 2017).

Despite these shortcomings, we believe this work amounts to a novel and effective design pattern for remote asynchronous collaboration on meticulous language work, serving a variety of documentary and pedagogical goals. The potential for computer supported cooperative language work remains relatively unexplored, and faces an egregious challenge: how do we go from minimally-viable research prototypes to robust, supported, and sustainable solutions (cf. Finlayson, 2016, p27)? We believe there remains a clear need for foundational research on technology for working with primarily oral, local languages, supporting a broad range of stakeholders, for the benefit of community goals in sustaining linguistic diversity.

5 Conclusion

We have described a system for cooperative language work, including speech transcription and language learning. It was developed during a period where Aboriginal community interactions were severely limited due to the COVID-19 pandemic, but where cooperative work and the underlying relationships needed to be sustained. We developed assistive technology to support (and even encourage) language acquisition in the course of transcription and the associated learner-speaker interactions. We set aside expert-defined practice, and instead designed for inclusive participation of learners and speakers, regardless of their technical competencies. In the process, we have demonstrated that the effort of systems engineering for specific sociolinguistic contexts has direct relevance for language data collection and for local language technologies in general.

Acknowledgements

We are grateful to the Bininj people of Northern Australia for the opportunity to work with them on the Kunwinjku language (ISO gup). This research has been supported by a grant from the Australian Research Council entitled *Learning English and Aboriginal Languages for Work*, and the Indigenous Languages and Arts Program entitled *Mobile Software for Oral Language Learning in Arnhem Land*. Our work with Bininj is covered by a research permit from the Northern Land Council and approvals from the board of Warddeken Land Management and the CDU Human Research Ethics Committee.

References

Oliver Adams. 2017. *Automatic Understanding of Unwritten Languages*. Ph.D. thesis, University of Melbourne.

Laurent Besacier, Etienne Barnard, Alexey Karpov, and Tanja Schultz. 2014. Automatic speech recognition for under-resourced languages: A survey. *Speech Communication*, 56:85–100.

Mat Bettinson. 2015. Towards Language Documentation 2.0: Imagining a Crowdsourcing Revolution. Presentation at the International Conference on Language Documentation and Conservation, `http://hdl.handle.net/10125/25302`.

Mat Bettinson. 2020. *Enabling Large-Scale Collaboration in Language Documentation*. PhD thesis, University of Melbourne, Melbourne, Australia.

Mat Bettinson and Steven Bird. 2017. Developing a suite of mobile applications for collaborative language documentation. In *Second Workshop on Computational Methods for Endangered Languages*, pages 156–164.

Mat Bettinson and Steven Bird. 2021a. Collaborative fieldwork with custom mobile apps. *Language Documentation and Conservation*, 15:411–432.

Mat Bettinson and Steven Bird. 2021b. Designing to support remote working relationships with indigenous communities. In *Proceedings of OzChi '21: 33rd Australian Conference on Human-Computer Interaction*.

Steven Bird. 2020a. Decolonising speech and language technology. In *Proceedings of the 28th International Conference on Computational Linguistics*, page 3504–19, Barcelona, Spain.

Steven Bird. 2020b. Sparse transcription. *Computational Linguistics*, 46:713–44.

Steven Bird. 2022. Local languages, third spaces, and other high-resource scenarios. In *Proceedings of the 60th Annual Meeting of the Association for Computational Linguistics*.

Steven Bird, Florian R Hanke, Oliver Adams, and Haejoong Lee. 2014. Aikuma: A mobile app for collaborative language documentation. In *Proceedings of the 2014 Workshop on the Use of Computational Methods in the Study of Endangered Languages*, pages 1–5. Association for Computational Linguistics.

Claire Bowern. 2008. *Linguistic Fieldwork: A Practical Guide*. Palgrave Macmillan.

Margaret Carew, Jennifer Green, Inge Kral, Rachel Nordlinger, and Ruth Singer. 2015. Getting in touch: Language and digital inclusion in Australian indigenous communities. *Language Documentation and Conservation*, 9:307–23.

MaryEllen Cathcart, Gina Cook, Theresa Deering, Yuliya Manyakina, Gretchen McCulloch, and Hisako Noguchi. 2012. LingSync: A free tool for creating and maintaining a shared database for communities, linguists and language learners. In *Proceedings of FAMLi II: Workshop on Corpus Approaches to Mayan Linguistics*, pages 247–250.

Vivian Cook. 2016. *Second Language Learning and Language Teaching*. Routledge.

Kees De Bot, Wander Lowie, and Marjolijn Verspoor. 2007. A dynamic systems theory approach to second language acquisition. *Bilingualism: Language and cognition*, 10:7–21.

Mark Alan Finlayson. 2016. Report on the 2015 NSF Workshop on Unified Annotation Tooling. Technical report, Computer Science and Artificial Intelligence Laboratory (MIT). http://hdl.handle.net/1721.1/105270, accessed February 2022.

Mark Gales, Kate Knill, Anton Ragni, and Shakti Rath. 2014. Speech recognition and keyword spotting for low-resource languages: BABEL project research at CUED. In *Workshop on Spoken Language Technologies for Under-Resourced Languages*, pages 16–23. ISCA.

Alvin Garcia and Herbert Gish. 2006. Keyword spotting of arbitrary words using minimal speech resources. In *Proceedings of the International Conference on Acoustics Speech and Signal Processing*. IEEE.

Carl Gutwin and Saul Greenberg. 1996. Workspace awareness for groupware. In *Conference Companion on Human Factors in Computing Systems*, pages 208–209.

Florian R Hanke. 2017. *Computer Supported Collaborative Language Documentation*. Ph.D. thesis, University of Melbourne. Http://hdl.handle.net/11343/192578.

Mark A Hasegawa-Johnson, Preethi Jyothi, Daniel McCloy, Majid Mirbagheri, Giovanni M di Liberto, Amit Das, Bradley Ekin, Chunxi Liu, Vimal Manohar, Hao Tang, et al. 2016. ASR for under-resourced languages from probabilistic transcription. *IEEE/ACM Transactions on Audio, Speech and Language Processing*, 25:50–63.

John Hatton. 2013. SayMore: Language documentation productivity. Talk at 3rd International Conference on Language Documentation and Conservation (ICLDC3). http://hdl.handle.net/10125/26153.

Setrag Khoshafian and Marek Buckiewicz. 1995. *Introduction to groupware, workflow, and workgroup computing*. John Wiley & Sons, Inc.

Stephen Krashen. 1992. The input hypothesis: An update. *Linguistics and Language Pedagogy: The State of the Art*, pages 409–431.

William Lane, Mat Bettinson, and Steven Bird. 2021. A computational model for interactive transcription. In *Proceedings of the Second Workshop on Data Science with Human in the Loop: Language Advances*, pages 105–111.

Éric Le Ferrand, Steven Bird, and Laurent Besacier. 2021. Phone based keyword spotting for transcribing very low resource languages. In *Proceedings of the The 19th Annual Workshop of the Australasian Language Technology Association*, pages 79–86.

Michael Levy. 1997. *Computer-assisted language learning: Context and conceptualization*. Oxford University Press.

Xinjian Li, Siddharth Dalmia, Juncheng Li, Matthew Lee, Patrick Littell, Jiali Yao, Antonios Anastasopoulos, David R Mortensen, Graham Neubig, Alan W Black, et al. 2020. Universal phone recognition with a multilingual allophone system. In *Proceedings of the International Conference on Acoustics, Speech and Signal Processing*, pages 8249–8253. IEEE.

Federico Marinelli, Alessandra Cervone, Giuliano Tortoreto, Evgeny A Stepanov, Giuseppe Di Fabbrizio, and Giuseppe Riccardi. 2019. Active annotation: Bootstrapping annotation lexicon and guidelines for supervised NLU learning. In *Proceedings of Interspeech 2019*, pages 574–578.

Felicity Meakins, Jenny Green, and Myfany Turpin. 2018. *Understanding Linguistic Fieldwork*. Routledge.

Jakob Nielsen. 1994. *Usability Engineering*. Elsevier. This is the bible for any discussion around producing easy-to-use products. It is vital to cite this is if one is talking about usability.

David Nunan. 1999. *Second Language Teaching & Learning*. Heinle & Heinle Publishers.

Walter Ong. 1982. *Orality and Literacy: The Technologizing of the Word*. Routledge.

Racquel-María Sapién. 2018. Design and implementation of collaborative language documentation projects. In *Oxford Handbook of Endangered Languages*, pages 203–24. Oxford University Press.

Jennyfer Lawrence Taylor, Wujal Wujal Aboriginal Shire Council, Alessandro Soro, Paul Roe, and Margot Brereton. 2019. A relational approach to designing social technologies that foster use of the kuku yalanji language. In *Proceedings of the 31st Australian Conference on Human-Computer-Interaction*, OZCHI'19, pages 161–172. Association for Computing Machinery.

Nicholas Thieberger. 2016. Language Documentation Tools and Methods Summit Report. Technical report, Centre of Excellence for the Dynamics of Language (CoEDL). `http://bit.ly/LDTAMSReport`, accessed February 2022.

Nicholas Williams, W. D. L. Silva, Laura McPherson, and Jeff Good. 2021. Covid-19 and documentary linguistics: Some ways forward. *Language Documentation and Description*, 20:359–377.

Marcely Zanon Boito, Alexandre Bérard, Aline Villavicencio, and Laurent Besacier. 2017. Unwritten languages demand attention too! Word discovery with encoder-decoder models. In *IEEE Workshop on Automatic Speech Recognition and Understanding*, pages 458–65.

John Zimmerman, Jodi Forlizzi, and Shelley Evenson. 2007. Research Through Design as a method for interaction design research in HCI. In *Proceedings of the SIGCHI Conference on Human Factors in Computing Systems*, pages 493–502. ACM.

Developing a Part-Of-Speech tagger for te reo Māori

Aoife Finn
Te Hiku Media
aoife@tehiku.co.nz

Peter-Lucas Jones
Te Hiku Media
peterlucas@tehiku.co.nz

Keoni Mahelona
Te Hiku Media
keoni@tehiku.co.nz

Suzanne Duncan
Te Hiku Media
suzanne@tehiku.co.nz

Gianna Leoni
Te Hiku Media
gianna@tehiku.co.nz

Abstract

This abstract discusses the development of a Part-of-Speech tagger for te reo Māori, which is the Indigenous language of Aotearoa - New Zealand. It mostly focuses on the creation of a tagset that is appropriate for Māori. This is in consideration of the fact that some tagsets have existing tags that are not suitable for some Māori word classes. Alternatively, the existing tagsets might lack entirely a suitable tag for some Māori word classes. And finally, some existing tagsets do not adequately reflect a Māori worldview. Emphasis is put on the importance of capturing the language according to the conceptualization of its speakers, and not imposing "traditional" grammatical categories where it is not appropriate. The solution involved changing how some existing tags are used and in some cases creating entirely new tags that are appropriate for Te reo Māori. The Part-of-Speech tagger was successfully built by a Māori Indigenous organisation and is being used as the foundation for other applications.

1. Introduction

This paper discusses the development of a Part-of-Speech tagger for Māori called *Whakairo Kupu*, meaning to *carve* or *sculpt words*. It specifically focuses on the creation of a tagset that was appropriate for Māori. Our current precision and recall scores are approximately 93%. Hereinafter, Māori will be referred to as te reo Māori or alternatively just Māori, and Universal Dependencies will be abbreviated to UD. Part-of-speech will be abbreviated as POS.

Furthermore in this paper, linguistic examples will consist of four to five lines. The first line will include a morpheme by morpheme te reo Māori phrase or sentence. The second line will see each morpheme with a linguistic gloss that gives information about the syntactic properties or meaning of the morpheme. A third line will show the POS tags that our tagger would assign to the morpheme. The fourth and typically final line will show the English translation. However, in the uncommon instance that a literal translation is needed, it will be shown on the fifth line. For an example of this, please see (1).

1) <u>Example</u>		<u>Glosses</u>
Haere	mai	*te reo*
go	DIR	*linguistic*
VERB	MOD	*POS*
"Welcome!"		*translation*
Lit: "Go hither"		*literal translation*

Moving on, te reo Māori is the Indigenous language of Aotearoa, also known as New Zealand, (Morrison, 2011). It is a member of the Eastern Polynesian branch of the Austronesian language family which itself has approximately 1200 members, (Harlow, 2007). Māori is related to other members of the Polynesian branch of Austronesian such as Rapanui, Rarotongan, Tahitian, Tuamotuan, Marquesan, Hawai'ian and Mangarevan, (Du Feu, 1996). Te reo Māori is a head-first and dependent- marking language, it is analytical with a high degree of polysemy.

Prior to the development of this tagger, there was no POS tagger for Māori from Aotearoa. POS taggers tag words according to their syntactic or grammatical category. However, many traditional syntactic categories, and by consequence POS labels, do not "work for" Māori, see (2). By this we mean for some of the traditional categories:

2)

a) The definition of, or guidelines for, an existing category is not suitable for Māori.

b) They do not have an existing category for certain word classes of Māori.

c) They do not reflect a Māori worldview of the Māori language.

We wanted a tagset that is usable with industry-wide tools, but we also needed a tagset that would meet the needs of te reo Māori. After researching various tagsets, we decided to base our tagset and guidelines on the UD tagset and tagging conventions. However, the categorization of words has been significantly altered to be appropriate for Māori. This is because at the time of development of our POS tagger, the UD conventions had still not been used to tag a Polynesian language such as te reo Māori, nor did it provide any guidelines about how to tag them.

Therefore the question arose as to how do we tag these words. Of course, we looked at how languages, other than the "big languages" such as English, were tagged. Yet, what works for other languages does not necessarily work for Māori. Furthermore, it would be a mistake to presume that the tagging solution for one Indigenous language should be applied to all Indigenous languages. As part of the re-Indigenization and decolonization, we do not homogenise Indigenous languages.

At this point, it is fitting to take a moment to digress and remind ourselves that at Te Hiku media our vision statement is *He reo tuku iho, he reo ora* which means *A living language transmitted intergenerationally*. This vision statement informs every decision that we make at every level. That means that it is of the utmost importance that we faithfully and accurately capture te reo Māori, as the language that has been passed down intergenerationally. In the same vein, we do not want to impose grammatical categories that are not correct or applicable.

To that end, we worked with highly-proficient, specially-selected Māori speakers and linguists who are specialists in Māori. This has ensured that our POS labels and guidelines conventions faithfully reflect a Māori speaker's conceptualization of their language.

We achieved this by simply asking speakers. We elicited answers without using questions that were influenced by academic theories of language or pedagogical methods of language teaching. The speakers reviewed our guidelines on a regular and consistent basis, they also partook in a survey to target special areas of interest. Furthermore, our guidelines are evergreen, meaning that they can and do change based on speaker feedback. This does not impact negatively on our tagged corpora as we have an automation system in place to retag words when necessary. We now briefly explore each point above in (2) seriatim.

2. Existing categories are not suitable for te reo Māori.

As mentioned above, some existing definitions and their guidelines for both syntactic categories and POS labels are not suitable for Māori.

The UD conventions follow a lexical approach, that is one-word equals one-tag. However, as mentioned previously, Māori is a highly analytic language in the sense that there are many words with multiple grammatical functions, as opposed to inflection. Sometimes a single concept is represented by many lexical words, see (3). Therefore we worked with our speakers to see when and where single or multiple labels were appropriate.

3)

Māori and POS label(s)				English
Kei te AUX				*present tense*
Mōku ADPRON				*for me*
He AUX	aha PRON	ai PART		*why*
I ADP	te DET	rā NOUN	nei DET	*today*

4) Ignoring white space between written words, in your mind is "i te rā nei"...

a) Made up of a single word "i te rā nei"

b) Made up of many separate words, "i", "te" and "rā" and "nei"

c) Other, please elaborate

We achieved this by asking non-leading questions. For example, in order to establish if the words of *i te rā nei*, meaning *today*, should receive a single or separate tags, we asked questions such as that in (4). If speakers had answered (a), then we could infer that *i te rā nei* should receive a single tag. On the other hand, if our speakers had answered (b), then the words should be tagged separately. We also left a blank space in (c) to allow our speakers to provide any other suggestions. As it happened, for time phrase adverbials with many lexical words such as *i te rā nei*, our speakers overwhelmingly chose to tag each word separately.

Crucially though, this was not the case for all concepts that were represented by many lexical words, as our speakers indicated that certain types should be tagged with a single word. As such, by working with our speakers we avoided making a blanket judgement and were able to give single or separate tags when and where appropriate, all according to the conceptualization of te reo Māori by speakers. Some developers of tagging guidelines for other languages choose a blanket approach for this type of problem. For example in the POS tagging of Griko, all apostrophes between words are treated as a single token, (Anastasopoulos et al, 2018). However this was not the right approach for us or te reo Māori, as evidenced by the fact that our speakers chose both single word and separate word tagging.

5)	Kua	hoko-na	e	au
	PFV	buy-PASS	ADP	1SG
	AUX	VERB	ADP	PRON

	he	whare
	DET	house
	DET	NOUN

"A house has been bought "

6)	Kua	whā	tau	au	ki
	PFV	four	year	1SG	ADP
	AUX	NUM	NOUN	PRON	ADP

Aotearoa
Aotearoa
PROPN

"I have been in Aotearoa for four years"

Lit: "Have been four years, I in Aotearoa"

Moving on, in example (5) tense is marked on the verb *hoko* with *kua*. The token *hoko* is given the POS tag VERB, and the separate tense-marker token *kua* is given the POS tag AUX. However, tense and aspect can also be marked on numbers in Māori, Harlow (2015: 256). This is the case in example (6) wherein *whā*, or *four*, is also marked with the perfect aspect marker *kua*. This is in the same way that verbs, such as *hoko* in (5) are tense-marked. This is not limited to te reo Maori, numbers that behave like verbs are also found in Choctaw and Jarawara (Dixon, 2012).

Whilst acknowledging that a number can be an "determiner, adjective or pronoun". The UD guidelines do not provide for numerals that behave like verbs. Yet, they state that verbs are often associated with "tense, mood" and "aspect". Therefore, under UD tagset guidelines, these numbers would likely be labelled as VERB.

Notwithstanding, tagging in this way would not be an accurate representation of te reo Māori. So as the POS gloss in (6) shows, we do not adhere to this. The tense-marked number token *whā* is tagged as numeral/NUM. Whilst, the separate tense-marker token *kua* is tagged as AUX .

3. Categories for certain word classes of Māori does not exist.

As stated above, UD conventions sometimes do not have a suitable existing category for certain classes of Māori words. Ergo, we have added POS labels that faithfully capture Māori, both the grammatical categories and the Māori view of te reo.

Māori has a word class commonly known as "particles" in linguistic literature, Harlow (2007: 24). These particles are small words such as *anō, iho, noa, pū, tonu* etc. Each particle can have meaning and many grammatical functions. Following our own analysis of over ninety particles, we found that grammatically they served many purposes, that their syntactic behaviour is wide, varied and commonplace. As such they do not fall under the remit of any "traditional" grammatical categories

For example, the "particle" *rawa* can modify nouns, pronouns, verbs, adjectives, numerals and negatives, (Harlow, 2015). We show a selection of these below. In example (7), *rawa* modifies the pronoun *koutou*. *Rawa* can also modify verbs like *hangaia* in (8), confirmation that verbal modification is taking place can be gleaned from the passive agreement that takes place on *rawatia*. The adjective *wera* is modified by *rawa* in (9). Whereas (10) and (11), show *rawa* modifying a negative and question word, i.e. *kāore* and *aha*, respectively.

7)	Mā	koutou	rawa	e
	ADP	3PL	MOD	TNS
	ADP	PRON	MOD	AUX

rangatira	te	kōrero
lead	DET.SG	discussion
VERB	DET	NOUN

"It is you who should lead the discussion"

8)

Hanga-ia	rawa-tia	he
build-PASS	MOD-PASS	DET.INDF
VERB	MOD	DET

whare	hou	mōna
house	new	ADP.3SG
NOUN	ADJ	ADPRON

"A new house was built especially for her"

9)

He	wera	rawa	te
PRED	hot	MOD	DET.SG
AUX	ADJ	MOD	DET

kai?
food
NOUN

"Is the food too hot?"

10)

Kāore	rawa	mātou	i	mōhio
NEG	MOD	3PL	PST	know
PART	MOD	PRON	AUX	VERB

"We really do not know"

11)

He	aha	rawa	te
PRED	what	MOD	DET.SG
AUX	PRON	MOD	DET

take?
reason
NOUN

"What is the reason?"

Of course, it is fair to ask why we did not use the UD POS tag "Particle", hereafter PART, for te reo Māori "particles". As per the UD guidelines, PART is said to often encode grammatical categories such as "negation, mood, tense", see UD guidelines, (References section below). However, crucially the "particles" of te reo Māori do not encode any of these categories. The UD PART tag is also a landing spot for words "that do not satisfy definitions of other universal parts of speech". For Indigenous or non-European languages, such as Māori, this in particular feels unsatisfactory. Rather than providing an accurate tag, anything that is deemed to fall outside of "universal" grammar is cast-off into the ambiguous PART category. Therefore, we chose to create a POS tag that would be fitting for this part of te reo Māori grammar. In a wider context, this fits with our vision statement mentioned above.

It should be noted however, that when and where the UD PART tag was applicable it was used and does appear in our tagset. This is the case for all the UD tags, we did not create new tags just for the sake of it. An example of the PART tag being used in our data is with te reo Māori words of negation, such as *kāore* in (10).

12)

Kāore	au	i	haere
NEG	1SG	PST	go
PART	PRON	AUX	VERB

"I did not go"

There is another class of words for which there is no suitable traditional label. When first-person singular, second-person singular and third-person singular pronouns, i.e. *ahau, koe* and *ia*, combine with certain adpositions, i.e. *tā, ā, tō, ō, mā* and *mō* they combine into a single word, (Bauer, 1997). These new combinations are concurrently both pronouns and adpositions. This can be seen in example (14) wherein *tō* and *ahau* have combined into *tōku*. By contrast, *tō* does not combine with *koutou* in (13).

13)

Me	hoki	au	ki
DEON	go_back	1SG	ADP
AUX	VERB	PRON	ADP

tō	koutou	whare
SG.POSS	3PL	house
ADP	PRON	NOUN

"I should go back to your house"

14)

Me	hoki	au	ki
DEON	go_back	1SG	ADP
AUX	VERB	PRON	ADP

tōku	whare
SG.POSS.1SG	house
ADPRON	NOUN

"I should go back go to my house"

These are not very common, but do occur in other languages, such as Irish, where they are commonly called *prepositional pronouns*. A UD Tagset that was developed for Irish simply tags these as preposition/PREP. Yet, this representation is not as accurate as it could be, they are at once both prepositions and pronouns in the grammar of Irish. Furthermore, the UD guidelines do not provide for such a word class.

With this in mind, we worked with our Māori speakers and linguists to faithfully capture and represent the equivalent te reo Māori word class. From working with our Māori speakers and linguists, it became clear that UD conventions do not have a suitable label for either "particles" or "adposition-pronouns". As such we created two new Māori specific labels for our tagset, i.e. modifier/MOD and adposition-pronoun/ADPRON.

4. Categories do not reflect a Māori worldview of the Māori language.

As has been said above, some UD conventions do not reflect a Māori worldview of the Māori language. For instance, the term Māori indicates Indigenous to Aotearoa. By contrast, *Pākehā* means of European origin, and *te reo Pākehā* is the Māori term for the English language. In our corpus, there are some instances of code-switching between Māori and English, and also between Māori and other Polynesian languages.

The UD guidelines recommend that foreign words receive the POS label "X", however this is problematic for us. Although the English language is not Indigenous to Aotearoa, to label English language words as "X" fails to capture the complex bi-cultural reality of modern-day Aotearoa. And to label other Polynesian languages as foreign disregards the historical, linguistic, cultural and genealogical ties among Pacific peoples. If we were to use "X" to tag all words that are not in te reo Māori, then English and other Polynesian languages would be conglomerated, or homogenised, into one group. Furthermore, it also limits the usefulness of our tagger for future applications where these languages are often mixed.

This resulted in the creation of two further Māori specific labels, Pākehā/PAKEHA for English language words, and MOANANUI for the cousin-languages of Māori. The creation of these Pākehā/PAKEHA and MOANANUI labels, allow us to distinguish other languages from te reo Māori, without disregarding the connections between the speakers of te reo Māori and other Polynesian languages.

The UD guidelines and tagsets have been used to tag languages where there is code-switching such as Turkish-German and Frisian-Dutch. It is our understanding that in such cases both languages are given UD tags. This approach would not work for us for two reasons. Firstly, as a small Māori Indigenous organisation, POS tagging English would not be a worthwhile use of our resources. Secondly, while we need to differentiate the other Polynesian languages from te reo Māori in our data, we would not create a tagset, nor presume to tag them without permission from the speakers of those languages.

In summation, the words in our Māori corpora have been categorised and labelled to reflect Māori in the minds of its speakers. At present, this same Māori lead approach is being expanded to include a feature layer that would include features relevant to Māori such as kupu mino and te reo ā-kāinga which are similar but different to loanwords and dialect respectively. Even at the most surface level of our tagging conventions, we do not use terms like dialect, when they are not appropriate to Maōri society.

5. Conclusion

Our tagset uses a total of 21 POS labels. They have been used to annotate our datasets, which contain over 40,000 tokens. The datasets cover many genres and are being constantly expanded. We have used our tagset and annotated datasets to build *Whakairo Kupu*, our POS tagger for te reo Māori. In our most recent *Whakairo Kupu* model, the precision was 92.5%, and the recall was 93.1%. These increased from 86.3% and 48.3% respectively in the very first model.

With regard to sharing our data, or allowing the use of Whakairo Kupu, Te Hiku Media operates under its *Kaitiakitanga* Licence. This quotation in (15) from our *Papa Reo* website best explains it. For more about the *Kaitiakitanga* Licence see our *Papa Reo* website (References section below).

15) Te Hiku Media have developed a Kaitiakitanga licence, which states that data is not owned but as cared for... Te Hiku Media are merely caretakers of the data and seek to ensure that all decisions made about the use of that data respect it's mana and that of the people from whom it descends...Māori data will not be openly released, but requests for access to the data, or for the use of the tools developed under the platform, will be managed using tikanga Māori.

In terms of applications for *Whakairo Kupu*, as it stands, not only does it POS tag te reo, but it has been used to build a grammar checker. It is also being used as a foundation for building a Named Entity Recognition tagger for te reo Māori.

6. References

Anastasopoulos, Antonis and Marika Lekakou, Josep Quer, Eleni Zimianiti, Justin DeBenedetto, David Chiang. 2018. *Part-of-Speech Tagging on an Endangered Language: a Parallel Griko-Italian Resource*. In Proceedings of the 27th

International Conference on Computational Linguistics, pages 2529–2539 Santa Fe, New Mexico, USA.

Bauer, Winifred. William Parker Te Kareongawai Evans, Te Aroha Noti Teepa. 1997. *The Reed Reference Grammar of Māori*. Auckland: Reed Books.

Dixon, R.M.W. *Basic Linguistic Theory 3*. Oxford: Oxford University Press.

Du Feu, V. 1996. Rapanui. London: Routledge

Harlow, Ray. 2007. *Māori A Linguistic Introduction*. Cambridge: Cambridge University Press.

Harlow, Ray. 2015. *A Māori Reference Grammar*. Wellington: Huia Publishers.

Morrison, Scotty. 2011. *The Raupō Phrasebook of Modern Māori*. Auckland: Penguin Group NZ

Te Hiku Media ~ PapaReo Kaitiakitanga License https://papareo.nz/#kaitiakitanga

7. Abbreviations

1	first-person	num	number
3	third-person	PART	particle
ADP	adposition	PASS	passive
ADPRON	adpositional -pronoun	PFV	perfect
AUX	auxiliary	PL	plural
DEON	deontic modality	POSS	possessum
DET	determiner	PRED	predicative
dir	directional	PRON	pronoun
INDF	indefinite	PST	past
MOD	modifier	SG	singular
NEG	negative	TNS	tense marker
NOUN	noun	VERB	verb

Challenges and Perspectives for Innu-Aimun within Indigenous Language Technologies

Antoine Cadotte
Université du Québec à Montréal
cadotte.antoine@courrier.uqam.ca

Ngoc Tan Le
Université du Québec à Montréal
le.ngoc_tan@uqam.ca

Mathieu Boivin
Université de Montréal
mathieu.boivin.2@umontreal.ca

Fatiha Sadat
Université du Québec à Montréal
sadat.fatiha@uqam.ca

Abstract

Innu-Aimun is an Algonquian language spoken in Eastern Canada. It is the language of the Innu, an indigenous people that now lives for the most part in a dozen communities across Quebec and Labrador. Although it is alive, Innu-Aimun sees important preservation and revitalization challenges and issues. The state of its technology is still nascent, with very few existing applications. This paper proposes a first survey of the available linguistic resources and existing technology for Innu-Aimun. Considering the existing linguistic and textual resources, we argue that developing language technology is feasible and propose first steps towards NLP applications like machine translation. The goal of developing such technologies is first and foremost to help efforts in improving language transmission and cultural safety and preservation for Innu-Aimun speakers, as those are considered urgent and vital issues. Finally, we discuss the importance of close collaboration and consultation with the Innu community in order to ensure that language technologies are developed respectfully and in accordance with that goal.

1 Introduction

In 2016, there were over 70 different indigenous languages in Canada, which together cumulated 260,550 speakers[1], for a total country population of 35,151,728[2]. This number of indigenous language speakers shows how light their demographic weight is, considering the length of indigenous people's presence throughout the country. Yet this number also hides important disparities between indigenous languages. While Cree, spoken in four of the country's provinces, counts over 96,000 speakers, other languages like Haida are only spoken by a few hundreds[3].

In this paper, we examine one specific indigenous language, spoken in Quebec and Labrador, Innu-Aimun (ISO code moe [4], Glottolog mont1268[5]). Like the aforementioned languages, its presence in the country's linguistic landscape is fragile, especially compared to the official languages (English and French). While linguistic resources do exist for Innu-Aimun, the development of its language technology and NLP applications is almost inexistent.

Our contributions to the current research consist in two main parts: (1) a survey of Innu-Aimun linguistic resources and technology, followed by (2) discussions and perspectives concerning how to develop Innu-Aimun language technology and the role it could have for the community.

The structure of this paper is described as follows: Section 2 describes Innu-Aimun and its linguistic situation, and surveys the available linguistic resources and technologies. Section 3 addresses the question of how Innu-Aimun language technology should be developed, including the importance of collaboration with the community, examining language-related social issues and discussing what role technology could have to help on these issues. Section 4 provides some ideas for short term and longer term developments, focusing on short term development perspectives and how they could be carried out. Finally, Section 5 concludes this paper and suggests future directions for further research.

2 Language Description and Survey

2.1 Innu-Aimun language

Innu-Aimun is a language spoken by the Innu, an indigenous people of Canada, formerly known as Montagnais (Mollen, 2006). It is a polysynthetic

[1] Statistics Canada: The Aboriginal languages of First Nations people, Métis and Inuit

[2] Statistics Canada: Census Profile, 2016 Census

[3] Statistics Canada: The Aboriginal languages of First Nations people, Métis and Inuit

[4] ISO 639-3 - moe

[5] Glottolog - mont1268

Proceedings of the Fifth Workshop on the Use of Computational Methods in the Study of Endangered Languages, pages 99 - 108
May 26-27, 2022

language and part of the Algonquian language family and of the Cree-Innu-Naskapi dialect continuum (Drapeau, 2014b). In 2017, the number of speakers was estimated at 12,000, spread over a dozen communities (Baraby et al., 2017).

As noted by Baraby et al. (2017), Innu-Aimun is "[...] alive but still fragile". Its state of preservation can be seen as part of the broader situation of indigenous languages in Canada. Generally speaking there is a transfer to the majority language (English in general, French mostly in the case of Innu) and indigenous language fluency is lower in younger age groups than in older ones (Drapeau, 2011). In some Innu communities, lexical erosion has been observed due to the high rate of bilingualism among speakers (Drapeau, 2014a).

Originally an oral language with several dialects, Innu-Aimun had its orthography standardized in 1989 (Mollen, 2006). This standardization work, done through a consultation between representatives of the different dialects, concerns only the written language; the differences in pronunciation between dialects remain (Mollen, 2006). The standard Innu-Aimun orthography is based on the Latin alphabet and includes a special character: the "superscript-u". This character has its own unicode code point [6], which has been incorporated in a keyboard developed specifically for Innu-Aimun [7].

2.2 Existing Innu-Aimun Resources and Technological Applications

While several linguistics resources are available, there are very few technological applications for Innu-Aimun. These were developed primarily for educational and language preservation purposes. This section describes existing linguistic resources for Innu-Aimun and applications that are part of a joint development effort with Cree language.

2.2.1 Primary linguistic resources

Despite its significant preservation challenges, Innu-Aimun is one of the best documented indigenous languages in Canada, and its documentation has become more technology-based in recent years (Baraby et al., 2017). Among the primary linguistic resources is the *Innu Grammar* (*Grammaire de la langue innue*) by Drapeau (2014b), which describes in detail many aspects of the Innu-Aimun grammatical structures.

The 1991 *Montagnais-French Dictionnary* (*Dictionnaire Montagnais-français*) by Drapeau (1991) was the first to use the standardized orthography (Mollen, 2006). The most up-to-date published dictionary available is the *Innu-French Dictionary* (2016, second edition) which includes more than 28,000 Innu-Aimun words [8]. However, an online version of this dictionary is available[9] and it is regularly expanded with new words (this tool is further discussed in the following section).

For conjugation, the guide *Conjugation of Innu verbs* (*Conjugaison des verbes innus*) by Baraby and Junker (2011) is available as a Website [10]. This guide is based on the work started with *Guide pratique des principales conjugaisons en montagnais* (Baraby, 1998) which has since been updated.

2.2.2 Integrated Web tools and Search Engine

With *Integrated Web tools for Innu language maintenance*, Junker et al. (2016) presented a series of Web tools intended primarily for bilingual speakers of Innu-Aimun and whose main goal was the preservation of the language. These included language learning games, several basic language resources (grammars, lexicons, etc.), a catalog of works in Innu-Aimun (including educational books, children's stories, etc.), an online dictionary and a verb conjugation application.

The verb conjugation application, developed by Baraby and Junker (2011), organizes verbs with respect to Innu-Aimun conjugation structure and includes audio clips for the pronunciation in the eastern and western dialects. The trilingual, pan-dialectal online dictionary (mentioned in the previous section) structures search results with respect to the Innu-Aimun morphology. Table 1 shows examples of entries from the Innu-Aimun-English part of dictionary. The dictionary uses the orthographic flexibility of the Innu-Aimun search engine developed by Junker and Stewart (2008).

In *Building search engines for Algonquian languages*, Junker and Stewart (2008) developed a search engine for East Cree (an Algonquian language related to Innu-Aimun) and then adapted it to Innu-Aimun. The authors' work consists of two parts: flexible orthographic search and verb search. The flexible orthographic search aims to solve different spellings problem for the same word, as the recent standardization of spelling, the existence of

[6] *Innu-Aimun.ca* - Writing and Technology (in French)

[7] Keyboard layout for Ilnu/Innu Aimun

[8] Tshakapesh Institute - *Dictionnaire Innu-Français*

[9] `https://dictionary.innu-aimun.ca/`

[10] `https://verbe.innu-aimun.ca`

Main verb (English)	Examples of bilingual entries	
	Innu-Aimun	English
see	eukuan	oh yeah!, I see!
	tepapameu	s/he has seen enough of him/her
	unapatam^u	s/he is mistaken about what s/he sees; s/he loses sight of it
make	tutam^u	s/he makes it
	tutamueu	s/he makes it for someone

Table 1: Example entries from the Innu-English online dictionary (Junker et al., 2016)

several dialects and the predominance of oral language mean that users will often look for a word with a different orthography than the standard one. The verb search component consists of a flexible search in a database of verbal paradigms, which identifies the most likely root and reconstructs the verb in its standard form. This aims to solve a challenge arising from the different forms of verb inflections in Cree and Innu-Aimun, as users can search for verbs in their non-canonical form.

Hasler et al. (2018) proposed an online terminology forum for multiple Algonquian languages, including Innu-Aimun, in order to provide translations and definitions for specialized terms in several fields such as healthcare, justice or environment. The forum is a tool for collaborative terminology development, with participation from communities and review from translators.

2.3 Existing Innu-Aimun digitized resources

To our knowledge, there is no publicly available annotated or aligned Innu-Aimun corpora, and few research works report on this subject. There exists however a certain amount of publicly available monolingual, bilingual and trilingual Innu-Aimun digitized texts.

2.3.1 Transcription and linguistic annotation

Citing the lack of linguistic documentation despite its importance to the preservation of the language, Drapeau and Lambert-Brétière (2013) presented a project to create and make available a corpus of linguistically analyzed Innu-Aimun texts. The corpus was built through the segmentation and transcription of oral recordings in standard orthography. The text analysis includes morphological segmentation and translation into French and English. The result is a multimodal, multilingual annotated Innu-Aimun corpus.

Kuhn et al. (2020) presented the language technology project by NRC Canada and its collaborators. This project aims to transcribe oral recordings for several indigenous languages in Canada, including Innu-Aimun.

2.3.2 Multilingual textual resources

The Tshakapesh Institute has an online catalog offering many texts in Innu-Aimun. This includes pedagogical books (primary and preschool), stories for children, novels, poetry, non-fiction and other types of works[11]. However, many of these texts are available only in non-digitized versions.

The publishing house *Mémoire d'encrier*, publishes bilingual Innu-Aimun-French works, such as novels (notably reeditions of works by Innu author An Antane Kapesh[12]) and collections of poems (notably by the Innu poet Joséphine Bacon[13]). Some of those titles are also published in bilingual Innu-Aimun-English versions[14]; those can thus be considered as trilingual Innu-Aimun-French-English texts.

On rarer occasions, texts in multiple indigenous languages are made available. The FNQLSDI (First Nations of Quebec and Labrador Sustainable Development Institute) produces documents in 6 languages including English, French, Innu-Aimun and other indigenous languages such as East Cree, and sometimes up to 12 languages [15].

[11]Tshakapesh Institute - Catalogue

[12]Mémoire d'encrier - An Antane Kapesh

[13]Mémoire d'encrier - Joséphine Bacon

[14]For example: Mawenzi House - *Message Sticks (Tshissinuatshitakana)*

[15]FNQLSDI - Multilingual books

3 Discussion: How Should Technology Be Developed for Innu-Aimun?

3.1 The imperative of respecting and collaborating with the community

Social and ethical aspects are of particularly great importance when it comes to practicing research involving indigenous languages in Canada. This should be emphasized not only considering the precarious situation of these languages, but also—and most importantly—in light of the well documented historical prejudices and subsisting societal issues indigenous communities have been subjected to. This includes the appalling legacy of the Indian Residential Schools system, as documented by the Truth and Reconciliation Commission of Canada[16]. Such considerations are crucial for indigenous languages in Canada in general and they should absolutely be kept in mind for Innu-Aimun language technology development.

As per the directives of the Social Sciences and Humanities Research Council (SSHRC) of Canada, "Whatever the methodologies or perspectives that apply in a given context, researchers who conduct indigenous research, whether they are indigenous or non-indigenous themselves, commit to respectful relationships with all indigenous peoples and communities."[17]

Indigenous research should as much as possible be done *by and for* the community. In the case of indigenous language technology development, this takes an even greater significance as such research aims first and foremost to have a concrete positive impact indigenous communities. Language technologies must address in their development the needs as well as the concerns of the community they serve.

If the developed technologies result in tools intended as applications with end users, evaluation of the technologies by members of the community should be a key component of a collaborative development. In the case of indigenous languages in Canada, an example of such an evaluation for a precise language is the one carried by Bontogon (2016) for a Plains Cree computer-aided language learning tool (CALL).

[16] Truth and Reconciliation Commission of Canada

[17] Social Sciences and Humanities Research Council - Definition of Terms, indigenous Research

3.2 Language and social issues

Among the most urgent linguistic issues expressed by some community members[18] is the need for better and safer interactions between Innu and health and social workers, as well as in the educational and justice systems. In the latter, ensuring the clarity of interactions with an indigenous person, by using an interpreter if need be, is not only important but a legal obligation, as described by Newashish and Boivin (2019).

Language plays an important role in culturally safe communications with health workers, as discussed by Møller (2016) in their study of language for nursing in Nunavut and Greenland. Cultural safety overall has been identified as important to ensure safe interactions with health workers: if interactions between indigenous patients and health workers are not adequate, this can lead to potentially disastrous situations like death, as has been recently concluded by a coroner inquiry following the death of an indigenous patient in Canada[19].

The Viens Commission final report[20] mentions that 54% of indigenous people in Quebec live in cities rather than in indigenous communities and that this makes access to services in their language all the more difficult. The need to improve the relation and interactions between Innu and non-indigenous in urban context has also been identified as an important matter by Leroux (2014) when examining cohabitation within Sept-Îles: difference in native language between non-indigenous and Innu is considered to play a role in the divide between the two.

The Innu-Aimun language is an integral part of Innu identity and this makes language preservation all the more important. As highlighted by Leroux (2014) through her interviews with Innu community members, the attempted assimilation of the Innu people to the dominant non-indigenous society is still profoundly felt and has had an impact on transmission of the language.

According to one Innu-Aimun teacher from the Uashat mak Mani-utenam community, with whom we exchanged, the language is highly endangered. Rare are the students that properly master their mother tongue and French dominates in day-to-day interactions. Not enough time in the curriculum,

[18] ITUM (Innu Takuaikan Uashat mak Mani-utenam) - Council of Uashat mak Mani-utenam

[19] Investigation Report on the Death of Joyce Echaquan (in French)

[20] Final report of the Viens Commission (in French)

she says, is allocated to teaching Innu-Aimun and preserving the language should overall be considered as a more pressing societal concern.

3.3 NLP and Innu-Aimun revitalization

As stated earlier, research in Innu-Aimun language technologies should first address the priorities and needs of the Innu communities, as expressed by them. For that matter, consultation with the community is a key part of such research. In this section, we offer ideas of roles Innu-Aimun language technology could play, as a first step towards further consulting the community—should it be to validate these ideas or to stimulate discussion on the matter and encourage other ideas.

Language preservation is a role commonly projected onto indigenous language technologies. We indeed believe language technologies could help preserve Innu-Aimun by acting as educational tools to native speakers and by acting as technologically-oriented language documentation. From the existing tools like online bilingual dictionaries to potential developments like machine translation, conversational agents and learning assistants, we think language technology could help support native speakers learn their language or improve their knowledge of it, and especially so in a context of prevailing bilingualism.

Some community members have said in discussions we held with them that in their view, an even more important role language technology could play is that of raising awareness and understanding within non-indigenous people. It is believed that gaining better knowledge of Innu-Aimun could help better raise awareness and understand Innu realities, which is of great importance for reconciliation. This becomes even more crucial for non-indigenous workers that interact with the community, as is often the case in the health and education sectors. When it comes to interactions in the context of health and education services, ensuring language knowledge becomes a matter of cultural safety. This need has already been recognized and some steps have been taken, like the recent creation of a program for translation and interpretation to and from Innu-Aimun [21]. We think the development of cross-lingual Innu-Aimun technologies is in line with those efforts and could be of great help to ensure cultural safety.

[21] Sept-Îles Cégep launches an Innu language translation program (in French)

4 Perspectives: Innu-Aimun and NLP

In light of the discussed roles for Innu-Aimun language technology, we present here our proposed vision for potential technological developments in collaboration with the ITUM group[22]. This vision is divided into two more accessible developments in the short term and two longer term developments.

4.1 Short term

4.1.1 Towards a first machine translation system

We consider machine translation could be a useful tool to the Innu community, both for language learning and to assist professional translators and teachers. On the language learning side, machine translation could serve as an extension or an enhancement of bilingual dictionaries. When it comes to forming Innu-Aimun words that correctly grasp the desired context, automated sentence translation could prove useful and machine translation can help reach that goal. On translation assistance, we concur with the view brought by Littell et al. (2018): that a general-purpose system like Google Translate is probably not achievable with the current state of resources and that translation assistance is a more accessible goal. Such an approach would also be more empowering for the community as it would aim to assist rather than replace Innu translators.

4.1.1.1 Parallel corpora

With the publicly available bilingual and trilingual Innu-Aimun texts, it is certainly possible to create experimental Innu-Aimun-French and Innu-Aimun-English parallel corpora. Some of the bilingual works mentioned earlier are only available in paper, while some are available in ebook and PDF formats. Naturally, books available in paper only would require a significant amount of work in order to be rendered usable as parallel data, as it would involve scanning the documents and using OCR (Optical Character Recognition) methods in order to obtain workable text. Considering only Innu-Aimun-French bilingual texts that are easily obtainable as ebook or PDF, we estimate that at least 3000 parallel Innu-Aimun-French sentences could be collectable with minimal effort. Such a

[22] ITUM (Innu Takuaikan Uashat mak Mani-utenam) - the council of Uashat mak Mani-utenam

small number of examples might not be enough to train an Innu-Aimun-specific translation model, but it could be put to contribution using machine learning techniques that are better adapted to low-resource or zero-shot settings and that harness data from other languages, as discussed in the following section.

Table 2 examines three bilingual corpora for the Innu-Aimun and French language pair: FNQLSDI books[23], Mémoire d'encrier poetry[24] and Mémoire d'encrier novels & essays[25]. The number of parallel sentences is an approximation and it might vary following proper alignment. Also in this table is the vocabulary size for each corpus and the percentage of words from this vocabulary that are absent from the most complete Innu-Aimun dictionary available [26]. We can observe that in all three cases, a very high proportion of the words found on the Innu-Aimun side (82-87%) are out-of-dictionary. Some of the out-of-dictionary words are simply proper nouns or words borrowed from other languages (e.g. French). But the main explanation probably resides in the polysynthetic nature of the language: as morphemes agglutinate to form longer words, a high proportion of the words will be in fact found in an inflected form that is not present in the dictionary. This observation also serves as a reminder of the importance of segmentation for the development of machine translation for Innu-Aimun.

The Innu-Aimun-French dictionary itself could be put to use as parallel data for Machine Translation. The 28K+ words and definitions found in the dictionary could probably not be counted as so many parallel sentences. But since many of these words are provided with translations that are as long as a sentence due to their high morphology, the parallel data found in the Innu-Aimun dictionary is certainly more useful to machine translation than that found in traditional bilingual dictionaries (where translation is usually provided as single corresponding words).

Since recent NMT (Neural Machine Translation) methods using auxiliary, higher-resourced languages have shown positive results for low-resource language pairs, even when the languages are unrelated (see Section 4.1.1.2), it is appropriate to survey other indigenous languages in Canada, with regard to their proximity and the availability of training data.

While the availability of open parallel corpora (and training data in general) is a major challenge for most indigenous languages in Canada, such a corpus has been published for the Inuktitut-English language pair and has made possible the development of machine translation models (Littell et al., 2018). This corpus contains in its third and latest version over 1.4 million pairs of aligned Inuktitut-English sentences, all collected from the proceedings of the Nunavut Hansard which is published in both languages (Joanis et al., 2020). This, according to the authors, constitutes the largest publicly available parallel corpus for a polysynthetic language.

Atikamekw, another indigenous language of Canada that belongs to the same family as Innu-Aimun (Algonquian languages) has a wikimedia project[27], which could help construct comparable corpora for these category of languages and thus enrich a multilingual neural machine translation framework. In addition, some of the FNQLSDI books available in Innu-Aimun are also available in Atikamekw, as well as in East Cree .

4.1.1.2 Applying methods for extremely low-resource language pairs

A large variety of methods have been proposed in different contexts to improve neural machine translation results for low-resource language pairs, as recent surveys show (Wang et al., 2021; Haddow et al., 2021). Several of these methods involve making use of data from auxiliary languages (such as transfer learning, multilingual modelling and others). Keeping in mind that the main goal of first experiments in machine translation is to assess feasibility, we focus here on the methods that allow the direct use of the parallel resources that have been mentioned so far.

Multilingual modelling, which aims at harnessing the most of many languages by sharing parameters between them, has shown good results for low-resource language pairs. This is done by Johnson et al. (2017), which show that it is possible to improve results for lower-resourced languages by combining them into a single model along with higher-resourced language pairs (with a total of 12 pairs). More recent contributions push

[23] FNQLSDI - Multilingual books
[24] Mémoire d'encrier - Joséphine Bacon
[25] Mémoire d'encrier - An Antane Kapesh
[26] Innu-Aimun online dictionary

[27] https://atj.wikipedia.org/wiki/Otitikowin

Corpus	Number of parallel sentences	Innu-Aimun vocabulary size	% of out-of-dictionary words
FNQLSDI books	1,450	4,453	87%
Mémoire d'encrier poetry	110	1,558	82%
Mémoire d'encrier novels & essays	1,670	4,170	87%

Table 2: Parallel Innu-Aimun - French corpora

the number of languages much higher and label the method "massively multilingual modelling". Aharoni et al. (2019) for example train models in one-to-many and many-to-one settings combining 102 languages and many-to-many models combining 59 languages. They improve previous results for low-resource pairs and show that adding more languages improves zero-shot performances, but point-out there exists a trade-off between the number of languages and overall translation performance, especially for higher-resourced pairs.

The goal of keeping a better performance for all language pairs in a multilingual model does not apply to our proposed experiments for Innu-Aimun translation: if adding more languages helps improve results for our low-resourced target language pairs, then there is no incentive not do so. Furthermore, recent results suggest that transfer learning can even be beneficial to unrelated languages that have different alphabets (Kocmi and Bojar, 2018).

Another method of interest is meta-learning, which Gu et al. (2018) applied on low-resource machine translation. They show meta-learning can significantly improve translation results for lower-resourced pairs, especially in zero-shot situations or when training with few examples.

4.1.2 Developing a morphological segmenter

We take the view that one of the first steps to take for Innu-Aimun language technology development is to consolidate and expand building blocks that are considered part of a basic language toolkit, as described for Plains Cree by Arppe et al. (2016). These building blocks, like lexical databases, written corpora and transcriptors, are not only important technological tools for languages but also form the basis for more advanced developments.

A fundamental building block to develop for Innu-Aimun is automated morphological segmentation. As stated earlier, the polysynthetic nature of Innu-Aimun makes some of its words equivalent to whole sentences in Indo-European languages. This trait makes the use of morphological segmentation almost inevitable for applications like machine translation, as described for Inuktitut and Inuinnaqtun, other indigenous languages in Canada (Le and Sadat, 2020b, 2021).

In the absence of a language-specific segmentation model, some unsupervised methods (i.e. learning methods that do not require annotated data) allow the training of a model using solely monolingual data from the target language. This is the case of the BPE (*Byte Pair Encoding*) method proposed for segmentation by Sennrich et al. (2016), which merges most frequent pairs of characters or n-grams (i.e. sequences of items like words, syllables, letters, etc.) found in the text to construct a subword vocabulary for the targeted language. However, such a method does not replace a language-specific segmentation model. For example, Le and Sadat (2020a) improve the translation results obtained by Joanis et al. (2020) on their Nunavut Hansard Inuktitut-English corpus by proposing their own Inuktitut-specific segmentation model.

A logical step to develop an Innu-specific segmentation model is to adapt to Innu-Aimun the Plains Cree FST model proposed by Snoek et al. (2014). The authors consider their model to be adaptable to other Algonquian languages, since the language structure would be similar. Another similar approach would be to use the same development method used by Snoek et al. (2014) and Harrigan et al. (2017) for Plains Cree or by Arppe et al. (2017) for East Cree, in order to develop an FST model specific to Innu.

Another possible approach for Innu-Aimun automated segmentation is the semi-supervised method, as used by Le and Sadat (2021) to develop their segmentation model for Inuinnaqtun (an endangered indigenous language of Canada). Semi-supervised methods are usually hybrid approaches that combine unsupervised methods with the use of available annotated data. In the case of Le and Sadat (2021), the proposed approach uses the Adaptor Grammars based framework by Eskander et al. (2020), which can learn a model based on a list of unsegmented words using grammar rules. These rules can also include a list of morphemes from the target language.

The semi-supervised approach is promising in the Innu-Aimun context, since enough linguistic documentation exists to define general grammar patterns as done by Le and Sadat (2021) and since a list of Innu-Aimun words and morphemes could be collected from the available dictionaries and verb conjugators. Counting the number of unique Innu-Aimun words currently found in the Innu-Aimun online dictionnary, combined with the words found the corpora analyzed in Table 2, a vocabulary size of 34K can be obtained and put to use in semi-supervised automated segmentation methods.

4.2 Longer term

4.2.1 Cross-lingual conversational agent

We propose the longer term development of a cross-lingual conversational agent whose primary purpose would be to act as an intelligent language tutor. This can be seen as being in line with the existing interactive learning games, proposed as part of the integrated web tools by Junker et al. (2016). First steps in the construction of the agent would involve collecting a Question-Answering dataset within educational and health groups/centers in Innu communities. Such a tool would assist not only native speakers in their learning of Innu-Aimun, but also non-native speakers in their communication and understanding of the communities' culture and realities. It could play a positive role especially for beginner-level learners and in contexts where access to an Innu-Aimun teacher is problematic—which is the case especially outside communities.

4.2.2 Automatic Innu-Aimun multimodal machine translation

As stated earlier, standardization of Innu-Aimun orthography is relatively recent (since 1989) (Mollen, 2006). This means many community members learned the language before the standardization occurred. Automated transcription could bridge the gap between how speakers use their language and how orthography-based tools function.

Among indigenous languages in Canada, an attempt was made with the development of an ASR (Automatic Speech Recognition) system for Inuktitut (Gupta and Boulianne, 2020). This project aimed to automatically transcribe Inuktitut and used 23 hours of transcribed Inuktitut oral stories to build an acoustic model.

However, relying on voice-based technologies brings significant challenges. Due to lack of data, dialect variances, and other restrictions, it is difficult to create strong ASR systems for indigenous languages (Jimerson and Prud'hommeaux, 2018). In the case of Innu-Aimun, not only is the writing far from its pronunciation, but the existence of multiple dialects means there are multiple ways to pronounce, depending on the region or community, as mentionned by Mollen (2006).

Despite significant challenges, developing multimodal systems would help to better represent cultural and ancestral data through voice—considering that Innu-Aimun is traditionally an oral language Mollen (2006). Fortunately, in the last few years, there have been efforts to digitise content in Innu-Aimun, both in text and in audio format, as stated in section 2.2.

5 Conclusion

Despite substantial challenges ahead, like the limited amount of resources available or the complexity of the language, we consider the development of more advanced Innu-Aimun technology to be feasible. We also consider such a development to be important, in view of the very real social issues related to Innu-Aimun. We believe language technologies like machine translation could be useful in the efforts to ensure language transmission and improve cultural safety in services. The first steps we proposed in this article, besides their goal of demonstrating feasibility, will help better understand the difficulties in processing Innu-Aimun texts and building technological modules like morphological and translation models. This will allow defining further steps towards the longer term goals like intelligent tutors, conversational agents and automatic transcription.

Acknowledgements

The authors are grateful to the community of Uashat Mak Mani-Utenam, Samuel Marticotte for his role in initiating this project, Mrs. Denise Jourdain for sharing her knowledge and experience, and Prof. Yvette Mollen for her precious advices and feedbacks. We also thank the anonymous reviewers for their valuable comments. This work has been partially supported by the The Centre for Research on Brain, Language and Music (CRBLM).

References

Roee Aharoni, Melvin Johnson, and Orhan Firat. 2019. Massively multilingual neural machine translation. In *Proceedings of the 2019 Conference of the North American Chapter of the Association for Computational Linguistics: Human Language Technologies, Volume 1 (Long and Short Papers)*, pages 3874–3884, Minneapolis, Minnesota. Association for Computational Linguistics.

Antti Arppe, Marie-Odile Junker, and Delasie Torkornoo. 2017. Converting a comprehensive lexical database into a computational model: The case of East Cree verb inflection. In *Proceedings of the 2nd Workshop on the Use of Computational Methods in the Study of Endangered Languages*, pages 52–56, Honolulu. Association for Computational Linguistics.

Antti Arppe, Jordan Lachler, Trond Trosterud, Lene Antonsen, and Sjur N. Moshagen. 2016. Basic Language Resource Kits for Endangered Languages: A Case Study of Plains Cree. In *Proceedings of the LREC 2016 Workshop "CCURL 2016 – Towards an Alliance for Digital Language Diversity"*, pages 1–8, Portorož (Slovenia).

Anne-Marie Baraby. 1998. Guide pratique des principales conjugaisons en Montagnais. *Sept-Iles: Institut culturel et éducatif montagnais.*

Anne-Marie Baraby and Marie-Odile Junker. 2011. Conjugaisons des verbes innus.

Anne-Marie Baraby, Marie-Odile Junker, and Yvette Mollen. 2017. A 45-year old language documentation program first aimed at speakers: the case of the Innu.

Megan A. Bontogon. 2016. *Evaluating nêhiyawêtân: A computer assisted language learning (CALL) application for Plains Cree.* Ph.D. thesis, University of Alberta.

L. Drapeau. 2011. *Les langues autochtones du Québec: Un patrimoine en danger.* Presses de l'Université du Québec.

Lynn Drapeau. 1991. *Dictionnaire montagnais-français.* Presses de l'Université du Québec.

Lynn Drapeau. 2014a. Bilinguisme et érosion lexicale dans une communauté montagnaise. In Pierre Martel and Jacques Maurais, editors, *Langues et sociétés en contact: Mélanges offerts à Jean-Claude Corbeil*, pages 363–376. Max Niemeyer Verlag.

Lynn Drapeau. 2014b. *Grammaire de la langue innue.* Presses de l'Université du Québec.

Lynn Drapeau and Renée Lambert-Brétière. 2013. The innu language documentation project. In *Proceedings of the 17th Foundation for Endangered Languages Conference.*

Ramy Eskander, Francesca Callejas, Elizabeth Nichols, Judith Klavans, and Smaranda Muresan. 2020. MorphAGram, evaluation and framework for unsupervised morphological segmentation. In *Proceedings of the 12th Language Resources and Evaluation Conference*, pages 7112–7122, Marseille, France. European Language Resources Association.

Jiatao Gu, Yong Wang, Yun Chen, Victor O. K. Li, and Kyunghyun Cho. 2018. Meta-learning for low-resource neural machine translation. In *Proceedings of the 2018 Conference on Empirical Methods in Natural Language Processing*, pages 3622–3631, Brussels, Belgium. Association for Computational Linguistics.

Vishwa Gupta and Gilles Boulianne. 2020. Automatic transcription challenges for inuktitut, a low-resource polysynthetic language. In *Proceedings of the 12th language resources and evaluation conference*, pages 2521–2527.

Barry Haddow, Rachel Bawden, Antonio Valerio Miceli Barone, Jindřich Helcl, and Alexandra Birch. 2021. Survey of low-resource machine translation.

Atticus G. Harrigan, Katherine Schmirler, Antti Arppe, Lene Antonsen, Trond Trosterud, and Arok Wolvengrey. 2017. Learning from the computational modelling of Plains Cree verbs. *Morphology*, 27(4):565–598.

Laurel Anne Hasler, Marie-Odile Junker, Marguerite MacKenzie, Mimie Neacappo, and Delasie Torkornoo. 2018. The Online Terminology Forum for East Cree and Innu: A collaborative approach to multiformat terminology development. In *LD&C Special Publication No. 20: Collaborative Approaches to the Challenges of Language Documentation and Conservation.* University of Hawai'i Press.

Robbie Jimerson and Emily Prud'hommeaux. 2018. Asr for documenting acutely under-resourced indigenous languages. In *Proceedings of the Eleventh International Conference on Language Resources and Evaluation (LREC 2018).*

Eric Joanis, Rebecca Knowles, Roland Kuhn, Samuel Larkin, Patrick Littell, Chi-kiu Lo, Darlene Stewart, and Jeffrey Micher. 2020. The Nunavut Hansard Inuktitut–English parallel corpus 3.0 with preliminary machine translation results. In *Proceedings of the 12th Language Resources and Evaluation Conference*, pages 2562–2572, Marseille, France. European Language Resources Association.

Melvin Johnson, Mike Schuster, Quoc V. Le, Maxim Krikun, Yonghui Wu, Zhifeng Chen, Nikhil Thorat, Fernanda Viégas, Martin Wattenberg, Greg Corrado, Macduff Hughes, and Jeffrey Dean. 2017. Google's multilingual neural machine translation system: Enabling zero-shot translation. *Transactions of the Association for Computational Linguistics*, 5:339–351.

Marie-Odile Junker, Yvette Mollen, Hélène St-Onge, and Delasie Torkornoo. 2016. Integrated web tools for Innu language maintenance. In *Papers of the 44th Algonquian Conference*, pages 192–210.

Marie-Odile Junker and Terry Stewart. 2008. Building search engines for Algonquian languages. *Algonquian Papers-Archive*, 39.

Tom Kocmi and Ondřej Bojar. 2018. Trivial transfer learning for low-resource neural machine translation. In *Proceedings of the Third Conference on Machine Translation: Research Papers*, pages 244–252, Brussels, Belgium. Association for Computational Linguistics.

Roland Kuhn, Fineen Davis, Alain Désilets, Eric Joanis, Anna Kazantseva, Rebecca Knowles, Patrick Littell, Delaney Lothian, Aidan Pine, Caroline Running Wolf, Eddie Santos, Darlene Stewart, Gilles Boulianne, Vishwa Gupta, Brian Maracle Owennatékha, Akwiratékha' Martin, Christopher Cox, Marie-Odile Junker, Olivia Sammons, Delasie Torkornoo, Nathan Thanyehténhas Brinklow, Sara Child, Benoît Farley, David Huggins-Daines, Daisy Rosenblum, and Heather Souter. 2020. The Indigenous Languages Technology project at NRC Canada: An empowerment-oriented approach to developing language software. In *Proceedings of the 28th International Conference on Computational Linguistics*, pages 5866–5878, Barcelona, Spain (Online). International Committee on Computational Linguistics.

Tan Ngoc Le and Fatiha Sadat. 2020a. Low-resource NMT: an empirical study on the effect of rich morphological word segmentation on Inuktitut. In *Proceedings of the 14th Conference of the Association for Machine Translation in the Americas (Volume 1: Research Track)*, pages 165–172, Virtual. Association for Machine Translation in the Americas (AMTA 2020).

Tan Ngoc Le and Fatiha Sadat. 2020b. Revitalization of indigenous languages through pre-processing and neural machine translation: The case of Inuktitut. In *Proceedings of the 28th International Conference on Computational Linguistics*, pages 4661–4666, Barcelona, Spain (Online). International Committee on Computational Linguistics (COLING 2020).

Tan Ngoc Le and Fatiha Sadat. 2021. Towards a first automatic unsupervised morphological segmentation for Inuinnaqtun. In *Proceedings of the First Workshop on Natural Language Processing for Indigenous Languages of the Americas*, pages 159–162, Online. Association for Computational Linguistics (NAACL 2021).

Shanie Leroux. 2014. Le point de vue des innus de sept-Îles, uashat et maliotenam sur les relations entre autochtones et allochtones en milieu urbain : vers une concitoyenneté. *Nouvelles pratiques sociales*, 27(1):64–77.

Patrick Littell, Anna Kazantseva, Roland Kuhn, Aidan Pine, Antti Arppe, Christopher Cox, and Marie-Odile Junker. 2018. Indigenous language technologies in Canada: Assessment, challenges, and successes. In *Proceedings of the 27th International Conference on Computational Linguistics*, pages 2620–2632, Santa Fe, New Mexico, USA. Association for Computational Linguistics.

Yvette Mollen. 2006. Transmettre un héritage: la langue innue. *Cap-aux-Diamants: la revue d'histoire du Québec*, 1(85):21–25. Publisher: Les Éditions Cap-aux-Diamants inc.

Helle Møller. 2016. Culturally safe communication and the power of language in arctic nursing. *Études/Inuit/Studies*, 40(1):85–104.

Maggie Newashish and Mathieu Boivin. 2019. Interprétation judiciaire atikamekw : ce que c'est; ce qu'il reste à faire... *Histoire Québec*, 24(4):12–14.

Rico Sennrich, Barry Haddow, and Alexandra Birch. 2016. Neural machine translation of rare words with subword units. In *Proceedings of the 54th Annual Meeting of the Association for Computational Linguistics (Volume 1: Long Papers)*, pages 1715–1725, Berlin, Germany. Association for Computational Linguistics.

Conor Snoek, Dorothy Thunder, Kaidi Lõo, Antti Arppe, Jordan Lachler, Sjur Moshagen, and Trond Trosterud. 2014. Modeling the Noun Morphology of Plains Cree. In *Proceedings of the 2014 Workshop on the Use of Computational Methods in the Study of Endangered Languages*, pages 34–42, Baltimore, Maryland, USA.

Rui Wang, Xu Tan, Renqian Luo, Tao Qin, and Tie-Yan Liu. 2021. A survey on low-resource neural machine translation. In *Proceedings of the Thirtieth International Joint Conference on Artificial Intelligence, IJCAI-21*, pages 4636–4643. International Joint Conferences on Artificial Intelligence Organization. Survey Track.

Using Speech and NLP Resources to build an iCALL platform for a minority language: the story of *An Scéalaí*, the Irish experience to date

Neasa Ní Chiaráin
Trinity College, Dublin
Ireland
neasa.nichiarain@tcd.ie

Oisín Nolan
Trinity College, Dublin
Ireland
oinolan@tcd.ie

Madeleine Comtois
Trinity College, Dublin
Ireland
comtoism@tcd.ie

Neimhin Robinson Gunning
Trinity College, Dublin
Ireland
nrobinso@tcd.ie

Harald Berthelsen
Trinity College, Dublin
Ireland
berthelh@tcd.ie

Ailbhe Ní Chasaide
Trinity College, Dublin
Ireland
anichsid@tcd.ie

Abstract

This paper describes how emerging linguistic resources and technologies can be used to build a language learning platform for Irish, an endangered language. This platform, *An Scéalaí*, harvests learner corpora – a vital resource both to study the stages of learners' language acquisition and to guide future platform development. A technical description of the platform is provided, including details of how different speech technologies and linguistic resources are fused to provide a holistic learner experience. The active continuous participation of the community, and platform evaluations by learners and teachers, are discussed.

1 Introduction

This paper presents our experience in developing an intelligent-Computer-Assisted Language Learning (iCALL) platform for the Irish language, *An Scéalaí* ('The Storyteller'). It promotes the study of Irish, an endangered language, in two distinct ways. Firstly, it deploys linguistic and computational resources to optimise the language learning process. Secondly, it harvests data about how language learners use the platform and stores learners' linguistic compositions, which is crucial for the study of the Irish acquisition process. The system is complex in that it integrates a number of linguistic and speech resources into a single user-friendly application for learners, while being hosted within a management system that enables high-level guidance by teachers and/or autonomous learning by individuals. A crucial feature is that *An Scéalaí* collects valuable learner data, hitherto unavailable, encompassing both the learners' linguistic output and their engagement with the language tools of the system.

An Scéalaí has entailed a cycle of design, implementation, testing, evaluation, redesign, and at the heart of the process has been an extensive collaboration with sectors of the language learning community. As an online system, it has been one of the fortuitous consequences of the global pandemic that an acute appetite for such a resource has resulted in a context which facilitated widespread testing. The present account provides a flavour of the developmental process and discusses the wider potential of this type of platform for many other minority and endangered languages.

An Scéalaí, as an iCALL platform, is *intelligent* in that it utilises speech and NLP knowledge and resources in an integrated platform that can opti-

Proceedings of the Fifth Workshop on the Use of Computational Methods in the Study of Endangered Languages, pages 109 - 118
May 26-27, 2022

mise the learners' acquisition of the four language skills (writing, listening, reading and speaking) in a holistic way. It is also *intelligent* in capturing the many dimensions of how learners progress in the development of their language skills, providing an intelligent learner corpus (*An Corpas Cliste*). This corpus will guide the future content and platform development.

The platform has involved the integration of different disciplines (linguistics, computational linguistics, engineering sciences) with expertise in the local language and its context. For us, and for many working with minority or endangered languages, getting such an integrated research environment has been very challenging (see more below). As mentioned, a crucial partner in the enterprise has been the active participation of the teaching and learning community. The platform and the experience described here hopefully demonstrates how such interdisciplinary research and development can work alongside a language community, to provide smart learning technologies that will serve future generations of learners and researchers in the field.

2 Background

2.1 Context: Irish, an Endangered Language

Irish, a Celtic language, is classified as 'definitely endangered' (Moseley, 2012). The communities of native speakers are clustered in small (Gaeltacht) regions, mostly in the West of Ireland. However, as an endangered language, it is unusual in being the first official language. It is a school subject for all, up until school-leaving age (c. 18 years), and hence, there is a large population of learners (c. 700,000 in the Republic of Ireland and unspecified numbers in Northern Ireland) (Ní Chiaráin, 2014). There are also many adult autonomous learners in Ireland and abroad.

There are many challenges for learners of Irish, the most pressing being that most learners do not have ready access to native speakers of the language, or genuine interactions using the language. Teaching resources are often very traditional and often criticized. As in the typical minority language teaching context, the teachers are themselves second language learners. Despite the many challenges, the large numbers of learners presents an opportunity to develop and test systems with large numbers of participants, as evidenced here.

2.2 Irish Speech and Language Technology

Despite some flourishing of speech and language resource development for Irish in recent years it remains, in the wider picture, very under-resourced. The lack of speech and language technologies has inevitable consequences in an increasingly digital world. Indeed, this deficit of resources for minority and endangered languages has been described as a digital timebomb (Ní Chasaide et al., 2020), in that it increasingly narrows the domains in which the language can be used, even by native speakers.

An Scéalaí is part of a wider initiative, ABAIR, whose mission is the development of linguistic resources, both to document the living language, and to underpin the development of core speech technologies. This initiative is particularly known for the provision of synthetic voices (TTS)[1] for the three main dialects of Irish (note there is no standard spoken variety, a common feature of minority languages). An automatic speech recognition system (ASR)[2] is also at prototype stage. A central concern is the development of the most urgently needed applications, unlike the case of technology in the major languages where development is profit-led. Of particular importance for language maintenance and transmission are sophisticated, interactive educational applications. A further related concern is the provision for those with speech/language or communication difficulties.

2.3 Motivation for *An Scéalaí* Design

As described in (Ní Chiaráin and Ní Chasaide, 2019) this platform currently involves the learner in sequential language learning activities. The learner writes some text, a story, and uses the language technologies to self-correct. The text can be listened to, via TTS, providing exposure to native speaker models of the language and enabling proof-listening as a self-correction tool. Spelling and grammar checkers also provide corrective feedback. A link to dictionaries, thesauri and grammar wizards enable the learner to further improve their composition. A facility is also provided for learners to record their own rendition of the story, and to compare it with a native speaker (TTS) rendition. The integration of these tools in the platform is intended to encourage a holistic ap-

[1] https://www.abair.ie

[2] https://phoneticsrv3.lcs.tcd.ie/rec/irish_asr

proach to language learning, where all language skills (writing, listening, reading and speaking) evolve simultaneously and reinforce each other.

Traditionally Irish learning was very text-based, with a focus on syntax, orthography and grammatical accuracy. One of the failures has been the nurturing of the spoken language and, as mentioned above, this has been exacerbated by the fact that most learners do not have access to native speaker models of the language. The inclusion of synthetic voice in a choice of dialect is, in our view, a novel core feature of the platform. Apart from the obvious need to acquire authentic pronunciation skills, it should be noted that the written form of Irish is opaque, in that that the link between the sounds and the orthographic forms are complex and typically not grasped by learners or their teachers. By constantly hearing the speech corresponding to their own written text, learners would have much more exposure and more readily grasp the fundamentally phonic structure key to the writing system (Ní Chasaide, 1999).

3 Description of the Platform

The platform is rather complex and includes a user-friendly interface where the learner has the benefit of access to feedback based on linguistic and speech resources. This integrated platform is targeting the parallel development of the four language skills (writing, speaking, listening, reading). The system also encompasses software for user and content management, which ensures that the platform is robust and user-friendly and is at all times harvesting learner data. The latter is key to a growing body of learner data, *An Corpas Cliste*, which will be used to study the stages of the acquisition process. This information will enable content development in line with acquisition stages, that can furthermore be personalised to the individual learner.

The platform development was an in-house collaboration where the software was written by our own students. These are pursuing an integrated programme in Computer Science, Linguistics and a Language, where Irish is an option[3]. (Note that this kind of programme provides the researchers with the key interdisciplinary skills and knowledge of the language, a fundamental prerequisite for developing sophisticated technologies for minority or endangered languages).

3.1 Platform Structure and Technologies Incorporated

An Scéalaí not only integrates speech and language resources, but provides a management framework that allows continuous communication between teachers and learners so that personalised guidance can be provided. The various aspects of this system are described here and implemented in a modular system where a set of independent services communicate via a REST API, which functions as one central *An Scéalaí* Node backend.

3.1.1 Speech and language technology

Text-to-speech

- For **text-to-speech** (TTS) functionality, A REST API is used to access the ABAIR TTS synthesiser (Ní Chasaide et al., 2017), which, when provided with a string of text, returns audio files containing the synthesised speech. The API provides a choice of HMM- and/or DNN-based synthesis in the three main dialects of Irish. Users can select their preferred dialect and speech engine.

- The TTS system also provides timing information about the speech, which is used to produce live text highlighting in sync with audio, to visually connect text and speech.

Grammar checker

- *An Gramadóir* (Scannell, 2013) is hosted as a microservice with a REST API that is called directly from the frontend to check text for grammar errors.

- An additional algorithm was added to check for a common spelling error in Irish, to do with vowel agreement within words.

- Further algorithms are being developed to fit with the grammar-checking framework.

- A custom module extending the *Quill*[4] text-editor (see below) was written to enable text highlighting and popup windows over the text. This module is used for displaying *grammar suggestions*, which consist of a text segment specified by *start* and *end* indices, information about the error, which may

[3] B.A. in Computer Science, Linguistics and a Language (Irish) https://www.scss.tcd.ie/undergraduate/computer-science-language/

[4] `https://quilljs.com/`

Figure 1: The *An Scéalaí* ('the Storyteller') homepage (English translation). The platform name, the tagline (tarraingíonn scéal scéal eile 'one story begets another') and the imagery on the homepage try to convey that all learners have a story to tell, continuing the well-known Irish storytelling tradition in a modern idiom.

optionally be colour-coded. This encoding of grammar suggestions is designed to be generic, and can be made compatible with a variety of grammar-checking algorithms, rendering a unified and coherent grammar-checker UI on the frontend, while maintaining a modular and extensible set of grammar checking algorithms on the backend.

- Given a grammar error, the highlighting module highlights the specified segment of text in the appropriate colour, and displays further information via popup when the user hovers over a piece of highlighted text.

Voice recording

- Students can record and listen back to their own voice reading segments of text. Each recording is associated with a piece of text, taken from a snapshot of the story at the time of recording. These recordings can then be archived for future reference, creating a history of voice recordings for a given story over time.

- Each segment of text is also synthesised via TTS, producing a 'gold standard' native speaker model, to which students can compare their own speech.

3.1.2 Managing users & content

The web application was developed using a JavaScript-centric *MEAN* stack, which deploys a MongoDB database, Node.js backend server, Express.js backend framework for API specification, and the Angular framework for the frontend. This choice in tech stack was made for quick prototyping, development, and deployment.

User management

- A user may register as either a student or a teacher. They must provide a unique username, password, and e-mail address, and verify these in order to log in.

- Passwords are encrpyted using SHA-512 so that passwords are not stored directly on the DB but may easily be validated for authentication.

- User details are stored in a JSON Web Token in the browser's local storage to keep the user authenticated.

- User accounts are assigned a *role* property upon registration (*student*, *teacher*, or *admin*) and the website presents different views tailored for the different types of user.

- *Classrooms* are effectively sets of students, whose stories a teacher will have access to.

Content management

- Story data is stored in standard Mongo documents. Additionally, snapshots of the story are saved when students interact with it in certain ways, for example performing a grammar check, or running TTS and listening back. These snapshots are basic elements of the *Corpas Cliste* (see section 3.4).

- The Quill JavaScript library[5] is used as a ready-to-go WYSIWYG editor, basic formatting options in stories. The formatting is encoded to a non-recursize subset of HTML for persistent storage.

- Audio recording is performed using the JavaScript *MediaStream Recording API*[6], which provides access to user recording devices via the browser. Audio files are stored and retrieved using MongoDB's *GridFS* specification to maintain a more uniform interface to data retrieval.

3.2 Student dashboard

- The central student dashboard consists of a text-editor that has been extended to incorporate a grammar-checking tool, text-to-speech synthesis, and a voice recording facility (see Section 3.1.1 for technical detail).

- The student may create and edit multiple texts, or *stories*, using these tools. The stories are associated with their individual accounts and saved on the cloud. They may also be exported to a variety of popular file formats for local storage.

- The text editor provides basic formatting options, producing a familiar writing environment for students.

- Live grammar-checking can be toggled on or off. When switched on, the checker will highlight grammatical errors as they are written. Hovering over a particular error will display information that should help the student resolve it. Students may filter which kinds of errors are flagged using a series of checkboxes below the editor, see Figure 2.

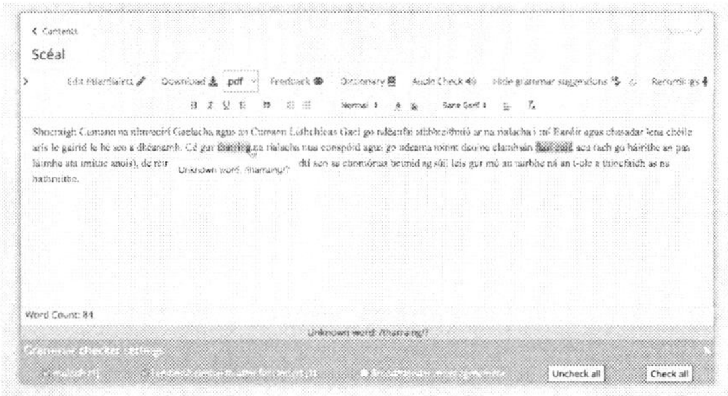

Figure 2: Central student dashboard, with grammar-checking toggled on.

- The story text may be synthesised using the ABAIR TTS system, enabling students to listen back to their story being read aloud. The synthetic utterance may simply be a word, sentence, or a paragraph, allowing students to focus on specific areas of the text.

- A voice recording facility is also provided, so that students may compare their own speech to that of the synthesis. Figure 3 shows the user interface for synthesis and recording.

Figure 3: Students may synthesise their stories, and compare recordings of their own speech.

- Given a unique code, a student may join their teacher's classroom, enabling the teacher to view their stories and provide textual or audio feedback.

3.3 Teacher dashboard

- The teacher dashboard is centered around *classrooms*, which are effectively collections of students whose stories the teacher can access and provide feedback on. Students are

[5] https://quilljs.com/

[6] https://developer.mozilla.org/en-US/docs/Web/API/MediaStream_Recording_API

notified when they have received either textual or audio (voice-note) feedback from their teacher.

- Each classroom has an associated code with which students can join.

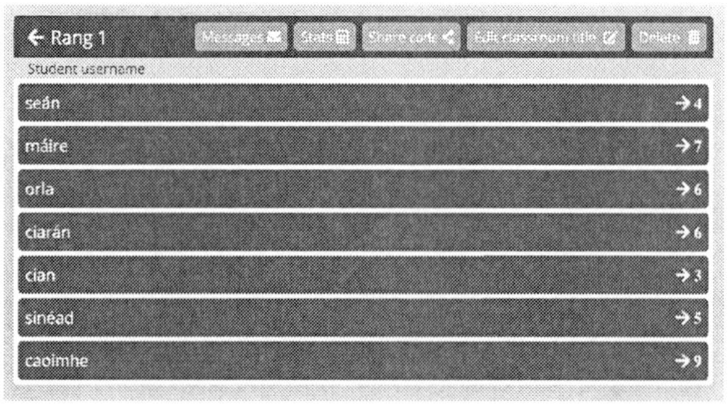

Figure 4: The classroom dashboard as seen by teacher accounts.

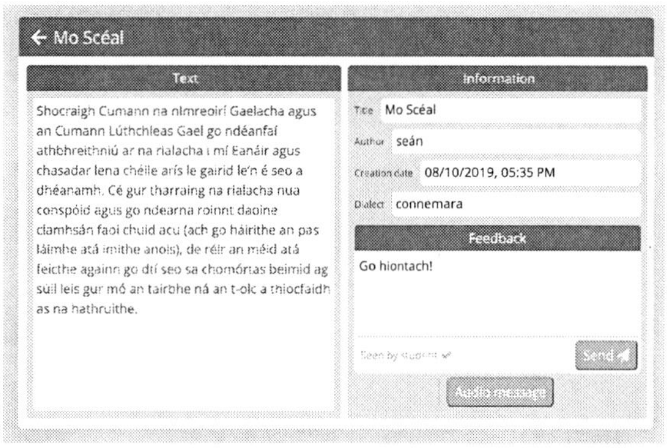

Figure 5: Teachers can directly access their students' stories, where they can leave textual and audio feedback.

- An analytics page provides information on the grammatical errors made by students in the associated classroom. This page also enables teachers to choose which kinds grammar errors are displayed for the students, producing classroom-level configurability for the grammar-checker. This configurability enables teachers to customise their students' experience to fit their lesson plans. In addition to each individual student's statistics, this page also provides an overview of how the class is performing by averaging the kinds and types of errors made by the class as a whole.

- On the messages page, teachers can communicate directly with the students in their classroom in using an interface similar to that of e-mail systems. They can send either textual or audio messages to individual students or to the entire class. Students who have any questions can then send a message back to their teacher.

3.4 The Learner Corpus (*An Corpas Cliste*)

- An engagement system is implement and tracks how *An Scéalaí* is used: each time the grammar checker, TTS, etc. are used, this is logged, along with a timestamp and a copy of the story at that point.

- These logs constitute a rich development history for each story, facilitating analyses of the ways in which TTS, grammar checker etc. are being used, and will allow researchers to examine how they are contributing to student learning, etc.

- Future development for the live grammar checking would be to provide finer time-resolution in grammar checking and correction. Also, in order to allow for more efficient storage, a method to track the difference between two versions of the text, rather than snapshotting the entire texts, will be implemented.

4 Community Evaluation > System Enhancement

Experienced Irish language teachers advised on aspects of the initial design of the platform. From prototype stage onwards, extensive consultation and evaluations has been carried out with the community of learners and teachers. The system grows as new/updated technologies come on stream and is being enhanced continuously in response to users' feedback. Groups of users who have contributed evaluations include trainee teachers in Ireland; second level pupils in Ireland; third level students in Ireland; Irish learners in America (part of a Fulbright scheme for Irish teaching in third level institutions in the US); the general public (recruited by word of mouth, as the system is online).

The total number of accounts registered to date is 4,428. The learner corpus now totals 42,542 stories; 5,596,257 words (an average of 131.55 words per story).

4.1 Trainee-Teacher Evaluation

We report here on system evaluations, which were carried out on the larger groups (n>50). These involved trainee-teachers at third level and their teachers over the period March – August 2021 (numbers in Table 1). As part of their training, these trainee-teachers are required to spend time among Irish-speaking communities (Gaeltacht), where they take part in an intensive Irish language immersion course. These trainee-teachers are learners of Irish in their own right, and will eventually be teachers of Irish at primary school level. A key element of the course involves a reflective journal, which is periodically reviewed by the teacher and which is used as the basis for an oral interview at the end of the course.

A Gaeltacht-based course was not possible in 2021 due to the pandemic and *An Scéalaí* provided an important core element of an online programme that was provided instead. The design of *An Scéalaí* fortuitously enabled course teachers to keep an overview of work being done in the form of an online reflective journal by learners, and it allowed them to interact with and guide individual learners on an ongoing basis. Note that for this cohort, *An Scéalaí* was being used both as a resource for their own language learning as well as a tool that they will deploy with their own pupils in the future.

We were fortunate in that the course directors engaged enthusiastically and saw the potential of the technology for their students. They collaborated continuously, e.g. facilitating additional workshops so that the system and its workings could be explained to the course teachers. Ongoing communication throughout the duration of the courses ensured that problems arising could be dealt with very promptly and the platform designers were receiving continuous feedback. Additionally, more formal evaluation of both the learner and teacher experience with the platform was elicited through voluntary responses to detailed questionnaires, presented via Google Forms and circulated on the last day of each course.

4.2 Learner Questionnaire

Section I elicited:

- learners' previous experience with online learning; the ease of use of *An Scéalaí*; learners' opinions on the usefulness of each of the tools embedded in the platform, using Likert scales and an open comment box.

Section II asked learners:

- in what context they felt *An Scéalaí* would be most useful; what the strengths/weaknesses of the platform are; their suggestions for improving the platform; whether they believed *An Scéalaí* enhanced their learning of Irish; whether it enhanced their confidence as learners; whether or not they'd like to continue using it in future. Open-ended comments were also invited, particularly to elaborate on any negative responses.

4.3 Teacher Questionnaire

This elicited teachers' level of experience of teaching online; whether *An Scéalaí* was found to be useful as a management system for the reflective journals; ease of use of the platform from a teachers' perspective; interest in using the platform with other classes in future. An open-ended comment box was included to elicit any feedback (positive/negative) teachers received from students during the course.

4.4 From Evaluation to System Enhancement

A total of 1793 learners and 85 teachers registered an account with *An Scéalaí* over the 5-month period. A great deal of information has been gleaned and a glimpse of some of the salient findings are presented here. Responses to some key questions are shown in Tables 1 and 2 below.

Pilot	March	April	May	June	July
(a) No. Accounts	384	293	51	498	603
(b) Respondents	187	222	21	254	494
(c1) Enhanced learning?	89.8% (168)	89.6% (199)	100% (21)	90.2% (229)	91.5% (452)
(c2) Improved confidence?	85% (159)	86% (191)	100% (21)	85.4% (217)	88% (435)
(c3) Use in future?	94.1% (178)	91.9% (204)	100% (21)	87% (221)	90.3% (446)

Table 1: Learner Responses: (a) overall number of accounts registered; (b) number of questionnaires returned; (c) % of positive responses to 3 of the questionnaire items

Responses are overwhelmingly positive from both learners and teachers. This is evidenced by not only the percentage positive responses but also in the open-ended comments, where terms like *réabhlóideach!* ('revolutionary') dominated.

We paid particular attention to any negative feedback and constructive comments emerging in the open-ended comment boxes. Many of these

Pilot	March	April	May	June	July
(a) No. Accounts	18	16	2	21	28
(b) Respondents	8	10	0	7	11
(c1) Useful management system?	100%	100%	-	87.5%	100%
(c2) Use in future?	100%	100%	-	100%	100%
(d) Ease of use?					
V easy:	3	3	-	2	4
Easy:	5	5	-	3	6
Moderate:	0	2	-	2	1
Difficult:	0	0	-	0	0
V difficult:	0	0	-	0	0

Table 2: Teacher Responses (a) number of accounts registered; (b) number of questionnaires returned; (c) % of positive responses to 3 of the questionnaire items; (d) breakdown of responses regarding ease of use on a five-point scale.

were acted on as the pilots were ongoing, during the six month period, so that there was a continuous cyclical process of learner/teacher feedback guiding intensive platform development. Samples of problems highlighted and responses to these problems are included here.

Text Display: in the earlier pilots, the most frequent criticism was of the simple plain text editor in the platform (which is the form needed to send data to our TTS servers). Learners wanted a Word-like layout with control over headings, fonts, layout, colour, etc. The solution was to implement a WYSIWYG Editor (see 3.2), which is mirrored by a plain text copy for the synthesis.

Email verification system: much time and resources were consumed in the earlier pilots by practical issues, e.g. lost password/lost data requests from learners. An automatic password retrieval system was put in place (see 3.1.2).

System Robustness: as the user numbers grew (we had not appreciated that Covid would last so long and that such large numbers would be using this system), the system crashed more frequently. Learners were quick to complain. This is a make-or-break feature to retain student users and, therefore, increasing the robustness is an ongoing priority, requiring continuous bug fixing and extensions to the system. This is a concern for the future, as maintaining this system in the longer term will require ongoing technical support.

Foregrounding of Oral/Aural skills: a core objective of this platform is the linkage of the spoken (native) language with the written forms. As mentioned, oral/aural skills have traditionally been neglected in Irish language teaching. *An Scéalaí* should offer a way for parallel development of the four language skills. However, our analysis of the data revealed that the synthetic speech output was relatively little used. While disappointing, on reflection this does not seem particularly surprising: the concept of proof-listening is novel and the platform design relegated this facility to a different tab from the main writing page, making it more likely to be overlooked. To rectify this, the system has been redesigned. In the forthcoming iteration, the option of listening to the spoken output (via TTS) is integrated into the main writing page.

These are relatively large ticket items. Myriads of small fixes were also implemented following feedback, items that would be unlikely to be spotted without user engagement, including: shifting the location of a textbox which obscured the learners' text; and allowing teachers to sort student names alphabetically A-Z, for attendance keeping.

5 Conclusions

Successful language transmission is key to language maintenance and revitalisation. In the Irish context, where the population at large receives Irish language instruction, there is the potential to make Irish a vibrant second language beyond the native speaker (or Gaeltacht) population. Computational approaches and the incorporation of linguistic and technology resources can turn the digital timebomb into a major stimulus to language pedagogy and indirectly to language maintenance. Besides its immediate use as a pedagogical platform, *An Scéalaí* will enable documentation and analysis of the stages of acquisition and it will stimulate future development and increasingly effective, technology-based interventions, where our linguistic knowledge is brought to bear.

Our experience has been that the language community is central to all aspects of the wider ABAIR initiative — in this case, the engagement of the educational sector — not a passive recipient but a vital partner in the enterprise, involved in every aspect from design to evaluation and dissemination.

The current platform is a work in progress. It integrates speech and language knowledge as well as core language technologies to provide a holistic learning environment. As further resources, such as ASR, come on stream, the aim is to expand the capacity of the platform in ways that will further enrich the learners' experience.

5.1 Future Directions

The platform as currently configured is potentially language independent (see below). A current focus is to increase the Irish language content. Towards this, we are actively investigating the use of avatars as a way of enhancing the delivery of the spoken output, including feedback on errors, etc. We are also developing independent grammar checking modules to cater for items not detected by the grammar checker currently in use, such as the genitive case marking. The system is also being linked to an interactive chatbot (e.g. to practice irregular verbs); a story starter (to kickstart the writing process); dictogloss (a text reconstruction exercise). A parallel development we have been involved with, the Learning and Reading Assistant (LARA) (Zuckerman et al., 2021), is currently integrated with *An Scéalaí*. The intention is to expand the content offered with a view to encouraging learners to read for pleasure.

Our future wishlist will include a redesign of the system for the mobile phone/tablet, as our analytics data shows that many learners are logging in using mobile phones and tablets. It is frequently pointed out that mobile phones/tablets are much more useful in a minority/endangered language context, where users may not have laptops.

5.2 *An Scéalaí*: a Model for Other Languages?

We increasingly see ourselves as part of a global movement where minority and endangered languages share common cause. To this end, *An Scéalaí* is developed as an open source platform, available on GitHub[7]. At its core it has a modular design. Once a given resource (such as TTS, dictionary, etc.) is available in a language, it should in principle be possible to clone *An Scéalaí* for a different endangered language, by slotting the resource in to the core framework. It would be particularly rewarding to find that we can share our experience and resources with other endangered language groups who strive to document, maintain and revive their linguistic heritage.

[7]https://github.com/OisinNolan/An-Scealai

6 Acknowledgements

Funding from the Department of Tourism, Culture, Arts, Gaeltacht, Sports and Media, Government of Ireland (*ABAIR*) and An Chomhairle um Oideachas Gaeltachta agus Gaelscolaíochta (*An Corpas Cliste*) is gratefully acknowledged. We would also like to thank Michelle de Bhailís and the community at Coláiste Ghaoth Dobhair for their enthusiastic involvement in the project to date.

References

Christopher Moseley. 2012. *The UNESCO atlas of the world's languages in danger*, 3rd edition. World Oral Literature Project.

Ailbhe Ní Chasaide. 1999. Irish. In *Handbook of the International Phonetic Association: a guide to the use of the international phonetic alphabet*, pages 111–116. Cambridge University Press, Cambridge.

Ailbhe Ní Chasaide, Neasa Ní Chiaráin, Christoph Wendler, Harald Berthelsen, Andy Murphy, and Christer Gobl. 2017. The abair initiative: Bringing spoken irish into the digital space. In *INTERSPEECH*, pages 2113–2117.

Ailbhe Ní Chasaide, Neasa Ní Chiaráin, Harald Berthelsen, Christoph Wendler, Andrew Murphy, Emily Barnes, and Christer Gobl. 2020. Can we defuse the digital timebomb? linguistics, speech technology and the irish language community. In *Proceedings of International Conference on Language Technologies for ALL (LT4All): Enabling Linguistic Diversity and Multilingualism Worldwide*, pages 177 – 181, UNESCO, Paris, France.

Neasa Ní Chiaráin. 2014. *Text-to-Speech Synthesis in Computer-Assisted Language Learning for Irish: Development and Evaluation (Unpublished doctoral dissertation)*. Ph.D. thesis, The School of Linguistic, Speech and Communication Sciences, Trinity College Dublin.

Neasa Ní Chiaráin and Ailbhe Ní Chasaide. 2019. An icall approach to morphophonemic training for irish using speech technology. In *CALL and complexity - short papers from EUROCALL 2019*, pages 314 – 320.

Kevin Scannell. 2013. *An Gramadóir: an open source grammar checking engine, Version 0.70*. https://cadhan.com/gramadoir/.

Ghil'ad Zuckerman, Sigurður Vigfússon, Manny Rayner, Neasa Ní Chiaráin, Nedelina Ivanova, Hanieh Habibi, and Branislav Bédi. 2021. LARA in the service of revivalistics and documentary linguistics: Community engagement and endangered languages. In *Proceedings of the Workshop on Computational Methods for Endangered Languages*, volume 1, pages 13–23.

Closing the NLP Gap: Documentary Linguistics and NLP Need a Shared Software Infrastructure

Luke Gessler
Department of Linguistics
Georgetown University
lg876@georgetown.edu

Abstract

For decades, researchers in natural language processing and computational linguistics have been developing models and algorithms that aim to serve the needs of language documentation projects. However, these models have seen little use in language documentation despite their great potential for making documentary linguistic artefacts better and easier to produce. In this work, we argue that a major reason for this NLP gap is the lack of a strong foundation of application software which can on the one hand serve the complex needs of language documentation and on the other hand provide effortless integration with NLP models. We further present and describe a work-in-progress system we have developed to serve this need, Glam.

1 Introduction

The labor that is required for documenting a language is complicated, repetitive, and time-consuming. As many have pointed out, methods from NLP and computational linguistics have great potential for expediting the documentary process (Bender et al., 2004; Gessler, 2019; Neubig et al., 2019, *inter alia*), and researchers in NLP/CL[1] have made great progress in advancing the ability of their models and algorithms to serve the needs of documentary linguistics. At the same time, interest in "low-resource languages" has surged in the past few years in the NLP research community, and there ought to be no better time than now for documentary projects to benefit from the contributions of researchers in NLP.

But somehow, most documentary linguistic work done even today in 2022 proceeds without any of the assistance that methods in NLP could be providing. This has been the state of affairs for quite some time—the introductory paragraph of the preface for the proceedings of the first ComputEL conference (Good et al., 2014) explains (emphasis ours):

> Contemporary efforts to document the world's endangered languages [...] are dependent on the widespread availability of [...] software to annotate [documentary data]. However, despite well over a decade of dedicated funding efforts aimed at the documentation of endangered languages, the **technological landscape** that supports the work of those involved in this research **remains fragmented**, and the **promises of new technology remain largely unfulfilled**. Moreover, **the efforts of computer scientists**, on the whole, are mostly **disconnected from the day-to-day work of documentary linguists**, making it difficult for the knowledge of each group to inform the other. On the one hand, **this deprives documentary linguists of tools making use of the latest research results to speed up the time-consuming task of describing an underdocumented language**. On the other hand, it severely limits the ability of computational linguists to test their methods on the full range of world's linguistic diversity.

Eight years later, at ComputEL-5, these words for the most part read as though they could have been written today.

Why is it that these "promises of new technology" remained unfulfilled for documentary linguists[2]? We argue here that the fundamental issue preventing vigorous exchange between documentary linguistics and NLP is a lack of application software which can adequately serve both communities: while it is true that apps exist and are commonly used in documentary linguistics, they are ill-suited for integration with NLP models. We therefore claim that **documentary linguistics will not benefit from advances in NLP until significant investments are made in developing application software which can compete with existing**

[1] We will simply write "NLP" in this work as a catch-all for any kind of computational work involving language, as a distinction between NLP and computational linguistics is fraught and not particularly important for the issues we discuss.

[2] For want of a better phrase, we will use "documentary linguist" as a flawed but useful shorthand for anyone involved in the documentary process who is not a computationalist, with the understanding that a linguist is only one kind of person who can be involved in a language documentation project.

Proceedings of the Fifth Workshop on the Use of Computational Methods in the Study of Endangered Languages, pages 119 - 126
May 26-27, 2022

apps in functionality and provide first-class support for NLP model integration.

In this work, we present and discuss this thesis, outlining ideals for what application software ought to accomplish for the documentary linguistics community. In addition, we present a work-in-progress system we have developed which attempts to implement these ideals as practical, usable application software aimed at catalyzing research relationships between documentary linguists and computationalists by taking the needs of both seriously and in equal proportion.

2 Related Work

2.1 NLP for Language Documentation

NLP researchers have grown steadily more more interested in work on what in the NLP community are referred to as "low resource languages", with the watershed moment perhaps being the advent of deep learning in NLP in the early 2010's (LeCun et al., 2015).[3] A full review of this work is out of scope of the present work, but suffice to say that leading NLP researchers believe enough progress has been made that the average language documentation project could benefit greatly from NLP assistance, though they also observe that adoption of methods in NLP in language documentation has been slow (Neubig et al., 2019, 2020).

2.2 Language Documentation Apps

Since the 90's, application software has entered use in language documentation, with many of them focusing particularly on speech transcription and linguistic annotation of transcribed speech (glossing, POS tagging, etc.).[4] Many apps have been created, but a few have emerged as favorites. ELAN (Wittenburg et al., 2006) is favored for transcribing speech from audio or video recordings, and SIL products, FLEx (Moe, 2008) and SayMore[5] foremost among them, are popular for analysis such as interlinearization and lexicon construction. Development of these apps all began well before methods in NLP were mature enough to be practically useful for the average low-resource language, and as a consequence, these apps were not designed to accommodate integration with NLP models and have struggled to expand to support them.

For example, Moeller and Hulden (2018) present an algorithm for automatic glossing of transcribed documentary data, but as they describe, it was impossible to integrate the model into FLEx itself—instead, data needed to be exported from FLEx so that it could be presented to the algorithm. This is a common limitation: in the area where there has been the most activity on providing usable NLP for documentary linguists, automatic speech recognition (ASR), the leading solution, ELPIS (Foley et al., 2018), requires that users close their ELAN file, present it to the model, then download a new ELAN file to replace the old one with the ASR output. Thus while it is sometimes possible today to use NLP models in conjunction with the leading software solutions for language documentation, support is limited to the NLP packages which explicitly support this option, and there are very few examples of language documentation apps providing in-app integration with NLP models.

The earliest example we are aware of of an app which attempts to provide rich in-app integration with computational tools work is Bender et al. (2004), where a vision for high-tech language documentation is given, accompanied by a prototype implementation. The system, Montage, describes a documentary workflow where the documentary workflow is tightly integrated with contemporary NLP techniques (specifically, "precision formal grammars"): for example, grammatical description is brought into the software, which allows users to construct a grammar in the app instead of "offline", and the implemented grammar becomes available for partial parsing of new textual inputs.[6] Critically, what is enabling the use of these advanced methods from computational linguistics in Montage is a foundation of application software: for example, the "markup tool" which enables the construction of the precision formal grammars would need to be a complicated piece of UI which can present

[3]What exactly counts as "low resource" is extremely variable, but its meaning is essentially that a language does not have nearly as much readily usable linguistic data as a "high resource" language such as Mandarin Chinese or Arabic, with respect to either quality or quantity. Thus even a language with many speakers, such as Luganda with 20M speakers, might count as a low resource language depending on context. Virtually all languages being documented by linguists would count as "low resource" from an NLP perspective.

[4]There are many other parts of the language documentation "pipeline" beyond these, such as metadata management, but since these are the tasks that have received disproportionate attention, we will mainly focus on them in this work.

[5]`https://software.sil.org/saymore/`

[6]Tangentially, it is also worth noting their discussion of software providing first-class support for the hypertextual links that inhere in documentary artefacts, e.g. between example sentences in a grammar and the texts the examples were drawn from, along the lines of Musgrave and Thieberger (2021).

itself and the content of precision formal grammars in a way that is approachable to documentary linguists.[7]

Beyond the apps that have been mentioned so far, some others have been developed through the years, though none of them have made it a major goal to tackle the issue of NLP integration. For example LingSync (Dunham, 2014; Dunham et al., 2015) is a newer app along the lines of FLEx; Hall (2022) presents a toolkit for empowering documentary linguists to tailor apps to their needs; and SayMore[8] and Aikuma (Bird et al., 2014) are apps aimed at spoken text collection and transcription. But none of these projects make it a major goal to tackle the NLP model integration problem.

In sum, while there is every indication that NLP models are ready to provide documentary linguists with great productivity gains, existing apps have not been able to accommodate them in a way that is ergonomic and complete, and no new apps have yet emerged which are competitive with the most popular apps on features and offer first-class support for integrating with NLP models. We term this disconnect between the availability of NLP models and the inability of existing apps to make effective use of them the NLP gap.

3 The NLP Gap

Why does the NLP gap exist? That is, why is it that language documentation is still being carried out without the help of NLP models despite their great potential to help? We argue here that the single most important reason why the NLP gap exists is a rather simple one: there is not a foundational infrastructure of application software that can serve both NLP researchers and documentary linguists.[9]

When one first thinks of language documentation, and NLP models in language documentation, one might suppose that it is the development of NLP models and their application that is hard. Indeed, developing these models is hard, and low-resource NLP is by no means solved. But we have reached a point where some models can be applied to any language and work with a respectable amount of accuracy even without any additional training, one such example being the universal phone recognizer of Li et al. (2020). Some logistical difficulties might remain (e.g. preparing and maintaining computers for them to run on, and finding stakeholders in the project who have the know-how to run them), but for many larger documentation projects these issues are not serious, and we still do not see them using these models.

If models are good enough to deliver value, and documentary linguists want to reap the benefits of NLP and know where in their workflows they'd like models to assist, and computationalists are often available to assist in getting their models to process documentary data, then what else remains? The only possible answer seems to be that it is the lack of support in language documentation apps that is to blame. As noted in §2, documentary linguists cite difficulty in using models, as to the extent that they are available at all, they are usable only in awkward ways which grate against their workflows. NLP models, if they are to be unobtrusive, must have deep integration with documentary workflows, and since these workflows occur in software, NLP models must be deeply integrated into documentary software, the only substrate in which vigorous exchange between these two communities may occur.

This is not a small challenge, as this software, if it were to succeed in its goal of catalyzing cooperation between computationalists and documentary linguists, would need to serve well the needs of both parties. From the perspective of the documentary linguists, the whole point of using an NLP model is that it ought to reduce their labor, and as we have seen, existing ways of using NLP models with apps like FLEx and ELAN are unergonomic to the point of often being more work than the alternative. From the perspective of NLP researchers, we must make it easy for them to do something more than make their model publicly available, which is a necessary but unfortunately insufficient step in making them usable by all but the most technically

[7] To our knowledge, Montage was never implemented, and nothing has been published on it since 2005, though some of its conceptual threads have been continued in the AGGREGATION project (`http://depts.washington.edu/uwcl/aggregation/`).

[8] `https://software.sil.org/saymore/`

[9] We must hasten to add that this is not the *only* reason for the NLP gap: there are broader problems to be solved, such as how to succeed in designing language technology in a way that includes and serves the many stakeholders in the documentary process (Bird, 2018), and how to do so in a way that will not reproduce the colonial legacy of disenfranchisement and extraction (Bird, 2020). But the lack of software is at least as important as these other issues—addressing the lack of software may not be sufficient for closing the NLP gap, but it is necessary. As such, we will focus here on the narrow, software problem, recognizing that there are broader problems that need to be solved in fully equip every party in a documentary process with language technologies.

experienced and motivated documentary linguists.

Beyond these design challenges, there is also the challenge of how to find the labor necessary to develop this software, which has been noted as a severe issue (Thieberger, 2016). Despite the fact that a path forward for excellent research and positive outcomes for language communities requires significant investment in application software infrastructure, the cultural currents within both linguistics and NLP, for better or worse, dictate that software engineering (which also happens to be incredibly time-intensive) does not constitute research activity. The obvious outcome is that no researcher in either discipline would be well advised to make this kind of work more than a side-interest in their research interests, and it is telling that the two most popular apps, FLEx and ELAN, were developed by software engineering staff at language-related organizations rather than academics themselves.

That is a bleak outlook—is a shift in how our fields reward software development too much to hope for? It is worth digressing for a moment here to note that academic communities do have the power to change how the field views and rewards software artefacts as contributions, if they choose to prioritize bringing about such a cultural shift. For example, in the field of astronomy, academics have been publishing software packages providing implementations of commonly needed statistical and simulation algorithms for decades, though traditionally, such packages were only viewed as "contributions" worthy of the attention of, say, a hiring or tenure committee if there was an associated publication in a journal (Chase, 2022). Securing such a publication could be difficult if a package was very specialized or small, and as the need for new packages has risen sharply, the field of astronomy has responded by lowering the requirements for a "software publication" (see Kelley 2021 for an example). In the future, the field may be moving towards treating a package in itself as a "publication" (in the academic sense, i.e. something that can appear on a C.V. or be indexed by Google Scholar). In sum, the field was able to recognize that its traditional assessment and treatment of certain research activity was no longer appropriate, and needed to be changed so that activity that used to be thought of as marginal would be recognized and rewarded as a first-class scholarly activity.

Despite these challenges, we believe it is possible and vitally important for researchers in language documentation and NLP to try to find ways of building the backbone of application software which is needed for interchange between the two fields to progress, which as we hope is clear by now is crucially necessary for achieving widespread use of NLP models in language documentation. In the short term, we hope that individuals will be able to overcome career risks that come with working on something that is not "research" by cooperating with others, thereby amortizing the loss of time spent on more traditional research topics. In the long term, we challenge senior academics, and especially senior academics in NLP who have presented their models and algorithms as beneficial for language documentation, to consider whether it is not time to reassess whether the software work we have described is deserving of more recognition and support, and if it is, how the community's cultural values and institutions could be changed to reward such work.

We close our discussion of the NLP gap on this note. In the remainder of this work, we turn to describe what we believe would be key goals for an app aimed at closing the NLP gap, and further describe a prototype-grade system we have constructed which aims to achieve these goals.

4 System Description

Glam is an alpha-quality system we have developed which aims to serve the needs we have described. While for the rest of this section we speak mostly of design instead of the state of the implementation, we take a moment to note its progress.

In its present state, Glam is capable of surface-level interlinear annotation of texts, and there is work underway to add support for lexical inventories (as in FLEx). This is the bare minimum necessary to conduct a small-scale language documentation project, such as for a semester-long field methods course that might be offered at a university. Support for NLP models has not yet been implemented, which may seem strange. The reason is that, as we have noted, it is important for this app to fully satisfy the needs of both documentary linguists and NLP researchers, and we have viewed the former as the much harder problem and prioritized solving it first. We have however naturally been considering the problem of NLP integration from the very initial stages of design, and have made implementation decisions with care in order to facilitate its eventual implementation. The latest state of the project can be tracked by visiting the repository.[10]

4.1 Core Goals

After considering the many and often conflicting needs that arise in language documentation and using models in language documentation, we arrived on these five goals, which we believe are some of the most important to achieve in order to make an app that documentary linguists will gladly use and will be easily integrable with models.

1. **Flexible Data**: all language documentation projects have different data needs, so you should be able to record however much data and whatever kind of data you desire. Annotating anything from good old-fashioned interlinear glossed text to more complicated formats like Universal Dependencies should be possible and easy.

2. **Seamless Collaboration**: working with others should be frictionless—you should be able to share data without even clicking a button, changes should be viewable by everyone in real time, and everyone should be able to pick the system up quickly.

3. **Durability**: data should never be lost—all past states of the database should be recorded and accessible.

4. **NLP Model Integration**: it should be easy to configure cutting-edge NLP models to provide best possible annotations to be corrected by humans, and have them train incrementally as new gold annotations become available.

5. **Pluggable UIs**: if you want to code new UIs for different kinds of annotation (e.g. entity recognition, syntax, and coreference), you should be able to do so just by writing JavaScript using the Glam API, with no back-end changes required.

4.2 Implementation

We will review some key points of our implementation of Glam here. It would take space beyond what is available here to describe exactly how documentary workflows are performed in Glam—instead, we will discuss only the fundamentals here, and refer readers to a video demo for more detail.[11]

[10]`https://github.com/lgessler/glam`

[11]`https://youtu.be/VXWPw91nTGY`

Platform Glam is implemented, in software engineering jargon, as a single-page web application. We chose to make Glam a web application because of the difficulty that comes with requiring local installation of apps: for example, some apps are not compatible with certain operating systems (FLEx, for instance, does not work on macOS), and others require some tricky installation steps (ELAN can require you to download supplementary software during installation). These difficulties are bypassed in a web application, where all that is required is a web browser and an internet connection (albeit at the cost of maintaining a publicly-accessible web server).

Database Data in Glam is stored in XTDB,[12] an immutable database which allows all past states of the database to be accessible. This means that data cannot be lost, and moreover that if there were demand for it, it would be relatively straightforward to allow users to see historical states of the database.[13]

Data Model The data model of Glam is designed to be extremely flexible: documents in the system are separated by project, and each project has a structure which is expressed just in terms of four basic constructs, which we call *layers*. A text layer holds a string representing the text that is to be analyzed. A token layer depends on a text layer and holds *tokens*, each of which is defined using the text layer with a begin and end index. A span layer depends on a token layer and holds *spans*, each of which refers to at least one token and has a value, such as a POS tag or an entity label. A relation layer depends on a span layer and consists of *relations*, each of which has a start and end span and has a value, such as a dependency relation or a coreference type. A vocabulary layer is a list of items which have at minimum a *form* and any number of additional fields, which may hold information such as part of speech or alternative spellings and may be open or closed depending on whether it is desirable for users to expand the vocabulary with more entries.

These layers are designed to be sufficient to express any kind of linguistic annotation, and we

[12]https://xtdb.com/

[13]Sometimes it might be desirable to destroy data, e.g. if a language consultant decides a text is too sensitive to share. XTDB provides technical means for accomplishing this (the *evict* operation), and implementation of data eviction using this database facility is planned for Glam.

believe this is possible because other researchers in corpus linguistics (Zipser and Romary, 2010) and NLP (Jiang et al., 2020) have convincingly argued that very similar data models are capable of expressing almost any linguistic structure. In practice, we expect that most projects will have a very similar structure, but the intention behind approaching data modeling this way is to give users good support no matter what their data looks like. In addition, we plan to expand the data model with document-level metadata, which will be useful for tracking information such as when a text was collected and who produced the data.

User System A basic user system with password authentication is used for maintaining security over data. Privileged users called administrators can set up projects and manage users, and may grant users either read-only or read-and-write privileges over any project. By default, projects are invisible to users.

NLP Integration Recall that the data model of Glam is composed of five fundamental layers. NLP integration is made general for any layer with the following procedure:

1. An NLP model is prepared for integration by making it contactable via generic protocols, such as HTTP(S), e.g. by wrapping it in a small web server (such as Flask for Python) and implementing an API specification provided by Glam which describes what methods must be supported to e.g. tokenize a string of text.

2. The model is registered within the Glam instance by an administrator, which will tell the instance how to contact the model (e.g. by URL, like `http://127.0.0.1:5128`). At this point, the system will attempt to contact the model and, if successful, register the *hooks* that are supported by that model. A *hook* is an action the model can take whenever a certain operation happens: for a span layer, this might be token creation, token boundary modification, or token deletion.

3. Every layer that depends on output from that model will be configured to contact that model using the model registration, and the exact hooks which are to be executed may be modified.

This strategy produces a loose coupling between NLP models and Glam: their only point of contact is HTTP(S) with a specified structure, meaning that as long as the model provides this it can be implemented in any way desired.

4.3 Outlook

At present, Glam has been receiving feedback from documentary linguists and is a few months from a beta release. Multiple field linguists have expressed interest in some of the design goals and features in Glam. Time will tell if the design and implementation choices we have made are the right ones, but our more important intent in this discussion is to demonstrate the kind of problems we think an app will need to solve in order to close the NLP gap.

5 Conclusion

We have discussed the problem of why NLP models have not seen more use in documentary linguistics, and concluded that the single most important barrier to adoption of NLP models is the lack of a substrate of application software that can serve the needs of both documentary linguists and NLP models well. We have moreover presented design goals and implementations of a system which we think shows potential to meet this need.

Regardless of the ultimate fortunes of our system, Glam, we reprise our invitation to readers to consider whether our assessment of the NLP gap is correct (i.e., that it cannot be closed without serious investment in application software, which in turn might require a cultural shift in some academic communities), and if it is, what there is to be done about it. NLP researchers have gained much from endangered languages, not least by sourcing unique data from them for publications—if they are in dire need of assistance that the NLP community is singularly able to provide, and which is not forthcoming from any other community or organization in the world, should the NLP community not act? Moreover, beyond this matter of deserts, there is also the exciting prospect of opportunity for new methods and models that could come from a deeper relationship between these two fields, mediated by a substrate of application software.

For junior researchers without a faculty position or tenure, a helpful action might be to find collaborators to work on this software problem with. For researchers in NLP working on low-resource NLP models aimed at application in documentation of endangered languages, it might be right to consider whether they ought to have more involvement in making this application actual instead of potential. For senior researchers with tenure, who wield the most influence, it may be appropriate to reexamine the reasons why the current norms around what constitutes "research activity" are what they are, and whether it might be right to reform them given the unmet needs of endangered languages.

Acknowledgements

We thank Andrew Harvey, Joey Lovestrand, and Patrick Hall for helpful comments on a draft of this work. We thank Patrick Hall and for feedback on both this work and a prelimary version of Glam. We thank Nathan Schneider, Amir Zeldes, Hannah Sande, William Croft, Andrew Cowell, Jin Zhao, Rosa Vallejos, Meagan Vigus, Jens Van Gysel, Lukas Denk, Joshua Birchall, and Alexis Palmer for critical feedback on preliminary versions of Glam. We thank Eve Chase for a helpful discussion on the nature of software contributions in linguistics/NLP and astrophysics.

References

Emily Bender, Dan Flickinger, Jeff Good, and Ivan Sag. 2004. Montage: Leveraging advances in grammar engineering, linguistic ontologies, and mark-up for the documentation of underdescribed languages. *Proc. of LREC.*

Steven Bird. 2018. *Designing mobile applications for endangered languages*, 1 edition, pages 842–861. Oxford University Press, United Kingdom.

Steven Bird. 2020. Decolonising speech and language technology. In *Proceedings of the 28th International Conference on Computational Linguistics*, pages 3504–3519, Barcelona, Spain (Online). International Committee on Computational Linguistics.

Steven Bird, Florian R. Hanke, Oliver Adams, and Haejoong Lee. 2014. Aikuma: A mobile app for collaborative language documentation. In *Proceedings of the 2014 Workshop on the Use of Computational Methods in the Study of Endangered Languages*, pages 1–5, Baltimore, Maryland, USA. Association for Computational Linguistics.

Eve Adde Chase. 2022. personal communication.

Joel Dunham, Jessica Coon, and Alan Bale. 2015. Lingsync: web-based software for language documentation. In *4th International Conference on Language Documentation and Conservation (ICLDC)*, Honolulu, Hawaii.

Joel Robert William Dunham. 2014. *The online linguistic database : software for linguistic fieldwork*. Ph.D. thesis, University of British Columbia.

Ben Foley, Josh Arnold, Rolando Coto-Solano, Gautier Durantin, T. Mark Ellison, Daan van Esch, Scott Heath, František Kratochvíl, Zara Maxwell-Smith, David Nash, Ola Olsson, Mark Richards, Nay San, Hywel Stoakes, Nick Thieberger, and Janet Wiles. 2018. Building Speech Recognition Systems for Language Documentation: The CoEDL Endangered Language Pipeline and Inference System (ELPIS). In *6th Workshop on Spoken Language Technologies for Under-Resourced Languages (SLTU 2018)*, pages 205–209. ISCA.

Luke Gessler. 2019. Developing without developers: choosing labor-saving tools for language documentation apps. In *Proceedings of the 3rd Workshop on the Use of Computational Methods in the Study of Endangered Languages Volume 1 (Papers)*, pages 6–13, Honolulu. Association for Computational Linguistics.

Jeff Good, Julia Hirschberg, and Owen Rambow, editors. 2014. *Proceedings of the 2014 Workshop on the Use of Computational Methods in the Study of Endangered Languages*. Association for Computational Linguistics, Baltimore, Maryland, USA.

Patrick James Hall. 2022. *Participatory Design in Digital Language Documentation: A Web Platform Approach*. Ph.D. thesis, University of California, Santa Barbara.

Zhengbao Jiang, Wei Xu, Jun Araki, and Graham Neubig. 2020. Generalizing Natural Language Analysis through Span-relation Representations. In *Proceedings of the 58th Annual Meeting of the Association for Computational Linguistics*, pages 2120–2133, Online. Association for Computational Linguistics.

Luke Zoltan Kelley. 2021. kalepy: a Python package for kernel density estimation, sampling and plotting. *Journal of Open Source Software*, 6(57):2784.

Yann LeCun, Yoshua Bengio, and Geoffrey Hinton. 2015. Deep learning. *Nature*, 521(7553):436–444.

Xinjian Li, Siddharth Dalmia, Juncheng Li, Patrick Littell, Matthew Lee, Jiali Yao, Antonios Anastasopoulos, David Mortensen, Graham Neubig, Alan Black, and Florian Metze. 2020. Universal Phone Recognition with a Multilingual Allophone System. In *2020 IEEE International Conference on Acoustics, Speech, and Signal Processing (ICASSP)*, Barcelona.

Ronald Moe. 2008. FieldWorks Language Explorer 1.0.

Sarah Moeller and Mans Hulden. 2018. Automatic Glossing in a Low-Resource Setting for Language Documentation. In *Proceedings of the Workshop on Computational Modeling of Polysynthetic Languages*, pages 84–93, Santa Fe, New Mexico, USA. Association for Computational Linguistics.

Simon Musgrave and Nick Thieberger. 2021. The language documentation quartet. In *Proceedings of the 4th Workshop on the Use of Computational Methods in the Study of Endangered Languages Volume 1 (Papers)*, pages 6–12, Online. Association for Computational Linguistics.

Graham Neubig, Patrick Littell, Chian-Yu Chen, Jean Lee, Zirui Li, Yu-Hsiang Lin, and Yuyan Zhang. 2019. Towards a General-Purpose Linguistic Annotation Backend. In *Proceedings of the 3rd Workshop on the Use of Computational Methods in the Study of Endangered Languages Volume 1 (Papers)*, Honolulu, Hawaii. Association for Computational Linguistics. ArXiv: 1812.05272.

Graham Neubig, Shruti Rijhwani, Alexis Palmer, Jordan MacKenzie, Hilaria Cruz, Xinjian Li, Matthew Lee, Aditi Chaudhary, Luke Gessler, Steven Abney, Shirley Anugrah Hayati, Antonios Anastasopoulos, Olga Zamaraeva, Emily Prud'hommeaux, Jennette Child, Sara Child, Rebecca Knowles, Sarah Moeller, Jeffrey Micher, Yiyuan Li, Sydney Zink, Mengzhou Xia, Roshan S Sharma, and Patrick Littell. 2020. A Summary of the First Workshop on Language Technology for Language Documentation and Revitalization. In *Proceedings of the 1st Joint Workshop on Spoken Language Technologies for Under-resourced languages (SLTU) and Collaboration and Computing for Under-Resourced Languages (CCURL)*, pages 342–351, Marseille, France. European Language Resources association.

Nick Thieberger. 2016. Language Documentation Tools and Methods Summit Report.

Peter Wittenburg, Hennie Brugman, Albert Russel, Alex Klassmann, and Han Sloetjes. 2006. ELAN: a Professional Framework for Multimodality Research. In *Proceedings of the Fifth International Conference on Language Resources and Evaluation (LREC'06)*, Genoa, Italy. European Language Resources Association (ELRA).

Florian Zipser and Laurent Romary. 2010. A model oriented approach to the mapping of annotation formats using standards.

Can We Use Word Embeddings for Enhancing Guarani-Spanish Machine Translation?

Santiago Góngora, Nicolás Giossa, Luis Chiruzzo
Facultad de Ingeniería
Universidad de la República
Montevideo, Uruguay
{sgongora,nicolas.giossa,luischir}@fing.edu.uy

Abstract

Machine translation for low-resource languages, such as Guarani, is a challenging task due to the lack of data. One way of tackling it is using pretrained word embeddings for model initialization. In this work we try to check if currently available data is enough to train rich embeddings for enhancing MT for Guarani and Spanish, by building a set of word embedding collections and training MT systems using them. We found that the trained vectors are strong enough to slightly improve the performance of some of the translation models and also to speed up the training convergence.

1 Introduction

In recent years the performance of machine translation systems has grown alongside with the rise of neural architectures (Zhang and Zong, 2020; Castilho et al., 2017) that infer the translation patterns while consuming a huge amount of data at training time. However, this high performance is hard to achieve when one (or both) of the languages is considered a low-resource language (Mager et al., 2018). That is the case for Guarani, an indigenous language spoken by nearly 10 million people in South America. It has the characteristic of being one of the few indigenous languages used for daily communication, both by people who identify with indigenous ethnicity as well as people who do not. According to the Paraguayan census office almost 70% of Paraguayans speak some form of Guarani at home[1], but despite this, it remains a low-resource language in the NLP community (Joshi et al., 2020), and the existing attempts at building machine translation systems for this language have not achieved very high results yet.

Qi et al. (2018) found that using pretrained word embeddings could be useful when building machine translation systems for low-resource scenarios. Considering the scarcity of Guarani-Spanish parallel text, the aim of this work is to evaluate if it is possible to enhance a MT system by incorporating word embeddings built with the available monolingual data. In order to do this, we first trained a set of word embedding collections and selected the best of these models according to some intrinsic tests. Finally we trained machine translation experiments using the different embeddings and compared them to the base scenario where no pretrained embeddings were used.

The intrinsic tests and other resources used in this paper are available on GitHub[2].

2 Related work

Although there have been some efforts on developing resources for Guarani, it remains largely under-explored in NLP. The current reference corpus for Guarani is COREGUAPA (Secretaría de Políticas Lingüísticas del Paraguay, 2019), it can be queried online but not be downloaded. Other resources include a Spanish-Guarani parallel corpus built from news sites and blogs (Chiruzzo et al., 2020), two corpora for sentiment analysis (Rios et al., 2014; Agüero-Torales et al., 2021), and a small Universal Dependencies corpus of the Mbya Guarani dialect (Thomas, 2019; Dooley, 2006). Except COREGUAPA, which cannot be downloaded, all of these resources are rather small for building accurate statistical models.

Interest towards machine translation for indigenous languages of the Americas has increased lately. An important antecedent is the First Workshop on NLP for Indigenous Languages of the Americas (AmericasNLP) (Mager et al., 2021), which organized a shared task on MT from Spanish to several indigenous languages, including Guarani, with several participants. The test set for this shared

[1] https://www.ine.gov.py/news/news-contenido.php?cod-news=505

[2] https://github.com/sgongora27/Guarani-embeddings-for-MT

Proceedings of the Fifth Workshop on the Use of Computational Methods in the Study of Endangered Languages, pages 127 - 132
May 26-27, 2022 ©2022 Association for Computational Linguistics

task was a subset of the XNLI corpus (Conneau et al., 2018) translated to all languages. However, Guarani-Spanish machine translation still remains under-explored. There are some works that take into account the lack of available data (Alcaraz and Alcaraz, 2020; Gasser, 2018; Rudnick et al., 2014; Abdelali et al., 2006), or try to use the rich Guarani morphology to enhance the translation results Borges et al. (2021).

The use of word embeddings to enhance machine translation in low-resource scenarios has been previously explored (Qi et al., 2018), obtaining good results overall. They report that using pre-trained embeddings for both the source and target languages seem to improve results for translating low-resourced languages, but the improvement is much lower for languages with large amounts of data. Furthermore, (Shapiro and Duh, 2018) explores alternatives to include pre-trained embeddings in MT systems for a morphologically rich language, and (Nguyen and Chiang, 2017) uses a transfer learning approach for enhancing translation for a low-resource pair, but considering data from other related low-resources pairs as well.

3 Word embeddings

In a previous work (Góngora et al., 2021) we carried a first round of experiments with Guarani word embeddings, collecting text from news sites, tweets and the Guarani Wikipedia[3]. We classified each tweet in one of three categories (A: very reliable, B: reliable, and C: unreliable) according to the probability of being in Guarani using a heuristic based on the number of Guarani tokens from a frequent words list. Finally, for evaluating the then trained embeddings, we also presented two sets of intrinsic tests based on the original tests from Mikolov et al. (2013). One of them is a translation of the original *capital-common-countries* (*ccc*) set, while the other is a new set for *family* relations, inspired in the original one.

In the current work, we collected more data from the different sources and added datasets such as *The Bible*[4] and *The book of Mormon*[5]. We also translated the classic similarity test MC-30 (Miller and Charles, 1991) to Guarani in order to have another intrinsic test to perform (in addition to the *family* and *capital-common-countries* tests).

We trained a set of 24 different word embedding models in Guarani with different configurations. All of them were built using the gensim library (Řehůřek and Sojka, 2010) implementation of the word2vec C-Bow algorithm (Mikolov et al., 2013). The configurations differ in how much text was used (see below), the embeddings size (150 or 300) and the window size (6, 7 or 8). The number of tokens used in the different experiments varies between 1.9M and 2.7M depending on the different data sets we use, as shown in table 1. The *base text* set is used in all models, while some models also include the A, A+B, or A+B+C tweet sets.

Set	Tokens	Sentences (s) or Tweets (t)
The Bible	760,697	99,689 s
The Book of Mormon	204,434	58,995 s
Guarani Wikipedia	504,730	28,123 s
News	433.134	51,753 s
Base text (the four sets above)	1,902,995	238,560 s
Very reliable tweets (A)	11,791	811 t
Reliable tweets (B)	75,493	6,498 t
Unreliable tweets (C)	706,907	71,767 t
Total	2,697,186	

Table 1: Number of tokens for each of the sets used for training the word embedding models.

3.1 Analogy and Similarity tests

In order to perform a preliminary evaluation of these models we used the previously mentioned analogy (*family* and *ccc*) and similarity (*MC-30*) tests. Table 2 shows the results for these tests, indicating the configuration of each of the twenty-four models. The results of the analogy tests (*family* and *ccc*) are precision using top 1 (T1) or top 5 (T5) matches, while the similarity test (*MC-30*) is Spearman's rank correlation. In order to compare the performance we also include a row for a *baseline* consisting of the best result for each of the intrinsic tests achieved by the models in our previous work (Góngora et al., 2021), which were trained with size 150, window 7 and did not use any of the tweet sets.

Overall we can see a great improvement over the results of the analogy tests reported in the previous work (*baseline*), which can be explained in part because we are using a larger amount of text for training the models. However, there is a noticeable gap between the results for *family* and the *ccc* tests. This difference may be due to the type and style of texts used during training: neither the Bible nor

[3] https://dumps.wikimedia.org/gnwiki/ - February 2021.

[4] https://biblics.com/gn - July 2021.

[5] https://www.churchofjesuschrist.org/study/scriptures/bofm?lang=grn - July 2021.

Size	W	Tweets	family T1	family T5	ccc T1	ccc T5	MC-30
150	6	none	42.86	52.38	6.52	18.58	0.515
150	6	A	45.24	57.14	7.11	17.39	0.527
150	6	AB	42.86	52.38	7.71	18.77	0.530
150	6	ABC	45.24	52.38	4.15	15.42	0.500
150	7	none	**54.76**	54.76	9.09	18.77	0.440
150	7	A	50.00	52.38	7.11	15.61	0.556
150	7	AB	40.48	54.76	8.10	18.38	0.499
150	7	ABC	45.24	54.76	4.35	14.43	0.502
150	9	none	45.24	54.76	9.09	**21.34**	0.495
150	9	A	45.24	54.76	6.92	18.38	0.475
150	9	AB	50.00	54.76	7.31	17.19	0.449
150	9	ABC	42.86	52.38	6.52	19.17	0.460
300	6	none	45.24	47.62	7.91	17.59	**0.569**
300	6	A	42.86	54.76	8.10	17.79	0.473
300	6	AB	40.48	50.00	5.93	17.00	0.552
300	6	ABC	40.48	47.62	4.74	17.98	0.541
300	7	none	42.86	52.38	7.71	20.95	0.403
300	7	A	45.24	52.38	7.51	20.16	0.511
300	7	AB	50.00	**59.52**	**9.49**	18.97	0.512
300	7	ABC	40.48	52.38	8.70	17.79	0.538
300	9	none	50.00	54.76	6.52	17.59	0.519
300	9	A	45.24	57.14	7.71	18.38	0.521
300	9	AB	47.62	52.38	8.10	19.76	0.543
300	9	ABC	38.10	54.76	6.32	20.16	0.513
Baseline			41.27	48.41	5.53	13.37	-

Table 2: Results for the intrinsic evaluation of the 24 models trained. Maximum scores in bold, minimum scores underlined. *Baseline* refers to the best result for each test reported in our previous work (Góngora et al., 2021).

the Book of Mormon include modern countries and cities in their sentences. Also the Guarani Wikipedia is really small, even having some articles containing just a single line, so the occurrence of these kind of words is pretty low. Lastly the *ccc* test does not take into account South American countries, which might be the more likely ones to appear in our news set.

The results for the similarity test (*MC-30*) are good enough, ranging from 0.403 to 0.569, even compared to the state of the art for English[6] which ranges from 0.618 to 0.92 but trained with much larger resources. For this test we could not compare the results with a previous baseline since it was not used in our previous work.

4 Machine translation experiments

We carried a series of machine translation experiments to compare the use of randomly initialized embeddings with the use of different pretrained embedding configurations. All experiments were done using OpenNMT[7] with its default configuration, an encoder-decoder model implemented with stacked LSTMs and an attention model, so that the difference between experiments would only be the embeddings initialization.

For those models using pre-trained word embeddings we had to choose both the Spanish embeddings and the Guarani embeddings. For Spanish we chose a collection of size 300 trained by Azzinnari and Martínez (2016) using a corpus of 6 billion words. Due to limitations of OpenNMT, the Guarani embeddings size must also be 300. Therefore we chose some of the twenty-four models trained according to their size (300), their Spearman's correlation score for the *MC-30* test (see table 2) and the subsets of tweets used for training them:

- `s300w6none`: size 300, window 6, no tweets
- `s300w9ab`: size 300, window 9, tweets A+B
- `s300w7abc`: size 300, window 7, tweets A+B+C

We trained three translation models in each direction (Guarani-Spanish and Spanish-Guarani) using them as pre-trained word embeddings. We also trained an additional model in each direction without using pre-trained word embeddings (i.e. using *randomly* initialized embeddings). In all cases the models were trained for 80K steps — saving a checkpoint every 5K steps — using the training set from Chiruzzo et al. (2020) (*Train2020*) and the training set from the parallel data we presented in our previous work (Góngora et al., 2021) plus 383 new parallel sentences collected for this work (we call this union *Train2021*).

We then chose, for each model, the checkpoint that maximized the ChrF metric for the dev set (*Dev2020+Dev2021*). The test results will be reported over the test set from (Chiruzzo et al., 2020) (*Test2020*), the test partition of our own parallel set (*Test2021*), and the dev and test sets from (Mager et al., 2021) (*ANLP Dev* and *ANLP Test*), using the BLEU (Papineni et al., 2002) and ChrF (Popović, 2015) scores. Table 3 shows the size of all the aforementioned datasets.

Corpus	Set Name	Sentences	Guarani Tokens	Spanish Tokens
Our parallel set	*Train 2021*	12,129	274,734	528,018
	Dev 2021	1,514	34,238	65,940
	Test 2021	1,532	34,597	68,805
(Chiruzzo et al., 2020)	*Train 2020*	11,501	214,727	304,012
	Dev 2020	1,481	26,606	37,355
	Test 2020	1,549	27,351	38,908
(Mager et al., 2021)	*ANLP Dev*	996	7,216	11,180
	ANLP Test	1,004	6,501	10,074

Table 3: Size of the parallel corpora partitions.

[6] https://aclweb.org/aclwiki/MC-28_Test_Collection_(State_of_the_art)

[7] https://opennmt.net/

Test Set	Test2020		Test2021		ANLP Dev		ANLP Test	
Models `Gn-Es`	BLEU	ChrF	BLEU	ChrF	BLEU	ChrF	BLEU	ChrF
`random`	21.90	37.26	15.12	37.71	0.41	12.22	0.37	11.75
`s300w6none`	22.64	**38.63**	15.75	**39.13**	0.48	13.44	0.51	12.85
`s300w9ab`	22.49	38.32	15.85	38.76	0.44	13.52	0.44	**12.93**
`s300w7abc`	22.54	38.46	15.75	38.94	0.57	**13.65**	0.50	12.75
(Borges et al., 2021)	20.30	-	-	-	-	-	-	-
Models `Es-Gn`	BLEU	ChrF	BLEU	ChrF	BLEU	ChrF	BLEU	ChrF
`random`	20.55	36.52	20.59	**37.08**	0.27	12.77	0.49	12.91
`s300w6none`	20.19	**36.95**	17.33	35.42	0.32	**13.10**	0.45	12.72
`s300w9ab`	19.75	35.13	20.24	36.23	0.36	12.49	0.17	**13.00**
`s300w7abc`	18.44	33.74	19.81	35.98	0.23	11.98	0.12	12.06
ANLP first place	-	-	-	-	-	-	6.13	33.6
ANLP *baseline*	-	-	-	-	-	-	0.12	19.3
ANLP last place	-	-	-	-	-	-	0.13	10.8

Table 4: BLEU and ChrF results of the translation experiments over the different test sets.

4.1 Guarani-Spanish

Figure 1 shows how BLEU and ChrF scores change at each checkpoint. We observe that, in general, models that use pretrained embeddings tend to converge earlier. This is particularly important when experimenting with several models and having little computing power available.

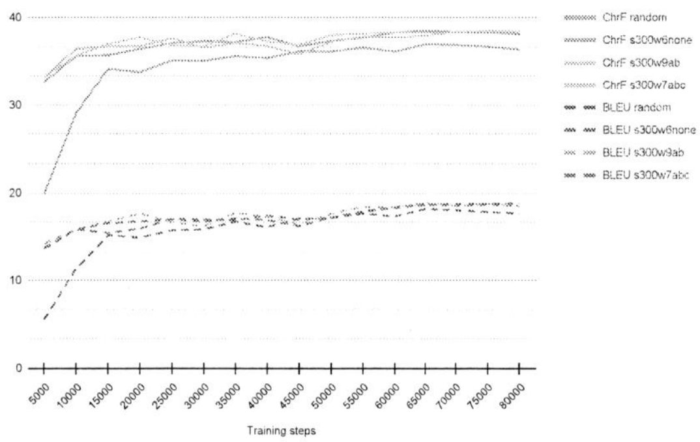

Figure 1: BLEU and ChrF evolution on the dev set for each checkpoint while training the `Gn-Es` models.

The top rows of table 4 shows the results over the test sets for the best model in each configuration. We also show the only result available for comparison in the direction `Gn-Es` (Borges et al., 2021), which used the (Chiruzzo et al., 2020) test corpus. We outperformed their results, which probably is because our models use more training data (they used only the train partition from Chiruzzo et al. (2020)).

We can also see that using pretrained word embeddings improved the performance with respect to the randomly initialized model on every test set. However, notice that the performance for the ANLP sets (Mager et al., 2021) drops dramatically. We think this could be explained by the more varied text styles present in these test sets, in contrast with the more uniform news text used for training.

4.2 Spanish-Guarani

Regarding the translation in the `Es-Gn` direction, figure 2 shows the results over the dev set and we can see the behavior is different. Although the faster convergence is observed again, the randomly initialized model performs as high as the pretrained ones. We can also see some performance stability problems as peaks in the graph. This behavior could be due to the target language embeddings being trained with fewer data, which is in line with what (Qi et al., 2018) reported.

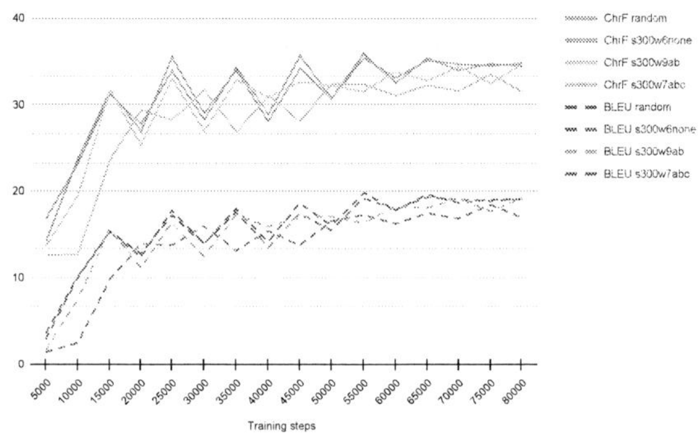

Figure 2: BLEU and ChrF evolution on the dev set for each checkpoint while training the `Es-Gn` models.

As can be seen in table 4 the results in this case are mixed, since the pretrained models do not outperform the randomly initialized model in all cases. Furthermore, the performance over the AmericasNLP sets also drops significantly, which probably has the same cause as the performance difference on the opposite direction.

In this direction it was possible to compare our best models with the performance obtained by AmericasNLP shared task participants (Mager et al., 2021). As shown in the bottom rows of table 4, our models perform between the bottom participants and the baseline. However, we did not aim to optimize the performance for this scenario: in this work we tried to focus only on analyze the use of pretrained word embeddings, and further work is needed to improve the training configurations with parameter tuning or different preprocessing techniques.

5 Conclusions

The results obtained in our experiments show that — with the currently available data — we can start to see some improvements when using pre-trained embeddings; at least in the `Gn-Es` direction. The performance of the `Gn-Es` models that used pre-trained embeddings was slightly better than the performance of the one that did not use them. Additionally, the developed systems converge faster when using pretrained embeddings, which is especially useful in the scenario that is common for low-resource research labs, that of having little computing power. However, in the `Es-Gn` direction the results were more mixed, which is aligned with the conclusions of Qi et al. (2018).

There are still many lines to explore. First, trying other methods and algorithms for building embeddings such as FastText, which could be better for morphologically rich languages such as Guarani (Bojanowski et al., 2017; Shapiro and Duh, 2018). Second, we must explore the different OpenNMT configuration possibilities. We could also use back-translation techniques as well, such as the approach explored by (Vázquez et al., 2021), the winning system in AmericasNLP shared task. Finally more diverse text is needed, considering the difference observed while evaluating over the AmericasNLP sets. This diversity is also needed for improving the word embeddings performance. The great differences between both analogy tests suggests that the words in the *capital-common-countries* test might not be suitable for Guarani, perhaps due to the topics covered in Paraguayan news which refer mainly to countries in the region.

References

Ahmed Abdelali, James Cowie, Steve Helmreich, Wanying Jin, Maria Pilar Milagros, Bill Ogden, Hamid Mansouri Rad, and Ron Zacharski. 2006. Guarani: a case study in resource development for quick ramp-up mt. In *Proceedings of the 7th Conference of the Association for Machine Translation in the Americas, "Visions for the Future of Machine Translation"*, pages 1–9.

Marvin Agüero-Torales, David Vilares, and Antonio López-Herrera. 2021. On the logistical difficulties and findings of jopara sentiment analysis. In *Proceedings of the Fifth Workshop on Computational Approaches to Linguistic Code-Switching*, pages 95–102, Online. Association for Computational Linguistics.

NB Alvarenga Alcaraz and PR Alvarenga Alcaraz. 2020. Aplicación web de análisis y traducción automática guaraní–español/español–guaraní. *Revista Científica de la UCSA*, 7(2):41–69.

Agustín Azzinnari and Alejandro Martínez. 2016. Representación de Palabras en Espacios de Vectores.

Piotr Bojanowski, Edouard Grave, Armand Joulin, and Tomas Mikolov. 2017. Enriching word vectors with subword information. *Transactions of the Association for Computational Linguistics*, 5:135–146.

Yanina Borges, Florencia Mercant, and Luis Chiruzzo. 2021. Using guarani verbal morphology on guarani-spanish machine translation experiments. *Procesamiento del Lenguaje Natural*, 66:89–98.

Sheila Castilho, Joss Moorkens, Federico Gaspari, Iacer Calixto, John Tinsley, and Andy Way. 2017. Is neural machine translation the new state of the art? *The Prague Bulletin of Mathematical Linguistics*, 108:109–120.

Luis Chiruzzo, Pedro Amarilla, Adolfo Ríos, and Gustavo Giménez Lugo. 2020. Development of a Guarani - Spanish parallel corpus. In *Proceedings of the 12th Language Resources and Evaluation Conference*, pages 2629–2633, Marseille, France. European Language Resources Association.

Alexis Conneau, Ruty Rinott, Guillaume Lample, Adina Williams, Samuel R. Bowman, Holger Schwenk, and Veselin Stoyanov. 2018. Xnli: Evaluating cross-lingual sentence representations. In *Proceedings of the 2018 Conference on Empirical Methods in Natural Language Processing*. Association for Computational Linguistics.

Robert A Dooley. 2006. Léxico guarani, dialeto mbyá com informações úteis para o ensino médio, a aprendizagem e a pesquisa lingüística. *Cuiabá, MT: Sociedade Internacional de Lingüística*, 143:206.

Michael Gasser. 2018. Mainumby: un ayudante para la traducción castellano-guaraní. *arXiv preprint arXiv:1810.08603*.

Santiago Góngora, Nicolás Giossa, and Luis Chiruzzo. 2021. Experiments on a Guarani corpus of news and social media. In *Proceedings of the First Workshop on Natural Language Processing for Indigenous Languages of the Americas*, pages 153–158, Online. Association for Computational Linguistics.

Pratik Joshi, Sebastin Santy, Amar Budhiraja, Kalika Bali, and Monojit Choudhury. 2020. The state and fate of linguistic diversity and inclusion in the NLP world.

Manuel Mager, Ximena Gutierrez-Vasques, Gerardo Sierra, and Ivan Meza-Ruiz. 2018. Challenges of language technologies for the indigenous languages of the Americas. In *Proceedings of the 27th International Conference on Computational Linguistics*, pages 55–69, Santa Fe, New Mexico, USA. Association for Computational Linguistics.

Manuel Mager, Arturo Oncevay, Abteen Ebrahimi, John Ortega, Annette Rios, Angela Fan, Ximena Gutierrez-Vasques, Luis Chiruzzo, Gustavo Giménez-Lugo, Ricardo Ramos, Ivan Vladimir Meza Ruiz, Rolando Coto-Solano, Alexis Palmer, Elisabeth Mager-Hois, Vishrav Chaudhary, Graham Neubig, Ngoc Thang Vu, and Katharina Kann. 2021. Findings of the AmericasNLP 2021 shared task on open machine translation for indigenous languages of the Americas. pages 202–217.

Tomas Mikolov, Kai Chen, Greg Corrado, and Jeffrey Dean. 2013. Efficient estimation of word representations in vector space.

George A. Miller and Walter G. Charles. 1991. Contextual correlates of semantic similarity. *Language and Cognitive Processes*, 6(1):1–28.

Toan Q Nguyen and David Chiang. 2017. Transfer learning across low-resource, related languages for neural machine translation. *arXiv preprint arXiv:1708.09803*.

Kishore Papineni, Salim Roukos, Todd Ward, and Wei-Jing Zhu. 2002. Bleu: a method for automatic evaluation of machine translation. In *Proceedings of the 40th Annual Meeting of the Association for Computational Linguistics*, pages 311–318, Philadelphia, Pennsylvania, USA. Association for Computational Linguistics.

Maja Popović. 2015. chrF: character n-gram F-score for automatic MT evaluation. In *Proceedings of the Tenth Workshop on Statistical Machine Translation*, pages 392–395, Lisbon, Portugal. Association for Computational Linguistics.

Ye Qi, Devendra Sachan, Matthieu Felix, Sarguna Padmanabhan, and Graham Neubig. 2018. When and why are pre-trained word embeddings useful for neural machine translation? In *Proceedings of the 2018 Conference of the North American Chapter of the Association for Computational Linguistics: Human Language Technologies, Volume 2 (Short Papers)*, pages 529–535, New Orleans, Louisiana. Association for Computational Linguistics.

Radim Řehůřek and Petr Sojka. 2010. Software Framework for Topic Modelling with Large Corpora. In *Proceedings of the LREC 2010 Workshop on New Challenges for NLP Frameworks*, pages 45–50, Valletta, Malta. ELRA. `http://is.muni.cz/publication/884893/en`.

Adolfo A. Rios, Pedro J. Amarilla, and G. Giménez-Lugo. 2014. Sentiment categorization on a creole language with lexicon-based and machine learning techniques. *2014 Brazilian Conference on Intelligent Systems*, pages 37–43.

Alex Rudnick, Taylor Skidmore, Alberto Samaniego, and Michael Gasser. 2014. Guampa: a toolkit for collaborative translation. In *LREC*, pages 1659–1663.

Secretaría de Políticas Lingüísticas del Paraguay. 2019. Corpus de Referencia del Guaraní Paraguayo Actual – COREGUAPA. `http://www.spl.gov.py`. Accessed: 2021-03-13.

Pamela Shapiro and Kevin Duh. 2018. Morphological word embeddings for arabic neural machine translation in low-resource settings. In *Proceedings of the Second Workshop on Subword/Character LEvel Models*, pages 1–11.

Guillaume Thomas. 2019. Universal dependencies for mbyá guaraní. In *Proceedings of the Third Workshop on Universal Dependencies (UDW, SyntaxFest 2019)*, pages 70–77.

Raúl Vázquez, Yves Scherrer, Sami Virpioja, and Jörg Tiedemann. 2021. The Helsinki submission to the AmericasNLP shared task. pages 255–264.

Jiajun Zhang and Chengqing Zong. 2020. Neural machine translation: Challenges, progress and future.

Faoi Gheasa: an adaptive game for Irish language learning

Liang Xu[1], Elaine Uí Dhonnchadha[2] and Monica Ward[1]

[1]Dublin City University, Ireland
[2]Trinity College Dublin, Ireland

Abstract

In this paper, we present a game with a purpose (GWAP) (Von Ahn, 2006). The aim of the game is to promote language learning and 'noticing' (Skehan, 2013). The game has been designed for Irish, but the framework could be used for other languages. Irish is a minority language which means that L2 learners have limited opportunities for exposure to the language, and additionally, there are also limited (digital) learning resources available. This research incorporates game development, language pedagogy and ICALL language materials development. This paper will focus on the language materials development as this is a bottleneck in the teaching and learning of minority and endangered languages.

1 Introduction

The primary aim of the research is to develop a game which learners (players) will want to continue playing for enjoyment which will also improve their vocabulary and grammar skills through noticing, reading and writing in a novel and fun way. From our point of view, the language learning aspect is paramount, but from the player's point of view it should appear to be a side effect of playing the game, rather than the purpose of the game. Therefore the 'game' narrative and game 'world' are of utmost importance. The inspiration for this game is the Cipher game (Xu & Chamberlain, 2020) which was developed to find errors in English Corpora through 'game with a purpose' (GWAP) methodology and crowdsourcing. In the process of annotating errors in text some players remarked that they felt this would be an effective way to learn a language. This current research seeks to test that hypothesis. To do this, we create a game environment that is conducive to language learning, where the learning challenges and trajectory conform to sound pedagogical principles and where the learner experience is adapted to the individual learner's needs. We also strive to make the game culturally relevant, and complementary to the school curriculum.

In this paper we describe the game, the linguistics challenges and the material development challenges.

2 Game aspects

The game world is a magical one in which ancient evil spirits are attempting to deny access to the ancient mythological tales by placing them under a spell, to cause people to lose their memory of their past. The player's challenge is to decipher these spells in order to restore the tales before they are sealed and lost forever. There are many different spells (ciphers) and stages before all the evil spells can be lifted and the story is restored.

Figure 1 Game Interface

Players accumulate points when they correctly identify ciphered words and lose points when they fail to spot a ciphered word or incorrectly identify

Proceedings of the Fifth Workshop on the Use of Computational Methods in the Study of Endangered Languages, pages 133 - 138
May 26-27, 2022

a ciphered word. Players can use their points to buy hints if they wish, which means that players with a minimal amount of Irish can enjoy playing the game. If a player cannot find all of the ciphered words on a page, they are given the choice to 'change the ending' by writing some text in Irish, or to abandon the attempt in which case they will be presented with the same page but with easier ciphers. The game is developed using Unity (client) and Photon (server).

Previous work on language learning games for Irish include multi-media games such as Fios Feasa[1], and CALL applications (Monica Ward, 2016; Monica Ward, Mozgovoy, & Purgina, 2019), (Neasa Ní Chiaráin & Ní Chasaide, 2016; Neasa Ní Chiaráin & Ní Chasaide, 2019). The *Faoi Gheasa* (Under a spell) game is different in terms of its adaptive educational content and game elements and its reuse of existing language materials.

For many years it has been known that games can contribute to learning (Dixon, Dixon, & Jordan, 2022; Prensky, 2003). They can be motivational for students and they encourage self-efficacy. Motivation is especially important in any language learning context (Dörnyei & Ushioda, 2013) and there has been a lot of focus on motivation in the language learning literature, e.g. (Hattie, 2008; Lightbown & Spada, 2021). Self-efficacy is important in learning contexts as it promotes student engagement and learning (Linnenbrink & Pintrich, 2003). Our *Faoi Gheasa* game leverages these motivational and engaging aspects of digital games to make the game playing (and learning) more enjoyable for learners.

3 Pedagogical aspects

This game employs the pedagogical technique of using storytelling as a means of language learning. According to Harris, Ó Néill, Uí Dhufaigh, and Ó Súilleabháin (1996:9:9) it is important that authentic materials be used, and that stories, songs, poems, and proverbs are of particular importance as they have cultural and traditional value. They also state that when suitable authentic material is not available then there is no alternative but to compose Irish versions of materials that children enjoy. Tierney and Dobson (1995) cited in (Mhic Mhathúna, 2004) also recommend listening to familiar stories in the second or foreign language.

Regarding the difficulty levels of stories, Harris et al. (1996:16-17) remind us that young learners who are acquiring Irish as a second language are still in the process of acquiring their first language. Therefore, they are generally not concerned about understanding every word they hear (in their first or second language), as long as there are sufficient hints in the context to allow them to get the general meaning. Harris et al. (1996) recommend that rather than focusing on simplifying the language, it is more important to provide a sufficient quantity of language input with the necessary contextual clues. They also suggest that the input needs to be challenging to provide opportunities for learning. Furthermore, they caution that over-simplification of written texts can result in stories that are somewhat bland and unnatural, and that there is scope for using more complex language particularly in the context of stories which are already familiar to the learners. We believe that these principles can also apply to written language in our game where learners will be familiar with some of the stories.

In relation to classroom teaching Harris et al. (1996:10:10) say that in order to cultivate a positive attitude to the learning of Irish, the teaching materials should be attractive, interesting, funny and that game-playing should be part of the process. We believe that our *Faoi Gheasa* game fulfils these criteria and that it can complement both classroom and non-classroom based learning. It leverages aspects of noticing (Skehan, 2013), consciousness raising (Smith, 1981), research on error correction (Chaudron, 1988) and incorporates elements from Games with a Purpose (Von Ahn, 2006).

3.1 L1-L2 learning issues

Irish has a complex role in Irish society. While not all members of society value the language for cultural and heritage reasons, for many Irish citizens and the Irish diaspora around the world, the Irish language has great cultural significance and they have a strong desire to acquire and improve their Irish language skills, and to ensure that their children are confident users of the language.
In learning a second language (L2), features which are not present in their first language (L1) often

[1] https://fiosfeasa.com/

present additional challenges for the learner (Laufer & Eliasson, 1993; Schepens, Van Hout, & Van der Slik, 2022; Vainio, Pajunen, & Hyönä, 2014). The majority of L2 learners of Irish have English as their L1. There are many linguistic differences between Irish and English, all of which can create barriers to the learning of Irish, a minority language in the shadow of English.

One difficulty for L1 English language speakers learning Irish is that orthography system is different from English yet uses the same Latin alphabet. While the Irish orthography system is opaque, it is more regular than English. However, the rules of the orthography system are not generally taught to students, and they are often left to decipher it themselves. Often, students do not see the patterns, and this hampers their learning. They automatically 'map' the English sound-orthography system to Irish, which is not always a successful approach. For example, the word *teach* meaning 'house' in Irish is pronounced quite differently from the word 'teach' in English.

Another difficulty for Irish language learners is that Irish has a complex system of initial mutations. This is a defining feature of the Celtic languages, which affects the initial phonemes of verbs, nouns, pronouns, adjectives, and some functional categories. The initial mutations on nouns, (and the word classes which modify and agree with a head noun), vary according to the gender of the noun i.e., whether the noun is masculine or feminine. At the level of morphology, Irish verbs are inflected for tense/mood, person and number, and nouns are inflected for number and case, the formation of which varies according to the gender of the noun. Features of Irish such as initial mutation, gender agreement, and case marking will be unfamiliar to learners whose first language is English.

Often Irish language learners are oblivious to the morphological and grammatical information encoded in a word and therefore lose vital clues when trying to understand written and spoken language. For example, in (1) *Bhí* 'was' has an initial mutation for past tense, *mhór* 'big' has an initial mutation to signal agreement with a feminine noun *tine* 'fire', *mbradán* 'salmon' has initial mutation as it is the object of the preposition and definite article *faoin* 'under the', and *feasa* 'knowledge' is in the genitive case to signify its relationship to *mbradán* 'salmon'.

(1) Bhí tine mhór faoin mbradán feasa.
Was fire big under.the salmon knowledge.
'There was a big fire under the salmon of knowledge'

In this game we encourage noticing of spelling orthography by introducing cipher errors into the stories. Most cipher errors are not errors which a learner would naturally make e.g., swapping the first half of a word with the second half, doubling the last letter, or removing all vowels. These types of errors encourage noticing, are relatively easy to spot, and minimise the risk of familiarising the learners with misspellings. In Figure 2 we have an example of the "Double Tail" cipher which doubles the last letter of a word, e.g. *Is* 'is' has become *Iss* and *mé* 'me' has become *méé*.

Figure 2 Example of a cipher and noun gender colour coding

In this experiment we encourage the noticing of noun gender which is a central feature of the morpho-syntax of Irish. English language speakers are generally unfamiliar with this grammatical feature of Irish. We do this as part of the game narrative by presenting nouns in distinct colours depending on their gender. In this way we facilitate the noticing of the two distinct types of noun. Some of the more complex ciphers remove the colour coding from nouns, and certain ciphers affect nouns of one gender or the other. Therefore noticing and remembering that individual words are affiliated to either the Water Spirit (blue, masculine nouns) or the Fire Spirit (red, feminine nouns) is an advantage in later stages of the game. In Figure 2 we see that *marúch* 'mermaid' is red and *dúlachán* 'dark one' is blue.

4 Materials development

As the game centres on stories which have been made unreadable by an evil spirit and which must be restored, an important requirement of the game is a bank of suitable stories. We decided on the theme of magic and mythology, for several reasons. Firstly, we hope that it has universal appeal to both young and old – all generations can enjoy a good story. Secondly a mythological theme can be made culturally relevant in different language settings, which should make the stories more interesting and significant for learners. Thirdly, some folklore stories can raise learners' cultural and heritage awareness which can motivate learners through reconnecting to the spirit of indigenous languages (Restoule, Archibald, Lester-Smith, Parent, & Smillie, 2010). A culturally responsive approach to learning is usually discussed in the context of marginalization e.g., (Sleeter, 2012), but it is relevant in all learning contexts, including Irish. Finally, we prefer stories and tales which are free from copyright restrictions.

We require the materials with difficulty levels ranging from beginner level to more advanced language learner levels. For younger children (6 to 8 years) who are just beginning to read, we use simple stories based on well-known fairy tales that they will be already familiar with in English. For more advanced learners we use more complex mythological stories and folk takes. For older children (10-12 years) we use simple versions of Irish mythological tales, and for the higher levels we use folk tales and legends with more sophisticated language constructions and vocabulary. This levelling of texts is currently a focus of our pilot study. Initially we have four levels of text difficulty: beginner, improver, intermediate and advanced. These are similar to CEFR levels A1, A2/B1, B2 and C1. When players sign up to play the game, they are asked for their age (we include the category 18+ for adults) and their school class/year and school type. Based on this information we assign them to an initial level, and they will move up or down levels depending on their performance in the game. Adults (18+) start in the improver category initially.

4.1 Sources of material

Ideally, we want to reuse resources where possible. However, while some stories are included in existing corpora (Kilgarriff, Rundell, & Uí Dhonnchadha, 2007) they are subject to copyright issues, which is also the case for published books and textbooks. In addition, we prefer that the stories (at the higher levels) are not already familiar to the game players. Where possible, we want to source texts which are already in electronic format, however some translating or composing of stories is envisaged.

One valuable source of online story material is the Dúchas.ie project which includes "The Schools Collection[2]". This collection was initiated in the 1930's by the Irish Folklore Commission in co-operation with the Department of Education. During that time, primary school children, aged approximately 12-14 years of age, collected folklore and tradition in their local areas and wrote it down in their school copybooks. The collection contains approximately 740,000 pages of handwritten pages compiled by pupils from 5,000 primary schools in Ireland between 1937 and 1939. Currently this collection is being transcribed through the Dúchas.ie crowdsourcing transcription project[3] and the transcribed material is publicly available online. This collection contains material written in both English and in Irish. Of particular interest to us are the folktales and Irish mythology legends written down almost ninety years ago by children who were native speakers of Irish. These stories fit into the 'intermediate' and 'advanced' categories. The collection contains a wealth valuable material at these levels which is ideal for our purposes. It does however require pre-processing as the texts are written down prior to the modern standardised orthography and they also contain some spelling and grammar errors. For the 'beginner' and 'improver' level we have translated some well-known fairy tales based on English versions, and we are currently seeking other sources of magical stories and tales. There is also a small amount of advanced level material dating from the early 1900's available on gutenberg.org[4], which also requires spelling standardisation.

[2] https://www.duchas.ie/en/info/cbe

[3] https://www.duchas.ie/en/meitheal/

[4] https://www.gutenberg.org/browse/languages/ga

4.2 Preparation of materials

In the case of Duchas.ie and Gutenberg.org stories the language was normalised to the modern spelling and grammar standards. Fairy tales were composed based on English versions. In order to avoid applying ciphers to proper nouns, and to facilitate the highlighting of noun genders, all stories were tagged with part-of-speech (POS) categories using the Irish POS tagger by Uí Dhonnchadha and van Genabith (2006). The POS tagged text was manually checked. The XML formatted POS tagged texts are imported into Unity and stories are divided into numerous screens (pages) and displayed in game. The game engine applies ciphers automatically and randomly to the texts. This means that if a player retries the same story, they will not encounter the same ciphers (enchantments). Figure 3 shows the *Faoi Gheasa* pipeline.

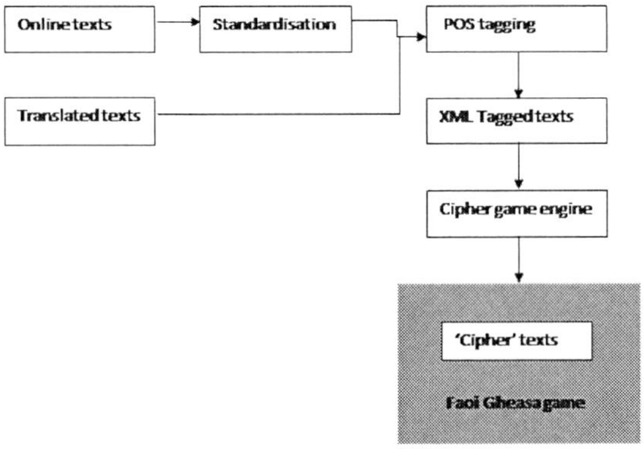

Figure 3 *Faoi Gheasa* pipeline

5 Conclusions and Future Work

In this paper we present a language learning game which will help players to improve their Irish language noticing skills and encourage reading for fun. The game is currently being piloted in a small number of primary and secondary schools and initial reactions are positive (74% of players who have filled in the survey questionnaire to date are interested in improving their language skills while playing a game). We are currently seeking new sources of material and fine-tuning the game adaptivity based on user feedback.

6 Acknowledgements

This work was conducted with the financial support of the Science Foundation Ireland Centre for Research Training in Digitally-Enhanced Reality (d-real) under Grant No. 18/CRT/6224. We would also like to express our special thanks to Tianlong Huang, who provided support for game development.

References

Chaudron, C. (1988). *Second language classrooms: Research on teaching and learning.*: Cambridge University Press.

Dixon, D., Dixon, T., & Jordan, E. (2022). Second language (L2) gains through digital game-based language learning (DGBLL): A meta-analysis. *Language Learning & Technology, 26*(1).

Dörnyei, Z., & Ushioda, E. (2013). *Teaching and researching: Motivation*: Routledge.

Harris, J., Ó Néill, P., Uí Dhufaigh, M., & Ó Súilleabháin, E. (1996). *Cúrsaí nua Gaeilge na bunscoile: móltaí agus ábhar samplach. Iml. 1 Naíonáin shóisearacha - rang 2.* Retrieved from Baile Átha Cliath:

Hattie, J. (2008). *Visible learning: A synthesis of over 800 meta-analyses relating to achievement*: Routledge.

Kilgarriff, A., Rundell, M., & Uí Dhonnchadha, E. (2007). Efficient corpus creation for lexicography. *Language Resources and Evaluation Journal.*

Laufer, B., & Eliasson, S. (1993). What Causes Avoidance in L2 Learning: L1-L2 Difference, L1-L2 Similarity, or L2 Complexity? *Studies in Second Language Acquisition, 15*, 35-48. doi:10.1017/S0272263100011657

Lightbown, P. M., & Spada, N. (2021). *How Languages Are Learned* (5 ed.): Oxford University Press.

Linnenbrink, E. A., & Pintrich, P. R. (2003). The role of self-efficacy beliefs instudent engagement and learning in the classroom. *Reading & Writing Quarterly, 19*(2), 119-137.

Mhic Mhathúna, M. (2004). *Storytelling As Vehicle for Second Language Acquisition: Learning Irish In a Naionra.* (PhD), University of Dublin, Trinity College, Dublin.

Ní Chiaráin, N., & Ní Chasaide, A. (2016). *The Digichaint interactive game as a virtual learning environment for Irish* Paper presented at the CALL communities and culture - short papers from EUROCALL 2016, Limassol, Cyprus.

Ní Chiaráin, N., & Ní Chasaide, A. (2019). *An Scéalaí: autonomous learners harnessing speech and language technologies.* Paper presented at the SLaTE 2019: 8th ISCA Workshop on Speech and Language Technology in Education, Graz, Austria.

Prensky, M. (2003). Digital game-based learning. *Computers in Entertainment (CIE), 1*(1).

Restoule, J., Archibald, J., Lester-Smith, D., Parent, A., & Smillie, C. A. (2010). Connecting to spirit in indigenous research. *Canadian Journal of Native Education, 33*(1).

Schepens, J., Van Hout, R., & Van der Slik, F. (2022). Linguistic dissimilarity increases age-related decline in adult language learning. *Studies in Second Language Acquisition*, 1-22. doi:10.1017/S0272263122000067

Skehan, P. (2013). Nurturing noticing. In *Noticing and second language acquisition: Studies in honor of Richard Schmidt*.

Sleeter, C. E. (2012). Confronting the marginalization of culturally responsive pedagogy. *Urban education, 47*(3), 562-584.

Tierney, D., & Dobson, P. (1995). *Are You Sitting Comfortably? Telling Stories to Young Language Learners.* London: CILT.

Uí Dhonnchadha, E., & van Genabith, J. (2006, May 2006). *A Part-of-speech tagger for Irish using Finite-State Morphology and Constraint Grammar Disambiguation.* Paper presented at the LREC 2006, Genoa.

Vainio, S., Pajunen, A., & Hyönä, J. (2014). L1 And L2 Word Recognition in Finnish: Examining L1 Effects on L2 Processing of Morphological Complexity and Morphophonological Transparency. *Studies in Second Language Acquisition, 36*(1), 133-162.

Von Ahn, L. (2006). Games with a purpose. *Computer, 36*(6), 92–94.

Ward, M. (2016). *CALLIPSO - Computer Assisted Language Learning for Parents Students and Others.* Paper presented at the Celtic Language Technology Workshop JALT-TALN 2016, Paris, France.

Ward, M., Mozgovoy, M., & Purgina, M. (2019). Can WordBricks Make Learning Irish More Engaging for Students? *International Journal of Game Based Learning, 9*(2), 20-39.

Xu, L., & Chamberlain, J. (2020). *Cipher: A prototype game-with-a-purpose for detecting errors in text.* . Paper presented at the LREC2020 Workshop on Games and Natural Language Processing.

Using Graph-Based Methods to Augment Online Dictionaries of Endangered Languages

Khalid Alnajjar[1,2,3], Mika Hämäläinen[1,2,3], Niko Partanen[1] and Jack Rueter[1]
[1]University of Helsinki, Finland
[2]École Normale Supérieure & CNRS, France
[3]Rootroo Ltd, Finland
firstname.lastname@helsinki.fi

Abstract

Many endangered Uralic languages have multilingual machine readable dictionaries saved in an XML format. However, the dictionaries cover translations very inconsistently between language pairs, for instance, the Livonian dictionary has some translations to Finnish, Latvian and Estonian, and the Komi-Zyrian dictionary has some translations to Finnish, English and Russian. We utilize graph-based approaches to augment such dictionaries by predicting new translations to existing and new languages based on different dictionaries for endangered languages and Wiktionaries. Our study focuses on the lexical resources for Komi-Zyrian (kpv), Erzya (myv) and Livonian (liv). We evaluate our approach by human judges fluent in the three endangered languages in question. Based on the evaluation, the method predicted good or acceptable translations 77% of the time. Furthermore, we train a neural prediction model to predict the quality of the automatically predicted translations with an 81% accuracy. The resulting extensions to the dictionaries are made available on the online dictionary platform used by the speakers of these languages.

1 Introduction

For many endangered languages there are several existing dictionaries and other bilingual lexical resources for different language pairs. For example, for many Uralic languages there are German dictionaries, as that has traditionally had a strong role as a scientific language of the field. Also the dictionaries in local majority languages such as Finnish, Estonian, Latvian and Russian are very common. Although the fact that a great many of them exist only as printed copies limits their use in the digital era.

Nevertheless, dictionaries play an important role in language documentation and revitalization efforts. For endangered Uralic languages, Akusanat online dictionary (Hämäläinen and Rueter, 2019) collects multilingual dictionary resources in multiple endangered languages such as the ones in focus of our paper: Komi-Zyrian, Livonian and Erzya. Making it possible for native speakers and language learners to access such a resource has a very big societal impact within the language communities.

Furthermore, online resources such as Wiktionary have gathered very large amounts of lexical data for majority languages. This data does not necessarily represent a fully curated and finalized product in which all entries would be of an equal quality. Only more recently has there been interest in building such resources in the languages that are nowadays more widely used, such as English. As creating these resources is an enormous undertaking, we investigate in this study the possibility of predicting translations from endangered languages to resource-rich languages automatically from existing translations in these high-resource language Wiktionaries.

We would like to point out that the languages we are working with in this paper are endangered, not just low-resourced (see Hämäläinen 2021). According to UNESCO Atlas of World languages (Moseley, 2010), Komi-Zyrian (kpv) has 217,316 native speakers and Erzya (myv) 400,000 native speakers. Livonian (liv), however, does not have any surviving native speakers[1], but has a small community of second language speakers.

Apart from Livonian, these languages have received some digital language documentation interest. Erzya (Rueter and Tyers, 2018) and Komi-Zyrian (Partanen et al., 2018) have small Universal Dependencies tree banks and morphological transducers (Rueter et al., 2020).

[1]https://www.thetimes.co.uk/article/death-of-a-language-last-ever-speaker-of-livonian-passes-away-aged-103-8k0rlplv8xj

Proceedings of the Fifth Workshop on the Use of Computational Methods in the Study of Endangered Languages, pages 139 - 148
May 26-27, 2022 ©2022 Association for Computational Linguistics

In the method we investigate in this study, the translations for a word in different languages are represented as graphs. This allows for an effective use of a large number of lexical resources that are not complete, but support one another.

Our main contributions in this work are:

1. We describe a method for inferring translations by combining different graph-based link prediction methods in endangered language data.

2. We evaluate their performance and applicability by conducting a manual evaluation, followed by detailed analyses and discussions.

3. We implement an artificial neural network model to determine the quality of predictions by the algorithmic methods automatically.

4. The prediction results of our method are published in an online dictionary after being verified by lexicographers to have a direct impact on the endangered language communities in question.

Our approach makes it possible for lexicographers to bootstrap new languages into existing multilingual dictionaries. This saves time as instead of building a lexicon from the ground up, their task becomes more of a post-editing, where new translations need only to be verified rather than written from scratch. In the context of larger languages, post-editing has become mainstream in lexicographic work (see Jakubicek et al. 2018), however in the context of endangered languages post-editing has thus far received less lexicographic interest.

2 Related Work

There is a plethora of NLP work out there relating to endangered languages ranging from rule-based approaches (Tyers, 2010; Zueva et al., 2020; Rueter and Hämäläinen, 2020) to latest neural models (Ens et al., 2019; Alnajjar, 2021; Wiechetek et al., 2021). In this section, however, we focus more on work on extending dictionaries.

There has been several attempts in the past in predicting new translations in bilingual and multilingual dictionaries. In this section, we describe the most relevant ones to our work. There has been related approaches to extending semantic knowledge bases (Raganato et al., 2016; Pasini and Navigli, 2017; Gesese et al., 2020), but we leave their detailed description out of this section as the problem the approaches try to solve is fundamentally different in terms of the availability and magnitude of the data.

Lam and Kalita (2013) have proposed a method for reversing bidirectional dictionaries (e.g., reversing Hindi-English to English-Hindi). Their approach requires WordNet[2] (Fellbaum, 1998) for at least one of the languages, and uses the similarities between the words and their synonyms, hyponyms and hypernyms in WordNet to estimate the quality of the reverse translations. They have tested the method by reversing resource-poor and endangered language dictionaries (e.g. Karbi, Hindi and Assamese) to have English as the source language instead of the destination language. It is worth noting that this approach is not capable of producing dictionaries or translations in new languages.

Lam et al. (2015) proposed a method for creating new dictionaries for resource-poor languages. In their work, a dictionary of a low-resource language to a resource-rich language with a high-quality WordNet is needed. To translate a word from the source language to a new language (e.g. Arabic), their method uses links between the English WordNet and existing multiple intermediate WordNets of other languages such as Finnish and Japanese to highlight the relevant words in the WordNets. Thereafter, each of these words are translated to the desired destination language using existing machine translation systems such as Google Translate. The higher the agreement between multiple machine translation systems, the higher the score given to the translation.

A constraint-based approach for inducting new bilingual dictionaries for low-resource languages that are share the language family has been proposed by Wushouer et al. (2015). In their approach, a graph is constructed from two bilingual dictionaries (i.e. A-B and B-C, where B is the intermediate language), and new potential translation links are examined by treating the problem as conjunctive normal form (CNF) and using WPMaxSAT solver to identify the new translations. This work has been extended further in (Nasution et al., 2016) to generalize the method to work for a larger group of languages and identify the best constraint set according to the language pairs.

A graph-based method for combining multiple

[2]https://wordnet.princeton.edu/

Wiktionaries and inferring new translations using graph-based probabilistic inference measured by random walks was proposed by Soderland et al. (2009). The goal of their work is to construct a huge dictionary covering the well-resourced languages (e.g., English, French, Spanish, ... etc) and suggest new dictionary translations; nonetheless, their work does not address endangered or resource-poor languages. Another graph-based method was embraced by Alnajjar et al. (2021).

Donandt et al. (2017) have trained a Support Vector Machine (SVM) model to predict whether a new translation is valid or not. Given multiple bilingual dictionaries, a directed graph is constructed where nodes are unique words with their language and part-of-speech tag. Depth-first search is applied to find cycles in the graph. Translations found in cycles with a translation in the dictionary from the target word back to the source are considered to be positive examples, whereas translations found in paths but not cycles are treated as negative instances. Additional features are passed to the model as well, such as the frequency of source word in a dictionary, number of available paths between the source and target words, and, in the case of sharing the language family, the average Levenshtein distance between all the words in the path. This method was not investigated nor evaluated for endangered languages.

3 Data

Two types of resources are used in our approach, 1) XML dictionaries of endangered languages (such as Komi-Zyrian, Livonian and Erzya, with kpv, liv and myv as ISO 639-3 codes respectively) and 2) Wiktionaries[3] of resource-rich languages (such as English and French). While we could utilize the Finnish WordNet (Lindén and Carlson, 2010) as an additional resource in this task as done in some of the previous work, however, in practice it would introduce more noise due to the relatively low quality of the Finnish WordNet[4].

3.1 XML Dictionaries

The XML dictionaries have been created in connection with the development work at morphological analysers, and they contain both materials from already published dictionaries and also individually added entries. In this work, we use dictionaries of three endangered languages Komi-Zyrian, Livonian and Erzya. The Komi and Erzya dictionaries are built as part of the Giella Project (Moshagen et al., 2014)[5] and they are available through UralicNLP (Hämäläinen, 2019), while the Livonian dictionary has been outlined in Rueter (2014).

```
<e id="None" meta="">
  <lg>
    <l pos="V" val="IV">аволямс</l>
    <stg>
      <st Contlex="IV_KUNDAMS">аволя</st>
    </stg>
  </lg>
    <sources>
      <book name="Olga01"/>
    </sources>
  <mg relId="0">
    <semantics>
    </semantics>
    <tg xml:lang="eng">
      <t pos="V">waive</t>
    </tg>
    <tg xml:lang="fin">
      <t pos="V" val="IV">huiskuttaa</t>
      <t pos="V" val="IV">heiluttaa</t>
      <t pos="V" val="IV">lakaista</t>
    </tg>
    <tg xml:lang="rus">
      <t pos="V" val="IV">махать</t>
    </tg>
    <defNative>Аволдамс ламокстЬ.</defNative>
  </mg>
</e>
```

Figure 1: An example of the XML structure in the Erzya dictionary.

As seen in Figure 1, an XML dictionary contains lexemes, their parts-of-speech, and translations grouped by the meaning group. Out of the three, the Livonian dictionary is the most consistent dictionary with multi-translations to Finnish (19,210), Latvian (18,064) and Estonian (18,684). Komi-Zyrian mostly has Russian (32,744) and Finnish (11,745) translations, and some English (6,702). Erzya has Finnish (12,631), Russian (7,572) and English (3,739).

While in theory these multilingual dictionaries have their translations divided into meaning groups that group semantically similar translations together, in practice these meaning groups are of a poor quality (see Hämäläinen et al. 2018) and thus omitted in our approach. The problem can already be seen in Figure 1 with the Erzya word аволямс where Finnish words *huiskuttaa* (to wave) and *heiluttaa* (to wave) are in the same meaning group as *lakaista* (to sweep).

[3]https://www.wiktionary.org/

[4]For instance, the word for a *dog* (koira) is linked as a synonym for a *pig* (sika), and unacceptably the word for a *woman* (nainen) is linked as a synonym for *whore* (huora) among others.

[5]https://giellalt.uit.no

3.2 Wiktionary

Wiktionaries are rich multilingual online dictionaries consisting of an enormous number of words, translations, examples. There are Wiktionaries for many resource-rich languages and they are publicly available.

We have crawled and parsed the Finnish (fin), Estonian (est), French (fra), Latvian (lav) and Russian (rus) Wiktionaries to extract all words and translations provided in them. Despite the humongous linguistic data supplied, the data in each Wiktionary is structured differently and is not well aligned with other dictionaries (e.g. a given translation does not necessary exist in the reverse direction). These dictionaries do not have many translations in our endangered languages of interest, but they serve as an important resource for our link prediction approach.

4 Inferring New Translation Candidates

Representing translations in a graph, where words are represented as nodes and translations between words as edges, is intuitive and has been successfully used for the task in the past, as described in the related work. In fact, some of the modern approaches to lexicography have also rejected the traditional tree structure of a dictionary in favor of a graph representation (Mechura, 2016). Similarly, we represent both types of dictionaries, XMLs and Wiktionaries, in a graph-based network using NetworkX library (Hagberg et al., 2008). Unlike some of the previous work such as (Donandt et al., 2017), the graph is not directional, given that nearly all lexical translations work bidirectionally.

Let $G = (V, E)$ denote the graph, where V is all the vertices/nodes in the graph and E is all undirected edges/links between two nodes. We initialize the graph with all translations from the five Wiktionaries in such a way that their entries become interconnected based on words and their translations.

To predict new translations from the source language S to the target language T, we load the XML dictionary of the desired endangered language to the graph while omitting any existing translations to the target language. This is done to ensure that all translations to the target language are projected by the method.

Once the graph is constructed, we iterate over all nodes from the source language $V_S = \{s|s \in V \cap S\}$ and their neighbouring nodes $N(s) = \{n|ns \in E\}$. For all the neighbouring nodes linked to the source language n, we examine whether they belong to the target language, i.e. $n \in T$. When such a constraint is satisfied, a new translation between the source lexeme s and n is considered as a candidate translation and assessed using link predictions methods. All candidates scoring zero on any of the link predictions methods described below are pruned out.

We employ four link prediction methods to discover new translations; these are 1) Jaccard coefficient (Jaccard, 1912), 2) Adamic-Adar index (Adamic and Adar, 2003), 3) resource allocation index (Zhou et al., 2009), and preferential attachment score (Liben-Nowell and Kleinberg, 2007). In short, Jaccard coefficient computes a score based on the common neighbours between the source and target nodes with respect to the total number of their neighbours. The Adamic-Adar index is defined as:

$$\sum_{w \in N(s) \cap N(n)} \frac{1}{log|N(w)|}$$

The resource allocation index is defined similarly but without taking the log of the denominator. Lastly, the preferential attachment score measures the magnitude of the neighbours of each node, which is defined as $|N(s)||N(n)|$.

An example of a sub-graph containing the Livonian lexeme (Japān) along with links to existing translations in the XML dictionary (which are Japani in Finnish, Jaapan in Estonian and Japāna in Latvian) is shown in Figure 2. All the remaining nodes in the graph and their black connections to the other nodes are from Wiktionaries. By running the link prediction methods described above to infer translations from Livonian to English, two new links are suggested and they point to the lexemes Japan and Nippon, shown in red dashed lines. The methods were able to recommend the link to the Japan with high confidence as there is a strong support based on their neighbouring nodes (i.e. liv_Japāna, fin_Japani and est_Jaapan), whereas the link to Nippon had a low confidence as only one node supports it (i.e. est_Jaapan).

5 Manual Evaluation

In our evaluation, we run the link prediction method for the following four language pairs, 1) Erzya and English 2) Livonian and English, 3) Komi-Zyrian and English and 4) Komi-Zyrian and

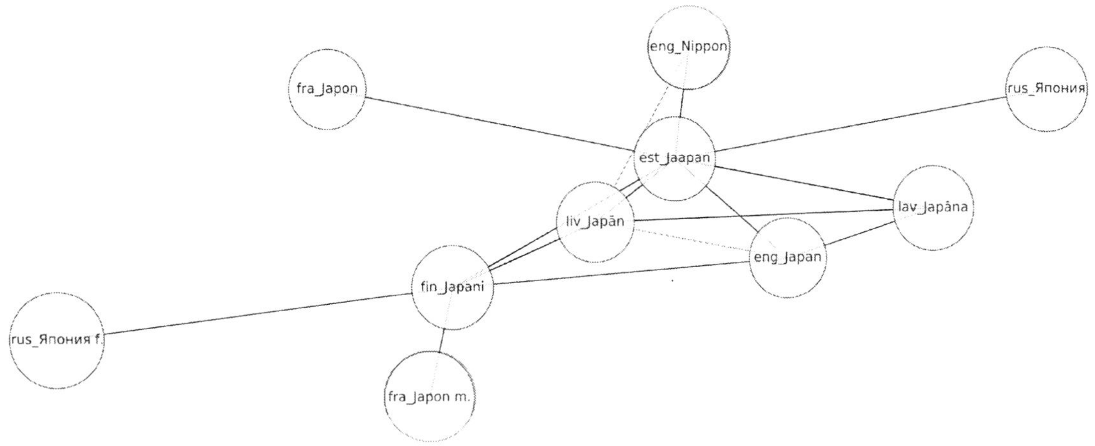

Figure 2: A sub-graph illustrating an example for inferring new translations from Livonian (Japān) to English (Japan and Nippon) by the methods (highlighted in red).

French. Which resulted in 17,042, 22,911, 9,611 and 7,765 translation suggestions for the four language pairs, respectively.

To evaluate the method, we have reached to fluent speakers in the source and target languages and requested them to manually annotate 200 randomly selected predictions. None of these predictions existed before in the XML dictionaries between each language pair. For each translation, they were instructed to indicate whether it is 1) good, 2) acceptable, 3) incomplete or 4) bad. Good translations are dictionary-ready entries and can be automatically populated as they are. Acceptable instances are correct predictions but may contain ambiguity due to, for example, synonymy or polysemy. Incomplete translations are close to the desired translation but require manual modifications, while bad translations are completely off predictions and should be removed.

In total, we obtained 800 annotated predictions. Table 1 shows the summary of annotations per language pairs. The annotations point out that the majority (44.62%) of inferred translations are good and can be used as they are. 16.62% and 15.5% of the predictions were seen as acceptable and incomplete, in the given order. Overall, this demonstrates the effectiveness of the method in predicting translations for endangered languages, with 76.75% good or potential translations, and only 23.25% bad translations.

We can see some examples of the predictions and human annotations in Table 2. In the table, we can see examples of all four annotation categories for

Pair	Good	Acceptable	Incomplete	Bad	Total
myv-eng	76	34	36	54	200
liv-eng	88	23	39	50	200
kpv-eng	102	35	29	34	200
kpv-fra	91	41	20	48	200
Total	357	133	124	186	800

Table 1: A summary of the manual annotation of predicted translations from endangered languages to resource-rich languages.

Komi-Zyrian to English translations. The annotator also wrote notes for non-good translations.

Next, we calculate the Pearson correlation coefficient to determine if there is a linear correlation between each of the four link prediction methods and the manual annotations. We assigned the annotation a value of from 3 (for good) to 0 (for bad). Our results indicate that there is a positive weak correlation between the annotation values and the predicted scores for three methods Jaccard coefficient, Adamic-Adar index, and resource allocation index. For preferential attachment, no correlation existed. All of the four correlations are with very strong statistical significance, i.e. p-value < 0.001. These correlation scores indicate the importance of considering the total and common neighbouring translations of the source and target words, something that is not taken into consideration in the preferential attachment method.

5.1 An automated evaluation attempt

Komi-Zyrian and Erzya dictionaries contain some English translations. As these translations were ignored during the automatic prediction phase, we

Komi-Zyrian	English	Annotation	Note
норматив	norm	good	
во пом	year	incomplete	end of the year
чуксасьны	crow	acceptable	verb
сӧгластӧм	indeclinable	bad	uncompromising

Table 2: Examples of Komi-Zyrian to English predictions and annotations.

can use them as a simplistic automatic evaluation metric to test if the method infers them correctly. To do so, we only consider English translations which exist in the initial graph (i.e., constructed from Wiktionaries) because some of these translations are placeholders (i.e., 'YY') or contain additional meta-data (e.g., the context or specification), not to mention that Wiktionaries are not complete resources and some words will be missing. This filtering resulted in 4,096 and 3,386 Komi-English and Erzya-English translation pairs to be assessed by the link prediction methods. For Komi-Zyrian to English, 2,419 (59%) of translations were predicted correctly; however, we were able to verify only 423 (13% of) Erzya to English translations by the existing XML dictionary.

These numbers indicate that at least this many translations were correct based on this automated evaluation method, however, this method cannot assess how many of the predicted translations that were not in the dictionaries, were correct as well. In our experience, dictionaries (even larger Wiktionaries) have an inconsistent coverage of synonyms in the translations. Which means that if our method predicts a synonym of an existing translation that is not in the dictionary, this simplistic automated evaluation cannot capture that. With a quick look into the data, we were able to see several of these cases.

Because no dictionary is perfect, and even less so in the context of endangered languages, it is difficult to conduct the kind of automated evaluation that would be functional in assessing the degree to which our predictions are correct. For this reason, we believe that the manual evaluation by people knowledgeable in the languages in question is the best way of evaluating the performance of the method. This also creates a very useful gold standard dataset that can be used in further evaluation of different approaches.

Layer (type)	Output Shape	Param #
Linear-1	[-1, 64, 64]	320
ReLU-2	[-1, 64, 64]	0
BatchNorm1d-3	[-1, 64, 64]	128
Linear-4	[-1, 64, 64]	4,160
ReLU-5	[-1, 64, 64]	0
BatchNorm1d-6	[-1, 64, 64]	128
Linear-7	[-1, 64, 64]	4,160
ReLU-8	[-1, 64, 64]	0
BatchNorm1d-9	[-1, 64, 64]	128
Dropout-10	[-1, 64, 64]	0
Linear-11	[-1, 64, 1]	65

Table 3: A summary of the architecture of the neural network.

6 Automatic Detection of Good Predictions

To further aid lexicographers in creating dictionaries, especially for endangered languages, we build an artificial neural network model for detecting whether a predicted translation by the methods is a good one. An automated way of filtering out the bad translations cuts the time needed for going through the predictions manually.

We have experimented with different neural architectures and techniques. For the scope of this work, we describe the outperforming model which is a multilayer feedforward neural network (for a summary of the architecture, see Table 3). The input to the network is the prediction scores computed by the link prediction methods and the output is a binary score, 1 denoting a good prediction and 0 a bad one. We follow the rule-of-thumb of introducing hidden layers based on 70-90% of the size of the input (Boger and Guterman, 1997), which yields three hidden layers and each layer consists of 64 neurons. Rectified linear unit (ReLU) is used as an activation function after each layer. Subsequently, batch normalization (Ioffe and Szegedy, 2015) and dropout (Srivastava et al., 2014) (with a probability of 10%) are applied to accelerate train-

	Precision	Recall	F1-score	N
		Baseline		
Good	77%	51%	61%	124
Bad	22%	47%	30%	36
Accuracy		50%		160
		Neural Model		
Good	81%	98%	89%	124
Bad	73%	22%	34%	36
Accuracy		81%		160

Table 4: The accuracy, precision, recall and F1-score of a random baseline and our neural model for detecting good translation candidates.

ing, and reduce internal covariate shift and overfitting. In total, the network had 9,089 trainable parameters.

In our model, we utilize Adam optimizer (Kingma and Ba, 2014) and a sigmoid layer combined with binary cross entropy as the loss function due to its suitability for the binary classification task. To obtain the classification from the model, a sigmoid function followed by rounding the result is applied post inference.

For the problem we are tackling, there are no available training datasets, neither for endangered languages nor resource-rich languages. To overcome this, we exploit our manual annotations and split them into 80-20 splits for training and testing. To convert the annotations into binary classes, we treat all good, acceptable and incomplete translations as positive instances and bad ones as negative.

After 1,000 epochs of training with a learning rate of 0.001, the model reached an accuracy of 81%. Table 4 reports a summary of the performance metric of the model in comparison to a random classifier as a baseline.

7 Discussion

When looking at the bad candidate translations, the reasons why they were predicted by our method can be divided roughly into two categories: polysemy and wrong translations in the original XML dictionaries. A polysemy of a word in one language can cause a wrong translation to appear in another language that does not exhibit the same polysemy. For example the Komi-Zyrian word гол had been translated into *paint* instead of the correct translation *goal*. This is due to polysemy in Finnish as the Finnish word *maali* means both *goal* and *paint*. Had there been more translations in between languages for these words that do not have the Finnish polysemy, the graph based model would have been less likely to predict this translation.

We have attempted to test the method by focusing solely on Wiktionary data, where we would omit all existing translations from a particular source language to another (e.g., Finnish to French or English). Nonetheless, many of the predicted translations were good but were missing from the Wiktionary of the source language, making it infeasible to assess the effectiveness of the method. Despite that, this is a strong indication that the proposed method with our model could be employed to enrich existing Wiktionaries further.

An idea we had for training a neural model for predicting whether the new predictions are good or bad was to generate synthetic training data automatically. In practice, collecting examples of good translations from Wiktionaries is easy, but producing automatically examples of bad translations is more difficult. Predicting random links between words would result in all of the link prediction models outputting such a low score that it would hardly be representative of the real case of bad translations that are mainly due to polysemy or wrong initial translations.

We tried out producing a dataset of bad translations with the idea that if an English word, for instance *can* is translated into *voida* (be able to) and *purkki* (can as a container) in Finnish and *võima* (be able to) and *purk* (can as a container) in Estonian, then predicting *voida* as a translation of *purk* and *purkki* as a translation of *võima* would make our synthetic data have very representative examples of bad translations. However, in practice, we ran into a coverage issue in Wiktionaries. For example, the English Wiktionary did not have any entry that would have had at least two translations into Finnish and Estonian. This made our good idea in theory impossible in practice.

While quality and coverage of the existing data pose challenges, our work has provided some insight for the lexicographers working with these resources about the limitations of the current state of the lexical resources. This has been well received as a form of a sanity check among the lexicographers in question given that the lexicographic resources have been built by different people depending on their funding situation. This means that a lot of the work done in the dictionaries has been there before the current people working with the resources have started extending them.

In our graphs, we have omitted the part-of-speech because it is not present for all lexemes, whether in the XML dictionaries or Wiktionaries. Taking them into consideration would have resulted in inferring low-quality translations in smaller magnitudes. Therefore, we believe that incorporating part-of-speech tags is a crucial step, once new translations are inferred. As this would assist in detecting some ambiguous cases where a miss-match between the parts-of-speech is sufficient to prune them out. The part-of-speech tags could be automatically predicted by taking advantage of neural- and graph-based methods (Angle et al., 2018; Das and Petrov, 2011; Thayaparan et al., 2018). However, in some cases, ensuring the same part-of-speech tag, might lead to correct translations being filtered out. For instance, the Finnish word *alla* may be an adverb or a postposition, whereas its English translation *under* is a preposition.

In terms of the features used in our neural model, we use the prediction scores returned by the link prediction methods. This causes the neural model to act as an expert voter observing the various scores and to make the executive decision of whether the prediction is valid or not. Additional features could be passed to the model, such as the strings of both source and target words, and meta-information about their nodes (e.g., the number of their distinct and common neighbours). Based on Donandt et al. (2017) work, using the Levenshtein distance between source and target words resulted in poor classifications. Such features contribute differently to the performance of the model depending on the languages and would limit the model to closely related languages with a high number of cognates. This motivated our choice of judging the quality of predictions based on the link prediction scores, which causes our model to be generic and appropriate for many different language pairs as we assume no phylogenetic relation between the languages in question. This also makes it possible for our approach to work across writing systems as we are dealing with languages written in Latin and Cyrillic alphabets.

8 Conclusions and Future Work

We have released the source code of our method and its predictions on Github[6]. Our method could, in the future, be integrated with the existing dictionary editing infrastructures for Uralic languages such as Giella (Moshagen et al., 2014) and Ve'rdd (Alnajjar et al., 2020). This would make link prediction an active part of the process of building lexical resources, making it a more dynamic human-in-the-loop task.

We have presented our work on extending the existing lexical resources for several endangered languages. For the time being, human annotators are needed to go through the predicted translations, although we have perceived promising results with our neural approach.

Regardless of the accuracy of the current method for identifying good predictions or what any future method might reach, we believe that a lexicographer needs to go through the predictions at any rate. Compiling dictionaries for an endangered language is an important step in the language documentation and, if done right, can greatly benefit the native speakers of the language in learning foreign languages, and also anyone interested in learning the endangered language in question. This being said, any fully automatically produced lexicon will have errors that ultimately lead to misunderstandings and can be harmful for the language community.

We envision that our work opens the door for constructing aligned multilingual word-embeddings between endangered languages and high-resource languages. This would narrow the gap between severely scarce-resource languages and the latest neural machine translation techniques, making it possible to build a functional neural translation system from languages at the risk of dying to a vast number of big languages which in return would greatly benefit the communities of endangered language.

The results produced by our method will be manually filtered by lexicographers and included in the Akusanat online dictionary[7]. The goal of our paper has been that of extending existing lexicographic resources so that the language communities can directly benefit from our research. Without releasing our results and having them manually verified, we would be embracing an unethical research tradition that relies on cultural and linguistic appropriation for a purely academic benefit.

Acknowledgments

Many thanks to our Livonian evaluators Uldis Balodis and Valts Ernštreits. This work was funded in part by the French government under manage-

[6]https://github.com/mokha/translation-link-prediction/

[7]https://www.akusanat.com/

ment of Agence Nationale de la Recherche as part of the "Investissements d'avenir" program, reference ANR-19-P3IA-0001 (PRAIRIE 3IA Institute).

References

Lada A Adamic and Eytan Adar. 2003. Friends and neighbors on the web. *Social networks*, 25(3):211–230.

Khalid Alnajjar. 2021. When word embeddings become endangered. *Multilingual Facilitation*, pages 275–288.

Khalid Alnajjar, Mika Hämäläinen, Jack Rueter, and Niko Partanen. 2020. Ve'rdd. narrowing the gap between paper dictionaries, low-resource nlp and community involvement. In *Proceedings of the 28th International Conference on Computational Linguistics: System Demonstrations*, pages 1–6.

Khalid Alnajjar, Jack Rueter, Niko Partanen, and Mika Hämäläinen. 2021. Enhancing the erzya-moksha dictionary automatically with link prediction. *Folia Uralica Debreceniensia*, 28:7–18.

Sachi Angle, Pruthwik Mishra, and Dipti Mishra Sharma. 2018. Automated error correction and validation for POS tagging of Hindi. In *Proceedings of the 32nd Pacific Asia Conference on Language, Information and Computation*, Hong Kong. Association for Computational Linguistics.

Z. Boger and H. Guterman. 1997. Knowledge extraction from artificial neural network models. In *1997 IEEE International Conference on Systems, Man, and Cybernetics. Computational Cybernetics and Simulation*, volume 4, pages 3030–3035 vol.4.

Dipanjan Das and Slav Petrov. 2011. Unsupervised part-of-speech tagging with bilingual graph-based projections. In *Proceedings of the 49th Annual Meeting of the Association for Computational Linguistics: Human Language Technologies*, pages 600–609, Portland, Oregon, USA. Association for Computational Linguistics.

Kathrin Donandt, Christian Chiarcos, and Maxim Ionov. 2017. Using machine learning for translation inference across dictionaries. In *LDK Workshops*, pages 103–112.

Jeff Ens, Mika Hämäläinen, Jack Rueter, and Philippe Pasquier. 2019. Morphosyntactic disambiguation in an endangered language setting. In *Proceedings of the 22nd Nordic Conference on Computational Linguistics*, pages 345–349, Turku, Finland. Linköping University Electronic Press.

Christiane Fellbaum, editor. 1998. *WordNet: An Electronic Lexical Database*. Language, Speech, and Communication. MIT Press, Cambridge, MA.

Genet Asefa Gesese, Mehwish Alam, and Harald Sack. 2020. Semantic entity enrichment by leveraging multilingual descriptions for link prediction. In *arXiv preprint arXiv:2004.10640*.

Aric A. Hagberg, Daniel A. Schult, and Pieter J. Swart. 2008. Exploring network structure, dynamics, and function using networkx. In *Proceedings of the 7th Python in Science Conference*, pages 11 – 15, Pasadena, CA USA.

Mika Hämäläinen. 2019. Uralicnlp: An nlp library for uralic languages. *Journal of open source software*, 4(37).

Mika Hämäläinen. 2021. Endangered languages are not low-resourced! *Multilingual Facilitation*.

Mika Hämäläinen and Jack Rueter. 2019. An open online dictionary for endangered uralic languages. In *Electronic lexicography in the 21st century Proceedings of the eLex 2019 conference*. Lexical Computing CZ sro.

Mika Hämäläinen, Liisa Lotta Tarvainen, and Jack Rueter. 2018. Combining concepts and their translations from structured dictionaries of uralic minority languages. In *Proceedings of the Eleventh International Conference on Language Resources and Evaluation (LREC 2018)*, pages 862–867. European Language Resources Association (ELRA).

Sergey Ioffe and Christian Szegedy. 2015. Batch normalization: Accelerating deep network training by reducing internal covariate shift. In *Proceedings of the 32nd International Conference on International Conference on Machine Learning - Volume 37*, ICML'15, page 448–456. JMLR.org.

Paul Jaccard. 1912. The distribution of the flora in the alpine zone. 1. *New phytologist*, 11(2):37–50.

Milos Jakubicek, Michal Měchura, Vojtech Kovar, and Pavel Rychly. 2018. Practical post-editing lexicography with lexonomy and sketch engine. In *The XVIII EURALEX International Congress*, page 65.

Diederik P Kingma and Jimmy Ba. 2014. Adam: A method for stochastic optimization. In *arXiv preprint arXiv:1412.6980*.

Khang Lam, Feras Al Tarouti, and Jugal Kalita. 2015. Automatically creating a large number of new bilingual dictionaries. In *AAAI Conference on Artificial Intelligence*.

Khang Nhut Lam and Jugal Kalita. 2013. Creating reverse bilingual dictionaries. In *Proceedings of the 2013 Conference of the North American Chapter of the Association for Computational Linguistics: Human Language Technologies*, pages 524–528, Atlanta, Georgia. Association for Computational Linguistics.

David Liben-Nowell and Jon Kleinberg. 2007. The link-prediction problem for social networks. *Journal of the American society for information science and technology*, 58(7):1019–1031.

Krister Lindén and Lauri Carlson. 2010. Finnwordnet–finnish wordnet by translation. *LexicoNordica–Nordic Journal of Lexicography*, 17:119–140.

Michal Mechura. 2016. Data structures in lexicography: from trees to graphs. In *RASLAN 2016 Recent Advances in Slavonic Natural Language Processing*, page 97.

Christopher Moseley. 2010. *Atlas of the World's Languages in Danger*, 3rd edition. UNESCO Publishing. Online version: http://www.unesco.org/languages-atlas/.

Sjur Moshagen, Jack Rueter, Tommi Pirinen, Trond Trosterud, and Francis M. Tyers. 2014. Open-Source Infrastructures for Collaborative Work on Under-Resourced Languages. In *The LREC 2014 Workshop "CCURL 2014 - Collaboration and Computing for Under-Resourced Languages in the Linked Open Data Era"*, pages 71–77.

Arbi Haza Nasution, Yohei Murakami, and Toru Ishida. 2016. Constraint-based bilingual lexicon induction for closely related languages. In *Proceedings of the Tenth International Conference on Language Resources and Evaluation (LREC'16)*, pages 3291–3298, Portorož, Slovenia. European Language Resources Association (ELRA).

Niko Partanen, Rogier Blokland, KyungTae Lim, Thierry Poibeau, and Michael Rießler. 2018. The first Komi-Zyrian universal dependencies treebanks. In *Second Workshop on Universal Dependencies (UDW 2018), November 2018, Brussels, Belgium*, pages 126–132.

Tommaso Pasini and Roberto Navigli. 2017. Train-O-Matic: Large-scale supervised word sense disambiguation in multiple languages without manual training data. In *Proceedings of the 2017 Conference on Empirical Methods in Natural Language Processing*, pages 78–88, Copenhagen, Denmark. Association for Computational Linguistics.

Alessandro Raganato, Claudio Delli Bovi, and Roberto Navigli. 2016. Automatic construction and evaluation of a large semantically enriched wikipedia. In *IJCAI*, pages 2894–2900.

Jack Rueter. 2014. The livonian-estonian-latvian dictionary as a threshold to the era of language technological applications. *Eesti ja soome-ugri keeleteaduse ajakiri. Journal of Estonian and Finno-Ugric Linguistics*, 5(1):251–259.

Jack Rueter and Mika Hämäläinen. 2020. Fst morphology for the endangered skolt sami language. In *Proceedings of the 1st Joint SLTU and CCURL Workshop (SLTU-CCURL 2020)*, pages 250–257, France. European Language Resources Association (ELRA).

Jack Rueter, Mika Hämäläinen, and Niko Partanen. 2020. Open-source morphology for endangered mordvinic languages. In *Proceedings of Second Workshop for NLP Open Source Software (NLP-OSS)*. The Association for Computational Linguistics.

Jack Michael Rueter and Francis M Tyers. 2018. Towards an open-source universal-dependency treebank for erzya. In *International Workshop for Computational Linguistics of Uralic Languages*.

Stephen Soderland, Oren Etzioni, Daniel Weld, Michael Skinner, and Jeff Bilmes. 2009. Compiling a massive, multilingual dictionary via probabilistic inference. In *Proceedings of the Joint Conference of the 47th Annual Meeting of the ACL and the 4th International Joint Conference on Natural Language Processing of the AFNLP*, pages 262–270, Suntec, Singapore. Association for Computational Linguistics.

Nitish Srivastava, Geoffrey Hinton, Alex Krizhevsky, Ilya Sutskever, and Ruslan Salakhutdinov. 2014. Dropout: A simple way to prevent neural networks from overfitting. *Journal of Machine Learning Research*, 15(56):1929–1958.

Mokanarangan Thayaparan, Surangika Ranathunga, and Uthayasanker Thayasivam. 2018. Graph based semi-supervised learning approach for Tamil POS tagging. In *Proceedings of the Eleventh International Conference on Language Resources and Evaluation (LREC 2018)*, Miyazaki, Japan. European Language Resources Association (ELRA).

Francis Tyers. 2010. Rule-based Breton to French machine translation. In *Proceedings of the 14th Annual conference of the European Association for Machine Translation*, Saint Raphaël, France. European Association for Machine Translation.

Linda Wiechetek, Flammie Pirinen, Mika Hämäläinen, and Chiara Argese. 2021. Rules ruling neural networks - neural vs. rule-based grammar checking for a low resource language. In *Proceedings of the International Conference on Recent Advances in Natural Language Processing (RANLP 2021)*, pages 1526–1535, Held Online. INCOMA Ltd.

Mairidan Wushouer, Donghui Lin, Toru Ishida, and Katsutoshi Hirayama. 2015. A constraint approach to pivot-based bilingual dictionary induction. *ACM Transactions on Asian and Low-Resource Language Information Processing (TALLIP)*, 15(1).

Tao Zhou, Linyuan Lü, and Yi-Cheng Zhang. 2009. Predicting missing links via local information. *The European Physical Journal B*, 71(4):623–630.

Anna Zueva, Anastasia Kuznetsova, and Francis Tyers. 2020. A finite-state morphological analyser for Evenki. In *Proceedings of the 12th Language Resources and Evaluation Conference*, pages 2581–2589, Marseille, France. European Language Resources Association.

Reusing a Multi-lingual Setup to Bootstrap a Grammar Checker for a Very Low Resource Language without Data

Inga Lill Sigga Mikkelsen **Linda Wiechetek** **Flammie A Pirinen**
UiT Norgga árktalaš universitehta
Divvun
Norway
inga.l.mikkelsen@uit.no tommi.pirinen@uit.no
linda.wiechetek@uit.no

Abstract

Grammar checkers (GEC) are needed for digital language survival. Very low resource languages like Lule Sámi with less than 3,000 speakers need to hurry to build these tools, but do not have the big corpus data that are required for the construction of machine learning tools. We present a rule-based tool and a workflow where the work done for a related language can speed up the process. We use an existing grammar to infer rules for the new language, and we do not need a large gold corpus of annotated grammar errors, but a smaller corpus of regression tests is built while developing the tool. We present a test case for Lule Sámi reusing resources from North Sámi, show how we achieve a categorisation of the most frequent errors, and present a preliminary evaluation of the system. We hope this serves as an inspiration for small languages that need advanced tools in a limited amount of time, but do not have big data.

1 Introduction

Language tools for very low resource languages are urgently needed to support language maintenance, but also it takes a long time to develop them. An existing multilingual infrastructure and existing tools that can be reused can speed up the process. In this article, we describe the process of making a Lule Sámi GEC together with a preliminary categorization of frequent Lule Sámi errors. Lule Sámi is on the lower end of lower resource language. It can benefit from North Sámi which is closely related and has a well-functioning grammar checker.

The reuse of existing knowledge is an important concept in effective development of new grammar checkers in multilingual infrastructures. With this work we would like to set an example of how high-end complex NLP tools can be made, in less time, by taking existing tools as a frame. The following tools were already ready-made: an FST-based morphological analyser, a morpho-syntactic disambiguator developed for correct text, and a multi-lingual infrastructure that contains scripts to build the grammar checker (among other applications). Our work took altogether 120 hours, (40 hours of meetings of two linguists (one of them native speaker) and 40 hours of work of one native speaker linguist).

For related languages we can even reuse rules and sets (prenominal modifiers, sentence barriers). But for example, lexemes have to be translated. This article will show in detail what can be reused, and which factors need special focus as they are language specific – many times it is systematic homonymies, and definitely idiosyncratic homonymies. In addition, we will evaluate the Lule Sámi grammar checker and point out future steps for improvement.

2 Background

2.1 Language and resources

Lule Sámi is spoken in northern Sweden and Norway, with an estimated 800-3,000 speakers (Sammallahti, 1998; Kuoljok, 2002; Svonni, 2008; Rydving, 2013; Moseley, 2010). The Lule Sámi written language was approved in 1983 (Magga, 1994). The first Lule Sámi spell checker was launched in 2007. Lule Sámi is a morphologically complex language, for more details see Ylikoski (2022).

In 2013 the Lule Sámi gold corpus of writing errors was built.[1] The gold corpus consists of 32,202 words with 3,772 marked writing errors. The goal of this error marked-up corpus was to test if the spellchecker corresponds to relevant quality requirements, by running the spell checker

[1] https://github.com/giellalt/lang-smj/

Proceedings of the Fifth Workshop on the Use of Computational Methods in the Study of Endangered Languages, pages 149 - 158
May 26-27, 2022 ©2022 Association for Computational Linguistics

on an error corpus, where spelling errors were manually marked and corrected. It was supposed to be usable for testing grammar checkers with some processing, and therefore also marked syntactic, morpho-syntactic and lexical errors. The texts gathered for the gold corpus were written by native Lule Sámi speakers and had neither been spellchecked nor proofread.

Speakers of Lule Sámi do not have a long written tradition, this amount of errors in the gold corpus show that native speakers of Lule Sámi are in need of tools helping them in the writing process. 1,774 of the errors in the gold corpus are non-word errors (i.e. misspellings that result in a non-existent form, non-word error, as opposed to real word errors where the misspelling results in an existing 'wrong' form), found by the spellchecker, the remaining 1,998 errors are morpho-syntactic, syntactic, word choice and formatting errors, which only a grammar checker can detect and correct. Lule Sámi is by UNESCO classified as a severely endangered language. For the (re)vitalisation of a language, it is important that the language is actually being used. With a (re)vitalisation perspective, a grammar checker for Lule Sámi will make it easier for people to use Lule Sámi in writing, which will increase the use of written Lule Sámi.

The marking and correcting of errors for the gold corpus is the first systematic work on Lule Sámi writing errors. So far, this gold corpus has not been used to analyse and describe error types characteristic for Lule Sámi. Our own experiences from proofreading and from the work with North Sámi were therefore the starting point for developing grammar rules.

2.2 Framework

The technological implementation of our grammar checker is based on well-established technologies in the rule-based natural language processing: finite-state automata for morphological analysis (Beesley and Karttunen, 2003; Lindén et al., 2013) and constraint grammar (Karlsson, 1990b; Didriksen, 2010) for syntactic and semantic as well as other sentence-level processing. The Lule Sámi has an existing morphological analyser and lexicon publicly available[2], which were originally imported from North Sámi with all rules and set specifications and then adapted to Lule Sámi. Antonsen et al. (2010) report F-scores of 0.95 for part-of-speech (PoS) disambiguation, 0.88 for disambiguation of inflection and derivation, and 0.86 for assignment of grammatical functions (syntax) for the Lule Sámi analyser.

The system is built on a pipeline of modules: we process the input text with morphological analysers and tokenisers to get annotated texts, then disambiguate and then apply grammar rules on the disambiguated sentences, c.f. Figure 1.

It is noteworthy, that the system is part of a multilingual infrastructure *GiellaLT*, which includes numerous languages — 130 altogether.

The grammar checker takes input from the finite-state transducer (*FST*) to a number of other modules, the core of which are several Constraint Grammar modules for tokenisation disambiguation, morpho-syntactic disambiguation and a module for error detection and correction. The full modular structure (Figure 1) is described in Wiechetek (2019). We are using finite-state morphology (Beesley and Karttunen, 2003) to model word formation processes. The technology behind our *FSTs* is described in Pirinen (2014). Constraint Grammar is a rule-based formalism for writing disambiguation and syntactic annotation grammars (Karlsson, 1990a; Karlsson et al., 1995). In our work, we use the free open source implementation VISLCG-3 (Bick and Didriksen, 2015). All components are compiled and built using the *GiellaLT* infrastructure (Moshagen et al., 2013). The code and data for the model is available for download [3].

The syntactic context is specified in handwritten Constraint Grammar rules. The ADD-rule below adds an error tag (identified by the tag `&real-negSg3-negSg2`) to the negation verb *ij* '(to) not' as in example (1) if it is a 3rd person singular verb and to its left there is a 2nd person singular pronoun in nominative case. The context condition further specifies that there cannot be any tokens specifying a sentence barrier, a subjunction, conjunction or a finite verb in between for the rule to apply.

(1) Dån **ittjij** boade guossáj.
you NEG.PAST.SG3 come guest.ILL
'You didn't visit.'

```
ADD (&real-negSg3-negSg2) TARGET ("ij")
IF (0 (Sg3))
```

[2] `https://github.com/giellalt/lang-smj/`

[3] `https://github.com/giellalt/lang-smj/`

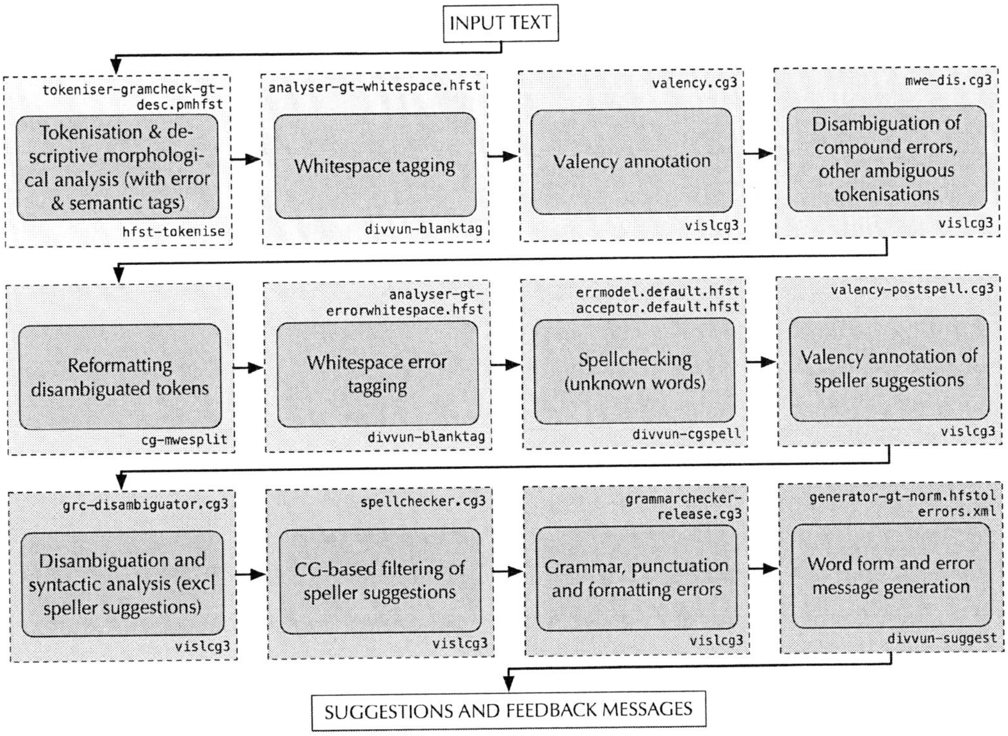

Figure 1: Structure of a grammar checker

```
(*-1 (Pron Nom Sg2)
BARRIER S-BOUNDARY OR
CS OR CC OR VFIN) ;
```

3 Setup

In this section, we answer the question of how to set up a grammar checker for a new language in *GiellaLT*. The resources we need are:

1. Word-based tools:
   - a tokeniser / handling of multiword entities etc.
   - an FST-based morphological analyser
   - a spellchecker
2. Sentence-based tools:
   - a disambiguator (that can deal with erroneous input)
   - a syntactic analyser
   - a number of phonological or morphosyntactic sets to categorise groups of words
   - error detection/correction rules for a set of frequent errors
3. A set of frequent error types
4. Regression tests (error-marked up test sentences)

Unlike machine learning, this approach is not dependent on a large amount of text data or a gold corpus. To develop a grammar checker, we only need several test sentences containing the errors in question. (Wiechetek et al., 2021) However, in the absence of a fully error marked-up text corpus, finding frequent errors is a challenge. We therefore provide a scheme based on our experience with finding common errors (for the North Sámi grammar checker) as a guideline for work on new languages. This scheme serves any language, but our experience is based on morphologically richer languages.

Error types can be divided into three main categories:

1. phonology-/typography-based errors
2. (morpho-)syntactic errors
3. writing convention-based errors

Phonology-/typography-based errors can be based on diacritics, vowel/consonant length, silent endings in certain contexts (*-ij* pronounced *-i*), divergence pronunciation/writing and homophone words.

Writing/formatting conventions apply to compounding (one vs. several words, hyphen), quotation marks, comma and punctuation in general. Morpho-syntactic and syntactic errors can be subdivided into verb-, NP-internal and VP-internal issues. NP-internal issues can be about prepositions and postpositions and their case restrictions, adjective agreement /forms in attributive/predicative positions, and relative pronoun agreement with its anaphora in number, gender and animacy.

Verb internal issues concern the auxiliary construction, negation phrases (where negation is expressed by a verb) and other periphrastic verb constructions.

VP internal issues, on the other hand, are more global and concern subject-verb agreement, subclauses formation, subcategorisation in general and case marking of object/adverbial and word order.

In addition to that, the choice of error types will depend on efficiency as well, that means which error types can rules generalize over, and which error types are very word specific. Very word specific work that cannot be generalized may not be so efficient.

3.1 Reuse of resources

Reusing (particularly North Sámi) resources to create Lule Sámi tools goes back as far as 2005, where the North Sámi descriptive morphosyntactic analyser/disambiguator was used to disambiguate Lule Sámi text and adapting work started. A disambiguator is a tool that resolves homonymy in a given syntactic context, and is an essential tool in sentence-level text processing. This tool was already available when we started our work. However, the initial goal of sentence analysis is based on correct input. We therefore had to adapt the tool to fit error input, e.g. by removing rules that were too strict and paying closer attention to misspelled word forms that can be confused with correct forms. In the course of time, other tools or modules have been copied over to Lule Sámi and been reused with or without adaptations, thereby creating lower-cost tools for Lule Sámi, cf. Table 1. Another tool that was already available when we started to build our GEC was the Lule Sámi morphological analyser. It had previously been constructed from scratch, starting from a common template used in the *GiellaLT* infrastructure.

Tool	**Reuse**	**Adaption**
	Analysis tools	
FST	existing	NONE
disambiguator	from sme	set specs rules
tokeniser	from sme	NONE
	Error detection/correction tools	
disambiguator	from sme	to fit err input
real w err rules	NEW	-
congr rules	from sme	sets
	from sme	homonymies
	Other	
regression tests	NEW	-
corpus mark-up	from sme	applied to smj text

Table 1: Reuse of resources for Lule Sámi (sme= North Sámi, smj= Lule Sámi)

Based on our experience, we have found a following workflow to be very effective in creating a new grammar checker: We use the normative morphological analyser and a tokeniser with grammatical tokenisation disambiguation. This is relevant when deciding if two words written apart have a syntactic relation or are simple compound errors. In addition, there, we use a FST-based spellchecker. The descriptive disambiguator/syntactic analyser was first taken as it is to be included in the Lule Sámi grammar checker. However, we found that the need for adaptions was urgent, and we needed a separate version of it specifically for potentially erroneous input. The difference to the descriptive disambiguator lays in the objective. The descriptive disambiguator aims at a reduction of homonymy (risking to some degree that correct analyses get lost). The grammar checker disambiguator, on the other hand, needs disambiguation only to get an idea of the sentence to find the error, but is dependent on finding error-analyses even if they do not make sense in the context, so homonymy is not to be reduced to a point where error readings disappear. The descriptive disambiguator is adapted on the fly, so basically every time testing runs into problems, the respective rules are traced and either eliminated or adapted to erroneous input. In some cases, we also noticed general errors in the rules that lead to an improvement of the descriptive disambiguator.

The error detection/correction module needed to be written from scratch at first glance. However, at second glance, there are parts that could be reused as well. Simple sets and lists were copied over from the Lule Sámi descriptive disambiguator. Semantic groupings of words developed in the process of North Sámi grammar checking were directly copied over from the North Sámi grammar checker, and lexical items translated to Lule Sámi as in the case of the following set *DOPPE* (the first of which is the North Sámi original, and the second of which is the translated Lule Sámi one), which generalises over static place-adverbs:

```
LIST DOPPE = "badjin" "bajil"
"dakko" "dá" "dákko" "dáppe" "dás"
"diekko" "dieppe" "do" "dokko"
"doppe" "duo" "duokko" "duoppe"
"olgun" ;

LIST DOPPE = "badjen" "dáppe"
"duoppe" "dåppe" "dággu" "daggu"
"duoggu" "dåggu" "dánna" "danna"
"duonna" "dånna" "dåhku" "duohku"
"ålggon" ;
```

As regards rules, the error types based on orthographic or phonetic similarity needed to be written from scratch, as they differ in North Sámi and Lule Sámi, as do possible contexts of errors that need to pay attention to homonymies. Especially systematic homonymies are partly different to North Sámi. However, some of them are the same in North Sámi and Lule Sámi, cf. Table 2. One of them is the homonymy between plural inessive (Lule Sámi) /locative (North Sámi) and singular comitative nouns, and between singular elative (Lule Sámi) /locative (North Sámi) and 3rd person singular possessive accusative singular nouns.

Not all rules needed to be written from scratch, certain rule types were reused from North Sámi. Subject-verb agreement rules are well-suited to be copy-pasted from North Sámi to Lule Sámi. With some tag adaptations, they were included into the Lule Sámi grammar checker.

3.2 Errors in Lule Sámi

When working with the Lule Sámi grammar checker, we wanted to start with errors made by high proficiency writers rather than language learners. That way we can have a functioning grammar checker for texts with very few errors and introduce more complex errors along the way.

Homonymy	Lule S.	North S.
Verbs		
PRS PL3 – PRT SG2	sjaddi	–
INF – PRS PL1	-	šaddat
PRS SG2 – PRS SG3	la	-
PRS SG2 – INF PRS CONNEG	–	leat
Nouns		
PL NOM – SG GEN	dile/mánno	–
PL INE – SG COM	gielajn	gielain
SG ELA – SG ACC PXSG3	girkus	girkkos

Table 2: Homonymies comparison between Lule Sámi and North Sámi

Texts written by second language learners or students generally have more and other types of errors and more complex errors, which will require a different grammar checker.

Typical errors of high proficiency writers happen when the written norm deviates from the spoken dialectal variation. One example for that is the negation paradigm, which in some dialects resembles the North Sámi paradigm rather than the norm of written Lule Sámi.

In the Lule Sámi written norm, the negation verb is inflected for both person, number and tense (present and past) followed by the main verb in connegative form, which is always the same, whilst in North Sámi only person and number is marked on the negation verb. Tense is marked on the main verb with two different connegative forms, see Table 3.

Lule Sámi		North Sámi	
Present	**Past**	**Present**	**Past**
iv vuolge	ittjiv vuolge	in vuolgge	in vuolgán
i vuolge	ittji vuolge	it vuolgge	it vuolgán
ij vuolge	ittjij vuolge	ii vuolgge	ii vuolgán

Table 3: Negation comparison for ‘not leave’

There is no full consensus on the exact border between North Sámi and Lule Sámi (Ylikoski, 2016), so in Lule Sámi text one can find variation regarding negation that reflects dialectical variation. In Lule Sámi text both the North Sámi negation system, as ex. (2), and a system with ‘double’ past marking on both the negation verb and with the main verb (3) are used.

(2) Aktak **ij** **vuolggám**
someone not.NEG.PRES.3SG go.PASTP
nuorráj dan biejve.
sea.SG.ILL that day
'No one went on the sea that day.'

(3) Gå ålgus vuolggi, de
when outside go.PAST.2SG, then
ittji **vuojnnám** åvvå majdik.
not.NEG.PAST.2SG see.PASTP all nothing
'When you went outside, you didn't see anything at all'

Most of the systematic morpho-syntactic errors made by high proficiency writers reflect ongoing languages changes and might not even be corrected by a proofreader. A grammar checker is a good way of making people aware of such changes.

Soajttet is a modal verb meaning '(to) maybe' and usually stands with the infinitive form of the main verb. However, the present singular third-person form *soajttá* '(s/he) maybe' is by many writers being used as an adverb, not as a modal verb, as example (4) shows. The modal auxiliary is not followed by an infinitive as it should, but a finite verb in third-person singular.

(4) EU **soajttá** máhtti mijáv
EU may.PRES.3SG can.PRES.3PL us
viehkedit.
help.INF
'EU might be able to help us'

Within noun phrases, writers frequently make agreement errors. According to the norm the noun should be in singular with numerals and demonstratives agreeing in case and number, according to (Ylikoski, 2022) there is variation in the contemporary language indicating that this agreement system is changing. The errors in the Divvun gold corpus show us that the change has gone further than described in (Ylikoski, 2022), and numerals are handled in the same way as attributive adjectives, see Table 4. Some writers seem to make use of this "new" paradigm, as in ex. (5), while others seem to be somewhere in between, as ex. (6) shows. In this last example, the case of the numeral is correct, but the noun is in plural.

(5) Alvos Státtáv máhtá vuojnnet gåjt
colossal Stáddá can see at.least
gietjav **báhppagieldajs**.
seven.NUM.NOM.SG parish.PL.ELA
'You can see the colossal Stáddá from at least seven parishes'

(6) Suohkana juogeduvvin
municipality divide
gietja sáme
seven.NUM.ILL.ATTR outskirt.area.PL.ILL.
rabdaguovlojda.

'The municipalities got divided into seven outskirt areas.'

	'(these) two cows'	
	Norm	**Systematical errors**
Nom	(dá) guokta gusá	(dá) guokta gusá
Gen	(dán) guovte gusá	(dáj) guokta gusáj
Acc	(dá) guokta gusá	(dájt) guokta gusájt
Ine	(dán) guovten gusán	(dájn) guokta gusájn
Ill	(dán) guovte gussaj	(dájda) guokta gusájda
Ela	(dát) guovtet gusás	(dájs) guokta gusájs
Com	(dájna) guovtijn gusájn	(dáj) guokta gusáj

Table 4: NP with demonstrative pronouns and numerals

Another noun phrase internal error is the use of and adjective in predicative form in an attributive position, as example (7). This is not a very common error, but might be more frequent in texts written by second language learners, since the predicative form is the one in dictionaries and the adjective inflection system is one of the most complex area of the morphology (Ylikoski, 2022). Along with this rule, we also made rules for correcting errors where the attributive form of an adjective is used in a predicative position.

(7) Mij tjuovojma **roaŋkok** bálggáv.
We follow crooked.SG.NOM path.SG.ACC
'We followed a crooked path'

There are also agreement errors where relative pronouns fail to agree with their anaphora in number, as in ex. (8), and not agreeing with its anaphora in animacy, as in ex. (9). A similar error regards the agreement of reflexive pronouns with their anaphora in number.

(8) Da sáme **gænna** ietjanisá
Those s.PL.NOM who.SG.INE themselves
ællim muorravuovdde
have.not wood.forrest
'Those s without their own wood forrest'

(9) Åhtsåp jådediddjev **mij**:
Search leader.SG.ACC which.NHUM.SG.NOM
'We are looking for a leader who:'

Conditional mood is according to (Ylikoski, 2022) largely missing in Lule Sámi, and instead a periphrastic conditional consisting of the auxiliary lulu- 'would' and the infinitive is used. The conditional auxiliary *lulu-* is by some writers handled as if it is a separate verb with present and past tense, not a mood, making errors like (10) and the non-word error (11).

(10) Vuorasulmutja **lulu** huvsov
old.people.PL.NOM be.COND.2SG care
ja sujtov oadtjot.
and nursing get.IF
'Old people would get care and nursing '

(11) ...sávvá ienebu **lulujin** kursajda
...wish more *would.3PL course
oassálasstet.
attend.
'...wishes more people would attend courses.'

Another big group of errors are real-word errors. These are mostly based on phonetic similarity between the confused forms. In this work, we focused on general rules that are not limited to one single word, but rather forms that apply to a group of lemmata. In Table 5 the first error (*álgge-álkke*) is an error limited only to this specific word. When in a hurry of building resources for very low resource languages, one has to make sure to work in an efficient way, and writing rules for correcting specific words does not get us fast-forward. The rest of errors in Table 5 are errors being corrected by rules that generalise over groups of words, or for the frequent negation auxiliary (function words are more efficient).

The errors we have worked with in Table 5 are all real word errors with the ij-sound written 'i', or the other way around, with 'i' written 'ij'. We classified them as real word errors, even though some errors can also be seen as agreement errors. High proficiency writers are typically not insecure about agreement, but errors of this type can still happen when typing fast. Another complicating factor is that the -i sound can also be written -ij. Odd syllable nouns in illative case end in -ij, even though the pronouncation is not -ij. 'To the dog' is spelled *bednagij* even though the actual pronounced more like *bednagi*. However, the spelling error *bednagi* will be picked up by the spell checker since it is a non-word.

Both Lule Sámi and North Sámi verbs are inflected with three persons and three numbers in past and present tense. The subject verb agreement rules were copied from North Sámi to the Lule Sámi grammar checker.

4 Evaluation

The first version of the Lule Sámi grammar checker has 64 rules and 17 rule types, three of which have a regression test of 50 or more test sentences. We also ran an initial evaluation of each regression test, and plan to run the grammar checker on the error-marked up corpus of 32,202 words[4].

Figure 6 shows an evaluation of three error types with a sufficiently large regression tests. The other error types will be evaluated in the final version of the paper. The rules for relative pronoun and numeral/determiner agreement and for modal verb maybe-constructions give good results for both precision and recall. Precision and recall of the modal verb constructions are as good as 98%. We are aware that this still needs to be tested on an independent corpus. The quality is measured using basic precision, recall and f_1 scores, such that recall $R = \frac{t_p}{t_p+f_n}$, precision $P = \frac{t_p}{t_p+f_p}$ and f_1 score as harmonic mean of the two: $F_1 = 2\frac{P \times R}{P+R}$, where t_p is a count of true positives, f_p false positives, t_n true negatives and f_n false negatives.

We also ran a test run of the automatic evaluation on the marked-up gold corpus of Lule Sámi, to see if the grammar checker finds true errors and also to improve the error mark-up of grammatical errors in the corpus, keeping in mind that the corpus had been originally marked up for predominantly spelling errors.

A lot of errors found by the grammar checker are true positives. Many of them were either not marked up or - more frequently - marked up with a different scope. Since the start of marking up the corpora for spelling errors, the mark-up guidelines have been developed further in connection with *GramDivvun*, the North Sámi grammar checker, and adapted to automatic evaluation, where the grammar checker output is tested against the corpus mark-up.

There are examples of when the grammar checker actually found grammatical errors that the human proof-reader missed out. Thirdly, there are examples where the original marking is not consistent with the newer guidelines for how much the scope of the error should be with regard to how much the grammar checker actually marks up. Example (12) is one of the cases where an error in relative pronoun agreement has been identified correctly by the grammar checker. This error type

[4] Can be found on GitHub: https://github.com/giellalt/lang-smj/tools/grammarcheckers

Error	Correct form	Type of error
álgge 'beginner'	**álkke** 'easy'	Only for this single word
hábbmima NOMACT SG GEN *'the designing's'*	**hábbmijma** PRT PL1 'we designed'	Systematic for all contracted -it verbs
bælosti PRS PL3 'they defend'	**bælostij** PRT SG3 's/he defended'	Systematic for all odd syllable -it verbs and auxiliary/copula *liehket*
i/ittji PRS/PRT SG2 'you do/did not'	**ij/ittjij** PRS/PRT SG3 's/he do/did not'	Missing "j" for negation verbs Sg2
ij/ittjij PRS/PRT SG3 's/he do/did not'	**i/ittji** PRS/PRT SG2 'you do/did not'	Extra "j" for negation verbs Sg3

Table 5: Real word errors comparison

	Precision	Recall	F_1
Rel pronoun agreement	81.43	83.82	82.61
Modal verb ('maybe')	98.00	98.00	98.00
Num/det agreement	74.14	67.19	70.49

Table 6: Performance of the grammar checker on three error types based on regression tests

had a particularly high number of true positives in our preliminary evaluation, showing that this is a frequent error type. Another very frequent true positive that has not been adapted to current mark-up standards regards numeral error types, as in (13). The old mark-up would have a bigger scope including context for the error, i.e. *daj gålmmå tiemáj birra>dan gålmå tiemá birra*. The current guidelines only mark up the form that is to be corrected, meaning *daj>dan*, *gålmmå>gålmå* and *tiemáj>tiemá* which are corrected in three steps and by three separate rules.

(12) Da ulmutja
Those people.PL.NOM
ma Hamsuna mielas li
which.NHUM.PL.NOM Hamsun mind is
buorre ulmutja Hamsun gåvvi buorak
good people Hamsun describe good
láhkáj.
way.
'Those people who, according to Hamsun, are good, he describes in a good manner'

(13) Tjállagin li artihkkala **daj**
Text is article these.DEM.PL.GEN
gålmmå **tiemáj** birra ma li
three.NUM.SG.NOM theme about which is
ássje majna Árran la barggam ...
topics with Árran is work ...
'In the text there are articles about these three themes, which are topics Árran has worked with'

However, there are also several false positives, as in ex. (14), where *gålmmå* is not an error. The difficulty here is that the subsequent noun form is homonymous between nominative and genitive, and the numeral should have only been corrected if it was a genitive phrase. False positives occurred specifically for this error type (in the case of nominative/genitive nouns), showing that more work with the respective rules is necessary to improve the performance of the grammar checker.

(14) Ja gå Knut lij **gålmmå**
And when Knut was three.SG.NOM
jage vuoras de jåhtin Hábmelij,
year.SG.GEN old then move Hábmel,
sadjáj Hamsund.
place Hamsund
'And when Knut was three years old, they moved to Hábmel, to a place called Hamsund'

In ex. (15), on the other hand, the agreement error finding of the grammar checker in *álgij* 's/he started' and its correction to *álggin* 'they started' is a false positive. This is based on there being two subject candidates, because of singular nominative and plural genitive being homonyms, (*cuhppa*) and the other one plural (*biejve*, which in this sentence is singular genitive). The grammar checker confuses the first of them for a subject and therefore wrongly adapts the verb to it.

(15) Bierjjedagá sjnjilltjamáno 20. biejve
Friday March 20. day.SG.GEN
álgij cuhppa, ja hiejtij
begin.PAST.SG3 cup.SG.NOM, and end
lávvodak iehkeda.
saturday evening
'The cup started Friday on March 20 and ended Saturday evening'

Additionally, we tested the grammar checker on

a manually proofread Lule Sámi corpus used for a new text to speech (TTS) tool. The grammar checker did find errors that the proofreader had missed and was therefore useful in a project where we want the text to be perfect. Most of the responses from the grammar checker on this corpus were however false positives, with the grammar checker marking correct forms as errors. These 'bad' results were in turn used to improve and fine tune the grammar checker rules. We find this a very beneficial way of working - using our tools to double-check a proofread corpus, and at the same time using the results of the corpus to improve our tools.

When running the grammar checker on a university level thesis, the grammar checker found many real errors. It was interesting that some highly frequent repeated errors were due to changes in the language norm.

The overall results show us that the grammar checker actually finds real errors, but the main challenge with making it usable to users is to restrict the rules. At this point there is too much noise with more false positives than true positives.

5 Conclusion

We have shown that by using a related language grammar checker as a starting point, we were able to create a basic level grammar checker for Lule Sámi, categorise a fair amount of frequent error types and collect regression tests for each of them in a reasonable amount of time (120 hours between two linguists, one of them a native speaker). The importance for language revitalisation cannot be measured before integrating the tools in the respective text processing programs for the language community to use. But we know from experience with the spell checker, that the tools have a wide group of users, and their importance can usually be felt in the number of complaints that are sent when something is wrong with the distribution or other technical issues. In the future, we want to offer a high-performance tool for the most common error types to the Lule Sámi users. We aim to release a beta version together with the commonly distributed spellchecker in 2022.[5] From the developer side we aim at regression tests of at least 100 examples per error type with at least 90 % precision and 70 % recall, so that the tool will be useful for a wider language community, be used in schools, by the government and for private users on mobile phones.

[5] c.f. https://divvun.no/en/index.html

Acknowledgments

We want to thank Børre Gaup for running the evaluation on the gold corpus and helping with the technical side of error mark-up and automatic evaluation.

References

Lene Antonsen, Linda Wiechetek, and Trond Trosterud. 2010. Reusing grammatical resources for new languages. In *Proceedings of the 7th International Conference on Language Resources and Evaluation (LREC 2010)*, pages 2782–2789, Stroudsburg. The Association for Computational Linguistics.

Kenneth R Beesley and Lauri Karttunen. 2003. *Finite State Morphology*. CSLI publications.

Eckhard Bick and Tino Didriksen. 2015. CG-3 – beyond classical Constraint Grammar. In *Proceedings of the 20th Nordic Conference of Computational Linguistics (NoDaLiDa 2015)*, pages 31–39. Linköping University Electronic Press, Linköpings universitet.

Tino Didriksen. 2010. *Constraint Grammar Manual: 3rd version of the CG formalism variant*. GrammarSoft ApS, Denmark.

Fred Karlsson. 1990a. Constraint Grammar as a Framework for Parsing Running Text. In *Proceedings of the 13th Conference on Computational Linguistics (COLING 1990)*, volume 3, pages 168–173, Helsinki, Finland. Association for Computational Linguistics.

Fred Karlsson. 1990b. Constraint grammar as a framework for parsing unrestricted text. In *Proceedings of the 13th International Conference of Computational Linguistics*, volume 3, pages 168–173, Helsinki.

Fred Karlsson, Atro Voutilainen, Juha Heikkilä, and Arto Anttila. 1995. *Constraint Grammar: A Language-Independent System for Parsing Unrestricted Text*. Mouton de Gruyter, Berlin.

Susanna Angéus Kuoljok. 2002. Julevsámegiella. *Bårjås: Julevsámegiella uddni - ja idet?*, pages 10–18.

Krister Lindén, Erik Axelson, Senka Drobac, Sam Hardwick, Juha Kuokkala, Jyrki Niemi, Tommi A Pirinen, and Miikka Silfverberg. 2013. Hfst—a system for creating nlp tools. In *International workshop on systems and frameworks for computational morphology*, pages 53–71. Springer.

Ole Henrik Magga. 1994. Hvordan den nyeste nordsamiske rettskrivingen ble til. *Festskrift til Ørnulv Vorren*, pages 269–282.

Christopher Moseley. 2010. *Atlas of the World's Languages in Danger*, volume 3. UNESCO.

Sjur N. Moshagen, Tommi A. Pirinen, and Trond Trosterud. 2013. Building an open-source development infrastructure for language technology projects. In *NODALIDA*.

Tommi A. Pirinen and Krister Lindén. 2014. State-of-the-art in weighted finite-state spell-checking. In *Proceedings of the 15th International Conference on Computational Linguistics and Intelligent Text Processing - Volume 8404*, CICLing 2014, pages 519–532, Berlin, Heidelberg. Springer-Verlag.

Håkan Rydving. 2013. *Words and varieties : lexical variation in Saami.* Société Finno-Ougrienne.

Pekka Sammallahti. 1998. *The Saami Languages: an introduction.* Davvi girji.

Mikael Svonni. 2008. Språksituationen för samerna i sverige. *Samiskan i Sverige, rapport från språkkampanjerådet*, pages 22–35.

Linda Wiechetek, Sjur Nørstebø Moshagen, Børre Gaup, and Thomas Omma. 2019. Many shades of grammar checking – launching a constraint grammar tool for North Sámi. In *Proceedings of the NoDaLiDa 2019 Workshop on Constraint Grammar - Methods, Tools and Applications*, NEALT Proceedings Series 33:8, pages 35–44.

Linda Wiechetek, Flammie A Pirinen, Børre Gaup, and Thomas Omma. 2021. No more fumbling in the dark - quality assurance of high-level NLP tools in a multi-lingual infrastructure. In *Proceedings of the Seventh International Workshop on Computational Linguistics of Uralic Languages*, pages 47–56, Syktyvkar, Russia (Online). Association for Computational Linguistics.

Jussi Ylikoski. 2016. Future time reference in lule saami, with some remarks on finnish. *Journal of Estonian and Finno-Ugric Linguistics*, 7(2):209–244.

Jussi Ylikoski. 2022. Lule saami. *The Oxford Guide to the Uralic Languages*, pages 130–146.

A Word-and-Paradigm Workflow for Fieldwork Annotation

Maria Copot[1], **Sara Court**[2], **Noah Diewald**[2], **Stephanie Antetomaso**[2], and **Micha Elsner**[2]

[1]Laboratoire de Linguistique Formelle, Université Paris Cité
[2]Department of Linguistics, Ohio State University

mcopot@etu.u-paris.fr, {court.22,diewald.21,antetomaso.2}@osu.edu, melsner0@gmail.com

Abstract

There are many challenges in morphological fieldwork annotation: it heavily relies on segmentation and feature labeling (which have both practical and theoretical drawbacks), it's time-intensive, and the annotator needs to be linguistically trained and may still annotate things inconsistently. We propose a workflow that relies on unsupervised and active learning grounded in Word-and-Paradigm morphology (WP). Machine learning has the potential to greatly accelerate the annotation process and allow a human annotator to focus on problematic cases, while the WP approach makes for an annotation system that is word-based and relational, removing the need to make decisions about feature labeling and segmentation early in the process and allowing speakers of the language of interest to participate more actively, since linguistic training is not necessary. We present a proof-of-concept for the first step of the workflow: in a realistic fieldwork setting, annotators can process hundreds of forms per hour.[1]

1 Introduction

A major component of current workflows for linguistic fieldwork is the creation and curation of Interlinear Glossed Texts (IGT), in which morphological forms are segmented into meaning-bearing units. These are expensive and time-consuming to produce, but constitute important training data for computational fieldwork methods. While IGT are a valuable resource for the study of endangered and under-described languages (Zamaraeva, 2016), annotations that directly segment and label morphemes may have both practical and theoretical shortcomings. Segmentation-based analyses may not always straightforwardly account for the diversity of phenomena attested in the world's languages, making them especially problematic in the early stages of understanding a morphological system. An alternative is provided by analyses that characterize morphological relations at the word level, such as those associated with Word-and-Paradigm approaches (WP; named by Hockett (1954); see Blevins (2016) for a general overview), which do not require segmentation and may allow for more efficient and informative morphological annotation in a low-resource fieldwork setting.

WP theories classify word forms in terms of the shared relationships they exhibit within a connected lexicon. These relationships may be conceptualised as tabular paradigms in which one axis groups items sharing a lexeme and the other groups items sharing a morphosyntactic cell.

PRS	PRS.3S	PST	PTCP.PRS
run	runs	ran	running
live	lives	lived	living

Table 1: A partial WP paradigm table in English

Note that paradigmatic tables would still be informative about the identities of morphosyntactic cells even without cell labels. Such an unlabeled table can be assembled first and then serve as an aid for post-hoc decisions about how to label the contrasts.

WP-style analyses inform recent work on unsupervised paradigm discovery (Kann et al., 2020b; Wiemerslage et al., 2021; Erdmann et al., 2020) as well as neural inflection and reinflection models without internal segmentation (Kann and Schütze, 2016; Anastasopoulos and Neubig, 2019; Silfverberg and Hulden, 2018). Since WP theories have proven to be such a good fit for "big data" morphology (Elsner et al., 2019), this paper asks whether they can also benefit the "small data" fieldwork setting. We see several potential advantages: modern computational tools can be used to provide initial analyses or suggestions for the annotator; grouping forms together as belonging to the same cells or

[1]All code for the paper can be found at https://github.com/CopotM/WP-workflow-ComputEL2022

Proceedings of the Fifth Workshop on the Use of Computational Methods in the Study of Endangered Languages, pages 159 - 169
May 26-27, 2022 ©2022 Association for Computational Linguistics

lexemes may be faster and easier than segmenting on a first pass; finally, segment-free annotations of some morphological phenomena may be preferable on theoretical grounds. We conduct pilot experiments in three languages, including a true under-resourced language, to show that trained human annotators can rapidly improve on the results of an unsupervised morphological analyzer (Jin et al., 2020). The workflow we propose takes these corrections as input to bootstrap iterated active learning. We collaborate with non-linguist native speakers of Wao Terero, a language isolate spoken in Ecuador, to evaluate the potential of the proposed methodology to increase community engagement in the annotation process. Finally, we discuss possible next steps in the design of an interactive annotation environment for Word-and-Paradigm morphology.

2 Background

2.1 Word-and-Paradigm Morphology

Linguistic theory necessarily informs documentary and descriptive methodology (Himmelmann, 1998). Standard workflows for linguistic fieldwork can be seen as theoretically aligned with Item-and-Arrangement (IA) analyses of morphological structure: field linguists often annotate collected texts or transcriptions by slicing words into morphemic subunits, each with a consistent form-meaning association. The resulting IGT can be useful for illustrating morphological structure in certain well-described languages, but IA-based approaches to morphological annotation have two main theoretical drawbacks. First, segmentation may not be able to capture important morphological generalizations, as many linguistic patterns are not strictly segmental. For example, an IA-style gloss b. below is unable to directly convey information about what exactly makes *caught* a past tense in the same way that is possible for *seemed*.

a.	*seem-ed*	b.	*caught*
	seem-PST		PST\catch

Second, it is not always the case that morphological systems exhibit reliable form-meaning correspondences. The meaning of a segmented unit may instead only be interpretable by contrasting it with other forms of the same word, or other words with the same grammatical function. Table 2 shows how the same segmental unit can have different (in this case, opposite) meanings which may only be interpreted in the context of other forms of the same lexeme: in Spanish, there is no unambiguous verb ending for IND.PRS.3SG, nor is there an unambiguous meaning for -a/-e. Instead, both segments are interpretable as IND.PRS.3SG markers only when contrasted with other related forms, like the SUBJ.PRS.3SG. In this case, if one is marked by -a, the other will be marked by -e.

	IND.PRS.3SG	SUBJ.PRS.3SG
TO EAT	com-e	com-a
TO BUY	compr-a	compr-e

Table 2: Morphological exchange pattern in Spanish

In addition to the theoretical shortcomings of segmentation-based approaches, IA-style annotation workflows may pose more concrete problems during descriptive or documentary fieldwork. Morphemic segmentation and labeling requires important decisions about the structure of a language's morphology to be made from the very start of the annotation process, even when the researcher lacks sufficient information to do so. WP theories instead take words themselves as the smallest meaning-bearing unit of analysis. By doing so, it is possible to characterize a morphological system as a set of parallel relationships among words. To derive the paradigmatic structure of a system (Bonami and Strnadová, 2019), one must start by establishing pairwise formal relationships that mark a functional contrast. For example, *run* ~ *runs* and *eat* ~ *eats* both mark PRS.NON3SG~PRS.3SG by means of the formal *X*~*Xs* relationship. Chains of words linked together by morphological relationships make up morphological families (e.g., {*run, running, ran, runner, runners*}; {*eat, eating, ate, eater, eaters*}), which may in turn be aligned according to word forms exhibiting parallel contrasts in meaning. In this way, paradigmatic structure gives rise to both morphological families (sets of inflectionally or derivationally related word forms) and paradigm cells (sets of forms that occupy the same place in the system of contrasts) as structured objects of morphological analysis.

Since decisions about the boundaries and labeling of subword units are unnecessary in such a framework, WP is well-suited to bootstrap morphological annotation. An annotation workflow that labels related structures of words and paradigms as opposed to segmented morphemes can help avoid the pitfalls of making incorrect assumptions about the system at an early stage, which can lead to problematic conclusions about the grammar of the language and be hard to recover from once adopted. Nevertheless, morpheme-style segmentations can still be extracted from WP alternations and paradigms, and morphosyntactic labels can easily be added to paradigmatic cells. In practice, a WP-based annotation system a) captures non-segmental morphological patterns just as naturally as segmental ones, since it's based on alternations at the word level and b) relies on judgements about which relationships are the same and which are different, a more straightforward task for untrained linguistic consultants. The latter aspect may in turn serve to boost community engagement and facilitate crowdsourcing data on a larger scale.

2.2 Machine-aided morphological annotation

Morphological annotation is part of a larger language documentation and description workflow which may be systematized as a sequence of data collection, transcription, analysis, annotation, and archival (Thieberger and Berez, 2012). Fieldwork projects are inherently collaborative in nature and their outcomes are ultimately shaped by the unique needs of the multiple stakeholders involved, including the community, the researcher, and the funding organization, among others. A project's goals may include the development of materials for language maintenance and revitalization, community access to digital language technologies, or the collection of language data for linguistic analysis. For this reason, field linguists often use software tools such as SIL's FLEx/FieldWorks (Rogers, 2010) to create digital lexica and collections of IGT that may serve as input for downstream applications or analyses and facilitate the creation of community-facing resources (Schreiner et al., 2020). To gloss a text using FieldWorks, the analyst separates each word into canonical morphemes, associating each one with a lexical or grammatical meaning.

While FieldWorks is perhaps the most widely used software for morphological annotation, other low-resource systems have successfully implemented rule-based finite state transducers (FST) for machine-aided development of IGT, digital lexica, and searchable corpora (Alnajjar et al., 2020; Kazeminejad et al., 2017; Arppe et al., 2016). While standard FSTs are limited in their ability to represent non-concatenative alternations and allomorphy, alignment-based transduction and two-level methods may be paired with probabilistic rule- or feature-based models to achieve higher performance using inflection tables or parallel texts (Hulden et al., 2014; Ahlberg et al., 2015; Palmer et al., 2010). Still other studies use IGT for morphological paradigm or grammar induction (Zamaraeva et al., 2019; Moeller et al., 2020). Since each of these methods assume pre-existing linguistic analyses of the data being processed, they may be suitable for later stages of annotation and resource development, but they run the risk of obscuring morphological patterns, hindering the discovery of important generalizations across word forms in the data early on in description and analysis.

For machine-assisted morphological annotation at the level of the unsegmented word, we draw on recent studies investigating low resource applications of neural sequence taggers for morphological analysis, POS tagging, and NER. While such models are known to require large amounts of consistently annotated data typically unavailable for under-described languages (Kann et al., 2020a), Garrette and Baldridge (2013) show that a POS tagger can be successfully trained with data annotated in as little as two hours when appropriate noise reduction techniques are applied. Experiments comparing model architectures suggest BiLSTMs with attention may be used for sequence tagging in low resource settings when combined with strategies for noise reduction and data augmentation, including character-level cross-domain and cross-lingual transfer methods (Adelani et al., 2021, 2020; Cotterell and Heigold, 2017; Hedderich et al., 2020), and data augmentation strategies involving external resources and collaborative curation (Adelani et al., 2021; Hedderich et al., 2021).

For linguistic fieldwork on languages that are not only under-resourced but also under-described, these methods may be complemented by unsupervised models to aid in the discovery of morphological phenomena and patterns that have yet to be documented or analyzed (Erdmann et al., 2020). For this reason, our proposed workflow utilizes unsupervised paradigm discovery methods to cluster and tag related word forms according to both lexeme and paradigm cell without the need for prior analysis or segmentation. Eventual implementation of an active learning component would allow for automated semi-supervised annotation to further increase efficiency and accuracy. Previous work on active learning for NER suggests the ideal model architecture may depend on the amount of data available for input (Erdmann et al., 2019). The modular nature of our proposed workflow would therefore allow for the option of interchanging models at different points within data collection and annotation. In summary, we believe WP-based annotation brings field linguistic representations closer to those used in the NLP community at large. This can speed up the early stages of the analytical process by enabling the use of unsupervised methods. Moreover, it enables relatively off-the-shelf adoption of new tagging models, rather than development of specific solutions for IGT.

2.3 Benefits for community engagement

In addition to allowing the fieldworker to begin annotation without committing to a segmentation-based analysis of the data, our proposed workflow aims to increase collaborative research with the language community by facilitating native speaker involvement in the annotation task. In conjunction with a growing focus on the ethical collection of linguistic data and collaborative fieldwork (Rice, 2006), we must remember that the diversity of language communities means there is no "one-size-fits-all" approach to ethical research or community engagement (van Driem, 2016). It is therefore important to position speakers as self-sufficient researchers of their own language by involving them at every step of the process, from data collection to analysis (Czaykowska-Higgins, 2009). Failure to engage with speakers of the language being studied can have far-reaching consequences.[2] We assume that the fieldworker is engaging with a community that desires resources such as dictionaries, grammars and educational materials. These are all the product of linguistic analysis. If the optimal outcome of community engagement is that community members have maximum agency in achieving their goals, lowering barriers to entry for non-specialists by providing more accessible tools and methods for analysis is one strategy for decreasing the community's reliance on outside specialists. Our proposal is only the first of many steps that would need to be taken to allow technology to facilitate such an outcome.

Existing fieldwork tools and methodologies may hinder community-based research by making data analysis difficult or inaccessible for native speakers of the language. One of the authors is involved in ongoing fieldwork on Wao Terero, a linguistic isolate spoken in the Ecuadorian Amazon. Education levels are low in rural Ecuador, and some of the native speakers involved in this project have less than a United States high school equivalent in formal schooling. The use of research tools that require extensive formal training or prior education in linguistic theory bars this subset of the community from fully participating in data analysis. Since these speakers are often older and monolingual, this can also skew scientific results, producing linguistic materials or analyses which may not represent the general Wao population.

Our proposed workflow directly contributes to the development of community-based research and linguistic tools. The relational WP approach, coupled with the concordance-based interface we propose, asks native speakers to identify patterns in the data by matching like with like, without requiring them to first learn technical vocabulary or a theory of morphemes. Section 4.1 presents the results of our collaboration with Wao Terero speakers to evaluate the potential of our workflow to increase community engagement in the field.

3 Workflow and experiments

We propose an annotation workflow (Figure 1) that begins with the collaborative collection of primary data within a language community. For morphological analysis, the model makes use of both naturalistic transcriptions or texts as well as a list of target lemmas for analysis. These files are used as input to an unsupervised model that identifies potential instances of lexemes and cells and outputs a sample of occurrences for each category to be annotated. The annotation process involves both excluding occurrences that don't belong in their assigned group and seeking out new occurrences to add to the group. The annotated output could then be used along with additional primary data as input to a supervised classifier within an active learning framework. Since the workflow is modular, each individual component can be updated over time in line with future advances in state of the art machine learning.

As a proof of concept that WP annotation is viable, we implement the first stage of our proposed workflow in which fieldworkers begin with the results of

[2] As one example, the ISO 639-3 codes used for identifying some languages, such as Wao Terero, Shuar (Chicham), and Ho-Chunk, are references to slurs for these communities. Since these codes are referenced by both the HTML and XML standards of the W3C, these communities cannot currently use the web in their language without reference to hate speech. A minimum of effort to engage with these communities could have avoided this.

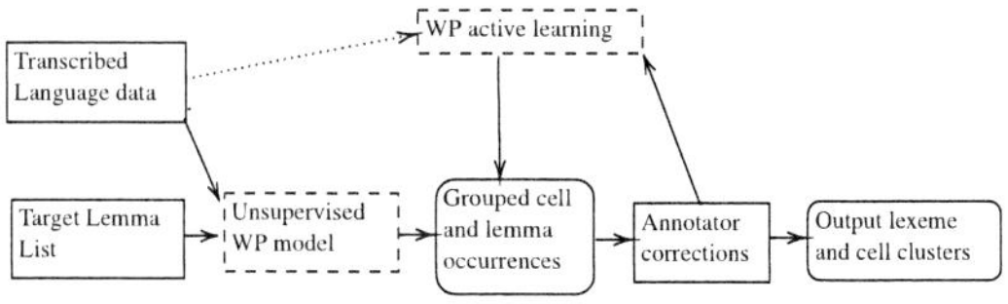

Figure 1: The proposed annotation workflow

an unsupervised analysis. We conduct a series of pilot experiments demonstrating that annotators can rapidly improve the results of such a system. While our full proposed workflow would integrate active learning within an interactive annotation environment, in the present work, we do not currently use these annotations as additional input to the model.

3.1 Model

Our initial annotation system is the baseline paradigm discovery system from SIGMORPHON 2020 Task 2 (Jin et al., 2020). Given raw text and a set of target lemmas, the model uses edit trees and an unsupervised HMM to identify and return potential inflected forms of those lemmas. The original model has both a retrieval and a generation component - the retrieval component uses edit distance to find potential forms of the given lemmas and cluster them into paradigm cells, while the generation component produces potential forms of the lemmas which are not present in the text. Because fieldworkers and language consultants must see forms in context in order to make decisions about their morphological status, we apply only the first (retrieval) component to cluster forms which are attested in the raw text corpus. For instance, the model produces the following paradigm for the English word HEAR: *hear, heard, hearing, heart* (each occupying a different numerically labeled cell). This model's requirements determine the amount of raw text necessary for our proposed workflow. While Jin et al. (2020) requires a moderate amount of text, a less resource-hungry method could be substituted for very early fieldwork where little transcribed text is available.

We generate concordance-style datasets for the annotation of each proposed lexeme and cell using the examples of their proposed forms identified within the corpus by the unsupervised model (Figure 2). These datasets are generated separately for each individual lexeme and paradigm cell proposed by the model. For lexemes, we aim for up to 7 examples per form; for cells, we sample 20 instances in total. These numbers were selected based on initial estimates to account for known trade-offs between annotation speed and quality.

Our annotation guidelines set the following rules: The annotator should ensure all accepted examples in a set correspond to the same lexeme or morphophonological paradigm cell. Incorrect instances include forms that are derivationally related, homophonous, or belong to other lexical categories or (non-syncretic) paradigm cells.[3] All of our experiments targeted verbs, and the annotators were instructed to reject any form they did not believe was a verb. By presenting examples within a concordance format, the annotator is able to use word context to filter out forms which do not occur in the correct paradigm as well as tokens which are homophonous with a member of the paradigm. For instance, when annotating files for the verbal lexeme *hear*, the annotator would exclude both *heart* (incorrect paradigm) and the noun *hearing* (homophonous with the V.PTCP.PRS form).

Inspection of these datasets allows annotators to correct precision errors in the model's output (incorrect forms added to paradigms/cells) but not recall errors (missing forms). We therefore give annotators the opportunity to include missing items for each paradigm cell in the dataset by showing them a few examples of forms from each of the other model-proposed paradigm cells. Because the number of lexemes is much larger than the number of cells, we cannot augment the lexeme datasets in the same way. Instead, we give the annotator a tool which conducts a regular expression search in the corpus and adds up to 20 detected examples to the annotation dataset. For instance, the annotator could type *hear.?* to find additional forms similar to *hears* that were not originally captured by the model. The annotator may then apply the same process of comparison to provide additional positive examples for a downstream classifier.

3.2 Data

In order to evaluate the effect of a human annotator on model performance, we experiment on two languages, English and Croatian, with gold standard annotations from the Universal Dependencies data set. For English, we use the GUM treebank (Zeldes, 2017) and for Croatian the SETimes treebank (Agić

[3]Especially from a WP perspective, there is no strong theoretical reason for positing that paradigms may not span derivationally related items and different lexical categories (Bonami and Strnadová, 2019). These choices were made for the current study so that the annotators' decisions could be compared to a gold standard.

LEXEME

annotator		form	model output	
	...you're still going to	hear	True	them.
	She thought she could	hear	True	Gomez laughing.
X	...signalling of problems of	hearing	True	and understanding.

CELL

annotator		form	model output	
	...mechanisms underlying the	learning	True	and processing of L2 grammar ...
	...periods of limited ... exposure	following	True	L2 training are not uncommon ...
	...may be found in different situations	including	True	when one studies a language ...
X	...such as listening and	reading	True	comprehension ...
	The training	lasted	False	varying lengths of time...

Figure 2: A selection of instances for annotation of the lexeme HEAR (top) and for a system-proposed morphological cell (bottom). Ellipses are for presentational purposes; the annotators saw full sentential contexts. The baseline's decision about the token is displayed as True/False in column 4, and the annotator marks an X in column 0 to indicate that they disagree.

and Ljubešić, 2015). In each case, we extract the entire treebank training file as raw text for model input. For the list of target lemmas, we select verbal lemmas with frequency ranks 10-111;[4] we skip the top 10 lemmas because they are the most likely to have atypical paradigms (Bybee, 1988), and the early stages of fieldwork should focus on identifying typical paradigm structure.

In each case, two annotators from a Linguistics Ph.D. program spent 30 minutes annotating lexeme data and 30 minutes on cell data. Experimenting on English, a language well known by the annotators, provides an upper estimate of model-plus-human annotator performance. The Croatian experiment provides a potentially more realistic example of model-plus-human performance on a language still relatively unknown to the fieldworker. While our annotators speak several Indo-European languages, neither of them is fluent in a Slavic language nor has ever studied Croatian.

It is relatively common to develop tools for endangered or under-resourced languages by applying them to small or unannotated datasets from well-resourced languages, since this allows for evaluation against a curated gold standard. However, well-resourced languages may differ typologically from real endangered languages, leading to poor generalization (Kann et al., 2019; Mager et al., 2018). Therefore, we conduct a third experiment on Wao Terero. The annotators for this experiment were native speakers of Wao Terero who have never taken a course in linguistics. Both were Spanish-Wao Terero bilinguals. One recently completed high school and the other has attended university courses. A Linguistics Ph.D. student who is currently conducting field research on Wao Terero but not a fluent speaker also performed annotations on the same data. To run the model, we use Wao Terero text of the New Testament as the raw text corpus. As the model did not perform well with single character verbs, the fieldworker specifically selected multi-syllable seed verbs for the model by searching for common inflectional endings with a regular expression search and compiled these into a list of 108 target lemmas. Six resulting lexeme files were removed since they had only two items and were potentially ambiguous. The annotators were provided approximately 10 minutes of instruction using Spanish verbal paradigms as examples before completing the task for Wao Terero. Instead of using the technical term "paradigm," the fieldworker described the concept as a collection of all the forms a verb might take while remaining the same word. Annotators were told that the goal was to assess the effectiveness of the annotation method, rather than tackling the issue of paradigm discovery directly. A guided practice preceded an hour of annotation. The guided practice featured the Spanish verb *cazar*, 'to hunt', with some errors that involved the homophone *casarse*, 'to marry', and a lexical-category-altering derivation *cazador*, 'hunter'. Speakers were allowed to ask any questions they wished during annotation and additionally provide clarification to one another. A request was made that they limit their communication among themselves so that it would be possible

[4]This selection procedure is not entirely unsupervised since we are guaranteed to select verbs as targets and our assessment of their frequency counts all their actual forms. However, it is similar to the task setup used in SIGMORPHON 2020, which also used only verbal targets; we believed that keeping this simplification from the shared task would help the baseline model to perform as reported.

to compare their annotation choices. They were given a directory with 102 annotation files named in a numerical order corresponding to the alphabetical order of stems, and instructed to annotate files in order until the hour was complete. Since we do not have an independently developed gold standard for Wao Terero, we focus our evaluation of the results of this experiment on measurements of annotation speed and additional qualitative observations.

3.3 Evaluation

For English and Croatian, we measure annotation accuracy at the token level. As in many unsupervised applications, this requires a preliminary mapping, since some of the model's proposed lexemes or cells may mix together multiple actual cells, from which the annotator must try to select one. We find the most likely interpretation of a set of forms by taking the most common gold label among its accepted instances. If a lexeme file contains *hear.V, hear.V, hear.V, hearing.N, heart.N*, the best interpretation is *hear.V*; If the annotator accepts examples 1, 2, and 4, they have 2/3 correct acceptances and 1/2 correct rejections, for an accuracy of 3/5. Annotator accuracies are micro-averaged across the dataset. Given the imposed time limits of the experiment, annotators did not inspect every annotation file output by the model. Final scores reflect the entire dataset; cases the annotator did not reach are left at their baseline values.[5]

4 Results

Table 3 shows lexeme evaluations before considering regular expression search results. Annotation in English is much faster than in Croatian. English annotators inspected an average of 444 lexeme tokens, including regex search results, in their 30 minutes, while Croatian annotators inspected 306. This is expected, since Croatian was selected to simulate the early stages of fieldwork in which the linguist is still relatively unfamiliar with the language being analyzed. However, annotators for each language are capable of reliably rejecting incorrect forms proposed by the model. Annotator mistakes on the English data tend to involve confusion between adjectival and verbal interpretations of forms like *leading*.

[5]We follow the SIGMORPHON 2020 task in grouping syncretic cells for evaluation. Thus, English has 5 valid paradigm cells (e.g., for the lexeme *show*: nonpast *show*, nonpast 3rd person *shows*, gerund/present participle *showing*, past participle *shown* and past active *showed*).

	Acc.	Marked	Corr.
English			
Base	81	-	-
A1	84	58	50
A2	83	43	33
Croatian			
Base	66	-	-
A3	67	19	19
A4	66	12	12

Table 3: Evaluation of lexeme annotations. Marked shows a count of instances altered from the baseline by annotators; Corr. shows a count of correct alterations.

	Acc.	Marked	Corr.
English			
Base	67	-	-
A1	97	129	120
A2	94	119	108
Croatian			
Base	90	-	-
A3	90	8	-1
A4	90	28	16

Table 4: Evaluation of cell annotations.

Table 4 shows cell evaluations. Annotation of cells in English is rapid and highly accurate; the English annotators were able to review all proposed cells in 30 minutes. The English baseline produces several candidate paradigm cells containing mostly function words or other non-verbal material. These are easily rejected, as are spurious members of real cells. Annotation in Croatian is slower and comparatively more error-prone. Annotators reviewed an average of 1384 items in 30 minutes, but without marking many forms. However, even with only 30 minutes, one annotator did contribute useful information on cell membership in Croatian.

Regular expression search did not contribute usefully to the results. While all four annotators labeled the results of their searches with high accuracy (≥ 80), it seems to have been too difficult to write good regular expressions that would elicit valid but undetected paradigm members. In English, annotators found 6 and 4 correct novel forms; in Croatian, 0 and 1. We believe an interactive environment for search and annotation could be more effective, a point we return to below.

4.1 Wao Terero results

The Wao Terero speaking annotators each made an assessment for all items in 4 files, constituting 67 tokens, in one hour. The linguist assessed 776 tokens. The speakers rejected 11 and 9 items respectively, agreeing on 3 items. The fieldworker rejected 15 items, agreeing with the speakers 6 and 5 times respectively. All annotators agreed on rejections for a total of 2 items. Notably, in one file consisting of four items, the linguist's annotations were the complement of one of the speaker's. This indicates that the file was ambiguous between two lexeme options and that finding ways to address ambiguity would increase annotator agreement. For instance, a specification of heuristics might be used. In this case simply choosing the option that resulted in the fewest rejections would have been adequate.

The difference in the number of items annotated by the speakers as compared to the fieldworker reflects the different approaches taken when completing the annotation task. Specifically, speakers attempted to understand the sentences that provided context for the words in question. Because the Bible constitutes atypical Wao Terero, one speaker complained that the data contained non-words.[6] This complicated the task for both speakers and may explain the low number of tokens assessed. The linguist instead assessed tokens based on orthographic regularities. Strictly speaking, this was exactly what the Wao Terero speakers were asked not to do, since they were provided homophones as examples of items that should be rejected.

In response to exit questions following the annotation task, the speakers stated that they had understood the task and its goals. One speaker stated that this type of investigation is valuable. Neither speaker claimed to find the task dull. One indicated that they didn't find it difficult except for when they had initially started. The other stated that it was very difficult because of unusual words. That is, one answered the question based on the conceptual difficulty of the task while the other answered according to practical issues with the data.

Despite issues with the data and what might be considered an initially slow annotation pace, our claim that speakers would find the task intuitive was borne out. Considering that existing IGT workflows require a great deal of specialist knowledge, the fact that speakers with no linguistic training can begin annotating using a WP-based workflow with only 10 minutes of training is notable.

5 Discussion

A more relational, word-based approach to morphological annotation for language documentation is desirable for both theoretical and practical reasons. Theoretically, Word-and-Paradigm annotation allows fieldworkers to avoid, or at least defer, difficult decisions about both morphological form and function. Our proposal separates the identification of a morphological cell from the application of a morphosyntactic label or set of features, a difficult analytical task often involving comparison of many related examples. For instance, distinguishing past tense from perfect aspect is a sensitive task (Bybee and Dahl, 1989) which might best be done once the forms in question can be reliably separated from the rest of the verbal paradigm. Thus, even if the desired end goal of annotation is IGT, we believe that our proposed annotation methodology can speed up the early stages of annotation and prevent the researcher from having to commit to an analysis too early.

From a practical standpoint, by starting with an automatically generated concordance set for each proposed cell and lexeme, the annotator can focus on making direct comparisons – is the proposed grouping coherent in terms of its surface form and distributional context? Annotating at the level of unsegmented words in context makes it possible for a native speaker who has no knowledge of technical or grammatical terms to easily identify the patterns represented by the concordances and contribute their expert knowledge. The proposed workflow is therefore designed to facilitate greater community involvement in the development of language resources and technologies in line with community needs. Our experiment results show that even in an unfamiliar language for which the

[6] The New Testament is not the optimal corpus for Wao Terero but there was little other choice. The language of New Testiment translations can be atypical and stylized, even in English. Given the distance between Mediterranean and Amazonian cultures the translation of the New Testament into Wao Terero is filled with neologisms, unfamiliar concepts and atypical phrasal constructions. Although there is a sizable Wao Terero deposit at the Endangered Language Archive (ELAR), the orthography of that collection is inconsistent and the restrictions placed on its use do not allow for practical use by researchers or Wao community members. One of the authors is currently involved in an effort to create an open corpus. This is in line with the wishes of Wao speakers, who have no access to ELAR materials. Unfortunately, this alternative corpus is still under development and the only suitably large corpus with a consistent orthography in existences is the New Testament.

annotator does not yet understand the functions of different morphological markers, there is still some capacity to weed out forms that do not belong. The tight integration of this workflow with unsupervised learning technology also means that any future improvements in unsupervised paradigm discovery can immediately benefit fieldworkers.

While our pilot experiment focuses on the initial steps of a computationally-aided field documentation project, our full proposed workflow envisions both an interactive environment and active learning. An interactive environment would allow annotators to view proposed paradigm tables alongside the text, helping to see where forms might be missing. Annotators could also search more effectively for forms that could fill in these gaps, for instance by viewing a word cloud of similar forms. This could make it easier to fix recall errors in system-proposed paradigms. Even a few labeled instances can vastly improve the performance of part of speech taggers (Stratos and Collins, 2015; Søgaard, 2010), and the same is true in a relational setting (Li et al., 2020). In our environment, we envision active learning directing the annotator's attention to the least certain distinctions, eliminating repetitive annotation of "easy" instances.

Our proposal shows promise as a faster and more theoretically grounded alternative to existing tools. Its modular structure makes it easy to integrate advances in the field of computational linguistics, and it allows the fieldworker to quickly and easily involve the intuitions of native speakers with little linguistic training, boosting community engagement.

6 Acknowledgements

We would like to thank Flora and Alberto Boyotai, the Wao Terero speakers who tested the annotation system and provided us with helpful feedback. A portion of this research was funded by the Lewis and Clark Fund for Exploration and Field Research from the American Philosophical Society, and by the Labex EFL.

References

David Ifeoluwa Adelani, Jade Abbott, Graham Neubig, Daniel D'souza, Julia Kreutzer, Constantine Lignos, Chester Palen-Michel, Happy Buzaaba, Shruti Rijhwani, Sebastian Ruder, et al. 2021. Masakhaner: Named entity recognition for african languages. *arXiv preprint arXiv:2103.11811*.

David Ifeoluwa Adelani, Michael A Hedderich, Dawei Zhu, Esther van den Berg, and Dietrich Klakow. 2020. Distant supervision and noisy label learning for low resource named entity recognition: A study on Hausa and Yorùbá. *arXiv preprint arXiv:2003.08370*.

Željko Agić and Nikola Ljubešić. 2015. Universal Dependencies for Croatian (that work for Serbian, too). In *The 5th Workshop on Balto-Slavic Natural Language Processing*, pages 1–8, Hissar, Bulgaria. INCOMA Ltd. Shoumen, BULGARIA.

Malin Ahlberg, Markus Forsberg, and Mans Hulden. 2015. Paradigm classification in supervised learning of morphology. In *Proceedings of the 2015 Conference of the North American Chapter of the Association for Computational Linguistics: Human Language Technologies*, pages 1024–1029, Denver, Colorado. Association for Computational Linguistics.

Khalid Alnajjar, Mika Hämäläinen, Jack Rueter, and Niko Partanen. 2020. Ve'rdd. narrowing the gap between paper dictionaries, low-resource nlp and community involvement. *arXiv preprint arXiv:2012.02578*.

Antonios Anastasopoulos and Graham Neubig. 2019. Pushing the limits of low-resource morphological inflection. In *Proceedings of the 2019 Conference on Empirical Methods in Natural Language Processing and the 9th International Joint Conference on Natural Language Processing (EMNLP-IJCNLP)*, pages 984–996, Hong Kong, China. Association for Computational Linguistics.

Antti Arppe, Jordan Lachler, Trond Trosterud, Lene Antonsen, and Sjur N Moshagen. 2016. Basic language resource kits for endangered languages: A case study of Plains Cree. In *Proceedings of the 2nd Workshop on Collaboration and Computing for Under-Resourced Languages Workshop (CCURL 2016), Portorož, Slovenia*, pages 1–8.

James P. Blevins. 2016. *Word and paradigm morphology*. Oxford University Press.

Olivier Bonami and Jana Strnadová. 2019. Paradigm structure and predictability in derivational morphology. *Morphology*, 29.

Joan Bybee. 1988. Morphology as lexical organization. In Michael Hammond and Michael Noonan, editors, *Theoretical morphology: Approaches in modern linguistics*, pages 119–142. Academic Press.

Joan L Bybee and Östen Dahl. 1989. *The creation of tense and aspect systems in the languages of the world*. John Benjamins Amsterdam.

Ryan Cotterell and Georg Heigold. 2017. Cross-lingual character-level neural morphological tagging. In *Proceedings of the 2017 Conference on Empirical Methods in Natural Language Processing*, pages 748–759, Copenhagen, Denmark. Association for Computational Linguistics.

Ewa Czaykowska-Higgins. 2009. Research models, community engagement, and linguistic fieldwork. *Language Documentation & Conservation*, 3(1):15–50.

Micha Elsner, Andrea D. Sims, Alexander Erdmann, Antonio Hernandez, Evan Jaffe, Lifeng Jin, Martha Booker Johnson, Shuan Karim, David L. King, Luana Lamberti Nunes, Byung-Doh Oh, Nathan Rasmussen, Cory Shain, Stephanie Antetomaso, Kendra V. Dickinson, Noah Diewald, Michelle McKenzie, and Symon Stevens-Guille. 2019. Modeling morphological learning, typology, and change: What can the neural sequence-to-sequence framework contribute? *Journal of Language Modelling*, 7(1):125–170.

Alexander Erdmann, Micha Elsner, Shijie Wu, Ryan Cotterell, and Nizar Habash. 2020. The paradigm discovery problem. In *Proceedings of the 58th Annual Meeting of the Association for Computational Linguistics*, pages 7778–7790, Online. Association for Computational Linguistics.

Alexander Erdmann, David Joseph Wrisley, Benjamin Allen, Christopher Brown, Sophie Cohen-Bodénès, Micha Elsner, Yukun Feng, Brian Joseph, Béatrice Joyeux-Prunel, and Marie-Catherine de Marneffe. 2019. Practical, efficient, and customizable active learning for named entity recognition in the digital humanities. In *Proceedings of the 2019 Conference of the North American Chapter of the Association for Computational Linguistics: Human Language Technologies, Volume 1 (Long and Short Papers)*, pages 2223–2234, Minneapolis, Minnesota. Association for Computational Linguistics.

Dan Garrette and Jason Baldridge. 2013. Learning a part-of-speech tagger from two hours of annotation. In *Proceedings of the 2013 Conference of the North American Chapter of the Association for Computational Linguistics: Human Language Technologies*, pages 138–147, Atlanta, Georgia. Association for Computational Linguistics.

Michael A. Hedderich, David Adelani, Dawei Zhu, Jesujoba Alabi, Udia Markus, and Dietrich Klakow. 2020. Transfer learning and distant supervision for multilingual transformer models: A study on African languages. In *Proceedings of the 2020 Conference on Empirical Methods in Natural Language Processing (EMNLP)*, pages 2580–2591, Online. Association for Computational Linguistics.

Michael A. Hedderich, Lukas Lange, and Dietrich Klakow. 2021. Anea: Distant supervision for low-resource named entity recognition.

Nikolaus P Himmelmann. 1998. Documentary and descriptive linguistics.

Charles F. Hockett. 1954. Two models of grammatical description. *Word*, 10:210–234.

Mans Hulden, Markus Forsberg, and Malin Ahlberg. 2014. Semi-supervised learning of morphological paradigms and lexicons. In *Proceedings of the 14th Conference of the European Chapter of the Association for Computational Linguistics*, pages 569–578, Gothenburg, Sweden. Association for Computational Linguistics.

Huiming Jin, Liwei Cai, Yihui Peng, Chen Xia, Arya McCarthy, and Katharina Kann. 2020. Unsupervised morphological paradigm completion. In *Proceedings of the 58th Annual Meeting of the Association for Computational Linguistics*, pages 6696–6707, Online. Association for Computational Linguistics.

Katharina Kann, Kyunghyun Cho, and Samuel R. Bowman. 2019. Towards realistic practices in low-resource natural language processing: The development set. In *Proceedings of the 2019 Conference on Empirical Methods in Natural Language Processing and the 9th International Joint Conference on Natural Language Processing (EMNLP-IJCNLP)*, pages 3342–3349, Hong Kong, China. Association for Computational Linguistics.

Katharina Kann, Ophélie Lacroix, and Anders Søgaard. 2020a. Weakly supervised pos taggers perform poorly on truly low-resource languages. In *Proceedings of the AAAI Conference on Artificial Intelligence*, volume 34, pages 8066–8073.

Katharina Kann, Arya D. McCarthy, Garrett Nicolai, and Mans Hulden. 2020b. The SIGMORPHON 2020 shared task on unsupervised morphological paradigm completion. In *Proceedings of the 17th SIGMORPHON Workshop on Computational Research in Phonetics, Phonology, and Morphology*, pages 51–62, Online. Association for Computational Linguistics.

Katharina Kann and Hinrich Schütze. 2016. Single-model encoder-decoder with explicit morphological representation for reinflection. In *Proceedings of the 54th Annual Meeting of the Association for Computational Linguistics (Volume 2: Short Papers)*, pages 555–560, Berlin, Germany. Association for Computational Linguistics.

Ghazaleh Kazeminejad, Andrew Cowell, and Mans Hulden. 2017. Creating lexical resources for polysynthetic languages—the case of Arapaho. In *Proceedings of the 2nd Workshop on the Use of Computational Methods in the Study of Endangered Languages*, pages 10–18, Honolulu. Association for Computational Linguistics.

Pengshuai Li, Xinsong Zhang, Weijia Jia, and Wei Zhao. 2020. Active testing: An unbiased evaluation method for distantly supervised relation extraction. In *Findings of the Association for Computational Linguistics: EMNLP 2020*, pages 204–211, Online. Association for Computational Linguistics.

Manuel Mager, Ximena Gutierrez-Vasques, Gerardo Sierra, and Ivan Meza-Ruiz. 2018. Challenges of language technologies for the indigenous languages of the Americas. In *Proceedings of the 27th International Conference on Computational Linguistics*, pages 55–69, Santa Fe, New Mexico, USA. Association for Computational Linguistics.

Sarah Moeller, Ling Liu, Changbing Yang, Katharina Kann, and Mans Hulden. 2020. IGT2P: From interlinear glossed texts to paradigms. In *Proceedings of the*

2020 Conference on Empirical Methods in Natural Language Processing (EMNLP), pages 5251–5262, Online. Association for Computational Linguistics.

Alexis Palmer, Taesun Moon, Jason Baldridge, Katrin Erk, Eric Campbell, and Telma Can. 2010. Computational strategies for reducing annotation effort in language documentation. *Linguistic Issues in Language Technology*, 3(4):1–42.

Keren Rice. 2006. Ethical issues in linguistic fieldwork. *Journal of Academic Ethics*, 4:123–155.

Chris Rogers. 2010. Review of fieldworks language explorer (flex) 3.0. *Language Documentation & Conservation*, 4:78–84.

Sylvia LR Schreiner, Lane Schwartz, Benjamin Hunt, and Emily Chen. 2020. Multidirectional leveraging for computational morphology and language documentation and revitalization. *Language documentation and conservation*, 14.

Miikka Silfverberg and Mans Hulden. 2018. An encoder-decoder approach to the paradigm cell filling problem. In *Proceedings of the 2018 Conference on Empirical Methods in Natural Language Processing*, pages 2883–2889, Brussels, Belgium. Association for Computational Linguistics.

Anders Søgaard. 2010. Simple semi-supervised training of part-of-speech taggers. In *Proceedings of the ACL 2010 Conference Short Papers*, pages 205–208, Uppsala, Sweden. Association for Computational Linguistics.

Karl Stratos and Michael Collins. 2015. Simple semi-supervised POS tagging. In *Proceedings of the 1st Workshop on Vector Space Modeling for Natural Language Processing*, pages 79–87, Denver, Colorado. Association for Computational Linguistics.

Nicholas Thieberger and Andrea L Berez. 2012. Linguistic data management. Oxford University Press.

George van Driem. 2016. Endangered language research and the moral depravity of ethics protocols. 10:243–252.

Adam Wiemerslage, Arya D. McCarthy, Alexander Erdmann, Garrett Nicolai, Manex Agirrezabal, Miikka Silfverberg, Mans Hulden, and Katharina Kann. 2021. Findings of the SIGMORPHON 2021 shared task on unsupervised morphological paradigm clustering. In *Proceedings of the 18th SIGMORPHON Workshop on Computational Research in Phonetics, Phonology, and Morphology*, pages 72–81, Online. Association for Computational Linguistics.

Olga Zamaraeva. 2016. Inferring morphotactics from interlinear glossed text: Combining clustering and precision grammars. In *Proceedings of the 14th SIGMORPHON Workshop on Computational Research in Phonetics, Phonology, and Morphology*, pages 141–150, Berlin, Germany. Association for Computational Linguistics.

Olga Zamaraeva, Kristen Howell, and Emily M. Bender. 2019. Handling cross-cutting properties in automatic inference of lexical classes: A case study of chintang. In *Proceedings of the 3rd Workshop on the Use of Computational Methods in the Study of Endangered Languages Volume 1 (Papers)*, pages 28–38, Honolulu. Association for Computational Linguistics.

Amir Zeldes. 2017. The GUM corpus: Creating multilayer resources in the classroom. *Language Resources and Evaluation*, 51(3):581–612.

Fine-tuning pre-trained models for Automatic Speech Recognition: experiments on a fieldwork corpus of Japhug (Trans-Himalayan family)

Séverine Guillaume[1] Guillaume Wisniewski[2] Cécile Macaire[1, 3]
Guillaume Jacques[4] Alexis Michaud[1] Benjamin Galliot[1]
Maximin Coavoux[3] Solange Rossato[3] Minh-Châu Nguyên[3] Maxime Fily[1, 5]

(1) LACITO, CNRS - Université Sorbonne Nouvelle - INALCO, France
(2) Université de Paris Cité, Laboratoire de Linguistique Formelle (LLF), CNRS, Paris, France
(3) LIG, CNRS - Université Grenoble Alpes - Grenoble INP - INRIA
(4) CRLAO, CNRS - École des Hautes Études en Sciences Sociales - INALCO
(5) Univ. Grenoble Alpes, CNRS, Grenoble INP, GIPSA-lab, 38000 Grenoble, France

severine.guillaume@cnrs.fr, guillaume.wisniewski@u-paris.fr, cecile.macaire@univ-grenoble-alpes.fr, rgyalrongskad@gmail.com, alexis.michaud@cnrs.fr, b.g01lyon@gmail.com, {maximin.coavoux, solange.rossato}@univ-grenoble-alpes.fr, minhchau.ntm@gmail.com, maxime.fily@gmail.com

Abstract

This is a report on results obtained in the development of speech recognition tools intended to support linguistic documentation efforts. The test case is an extensive fieldwork corpus of Japhug, an endangered language of the Trans-Himalayan (Sino-Tibetan) family. The goal is to reduce the transcription workload of field linguists. The method used is a deep learning approach based on the language-specific tuning of a generic pre-trained representation model, `XLS-R`, using a *Transformer* architecture. We note difficulties in implementation, in terms of learning stability. But this approach brings significant improvements nonetheless. The quality of phonemic transcription is improved over earlier experiments; and most significantly, the new approach allows for reaching the stage of automatic word recognition. Subjective evaluation of the tool by the author of the training data confirms the usefulness of this approach.

1 Introduction

The use of *Transformer*-type neural architectures to learn multilingual models of text and speech, coupled with methods for fine-tuning these generic representations, has opened up the possibility of developing tools for the many languages for which there is only a small amount of annotated data available. This approach has special appeal for linguistic documentation tasks: the development of semi-automatic or even automatic transcription and annotation methods based on a small amount of annotated data would reduce the annotation effort of field linguists and language workers, who could then focus their attention on linguistically and relationally meaningful tasks during fieldwork (Thieberger, 2017; Michaud et al., 2018; Partanen et al., 2020; Prud'hommeaux et al., 2021). In this multidisciplinary endeavour, it is clear that "linguists and Natural Language Processing (NLP) scientists may want to adjust their expectations and workflows so that both can achieve optimal results with endangered data" (Moeller, 2021).

The present work reports on our experiments using a pre-trained model of speech, `XLS-R` (Conneau et al., 2020), to develop a phonemic recognition system for a minority language of China: Japhug (Ethnologue language code: `jya`, Glottolog code: `japh1234`; see Jacques 2019, 2021). The transcription of recordings in a newly documented language is a key task for fieldworkers (linguists and language workers). It is also an interesting topic for the speech processing community, as it raises several challenges, epistemological as well as practical.

First of all, the amount of data available for such languages is very small: for instance, of the 197 languages in the Pangloss Collection (Michailovsky et al., 2014), which hosts audio recordings in various languages of the world (most of them endangered), only 44 corpora contain more than one hour of recordings. There is therefore a need for speech recognition methods that require as little training data as possible. In this respect, Japhug can be considered as an outlier, since there is a 32-hour transcribed corpus, freely available in the Pangloss

Proceedings of the Fifth Workshop on the Use of Computational Methods in the Study of Endangered Languages, pages 170 - 178
May 26-27, 2022 ©2022 Association for Computational Linguistics

Collection[1] as well as from Zenodo (Galliot et al., 2021)[2] and as a Huggingface dataset.[3] The size of this corpus is one of the reasons for choosing Japhug as the test case for the present investigations: we wanted to be able to evaluate the amount of data that is necessary to obtain an automatic transcription of *good* quality — an important criterion here being the linguist's evaluation of the usefulness of the automatically generated transcript, as will be discussed again below.

Research in the field of resource-constrained Automatic Speech Recognition (ASR) has brought out "the importance of considering language-specific and corpus-specific factors and experimenting with multiple approaches when developing ASR systems for languages with limited training resources" (Morris et al., 2021, 4354). To mention two such factors:

- Endangered/little-described languages have structural features of their own, which may be widely different from those of the languages routinely taken into account in the work of the speech processing community. (It has even been argued that highly elaborate linguistic structures and typological oddities are more likely to be found in minority languages, for sociolinguistic reasons: Haudricourt 2017 [original publication: 1961]; Trudgill 2011.) For example, Japhug has a degree of morphosyntactic complexity that is particularly impressive, especially in view of its areal context (Jacques, 2021, *passim*).

- Speakers of minority languages frequently use words (or multi-word expressions, or even entire sentences) from other languages — typically the majority language of the country, or of the area (Moore, 2018; Aikhenvald, 2020). The presence of various loanwords, as well as cases of code-switching in the recordings, are a challenge for the automatic transcription of linguistic fieldwork data.

Conversely, there is one aspect in which automatic transcription tends to be easier for fieldwork data than for widely studied languages: namely, their high degree of orthographic transparency. Most endangered languages are languages transmitted through oral tradition, without a widely used writing system, and the transcriptions are usually made by linguists and language workers either in the International Phonetic Alphabet or in an orthography that is very close to the pronunciation. Thanks to this last characteristic one may realistically hope to achieve good quality transcriptions, as the system does not have to learn a complex spelling — unlike in the case of orthographies which have less straightforward correspondences between graphemes and phonemes (e.g. Uralic languages in Cyrillic orthography have a high degree of grapho-phonematic complexity, raising some technical difficulties: Gerstenberger et al., 2016).

The sections below are organized as follows: we start out, in section 2, by briefly describing the model we have used. Then we move on to presenting, in section 3, the results of a first set of experiments on phonemic transcription, which show that `XLS-R` does indeed allow us to produce very good quality transcriptions from a small corpus of annotated data, and that these transcriptions meet a need from the linguists conducting language documentation and conservation work. However, a second set of experiments described in section 4 shows that this result is difficult to reproduce, which leads us to qualify our initial optimistic conclusion concerning the technological dimension of the work.[4]

2 Fine-tuning pre-trained models

Principle The approach implemented in this work is based on the fine-tuning of a multilingual signal representation model, a method introduced in the field of speech recognition by Conneau et al. (2020) to build speech recognition models from little data. This approach is today at the core of many NLP models and is considered by many to be the most promising way to develop NLP and speech systems beyond the thirty or so languages (representing only 0.5 % of the world's linguistic diversity) for which there are large amounts of annotated data (Pires et al., 2019; Muller et al., 2021).

The proposed approach is composed of two steps. In the first step, `XLS-R`,[5] a multilingual model

[1] `https://pangloss.cnrs.fr/corpus/Japhug`

[2] `https://doi.org/10.5281/zenodo.5521111`

[3] `https://huggingface.co/datasets/BenjaminGalliot/pangloss`

[4] The models and all the scripts used in our experiments are freely available `https://github.com/CNRS-LACITO/xlsr_for_pangloss`.

[5] Note that many other pre-trained models are available, such as `hubert-large-ls960-ft` and `wav2vec2-`

trained in an unsupervised way on a corpus of 56,000 hours of recordings in 53 languages, is used to automatically build a language-independent, 'generic' representation of the signal. In a second step, this representation is used as input to a phonemic recognition system, trained on audio data that are time-aligned with a manual transcription provided by the linguist. This second step allows to learn how to match the signal representations with labels: in this case, it is essentially the labels corresponding to the phonemes.

In our experiments, we used the `XLS-R` multilingual model[6] and the HuggingFace API (Wolf et al., 2020) to use and fine-tune it. We ran the fine-tuning for 60 epochs (i.e. 60 iterations over the training data) to be assured that the fine-tuning had converged, and we kept the last model.

Using the model for phoneme prediction In order to apply the method described in the previous paragraph to the task of phoneme recognition, we simply defined a set of labels corresponding to the set of characters composing the phonemes. More precisely, the set of labels used for fine-tuning is made of the 44 characters that appear in at least one Japhug phoneme.[7] This technical choice is based on the experiments reported by Wisniewski et al. (2020) showing that the prediction of the characters composing the phonemes (instead of the phonemes as units) allows to obtain good predictions, sidestepping the task of explicitly listing the phonemes of the language (for example to specify that /ʈʂʰ/ constitutes a single phoneme, noted by a trigraph: ʈ+ʂ+ʰ). For the sake of simplicity at an initial exploratory stage, we also removed from the manual transcriptions all the punctuation marks and the other miscellaneous symbols used by linguists in their transcriptions (symbols to note linguistic phenomena of emphasis or focus, for example).

To this set of grapho-phonemic labels is added the space, to delimit words, thereby coming a step closer to the development of a true speech recognition system for endangered languages. The addition of a special character marking the word boundaries is a novelty in our work;[8] it aims at allowing the system to recognize words directly. This avoids the need for post-processing or for a second system to segment the lattice of phonemes into words, such as the ones developed by Godard et al. (2018) and Okabe et al. (2021). To arrive at *bona fide* word recognition (and thus at full-fledged Automatic Speech Recognition), use of a language model is clearly the most efficient way to go, and this method has been successfully applied in the context of some minority/endangered languages (Partanen et al., 2020; Prud'hommeaux et al., 2021), but it should be remembered that there is huge diversity among the data sets available for endangered/low-resource languages, so that, surprising as it may seem, "no single ASR architecture outperforms all others" (Morris et al. 2021, 4354; see also Macaire et al. 2022 on two Creole languages). The use case addressed here is one in which the amount of text available is no greater than a few tens of thousands of words, i.e. an insufficient amount to train a language model according to standard workflows.

3 Evaluation on the Japhug language

In order to facilitate the reproduction of the experiments, the Japhug corpus is made available as a Huggingface dataset[9] which can be used off-the-shelf with the tools described here.

3.1 Experimental results

The quality of our system is evaluated using two classical metrics: the character error rate (CER), i.e. the edit distance between the reference and the prediction computed at the character level,[10] and the word error rate (WER), a similar metric computed at the word level. Note that what makes the use of the latter metric possible is that the systems we trained are capable of predicting word boundaries (which was not the case in previous work such as Adams et al. 2018).

Using a ten-hour corpus for fine-tuning `XLS-R`, the system obtains a CER of 7.4 % and a WER of 18.5 %. Figure 1 shows how the performances of a

`large-100k-voxpopuli`.

[6]This model is named `wav2vec2-large-xlsr-53` in Hugging Face API.

[7]This list is constructed simply by enumerating all the characters in the transcriptions and is not based on a phoneme inventory or a grapheme-to-phoneme mapping.

[8]Note that the use of a special character directly predicted by our model is only novel in the context of a low-resource/language documentation setting: it constitutes common practice in character-level ASR.

[9]`https://huggingface.co/datasets/BenjaminGalliot/pangloss`

[10]Our system is predicting a stream of characters and not of phonemes (as stated in §2, the label set is made of the characters used to write the phonemes) and the edit operations, at the heart of the CER computation, are defined directly on the characters. Computing the *phoneme error rate* in which each phonemes would be considered as an indivisible unit would weigh errors differently.

fine-tuned model evolve for training sets whose size is close to the corpora usually collected in fieldwork on endangered/minority languages. It turns out that the CER is already very low (12.5 %) for a training corpus containing two hours of annotated data.

These two results show that the proposed approach allows to obtain transcriptions of good quality, which reach the threshold at which the framework provided by the computer tool constitutes a useful starting point (preferable to the traditional method: a completely manual input). In particular, the performance is improved by 4 points compared to the results of Wisniewski et al. (2020), which were also based on a neural method of phonemic transcription, but which learned a signal representation only from the training data, without using a pre-trained model.

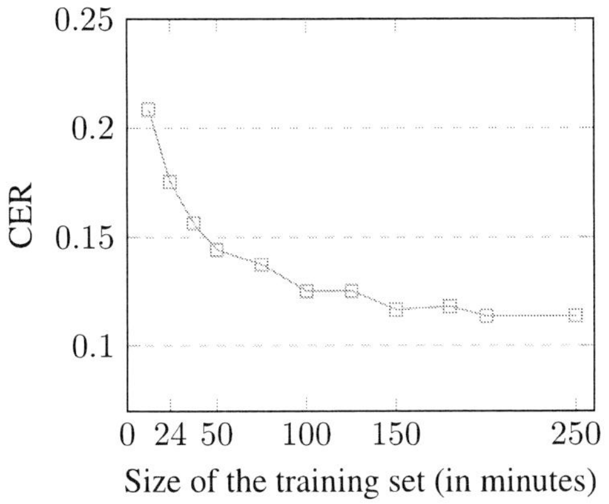

Figure 1: Evolution of performances as a function of the size of the training corpus.

The word-level error is much higher than the character-level error, but the difference is primarily due to the way in which the two evaluation metrics are defined. There are significantly fewer words than characters, so that an error at the character level (which naturally translates into an error at the word level containing it) will have a stronger impact on the WER than on the CER. A closer analysis of the results shows that our system makes few errors on word boundaries: nearly 90 % of spaces are correctly predicted.

3.2 Quality assessment of transcriptions by the linguist

To evaluate the usefulness of the system described in the previous section, a specialist of the Japhug language (Guillaume Jacques) corrected the automatic transcription of a recording that he had not yet transcribed. This pilot experiment is not systematized like that of Sperber et al. (2017) or other studies of post-editing processes in machine translation (Nitzke, 2021), and moreover concerns only 236 words, corresponding to a 2-minute recording of the Japhug language. The evaluation could therefore be dismissed as impressionistic and unreliable from the point of view of NLP tool evaluation. But it cannot be overemphasized that there is a "need for developers to directly engage with stakeholders when designing and deploying technologies for supporting language documentation" (Prud'hommeaux et al., 2021, 491). The point of view of end users is clearly significant and relevant to guide multidisciplinary team work of the type reported here.

The evaluation experiment, even though it is conducted in a way that is not standard in NLP evaluation, leads to a clear observation: the number of corrections to be made to obtain a quality transcription is much lower than the CER suggests. The linguist only had to correct 1.9 % of the characters. The figure becomes 4.2 % if punctuation is taken into account: punctuation marks are not predicted by the system – remember that they were removed from the training corpus at the preprocessing stage – and must therefore be added manually by the person taking up the automatic transcription for further processing. The corresponding WER is at 5.9 %. The difference between the estimated CER (computed on data that have been annotated beforehand) and the number of actual corrections is largely explained by the ambiguity inherent in the task of phonemic transcription: the linguist transcribing the data does not work at an exclusively phonetic-phonological level, but makes many decisions based on high-level information (in short: word identification based on context). Table 1 shows a sample of manual corrections made by the linguist to the output of our system.

The observation of a gap between the metrics and the evaluation by the user is reminiscent of similar findings obtained in the evaluation of machine translation (Wisniewski et al., 2013). Such observations are of great importance in the perspective of integrating the tools into workflows for linguistic documentation. It would seem that the actual degree of usefulness (the "real" quality) of the systems is higher than the evaluation metrics used so far would suggest. At least in the case of Japhug, the effort required to correct automatic transcrip-

①	tɕe kɯɕɯŋgɯ tɕe iɕqha @mingchao(u→)ɯraŋ nɯ tɕu pjɤŋu tɕendɤre iɕqha nɤki @yanguo kɤti rɟɤlkhɤβ ɣɯ nɯrɟɤlpu nɯ kɯ, iɕqha nɯ, iɕqha nɯ ɯftsa nɯnɯ rɟɤlpu lusɯndɤm pjɤsɯso. tɕe nɯ rɟɤlpu lusɯndɤm pjɤsɯso tɕe, tɕendɤre nɤkinɯ, sɤtɕha ra tosɤtʂoʁloʁnɯ ʑo ɕti tɕe. tɕendɤre iɕqha nɯ, @shandong nɯtɕu ɯrmi @zhangxiaobing kɯrmi ci tɯtsɣe ɯkɯβzu ci pjɤtu, tɤtɕɯ. tɕendɤre ɯrʑaβ nɯ ɯskhrɯ mɯɲɤβdi χsɯsla ma mɯtoβzu ri tɕendɤre ɯpɕi joɬoʁndʑi ɲɤphɣondʑi pjɤra matɕi sɤtɕha ra pjɤkɤtʂoʁloʁci qhe tɕe nɯra tɕetha kɯsɤɣʑi ra pɯme ma ɲɤsɯsondʑi qhe tɕe nɯ jophɣondʑi.
②	tɕe kɯɕɯŋgɯ tɕe iɕqha, @mingchao ɯraŋ nɯtɕu pjɤŋu, tɕendɤre iɕqha, nɤki, @yanguo kɤti rɟɤlkhɤβ ɣɯ, nɯrɟɤlpu nɯ kɯ, iɕqha nɯ(,→.) iɕqha nɯ, ɯftsa nɯnɯ rɟɤlpu lusɯndɤm pjɤsɯso. tɕe nɯ rɟɤlpu lusɯndɤm pjɤsɯso tɕe, tɕendɤre, nɤkinɯ, sɤtɕha ra tosɤtʂoʁloʁnɯ ʑo ɕti tɕe, tɕendɤre iɕqha nɯ, @shandong nɯtɕu, ɯrmi @zhangxiaobing kɯrmi ci, tɯtsɣe ɯkɯβzu ci pjɤtu, tɤtɕɯ. tɕendɤre ɯrʑaβ nɯ ɯskhrɯ, mɯɲɤβd(er,→i) χsɯsla, ma mɯtoβzu ri, tɕendɤre ɯpɕi joɬo(n→ʁ)ndʑi ɲɤphɣondʑi pjɤra matɕi, sɤtɕha ra pjɤkɤtʂoʁloʁci qhe tɕe nɯra tɕetha kɯsɤɣʑ(ɯ→i)ra pɯme ma ɲɤsɯson(ɯ→dʑi) qhe tɕe nɯ jophɣondʑi.

Table 1: An excerpt from the manual corrections made to automatic transcriptions. System ①, corresponding to the setup described in §3, does not predict punctuation, nor does it predict the symbol @ (which indicates Chinese loanwords), whereas system ② predicts these two elements.

tions is considered "very low" by our expert on Japhug. A linguist's assessment of the amount of effort depends of course on many factors, including the degree of command of the target language. This makes the comparison from one case to another problematic; this is one of the difficulties encountered in interdisciplinary work between computer scientists and linguists. This point will be briefly taken up in the following paragraph.

4 Taking a critical look at the process of training statistical models

The results presented in the previous section are, to say the least, highly encouraging. They show that it is possible to achieve very good quality automatic phonemic transcriptions, even for languages for which relatively little annotated data is available (about 2 hours). Not only is the quality of the transcriptions sufficient to serve as a basis for further linguistic documentation work, but approaches based on pre-learning of representations open up the possibility of recognition at the word level, a major advance for the intended use cases (documentation of endangered languages in fieldwork). In practice, a phoneme lattice is not the best basis for further work by a field linguist. For a phoneme transcription to be complete, each individual phoneme would have to be recognizable from the audio signal, which would be contrary to all expectations, given the well-documented variability in the phonetic realization of phonemes (Niebuhr and Kohler, 2011). This variability, which carries a non-negligible part of the information contained in the signal, is particularly extensive in spontaneous speech, the object of study privileged by field linguists (Bouquiaux and Thomas, 1971; Newman and Ratliff, 2001). Thus, the basic unit for the constitution of corpora of rare languages is clearly not the phoneme, but the morpheme (and the higher-level units: word, sentence...).

Our initial results led us to consider more complex transcription tasks in which the system must also predict punctuation, as well as Chinese loanwords (cases of code-switching with the national language) found in Japhug documents (where they are transcribed according to the romanization conventions of standard Mandarin). The goal is, as before, to reduce the annotation effort of field linguists. Taking punctuation and loanwords into account essentially involves changing the preprocessing performed on the transcriptions before training.

The difficulties which we encountered during the development of this new system led us to study in a systematic way the degree of *stability* of the learning process. Neural network training is a difficult task in that it involves a very large number of parameters and relies on the optimization of a non-convex objective function. In practice, the optimization methods at the heart of deep learning rely on a very large number of hyper-parameters,[11]

[11]Hyper-parameters are special parameters the optimal

the choice of which has a direct impact on the performance of the resulting system. Thus, for the task of fine-tuning the XLS-R model (used in the work reported here), it is possible to change the value of more than twenty parameters that include the initial value of the learning step, its scheduling, the optimization method, the size of the batches, as well as various parameters for dropout.

We have represented in Figure 2 the performances (evaluated by the CER) obtained on the validation set during the different trainings we have performed during the development of these systems. Note that the systems were fine-tuned on a three-hour corpus (10% of which, making up 18 minutes, were used as a validation set) in order to keep the training times to a reasonable duration. The experiments we conducted with a larger corpus did not lead to improvements in the results obtained. These learning curves were obtained by varying the various parameters for optimization (training step, values for dropout, choice of the training set), but also by trying various experimental conditions: in particular, by taking into account the punctuation or not.

Among the 91 training curves shown in Figure 2, the CERs obtained on the validation set vary between 8.8 % and 28.8 % ($M = 14.8$, $S = 2.2$). Most of the learned systems perform significantly worse than the system described in our first experiments: only 6 systems have a CER at validation that is below 12.0 %, and none of them reaches the performance of the system described in section 3. Although not all of these error rates are directly comparable, these results show not only that performance on the validation set is highly sensitive to the choice of hyper-parameters (as expected), but more importantly, that the optimal value of these parameters varies across corpora, train-test splits and configurations.

However, as the results in Table 2 show, if we apply the different models obtained to the corrected text of section 3.2, the quality of the transcriptions is such that it requires only a small number of corrections. This result is all the more remarkable since these systems were only learned on 3 hours of annotated data, a reasonable amount of data to expect in scenarios of language documentation. Above all, it appears that the performance of the models on the validation set does not seem to be a reliable indicator of their quality in practice. This makes their selection and more generally their development very difficult.

value of which can only be found by trial-and-error and training a system completely. Tuning hyper-parameters tends to be highly time-consuming and resource-intensive.

	①	②	③
CER validation		8.8 %	13.9 %
WER	5.9 %	19.5 %	21.6 %
CER	4.2 %	9.1 %	6.7 %
⊖ punctuation	1.9 %	6.8 %	4.5 %
⊖ Pinyin	0.7 %	2.9 %	4.0 %

Table 2: Detailed evaluation of the various systems for phonemic transcription: ① is the system described in section 3, ② and ③ are two of the systems from our second series of experiments (described in §4): ② is the systeme with lowest CER on the validation set, and ③ that with lowest CER on the test set. These last two systems predict punctuation and the @ symbol for loanwords.

In a more qualitative way, we have reported in Table 1 an extract of the transcription of this text by the system described in section 3 and by a system predicting the punctuation. It appears that, while the first system is able to achieve a perfect transcription except for Chinese words (romanized into *Pinyin*) and punctuation marks, the second system presents properties that may be quite interesting for innovative workflows for computational documentation of languages. First of all, it places the utterance boundaries (materialized by the dot) without errors. The division into sentences constitutes a fundamental dimension of the structure of linguistic documents, and an important dimension of the work curating transcriptions for electronic publication in language archives. Moreover, the model recognizes Chinese borrowings remarkably well, paving the way for their automatic identification. Such additional treatments down the line are key to a workflow that makes the most of a range of NLP tools. The ultimate aim is to arrive at Interlinear Glossed Texts (IGT), with annotation down to the level of the morpheme; in turn, IGT corpora have considerable usefulness in research, including possibilities for automatically inferring linguistic patterns from the glossed corpora (Zamaraeva et al., 2019).

5 Conclusion

In this work, we have described how the fine-tuning of a multilingual model could be used to learn an

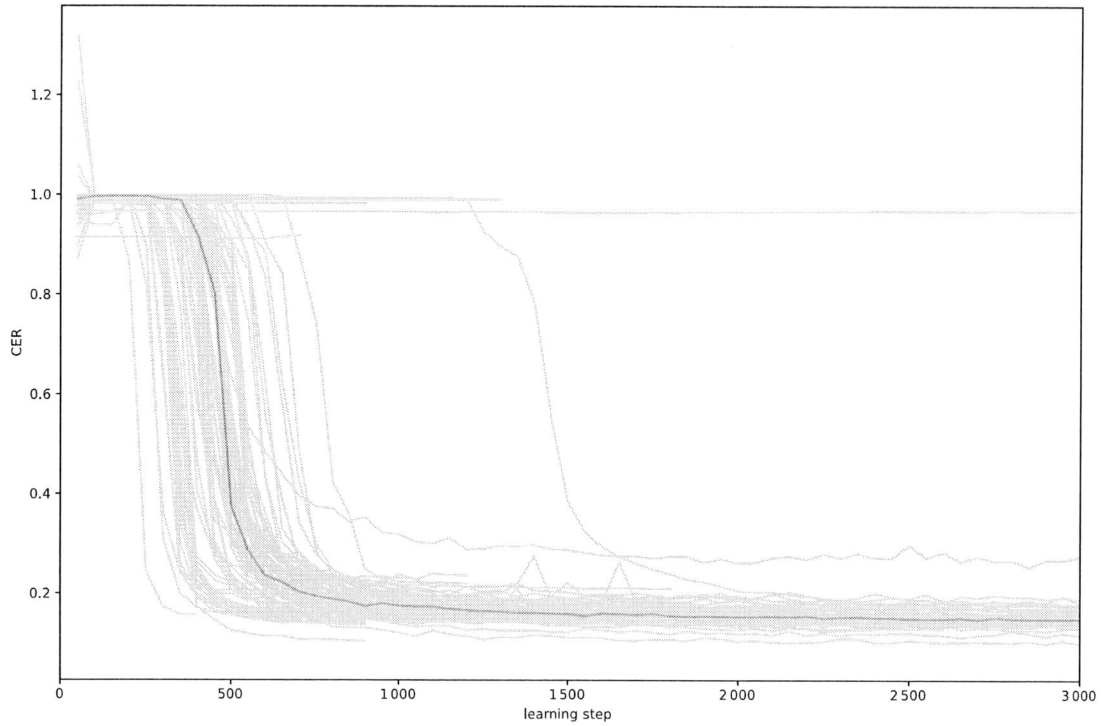

Figure 2: CER over the validation set in the course of various optimizations. The curve in red corresponds to the median value for CER at each stage.

automatic phonemic transcription system for an endangered language, and thus reduce the annotation effort of field linguists. Despite the large variability of the scores obtained on a validation set, we succeeded in developing systems whose predictions required only a small number of manual corrections by the linguist: a number that is much smaller than that estimated by the Character Error Rate (CER). This work shows the interest of this type of approach, and opens many perspectives. In particular, the approach seems to us to call for an extension of the experiments to other endangered languages (e.g. from other corpora hosted in archives of endangered languages, about which see Berez-Kroeker and Henke 2018), in order to evaluate more widely its usefulness for language documentation. We also wish, in our future work, to improve the quality of predictions at the word level, for example by integrating a language model.

Acknowledgments

We wish to express our deepest gratitude to the main Japhug language consultant, Tshendzin.

Financial support was given by *Agence Nationale de la Recherche* as part of grants ANR-10-LABX-0083 (*Laboratoire d'excellence* "Empirical Foundations of Linguistics", 2011-2024) and ANR-19-CE38-0015 ("Computational Language Documentation by 2025", 2019-2024). Financial support was also contributed by the Institute for Language Diversity and Heritage (ILARA-EPHE).

An important part of the linguistic resources used in the present work was collected in the course of the project "Himalayan Corpora: Parallel corpora in languages of the Greater Himalayan area" (ANR-12-CORP-0006).

References

Oliver Adams, Trevor Cohn, Graham Neubig, Hilaria Cruz, Steven Bird, and Alexis Michaud. 2018. Evaluating phonemic transcription of low-resource tonal languages for language documentation. In *LREC 2018 (Language Resources and Evaluation Conference)*, pages 3356–3365.

Alexandra Aikhenvald. 2020. Language contact and endangered languages. *The Oxford handbook of language contact*, pages 241–260.

Andrea L. Berez-Kroeker and Ryan E. Henke. 2018. Language archiving. In Kenneth L. Rehg and Lyle Campbell, editors, *The Oxford handbook of endangered languages*, pages 433–457. Oxford University Press, Oxford.

Luc Bouquiaux and Jacqueline Thomas. 1971. *Enquête et description des langues à tradition orale. Volume I : l'enquête de terrain et l'analyse grammaticale*, 1976 (2e) edition. Société d'études linguistiques et anthropologiques de France, Paris. 3 volumes.

Alexis Conneau, Alexei Baevski, Ronan Collobert, Abdelrahman Mohamed, and Michael Auli. 2020. Unsupervised cross-lingual representation learning for speech recognition. *CoRR*, abs/2006.13979.

Benjamin Galliot, Guillaume Wisniewski, Séverine Guillaume, Laurent Besacier, Guillaume Jacques, Alexis Michaud, Solange Rossato, Minh-Châu Nguyên, and Maxime Fily. 2021. Deux corpus audio transcrits de langues rares (japhug et na) normalisés en vue d'expériences en traitement du signal. In *Journées scientifiques du Groupement de recherche "Linguistique informatique, formelle et de terrain" (GDR LIFT)*, Grenoble.

Ciprian Gerstenberger, Niko Partanen, Michael Rießler, and Joshua Wilbur. 2016. Utilizing language technology in the documentation of endangered Uralic languages. *Northern European Journal of Language Technology*, 4:29–47.

Pierre Godard, Marcely Zanon Boito, Lucas Ondel, Alexandre Berard, François Yvon, Aline Villavicencio, and Laurent Besacier. 2018. Unsupervised word segmentation from speech with attention. In *Interspeech 2018*, Hyderabad, India.

André-Georges Haudricourt. 2017 [original publication: 1961]. Number of phonemes and number of speakers [translation of: *Richesse en phonèmes et richesse en locuteurs*]. *L'Homme*, 1(1):5–10.

Guillaume Jacques. 2019. Japhug. *Journal of the International Phonetic Association*, 49(3):427–450.

Guillaume Jacques. 2021. *A grammar of Japhug*. Number 1 in Comprehensive Grammar Library. Language Science Press, Berlin.

Cécile Macaire, Didier Schwab, Benjamin Lecouteux, and Emmanuel Schang. 2022. Automatic Speech Recognition and query by example for Creole languages documentation. In *Findings of the Association for Computational Linguistics: ACL 2022*, Dublin, Ireland.

Boyd Michailovsky, Martine Mazaudon, Alexis Michaud, Séverine Guillaume, Alexandre François, and Evangelia Adamou. 2014. Documenting and researching endangered languages: the Pangloss Collection. *Language Documentation and Conservation*, 8:119–135.

Alexis Michaud, Oliver Adams, Trevor Cohn, Graham Neubig, and Séverine Guillaume. 2018. Integrating automatic transcription into the language documentation workflow: experiments with Na data and the Persephone toolkit. *Language Documentation and Conservation*, 12:393–429.

Sarah Moeller. 2021. *Integrating machine learning into language documentation and description*. Ph.D. thesis, University of Colorado at Boulder.

Patrick Moore. 2018. Re-valuing code-switching: lessons from Kaska narrative performances. In *Activating the heart: Storytelling, knowledge sharing, and relationship*, Waterloo, Canada. Wilfrid Laurier University Press.

Ethan Morris, Robbie Jimerson, and Emily Prud'hommeaux. 2021. One size does not fit all in resource-constrained ASR. In *Interspeech 2021*, pages 4354–4358. ISCA.

Benjamin Muller, Antonios Anastasopoulos, Benoît Sagot, and Djamé Seddah. 2021. When being unseen from mBERT is just the beginning: Handling new languages with multilingual language models. In *Proceedings of the 2021 Conference of the North American Chapter of the Association for Computational Linguistics: Human Language Technologies*, pages 448–462, Online. Association for Computational Linguistics.

Paul Newman and Martha Ratliff. 2001. *Linguistic fieldwork*. Cambridge University Press, Cambridge.

Oliver Niebuhr and Klaus J. Kohler. 2011. Perception of phonetic detail in the identification of highly reduced words. *Journal of Phonetics*, 39(3):319–329.

Silvia Nitzke, Jeanand Hansen-Schirra. 2021. *A short guide to post-editing*. Number 16 in Translation and Multilingual Natural Language Processing. Language Science Press, Berlin.

Shu Okabe, François Yvon, and Laurent Besacier. 2021. Segmentation en mots faiblement supervisée pour la documentation automatique des langues. In *Journées scientifiques du Groupement de recherche "Linguistique informatique, formelle et de terrain" (GDR LIFT)*, Grenoble.

Niko Partanen, Mika Hämäläinen, and Tiina Klooster. 2020. Speech recognition for endangered and extinct Samoyedic languages. In *Proceedings of the 34th Pacific Asia Conference on Language, Information and Computation*.

Telmo Pires, Eva Schlinger, and Dan Garrette. 2019. How multilingual is multilingual BERT? In *Proceedings of the 57th Annual Meeting of the Association for Computational Linguistics*, pages 4996–5001, Florence, Italy. Association for Computational Linguistics.

Emily Prud'hommeaux, Robbie Jimerson, Richard Hatcher, and Karin Michelson. 2021. Automatic speech recognition for supporting endangered language documentation. *Language Documentation & Conservation*, 15:491–513.

Matthias Sperber, Graham Neubig, Jan Niehues, Satoshi Nakamura, and Alex Waibel. 2017. Transcribing against time. *Speech Communication*, 93:20–30.

Nick Thieberger. 2017. LD&C possibilities for the next decade. *Language Documentation and Conservation*, 11:1–4.

Peter Trudgill. 2011. *Sociolinguistic typology: social determinants of linguistic complexity*. Oxford University Press, Oxford.

Guillaume Wisniewski, Séverine Guillaume, and Alexis Michaud. 2020. Phonemic transcription of low-resource languages: To what extent can preprocessing be automated? In *Proceedings of the 1st Joint SLTU (Spoken Language Technologies for Under-resourced languages) and CCURL (Collaboration and Computing for Under-Resourced Languages) Workshop*, pages 306–315, Marseille, France. European Language Resources Association (ELRA).

Guillaume Wisniewski, Anil Kumar Singh, Natalia Segal, and François Yvon. 2013. Design and analysis of a large corpus of post-edited translations: Quality estimation, failure analysis and the variability of post-edition. In *Proceedings of Machine Translation Summit XIV: Papers*, Nice, France.

Thomas Wolf, Lysandre Debut, Victor Sanh, Julien Chaumond, Clement Delangue, Anthony Moi, Pierric Cistac, Tim Rault, Remi Louf, Morgan Funtowicz, Joe Davison, Sam Shleifer, Patrick von Platen, Clara Ma, Yacine Jernite, Julien Plu, Canwen Xu, Teven Le Scao, Sylvain Gugger, Mariama Drame, Quentin Lhoest, and Alexander Rush. 2020. Transformers: State-of-the-art natural language processing. In *Proceedings of the 2020 Conference on Empirical Methods in Natural Language Processing: System Demonstrations*, pages 38–45, Online. Association for Computational Linguistics.

Olga Zamaraeva, Kristen Howell, and Emily M. Bender. 2019. Handling cross-cutting properties in automatic inference of lexical classes: A case study of Chintang. In *Proceedings of the 3rd Workshop on the Use of Computational Methods in the Study of Endangered Languages Volume 1 (Papers)*, pages 28–38, Honolulu. Association for Computational Linguistics.

Morphologically annotated corpora of Pomak

Ritván Jusúf Karahóğa Panagiotis Krimpas Vivian Stamou Vasileios Arampatzakis Dimitrios Karamatskos Vasileios Sevetlidis Nikolaos Constantinides Nikolaos Kokkas George Pavlidis Stella Markantonatou

Institute for Language and Speech Processing, Athena R.C.
{ritvan.karachotza, p.krimpas, vistamou, vasilis.arampatzakis, dkaramatskos, vasiseve, n.konstantinidis, nikolkok, marks, gpavlid}@athenarc.gr

Abstract

The project Philotis is developing a platform to enable researchers of living languages to easily create and make available state-of-the-art spoken and textual annotated resources. As a case study we use Greek and Pomak, the latter being an endangered oral Slavic language of the Balkans (including Thrace/Greece). The linguistic documentation of Pomak is an ongoing work by an interdisciplinary team in close cooperation with the Pomak community of Greece. We describe our experience in the development of a Latin-based orthography and morphologically annotated text corpora of Pomak with state-of-the-art NLP technology. These resources will be made openly available on the Philotis site and the gold annotated corpora of Pomak will be made available on the Universal Dependencies treebank repository.

1 Introduction

In Philotis[1] we aim at supporting the researchers of living languages to develop annotated (linked) spoken and textual resources without external technical aid: ideally, speakers of the documented language and eager linguists alone would suffice. To this end, we take advantage of open-source NLP tools, semantic web technologies, annotation tools and universally adopted annotation and codification schemes. Pomak is our case study of endangered oral language. We make available existing and new textual and oral material of Pomak and develop annotated spoken and textual corpora. Here, we provide some information about Pomaks and their language and, briefly present our experience from the development of a Latin-based orthography and a morphologically annotated corpus of Pomak.

Several researchers have highlighted the interdisciplinary nature of language documentation work (to mention but a few: Woodbury 2003; McDonnell 2018; Rice 2018; Bird 2020) because different linguistic specialisations are required and linguistic activity can hardly be considered independent of its social and situational settings. Furthermore, the technical problems of resource development should not be underestimated. Back in 2003, Woodbury (2003) explained that ideally, language technology should support multimodal data and multilayered annotations that would be linked to each other so that they could be studied simultaneously. We would add that technical solutions have to be flexible, among other things because different languages may pose different documentation problems, in particular if the linguistic communities want to exploit legacy material.

State-of-the-art tools and methods greatly facilitate traditionally hard tasks such as morphological annotation of corpora (Anastasopoulos et al., 2018) and speech to text transcription (Lane et al., 2021). We have taken advantage of this technology and received excellent results but the overall experience was not devoid of problems. We proceed by introducing Pomak as an endangered oral language; next we discuss our experience with the development and morphological annotation of the corpora of Pomak.

2 About Pomak

Pomak (endonym: Pomácky, Pomácko, Pomácku or other dialectal variants) is a non-standardised East South Slavic language variety. Pomak is spoken in Bulgaria and Greece (mainly the Rhodope Mountain area), in the European part of Turkey and, in the places of Pomak diaspora (Constantinides 2007: 35). Pomak is included in the map of the European Languages Equality Network[2]. As is the case with all East South Slavic varieties, several of the linguistic features that appear in the Pomak dialectic continuum are due to mutual interaction and convergence with non - Slavic languages

[1] https://philotis.athenarc.gr/

[2] https://elen.ngo/languages-map/

Proceedings of the Fifth Workshop on the Use of Computational Methods in the Study of Endangered Languages, pages 179 - 186
May 26-27, 2022

of the Balkan Sprachbund (Papadimitriou 2013: 23), mostly Latin (Solta 1980) and Greek (Krimpas 2020). In comparison to all East South Slavic languages, Pomak seems to exhibit a more profound phonological, morphological, morphosyntactic and lexical influence by Medieval and Modern Greek (Krimpas 2020: 196) and, due to the predominantly Muslim religion of its speakers, a more profound lexical and phonotactical influence by Ottoman and Modern Turkish.

There is no widely accepted orthography of Pomak. The language is not taught in any of the countries where Pomaks reside.

Table 1 describes Pomak with the six factors of language vitality and endangerment proposed in Brenzinger et al. (2003). Note that "A language that is ranked highly according to one criterion may deserve immediate and urgent attention due to other factors" (Brenzinger et al. 2003: 9).

Factors of language vitality and endangerment	Scores for Pomak
1. Intergenerational Language Transmission	4
2. Absolute Number of Speakers	35000
3. Proportion of Speakers within the Total Population	3,2 %
4. Trends in Existing Language Domains	3
5. Response to New Domains and Media	1
6. Materials for Language Education and Literacy	2

Table 1: Factors of language vitality and endangerment for the Pomak language as of 2021.

1. Factor 1. "(4)" is defined as: "Most but not all children or families of a particular community speak their language as their first language, but it may be restricted to specific social domains (such as at home where children interact with their parents and grandparents)." (Brenzinger et al. 2003: 9).

2. The value of factor 2, and consequently of factor 3, is an estimation (Adamou and Fanciullo, 2018).

3. Factor 4. "(3)" is defined as: "The language is used in home domains and for many functions, but the dominant language begins to penetrate even home domains." (Brenzinger et al. 2003: 10).

4. Factor 5. "(1)" is defined as: "The language is used only in a few new domains." (Brenzinger et al. 2003: 11).

5. Factor 6. "(2)" is defined as: "Written materials exist, but they may only be useful for some members of the community; and for others, they may have a symbolic significance. Literacy education in the language is not a part of the school curriculum." (Brenzinger et al. 2003: 12).

3 Compiling textual corpora of Pomak

An oral/endangered language may have some textual and audio legacy (Gerstenberger et al., 2017). There are sporadic transcriptions and recordings of Pomak folk songs and tales; in addition, there are very few modern texts (journalistic texts and translations from Greek and English into Pomak). The texts are in a variety of alphabets ranging from Cyrillic to Greek to an English-based Latin alphabet. We collected these dispersed resources via a network of native speakers and Greek scholars who are close to the Pomak community. Following the requirements of the Pomak community, selected parts of this material was included in the developed corpora and the original material will be made available exactly as it was received. Our research center and the copyright owners (authors, publishing houses) have agreed, according to the Greek law, to ensure free distribution of the material for research purposes. Eventually, a corpus of about 130000 words was compiled. Table 2 shows the types of text included and the size of the respective corpora in words. Where possible, the geographical origins of the texts are given as a reliable indication of the dialect represented in the text.

Mature open-source NLP technology that would take full advantage of archived textual material is not available yet (Hutchinson 2020). Undoubtedly, a detailed TEI-conformant encoding of this material is the optimum approach but, at the moment, we have given priority to (spoken) material collection. We are in the process of defining Dublin Core and TEI-conformant metadata to declare the origins of the material in the corpus and to develop links of medium granularity between the resources.

Text types	Words	Geographical origins
Folk tales	43.817	Emonio, Glafki, Dimario, Echinos, Myki, Pachni, Oreo
Language description	19.524	mixed
Journalism	25.236	Myki
Translations into Pomak	24.208	Myki - Pachni
Folk songs	18.434	mixed
Proverbs	550	mixed
Other	5.325	Myki

Table 2: Pomak corpus: type, size and geographical origins of texts.

In addition to the above, an oral/endangered language may have resources that can be used to effectively improve the quality of its morphosyntactic annotation. In our work with Pomak we had the benefit of the electronic lexicon Rodopsky[3], which contains approximately 61.500 lemmas that correspond to about 3.5 x 10^6 unique forms (i.e., combinations of a lexical token and a PoS symbol) annotated for lemma, PoS and morphological features (Figure 1). We exploited Rodopsky to obtain mature morphological annotation of the corpora so we needed morphological annotation and evaluation facilities separate from the syntactic ones.

It goes without saying that, since Pomak has been sparsely documented by individuals who employed largely incompatible orthographies and in order to take advantage of Rodopsky, which also employs its own orthography, text homogenisation work was deemed necessary. The first step to this direction was the Krimpas et al. (2021) alphabet (K&K alphabet from now on, illustrated in Table 5). First Rodopsky was transcribed automatically to the K&K alphabet and corrected manually; the procedure helped us better define the orthography applied to the corpora. Finally, the morphological annotation of the corpus required additional orthographic refinements. The various orthographies used in the corpora were automatically mapped on the K&K orthography and the output was corrected manually.

[3]https://www.rodopsky.gr/

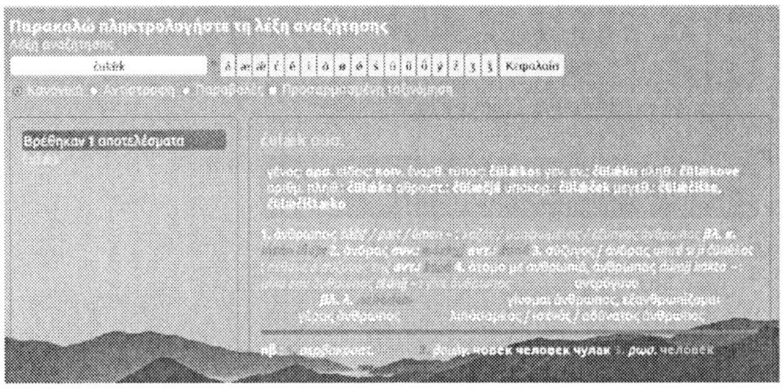

Figure 1: Rodopsky: Electronic lexicon of Pomak. Partial screenshot of the entry *čulæk* 'man' with morphological annotation encoded in Greek.

We proceed to a brief presentation of the adopted orthography of Pomak.

4 The orthography of Pomak

A key issue in developing the corpora of Pomak was the orthography. No alphabet of Pomak proposed so far, let alone orthography, has enjoyed any acceptability. A good alphabet would, at minimum, help maximise the possible impact of the developed resources on the sustainability of the documented language. In the case of Pomak, we have adopted the K&K alphabet (Table 5) that is the outcome of several years of manual work.

Cahill and Karan (2008) discuss good practices for developing orthographies for oral languages. Armostis et al. (2014) discuss the case of Cypriot Greek, which is a major dialect of Greek not adequately represented by the standard Greek alphabet. Their overall recommendation is that native speakers should participate in the definition of the orthography and have the final word in several decisions. Furthermore, they identify the, probably conflicting, good practices that are briefly introduced and discussed immediately below:

Phonetic transparency. The phonemic analysis of a language is indispensable for orthography design but detailed work with a multitude of languages suggests that the lexical level of phonology is also important. This is because while different phonological processes may result in given surface forms, native speakers may be aware of some phonological processes but not of others, so they may only be aware of the lexical form. After all, the script is meant to be used first and most by native speakers rather than by linguists. We exemplify the application of these ideas with the following Pomak words that form minimal pairs on the basis of sound to phoneme correspondence: *paláta* 'floor' vs. *palta* 'doused', *cíkom* 'squeak' vs. *číkom* 'cut; break', *samár* 'saddle' vs. *šamár* 'slap', *som* 'I am' vs. *søm* 'I sow', *grom* 'thunder' vs. *grøm* ' I heat', *pat* 'under' vs. *pæt* 'read (past passive participle)', *lóka* 'valley' vs. *lka* 'light (adj., acc.masc.sing.), *sénem* 'I shadow' vs. *šénem* 'I amuse myself', *vris* 'fountain; tap' vs. *vriš* 'you boil; you are full of'.

Systematic orthographies with reliable sound-symbol representation and consistent spelling enjoy enhanced acceptability, learnability, and usability by native speakers. Spelling should not be affected by pronunciation changes due to context. For instance, b [b], d [d], g [g] are devoiced in word-final position or before a voiceless consonant. We chose not to orthographically show this devoicing for the sake of consistency across declension (in the case of nominal forms) and conjugation (in the case of verbal forms). This is why we spell *hlæb* 'bread (Nom|Sg)' even though this form is pronounced [hlp] given the final position of the originally voiced consonant; in this way spelling is consistent with all other forms, e.g. *hlbu* 'of/to (the) bread', *chlba* 'bread (Acc|Sg), *hlbove* 'breads (Nom|Pl)' etc.

Easily discriminable symbols: Similar symbols or crowd adjoining letters, mirror–image symbols, overuse of a letter as part of various digraphs (e.g., bh, dh, ...), superimposing more than one diacritic are not recommended. For example, graphs denoting palato-alveolar sibilants are consistently spelled by adding a háček above their non-palato-alveolar counterparts (as in most other Latin-written Slavic languages), while graphs denoting palatalised sonorants are consistently indicated by means of a cedilla (or comma depending on the keyboard) below their non-palatalised counterparts as in Latvian; this system was preferred to Croatian *lj* and *nj* or Slovak *l'* and *ň* since the former requires two graphs and the latter is not consistent. Examples: *cístem* 'I clean' vs. *čeréša* 'cherry', *slónce* 'sun' vs. *šténe* 'puppy, cub', *zólezo* 'iron' vs. *žalvá* 'turtle; tortoise', *kópele* 'lad' vs. *kókaļe* 'bones (Pl)', *pésne* 'song' vs. *kámeņe* 'stones (Pl)'.

Portability of the alphabet. UNICODE is strongly recommended. The K&K alphabet of Pomak is encoded in Unicode.

Decisions might be needed as to where *word delimiters* should be put, often in the cases of compounds, clitics, pronouns, and prepositions. Distributional and phonological criteria are applied. For instance, various interrogative, indefinite and negative pronouns, conjunctions and adverbs, the first element of which is originally a preposition or a particle are normally used as a single word in most Slavic languages. However, given that there are quite a few cases where components are written as separate words in given contexts e.g., *at* 'from; out of', *kak* 'how; as; like', *kadé* 'where'), we chose to write them as two words irrespective of context. So, instead of writing *atkák* 'since', *níkutrí* 'nobody' and *nókade* 'somewhere' we write *at kak* 'since', *ní kutrí* 'nobody' and *nó kadé* respectively.

Dialectical issues. Most languages consist of dialect continua often exposing systematic phonological and morphosyntactic differences across dialects. In the uni-lectal approach one dialect serves as the basis for the written form and the others make a mental adjustment while reading and writing. In the multi-lectal approach the dialects are accommodated via consideration of the various varieties (Cahill and Karan, 2008). Pomak has several dialects. The K&K alphabet stands somewhere between the two approaches. For example, the vowel in the first syllable of *zmom* '(that) I take' is pronounced as [ø] in Myki, as [jo] in Echinos, and as [e] in Dimario. However, we chose to spell it as *ø* irrespective of dialect, given that speakers from Echinos or Dimario automatically pronounce [ø] as [jo] or [e], respectively, while speakers from Myki, if asked to read out the spellings *jo* and *e* respectively, would not automatically pronounce them as [ø], given that they do not have the [jo] and [e] sounds; moreover, there are words that are spelled and pronounced with [jo] or [e] in all dialects, e.g. *med* 'honey', *jok* 'non-'. Of course, since Pomak dialects are numerous and geographically dispersed, major vowel differences cannot sometimes be spelled by means of a 'neutral', i.e. hyperdialectal orthography.

5 The gold morphologically annotated corpus

We have already said that in our work with Pomak we had the benefit of the electronic lexicon Rodopsky (Fig. 1), which contains approximately 3.5 x 10^6 unique forms annotated, among other things, for lemma, PoS and morphological features. In order to take advantage of this rich source of linguistic knowledge of Pomak, some adaptation work was required: apart from transcribing it to the K&K orthography, the morphological annotation had to be mapped on the Universal Dependencies framework (UD)[4] and the CONLLU format had to be adopted. UD was chosen as a morphosyntactic annotation framework because of its large inventory of annotation features and because it is recognised by several open-source, state-of-the-art NLP tools that we planned to use for the morphosyntactic annotation of the corpus.

The mapping on UD revealed problems of which the most important were:

1. The analysis in Rodopsky did not include the UD PoS DET(erminer) and X(other). In addition, re-assignment of PoS to several lemmas was required, e.g., which participles would be considered adjectival or verbal forms.

2. Additional morphological features were necessary to describe (i) Degree modification of nouns, adjectives and adverbs (Degree modification should not be confused with Comparison), (ii) Determiners and adverbs that are formed with one of the particles *næ / nó, ní, sæ*; these are assigned the new feature "particle type" with values "indicative", "negative" and "total".

3. The tense and aspect system of Pomak required extra attention in order to be described with some accuracy.

The mapping of the morphological annotation of Pomak in Rodopsky on the UD framework was carried out by native speakers and linguists and the results will be uploaded on the UD language specifications area. Furthermore, it revealed interesting parallel phenomena of Greek and Pomak, in particular in the verb and the Degree modification systems that deserve a closer study.

Once Rodopsky was transcribed into a UD and CONLLU compatible form and was manually corrected, it was mapped on the corpora (both Rodopsky and the corpora had been transcribed into the K&K orthography). This initiated an about 30-days long cycle of manual corrections, this time of 6350 sentences and 86700 words selected from the Pomak corpus to form the gold tagged corpus that would be used for training and evaluating the NLP tools. This part of the annotation was performed by a native speaker and a linguist fluent in Pomak but not in UD, so the manual annotation time reported includes their training in the framework (Interannotation agreement kappa scores on 476 sentences: PoS tags 0.90, features 0.87, lemmas 0.93). The corpus will be uploaded to the UD language repository.

[4] `https://universaldependencies.org/`

Alternatively, we could have proceeded with the morphological annotation of gradually bigger corpora (Anastasopoulos et al. 2018). However, the selected procedure had clear merits:

1. We proceeded faster since the annotators worked on texts that were assigned morphological annotation of good quality.

2. Dedicated resources mitigate the effect of imposing knowledge from other languages onto the documented one through shared training language models.

3. It made room for the active participation of the community in the documentation process of their native language.

On the downside of the procedure are:

1. The overall procedure of transcribing Rodopsky into CONLLU cannot be generalised and made useful to other languages.

2. We faced extra problems with the NLP tools because some of them do not offer the option of separate morphological and syntactic annotations (see below).

6 Morphological annotation of the corpus of Pomak

The gold morphologically annotated corpus was used to train and evaluate NLP tools that would, in turn, be used to assign morphological annotations to the entire Pomak corpus and to future material from the spoken corpora. We conducted a series of experiments with four tools in an effort to identify the one that would yield the best morphological annotation results for Pomak.

The situation with state-of-the-art open-source NLP tools reminded of the description by (Arkhipov and Thieberger 2018:141): "... although basic principles are quite straightforward to master, the details of use of particular tools and interaction between tools in different setups are highly specific and can often be a source of frustration. Thus, not only an effort is required from the LD practitioners to invest in learning, but considerable effort is also required from the developers to invest in harmonisation of tools and making workflows more straightforward and robust."

Our experience confirms that even people with a training in programming must spend considerable time on state-of-the-art NLP tools. We ran four open-source tools, all implemented in Python. All tools provided a command line interface, but:

A. Instructions often were problematic: (a) Outdated compilation instructions (b) Instructions for training a model of a new language from scratch: (i) some tools provided insufficient documentation of the addition of languages new to the UD framework, and (ii) the alignment of the processes included in the pipeline was a hard task with some tools with incomplete instructions (c) Outdated README instructions required missing files; we had to correct the code.

B. Both the separation of morphological from syntactic annotation and the independent evaluation of the two annotation levels were hard.

We used Rodopsky for the morphological annotation of the Pomak corpus and we wanted to evaluate morphological annotation only, however some tools did not allow for this. Also, all tools assigned both morphological and syntactic annotation which may not be always desirable because when a new language is documented, the various levels of analysis (morphology, syntax, semantics etc) have not reached the same stage of maturity. Morphology is the basic annotation level and it is reasonable to address it first. We think that the unified annotation should be an option and not the rule. We had to rewrite the code of some NLP tools and comment out the parts handling dependency relations in order to obtain evaluation results for the morphological annotation.

This said, we would like to note that, probably, the assignment of false dependency relations might eventually be of no or little harm. We plan to compare the unified and the two-stage annotation strategy with future experiments on the corpora of Pomak.

There is a keen interest in incorporating contextual word embeddings as a functionality (Nguyen et al., 2021) but at the moment, pretrained transformer models are available with few tools only. Amongst the ones we tested, spaCy v3.2.2 allows for transformer based autoregressive models, while Udify supports only Bert like models.

One might note that pretrained multi-language models can be used by just one openly available NLP library. However, languages with no annotated corpora, such as Pomak, must have access to pretrained multi-language models in order to be assigned a reasonable (first) morphosyntactic annotation (Anastasopoulos et al., 2018).

We investigated the performance of the tools spaCy v3.2.2[5] (Honnibal et al., 2020), Stanza[6] (Qi et al., 2020), UDify[7] (Kondratyuk and Straka, 2019) and UDPipe[8] (Straka et al., 2016) on the gold morphologically annotated corpus of Pomak that was further split into training, development and test set (80:10:10). (Table 3).

Corpus	Train	Dev	Test
Sentences	5000	671	679
Tokens	67345	9736	9701

Table 3: Statistics on the training, development and test sets.

We experimented with the tasks of lemmatisation, PoS tagging and morphological annotation. The performance of each tool on the Pomak corpus is illustrated in Table 4.

Parser	Model	LEMM	UPOS	FEATS
SpaCy	XLM-Roberta-large	93.85	98.38	**95.54**
Stanza	Stanza	**97.82**	**98.73**	95.23
UDify	UDify-base	90.27	97.59	91.03
UDPipe	UDPipe v1.2	92.04	95.94	90.39

Table 4: Accuracy scores for the tasks of lemmatisation (LEMM), PoS tagging (UPOS) and morphological feature (FEATS) assignment. The highest scores in each column are in bold.

Table 4 shows that Stanza achieves the best accuracy scores in PoS tagging and lemmatisation and spaCy in feature assignment. We note that in the case of spaCy we ran (the large pretrained multilingual model) RoBERTa (XLM-RoBERTa). All tools returned reasonable PoS tagging results.

The entire annotated corpus of Pomak will be made available on Philotis. We are currently in the process of assigning syntactic annotation to the Pomak corpus according to the UD paradigm.

[5] `https://spacy.io/`

[6] `https://stanfordnlp.github.io/stanza/`

[7] `https://github.com/Hyperparticle/udify`

[8] `https://ufal.mff.cuni.cz/udpipe/1/models`

7 Conclusion

We have described the procedure of developing state-of-the-art textual resources for Pomak, an endangered, oral European language of the Slavic family. A group of linguists, computational linguists and engineers took full advantage of the Pomak legacy and cooperated closely with the native speaker community. In this way and in a short period of time (about 8 months), we produced reasonably sized morphologically annotated corpora of good quality and identified the open source NLP tools for the morphological annotation of Pomak.

We have also reported on our experience with using open NLP tools. We have observed that skilled programmers may still be needed in order to use these tools. Furthermore, powerful tools have not been fully exploited yet. In the overall, however, the huge progress in openly available state-of-the-art NLP technology has boosted the development of resources for endangered oral languages.

References

Evangelia Adamou and Davide Fanciullo. 2018. Why Pomak will not be the next Slavic literary language. In D. Stern, M. Nomachi, and B. Belić, editors, *Linguistic regionalism in Eastern Europe and beyond: minority, regional and literary microlanguages*, pages 40–65. Peter Lang.

Antonios Anastasopoulos, Marika Lekakou, Josep Quer, Eleni Zimianiti, Justin DeBenedetto, and David Chiang. 2018. Part-of-speech tagging on an endangered language: a parallel Griko-Italian resource. In *Proceedings of the 27th International Conference on Computational Linguistics*, pages 2529–2539, Santa Fe, New Mexico, USA. Association for Computational Linguistics.

Alexandre Arkhipov and Nick Thieberger. 2018. Reflections on software and technology for language documentation. In Andrea L. Berez-Kroeker Bradley McDonnell and Gary Holton, editors, *Reflections on Language Documentation. 20 Years after Himmelmann 1998 Language Documentation & Conservation Special Publication*, volume 15, pages 140–149.

Spyros Armostis, Christodoulou Kyriaci, Katsoyannou Marianna, and Charalambos Themistocleous. 2014. *Addressing writing system issues in dialectal lexicography: the case of Cypriot Greek*, page 23–38.

Steven Bird. 2020. Decolonising speech and language technology. In *Proceedings of the 28th International Conference on Computational Linguistics, COLING 2020, Barcelona, Spain (Online), December 8-13, 2020*, pages 3504–3519. International Committee on Computational Linguistics.

Matthias Brenzinger, Arienne M. Dwyer, Tjeerd de Graaf, Colette Grinevald, Michael Krauss, Osahito Miyaoka, Nicholas Ostler, Osamu Sakiyama, María E. Villalón, Akira Y. Yamamoto, and Ofelia Zepeda (UNESCO Ad Hoc Expert Group on Endangered Languages). 2003. Language vitality and endangerment. Paris, 10-12.

Michael Cahill and E. V. Karan. 2008. Factors in designing effective orthographies for unwritten languages. In *SIL Electronic Working papers 2008-001*.

Nikolaos Constantinides. 2007. *Units of the Pomak Civilization in Greek Thrace. Brief historical review,language and identities*. Democritus University of Thrace:MA Thesis.

Ciprian-Virgil Gerstenberger, Niko Partanen, and Michael Rießler. 2017. Instant annotations in elan corpora of spoken and written Komi, an endangered language of the Barents Sea region. In *Proceedings of the 2nd Workshop on the Use of Computational Methods in the Study of Endangered Languages, Honolulu, Hawai*, pages 57–66.

Matthew Honnibal, Ines Montani, Sofie Van Landeghem, and Adriane Boyd. 2020. spaCy: Industrial-strength Natural Language Processing in Python.

Tim Hutchinson. 2020. Natural language processing and machine learning as practical toolsets for archival processing. *Records Management Journal*, 30:155–174.

Dan Kondratyuk and Milan Straka. 2019. 75 languages, 1 model: Parsing Universal Dependencies universally. In *Proceedings of the 2019 Conference on Empirical Methods in Natural Language Processing and the 9th International Joint Conference on Natural Language Processing (EMNLP-IJCNLP)*, pages 2779–2795, Hong Kong, China. Association for Computational Linguistics.

Panagiotis Krimpas, Nikolaos Constantinides, Ritvan Karahoğa, Stella Markantonatou, and George Pavlidis. 2021. «Pomak: An idiosyncratic South East Slavic language?». In *VII Scientific Conference on "The Traditional Culture of Greece"»*, Lomonosov State University in Moscow.

Panagiotis G. Krimpas. 2020. Language and origin of Pomaks in the light of the Balkan Sprachbund. In A. Bartsiokas & N. Macha-Bizoumi M. Varvounis, editor, *The Pomaks of Thrace: Multidisciplinary and interdisciplinary approaches*, pages 167–204. Thessaloniki: K&M Stamoulis.

William Lane, Mat Bettinson, and Steven Bird. 2021. A computational model for interactive transcription. In *Proceedings of the Second Workshop on Data Science with Human in the Loop: Language Advances*, pages 105–111, Online. Association for Computational Linguistics.

Bradley McDonnell. 2018. Reflections on linguistic analysis in documentary linguistics. In Andrea L. Berez-Kroeker & Gary Holton Bradley McDonnell, editor, *Reflections on Language Documentation. 20 Years after Himmelmann 1998. Language Documentation Conservation Special Publication*, volume 20, pages 191–200.

Minh Van Nguyen, Viet Dac Lai, Amir Pouran Ben Veyseh, and Thien Huu Nguyen. 2021. Trankit: A light-weight transformer-based toolkit for multilingual natural language processing. In *EACL (System Demonstrations)*, pages 80–90.

Panayotis G. Papadimitriou. 2013. *Dialects of the Pomaks of the Greek Rhodope. Regional Analytical Slavic and Muslim speakers in Southeastern Europe.* Thessaloniki: Balkan Peninsula Research Institute. [In Greek].

Peng Qi, Yuhao Zhang, Yuhui Zhang, Jason Bolton, and Christopher D. Manning. 2020. Stanza: A python natural language processing toolkit for many human languages. In *Proceedings of the 58th Annual Meeting of the Association for Computational Linguistics: System Demonstrations*, pages 101–108, Online. Association for Computational Linguistics.

Sally Rice. 2018. Reflections on documentary corpora. In Andrea L. Berez-Kroeker & Gary Holton Bradley McDonnell, editor, *Reflections on Language Documentation. 20 Years after Himmelmann 1998. Language Documentation Conservation Special Publication*, 15, pages 157–172. University of Hawai'i Press.

Georg Renatus Solta. 1980. *Einführung in die Balkanlinguistik mit besonderer Berücksichtigung des Substrats und des Balkanlateinischen.* Darmstadt: Wissenschaftliche Buchgesellschaft.

Milan Straka, Jan Hajič, and Jana Straková. 2016. UDPipe: Trainable pipeline for processing CoNLL-U files performing tokenization, morphological analysis, POS tagging and parsing. In *Proceedings of the Tenth International Conference on Language Resources and Evaluation (LREC'16)*, pages 4290–4297, Portorož, Slovenia. European Language Resources Association (ELRA).

Anthony C Woodbury. 2003. Defining documentary linguistics. In Peter K. Austin, editor, *Language Documentation and Description*, volume 1, pages 35–51. London: SOAS.

A Appendices

Pronunciation	Character	Example word
[a], [ɐ]	A, a	**a**stávem 'leave'
[ɛɐ], [æ]	Æ, æ	l**æ**k 'drug'
[b]	B, b	**b**ába 'grand-mother'
[ts̑]	C, c	**c**ístem 'clean'
[ʧ]	Č,č	**č**eréša 'cherry'
[d]	D, d	**d**órvo 'wood'
[e]	E, e	pr**e**dávom 'sell'
[f]	F, f	**f**átom 'catch'
[g] [g^j]	G, g	**g**órlo 'throat'
[dẑ]	Ǵ, ǵ	**ǵ**væzda 'star'
[dʒ̑]	Ğ, ğ	**ğ**umajá 'mosque'
[x]	H, h	**h**ránem 'feed'
[i]	I, i	v**i**sok 'tall'
[j]	J, j	**j**áto 'food'
[k], [k^j]	K, k	**k**ukóška 'hen'
[ɫ], [l^j]	L, l	**l**ažýca 'spoon'
[ʎ]	Ḷ, ḷ	kóka**ḷ**e 'bones'
[m]	M, m	**m**agáre 'donkey'
[n], [n^j]	N,n	**n**us 'nose'
[ɲ]	Ṇ, ṇ	spa**ɲ**é 'sleep'
[o], [u], [a], [ɐ]	O, o	p**o**t 'road'
[ø]	Ø, ø	sp**ø**m 'to sleep'
[p]	P, p	**p**étal 'horse shoe'
[r]	R, r	**r**ábata 'work'
[s]	S, s	**s**órce 'heart'
[ʃ]	Š, š	**š**ápka 'cap'
[t]	T, t	**t**umafíl 'car'
[u]	U, u	**u**šá 'ear'
[y], [^{j}u]	Ü, ü	t**ü**rén 'train'
[v]	V,v	**v**orh 'top'
[ɨ]	Y, y	k**y**smét 'fortune'
[z]	Z, z	**z**imá 'winter'
[ʒ]	Ž, ž	**ž**alvá 'turtle'

Table 5: The A&A (2021) alphabet: phonemes, character set, usage examples.

Enhancing Documentation of Hupa with Automatic Speech Recognition

Zoey Liu
Boston College
zoey.liu@bc.edu

Justin Spence
University of California, Davis
jspence@ucdavis.edu

Emily Prud'hommeaux
Boston College
prudhome@bc.edu

Abstract

This study investigates applications of automatic speech recognition (ASR) techniques to Hupa, a critically endangered Native American language from the Dene (Athabaskan) language family. Using around 9h12m of spoken data produced by one elder who is a first-language Hupa speaker, we experimented with different evaluation schemes and training settings. On average a fully connected deep neural network reached a word error rate of 35.26%. Our overall results illustrate the utility of ASR for making Hupa language documentation more accessible and usable. In addition, we found that when training acoustic models, using recordings with transcripts that were not carefully verified did not necessarily have a negative effect on model performance. This shows promise for speech corpora of indigenous languages that commonly include transcriptions produced by second-language speakers or linguists who have advanced knowledge in the language of interest.

1 Introduction

The documentation of endangered and other less-studied languages typically involves the creation of high-quality audio and video recordings representing a variety of speech genres, with the long-term goal of generating general-purpose linguistic data that can be used by diverse audiences for different research and applied purposes (Himmelmann, 1998; Riesberg, 2018). With the advent of cheap, highly portable digital recording and storage technologies since the early 2000s, it is not uncommon for fieldwork projects to generate hundreds of hours of multimedia recordings.

While these collections of recordings are becoming increasingly accessible via web-based portals, in the sense that they can be downloaded, locating information of interest within them correctly and efficiently is another matter entirely. Coarse-grained catalog metadata describing the content of the recordings can provide users with some shallow guidance, but the identification of more specific information requires enormous investments of time and effort. Accordingly, it becomes essential to have adequate transcriptions of recordings for users to find the information they are interested in.

Transcribing recordings, however, is also an extremely time-consuming endeavor, leading to what is sometimes called the "transcription bottleneck" (Gupta and Boulianne, 2020; Zahrer et al., 2020; Ćavar et al., 2016; Shi et al., 2021), which refers to the situation where the language data is mostly in the form of (archival) recordings, and transcriptions of the data are not yet available.

Hupa (ISO 639-3 code: hup; Glottolog code: hupa1240), a critically endangered Native American language of northwestern California, provides a case in point. Since the early 2000s, Mrs. Verdena Parker, an elder from the Hoopa Valley Tribe, has generously shared her knowledge of the language with other community members and academic researchers. Recordings produced by and with Mrs. Parker include several hours of monolingual Hupa narratives and other texts, as well as over 800 hours of linguistic interviews that are a mixture of Hupa and English as the elicitation metalanguage. [1]

The sheer quantity of these Hupa recordings makes their transcription challenging, a situation that is exacerbated by other factors. First, the people who are considered first-language speakers of Hupa are older and tend not to be literate in the language. Therefore the pool of potential transcribers is limited to second-language speakers and linguists with advanced research knowledge. Second, while literacy is used as a tool for some pedagogical purposes in the contemporary Hupa community and there is a reasonably well-established practical orthography, many of the classes for learning Hupa

[1] Many of these recordings are now available through the California Language Archive web portal: https://cla.berkeley.edu/.

Proceedings of the Fifth Workshop on the Use of Computational Methods in the Study of Endangered Languages, pages 187 - 192
May 26-27, 2022

focus more on developing oral proficiency rather than on literacy skills per se. This means many of the younger people who have become second-language speakers of the language may not feel confident in their ability to produce accurate transcriptions of connected discourse.

In this work, we apply automatic speech recognition (ASR) technology to help address the transcription bottleneck for Hupa. In particular, we hope to develop effective techniques that would lend themselves to transcribing spoken Hupa. At this stage of the research, we are focusing primarily on monolingual narratives and other texts since these have the highest density of linguistic data and thus more value for research and language documentation.

2 Meet the Language Data

2.1 The Hupa Language

Hupa is the ancestral language of the Hoopa Valley Tribe in present-day Humboldt County, California. Since the mid-19th century, Hupa people have endured many hardships in the wake of the violent colonization of the region, including decades of educational policies that were designed to eradicate indigenous languages and other manifestations of traditional culture. As a result of this difficult history, by the mid-20th century most Hupa children grew up primarily speaking English as their first language, and today there are only a handful of elderly people (probably fewer than a dozen) who are considered first-language speakers of Hupa.

Nevertheless, at least since the 1970s, tribal members have been engaged in various kinds of language reclamation efforts (in the sense of Leonard (2011)), and today a number of people have developed a high degree of L2 proficiency in the language. Students at Hoopa Valley High School can take four years of Hupa language as part of their regular curriculum, and a practical orthography for the language developed in the 1980s and 1990s (Golla, 1996) is used in a number of pedagogically-oriented resources. Good descriptions of the linguistic features of Hupa are also obtainable from Golla (1970) and Sapir and Golla (2001) (see also Gordon (1996)), although there remains something of a disconnect between the highly technical descriptive materials produced by professional academics and the needs on the ground of language teachers and learners.

2.2 Audio data and transcriptions

The Hupa audio data in our experiments consists of a subset of audio recordings collected from fieldwork with Mrs. Verdena Parker (Table 1) that started in 2005 and is ongoing today. The majority of the recordings we use feature Mrs. Parker telling stories from different genres, including personal anecdotes from her life, oral-historical accounts of significant events in Hoopa Valley, and traditional stories that explain how the world came to be. Each recording has time-aligned transcriptions in the practical orthography of Golla (1996); the transcripts were produced by a human transcriber using annotation tools such as ELAN (Brugman and Russel, 2004).

Since the audio files had been transcribed gradually over a number of years by several researchers, each transcript was lightly edited and corrected by a linguist (an author of this paper), who has advanced research knowledge of the language. As of now, after removing utterances that are fully in English, the amount of spoken Hupa available for conducting ASR experiments totals 9h12m.

Although all transcriptions were checked in consultation with Mrs. Parker, each one typically goes through several stages of manual checking before being considered complete. As a result, some transcriptions have been subsequently examined more thoroughly than others. Based solely on transcription quality differences, we divided the audio data into two sets: the "verified" data (~1h35m) vs. the "coarse" data (~7h37m).

Overall, the transcriptions of the verified data are more accurate than those of the coarse data. That said, the verified transcriptions typically have undergone more orthographic normalization, which includes removing elements (e.g., word-final epenthetic vowels) that are audible in the recordings but are not part of the practical orthography (Golla, 1996). In a small number of instances, the verified transcriptions might have slight deviations from what was actually produced in the corresponding recording if Mrs. Parker felt strongly that she had misspoken. Therefore while the verified transcriptions tend to be more accurate, in some ways they are idealizations that are less faithful to the acoustic substance of their original recordings.

2.3 Digitized texts

In addition to the audio recordings and their transcriptions, we also included digitized texts for our

Data	N of words	N of types
verified transcriptions	9,265	2,024
coarse transcriptions	41,062	5,731
digitized written texts	41,381	8,205

Table 1: Descriptive statistics for the text data of Hupa applied in experiments.

experiments (Section 4); these texts were originally transcribed from dictation from Sapir and Golla (2001) and Goddard (1904) (Table 1).

3 Related Work

While research on ASR for endangered language documentation is still relatively rare, recently there has been growing efforts trying to mitigate this gap (Michaud et al., 2018; Prud'hommeaux et al., 2021). Shi et al. (2021) adopted end-to-end systems for Yoloxóchitl Mixtec, an endangered Mixtecan language. Using encoder-decoder architectures, they achieved the best word error rate (WER) ($\sim$16%) for over 55h of conversational speech from more than twenty speakers. Gupta and Boulianne (2020) applied neural ASR models for Cree, an indigenous language in Canada. Their data consists of 4h30m story retelling or reading from six speakers. Utilizing data from high-resource languages, Zahrer et al. (2020) performed cross-linguistic learning of phoneme recognition for the Muyu language. In a study of ASR for two tonal languages, Yongning Na and Eastern Chatino, Adams et al. (2018) proposed a neural architecture to jointly predict phonemes and tones without needing time-aligned transcripts and pronunciation dictionary.

ASR technologies have also been developed for some Dene languages (Littell et al., 2018), though in a limited way. For instance, speech recognition tools were incorporated into the Rosetta Stone language learning software for Diné Bizaad (Navajo). [2] The Persephone ASR software (Adams et al., 2018) was combined in ELAN (Brugman and Russel, 2004) for Tsuut'ina.

4 Experiments

4.1 Evaluation scheme

In (low-resource) ASR experiments [3], acoustic models are commonly evaluated with data from held-out speaker(s). This evaluation standard, however, is not applicable in our study here since all of the Hupa audio came from one speaker. Thus as alternatives, we designed two separate evaluation schemes for both the verified and the coarse data.

The first one utilized random splits, for which we randomly divided all the recordings into training and test sets at a 4:1 ratio for ten times. For the second scheme, taking into account the fact that the audio recordings were collected from distinct fieldwork dates (17 dates for the verified data and 34 dates for the coarse data), we used recordings from each held-out date as the test set and the rest of the data was employed as the training set. WER and character error rate (CER) were taken as evaluation metrics for model performance.

Note that the results obtained from these two evaluation methods are not directly comparable, given that the amount of training data and that of the test data for the two methods are different. On the other hand, the goal of employing separate evaluation schemes is to acquire more realistic estimates regarding the potential of the ASR systems in the case of Hupa.

4.2 Acoustic training data configuration

With the two evaluation schemes outlined above, we investigated different training settings with the goal of exploring: (1) the differences between the verified and coarse data; a(2) the utility of including all acoustic data, regardless of transcription quality.

In our first four experiments, we focused on the verified data, evaluating ASR performance with random splits then with held-out dates. We then included the coarse data for model training, keeping the test data the same in order to determine whether WER decreases with more training data, even when there is a mismatch in transcription quality between the test data and the training data. In our second set of experiments, we carried out the same model training procedures using the coarse data. Finally, we combined the coarse data and verified data to train and test acoustic models on random splits of this combined data.

4.3 Language and acoustic models

For each training/test set split of the audio data, we built one trigram language model with Witten-Bell discounting using the SRILM toolkit (Stolcke, 2002); the data used to train the language model also included the transcripts of the audio training data along with the digitized texts.

For acoustic modeling, we drew on the open-source Kaldi toolkit (Povey et al., 2011). The au-

[2] https://navajorenaissance.org/

[3] Code in quarantine at https://github.com/zoeyliu18/Hupa

Original utterance:	haya:ɬ keh do'ng haya: ch'in' *** tehɬ
Model prediction:	haya:ɬ *** do'ng haya: ch'in' te: niwhsing
Evaluation:	D I S

The original utterance has six words; compared to the original utterance; the utterance predicted by the ASR model contains one deletion (D), one insertion (I), and one substitution (S); therefore:

$\text{WER} = 100 * \frac{1+1+1}{6} = 50\%$

An example of WER calculation; I for insertion, D for deletion, and S for substitution.

Evaluation	Data	Training setting	WER (%)	CER (%)
random splits	train: 1h16m; test: 19m	*just verified data*	53.23	24.58
		add coarse data	36.89	12.20
held-out dates	train: 1h30m; test: 5m	*just verified data*	46.10	17.48
		add coarse data	37.96	13.57

Table 2: ASR evaluation results for the verified data.

Evaluation	Data	Training setting	WER (%)	CER (%)
random splits	train: 6h6m; test: 1h31m	*just coarse data*	45.13	21.37
		add verified data	35.13	12.65
held-out dates	train: 7h24m; test: 13m	*just coarse data*	37.70	12.58
		add verified data	35.60	12.37

Table 3: ASR evaluation results for the coarse data.

Evaluation	Data	WER (%)	CER (%)
random splits	train: 7h22m; test: 1h50m	35.26	12.38

Table 4: ASR evaluation results when combining all verified and coarse data together.

dio recordings were transformed to the standard 13 dimensional mel-frequency cepstral coefficients (MFCCs), as well as their delta- and delta-delta features. The delta- and delta-delta features are, respectively, numerical approximations of the first and second order derivatives of the MFCCs, both computed on a 25ms window with 10ms interval apart which enables modeling the trajectories of the audio signals. Linear Discriminant Analysis and Maximum Likelihood Linear Transform were then employed to reduce the dimensionality of the feature vectors.

The acoustic model architecture that we used is a fully connected deep neural network (DNN) (Miao et al., 2015), which has been demonstrated to have competitive performance when facing data limitation (Morris et al., 2021). The DNN had six hidden layers, each with 1024 hidden units. Sequence training was carried out with the default parameters in Kaldi using state-level minimum Bayes risk criterion and a per-utterance Stochastic Gradient Descent weight update. Decoding was performed with the finite state transducer-based decoder implemented in Kaldi.

5 Results

The average WER results for the verified data given each training setting and evaluation scheme are presented in Table 2. When only using the verified data for ASR training and evaluation, we obtained a WER of 53.23%; on the other hand, we see that combining coarse data with the training data of the verified set resulted in much lower WER values (and lower CER values as well), and accordingly better model performance; this pattern is consistent regardless of whether evaluating acoustic models with random splits or held-out dates. Similar observations hold when developing models for the coarse data with additional help of verified data (Table 3), which also led to lower WER values. These results indicate that including more training data, even when the transcription quality of the training data does not necessarily match that of the test data, is helpful to build better ASR models.

When combining all data from the verified set and the coarse set together, we reached a WER of 35.26% evaluated with random splits, which is comparable to the results of random splits for each data set separately.

6 Discussion & Ongoing Work

Leveraging ASR technologies, we investigate the possibility and effectiveness of automatically transcribing fieldwork recordings for Hupa. Through experimentation with different evaluation schemes and training settings, the acoustic models demonstrate reasonable WER results, showing promise for applying spoken language technology to document Hupa. Interestingly, training ASR models using recordings with transcripts that were not carefully verified did not negatively impact the performance, which bodes well for speech corpora of indigenous languages that include transcriptions produced by second-language speakers or linguists.

In ongoing work, we are extending our efforts in several directions. First, the transcripts of the coarse data are being manually checked periodically to improve transcription and gloss alignment quality. Second, as we are still in the preliminary stage of performing ASR for Hupa, the current study only used the DNN architecture from Kaldi. We plan to explore other more recent neural approaches (Watanabe et al., 2018) that have been found to be effective with limited amount of audio data (Shi et al., 2021); then apply the trained models to recordings that have not yet been transcribed in an iterative fashion to better combine ASR with documentation of Hupa. Even a WER as high as $\sim 35.26\%$ is expected to yield significant savings in the time required to make transcribed texts available.

Third, thus far our acoustic models are decoded with language models at the word level. However, given the complex morphological features of Hupa (Sapir and Golla, 2001), to reduce out-of-vocabulary rate in future experiments, we are working towards combining morphological segmentation or subword unit models Liu et al. (2019) into building ASR systems. Lastly, with better performing acoustic models and more transcriptions, we aim to develop a workflow to adapt these transcribed materials into pedagogically-oriented resources for use by members of the community.

Acknowledgements

We are grateful for the continuous support from the Hupa indigenous community. We would like to especially thank Mrs. Verdena Parker for her generous and valuable input for the documentation work of Hupa throughout the years. In addition, we thank the anonymous reviewers for their helpful feedback. This material is based upon work supported by the National Science Foundation under Grant #2127309 to the Computing Research Association for the CIFellows Project, and Grant #1761562. Any opinions, findings, and conclusions or recommendations expressed in this material are those of the author(s) and do not necessarily reflect the views of the National Science Foundation nor the Computing Research Association.

References

Oliver Adams, Trevor Cohn, Graham Neubig, Hilaria Cruz, Steven Bird, and Alexis Michaud. 2018. Evaluation Phonemic Transcription of Low-Resource Tonal Languages for Language Documentation. In *Proceedings of the Eleventh International Conference on Language Resources and Evaluation (LREC 2018)*, Miyazaki, Japan. European Language Resources Association (ELRA).

Hennie Brugman and Albert Russel. 2004. Annotating multi-media/multi-modal resources with ELAN. In *Proceedings of the Fourth International Conference on Language Resources and Evaluation (LREC'04)*, Lisbon, Portugal. European Language Resources Association (ELRA).

Malgorzata Ćavar, Damir Ćavar, and Hilaria Cruz. 2016. Endangered Language Documentation: Bootstrapping a Chatino Speech Corpus, Forced Aligner, ASR. In *Proceedings of the Tenth International Conference on Language Resources and Evaluation (LREC'16)*, pages 4004–4011, Portorož, Slovenia. European Language Resources Association (ELRA).

Pliny Earle Goddard. 1904. *Hupa texts*, volume 1. The University Press.

Victor Golla. 1996. Hupa Language Dictionary Second Edition.

Victor Karl Golla. 1970. *Hupa grammar*. Ph.D. thesis, University of California, Berkeley.

Matthew Gordon. 1996. The phonetic structures of Hupa. *UCLA Working Papers in Phonetics*, pages 164–187.

Vishwa Gupta and Gilles Boulianne. 2020. Speech Transcription Challenges for Resource Constrained Indigenous Language Cree. In *Proceedings of the 1st Joint Workshop on Spoken Language Technologies for Under-resourced languages (SLTU) and Collaboration and Computing for Under-Resourced Languages (CCURL)*, pages 362–367, Marseille, France. European Language Resources association.

Nikolaus P Himmelmann. 1998. Documentary and descriptive linguistics. *Linguistics*, pages 161–195.

Wesley Leonard. 2011. Challenging "extinction" through modern Miami language practices. *American Indian Culture and Research Journal*, 35(2):135–160.

Patrick Littell, Anna Kazantseva, Roland Kuhn, Aidan Pine, Antti Arppe, Christopher Cox, and Marie-Odile Junker. 2018. Indigenous language technologies in Canada: Assessment, challenges, and successes. In *Proceedings of the 27th International Conference on Computational Linguistics*, pages 2620–2632, Santa Fe, New Mexico, USA. Association for Computational Linguistics.

Chang Liu, Zhen Zhang, Pengyuan Zhang, and Yonghong Yan. 2019. Character-Aware Sub-Word Level Language Modeling for Uyghur and Turkish ASR. In *The Annual Conference of the International Speech Communication Association (Interspeech)*, pages 3495–3499.

Yajie Miao, Hao Zhang, and Florian Metze. 2015. Speaker adaptive training of deep neural network acoustic models using i-vectors. *IEEE/ACM Transactions on Audio, Speech, and Language Processing*, 23(11):1938–1949.

Alexis Michaud, Oliver Adams, Trevor Cohn, Graham Neubig, and Séverine Guillaume. 2018. Integrating automatic transcription into the language documentation workflow: Experiments with Na data and the Persephone toolkit. *Language Documentation & Conservation*, 12:393–429.

Ethan Morris, Robert Jimerson, and Emily Prud'hommeaux. 2021. One size does not fit all in resource-constrained ASR. In *The Annual Conference of the International Speech Communication Association (Interspeech)*, pages 4354–4358.

Daniel Povey, Arnab Ghoshal, Gilles Boulianne, Lukas Burget, Ondrej Glembek, Nagendra Goel, Mirko Hannemann, Petr Motlicek, Yanmin Qian, Petr Schwarz, et al. 2011. The Kaldi speech recognition toolkit. In *IEEE 2011 workshop on automatic speech recognition and understanding*, CONF. IEEE Signal Processing Society.

Emily Prud'hommeaux, Robbie Jimerson, Richard Hatcher, and Karin Michelson. 2021. Automatic Speech Recognition for Supporting Endangered Language Documentation. *Language Documentation & Conservation*, 15:491–513.

Sonja Riesberg. 2018. Reflections on descriptive and documentary adequacy. In Bradley McDonnell, Andrea L. Berez-Kroeker, and Gary Holton, editors, *SP15: Reflections on Language Documentation 20 Years after Himmelmann 1998*, chapter 15, pages 151–156. University of Hawai'i Press.

Edward Sapir and Victor Golla. 2001. Hupa texts, with notes and lexicon. *The Collected Works of Edward Sapir, ed. by Victor Golla & Sean O'Neill*, 14:19–1011.

Jiatong Shi, Jonathan D. Amith, Rey Castillo García, Esteban Guadalupe Sierra, Kevin Duh, and Shinji Watanabe. 2021. Leveraging End-to-End ASR for Endangered Language Documentation: An Empirical Study on Yolóxochitl Mixtec. In *Proceedings of the 16th Conference of the European Chapter of the Association for Computational Linguistics: Main Volume*, pages 1134–1145, Online. Association for Computational Linguistics.

Andreas Stolcke. 2002. SRILM-an extensible language modeling toolkit. In *Seventh international conference on spoken language processing*.

Shinji Watanabe, Takaaki Hori, Shigeki Karita, Tomoki Hayashi, Jiro Nishitoba, Yuya Unno, Nelson Enrique Yalta Soplin, Jahn Heymann, Matthew Wiesner, Nanxin Chen, Adithya Renduchintala, and Tsubasa Ochiai. 2018. ESPnet: End-to-End Speech Processing Toolkit. In *Proceedings of Interspeech*, pages 2207–2211.

Alexander Zahrer, Andrej Zgank, and Barbara Schuppler. 2020. Towards Building an Automatic Transcription System for Language Documentation: Experiences from Muyu. In *Proceedings of the 12th Language Resources and Evaluation Conference*, pages 2893–2900, Marseille, France. European Language Resources Association.

Author Index

Association for Computational Linguistics
209 N. Eighth Street
Stroudsburg, Pennsylvania 18360

ISBN 978-1-7138-6730-2

CURRAN ASSOCIATES INC.
proceedings.com